Thomas May

The Reigne of King Henry the Second
Written in Seauen Bookes

MEDIEVAL AND RENAISSANCE

TEXTS AND STUDIES

VOLUME 195

RENAISSANCE ENGLISH TEXT SOCIETY

SEVENTH SERIES
VOLUME XXII (for 1997)

Henry the 2ᵈ ſurnamed Shortmantle, King of England, Duke
of Normandy, and Aquitaine, Earle of Poicteres, and Anjov: Lord
of Ireland. He raigned 34 yeares 9 months, died the 6ᵗʰ of July
1189 at the age of 61 yeares, and lieth buried at Fonteverard
in Normandy.

Levis 5, I

Renold Elstrack, *Henry II of England*, Rosenwald Collection.
© 1997 Board of Trustees, National Gallery of Art, Washington.

Thomas May

The Reigne of King Henry the Second
Written in Seauen Bookes

edited by

Götz Schmitz

Arizona Center for Medieval and Renaissance Studies
in conjunction with
Renaissance English Text Society
Tempe, Arizona
1999

Library of Congress Cataloging-in-Publication Data
May, Thomas, 1595–1650.
    The reigne of King Henry the Second, written in seauen books / Thomas May ; edited by Götz Schmitz.
        p. cm. — (Medieval & Renaissance Texts & Studies ; v. 195) (Renaissance English Text Society ; 7th ser., v. 22)
    Includes bibliographical references (p.) and index.
    ISBN 0-86698-237-X
        1. Great Britain—History—Henry II, 1154–1189–Poetry. 2. Henry II, King of England, 1133–1189—Poetry. 3. May, Thomas, 1595–1650. Reigne of King Henry the Second. 4. Henry II, king of England, 1133–1189—In literature. I. Schmitz, Götz, 1944– II. Title. III. Medieval & Renaissance Texts & Studies (Series) ; v. 195. IV. Renaissance English Text Society (Series) ; vol. 22.
    PR2709.M3 A76 1999
    821'.4—dc21   99–055552

Table of Contents

List of Illustrations   ix

Acknowledgements   xi

INTRODUCTION

The Manuscript Copy of *King Henry the Second*
    Description and Collation   xv
    Provenance   xvi
    Scripts and Scribes   xxiv
    The Autograph Copy of May's *Tragœdy of Cleopatra*   xxxii

The Printed Edition (1633)
    Description and Collation   xli
    The Printers   xlii
    The Huntington Library Copy   xlix
    Additions to the Printed Edition:
        Frontispiece, Motto, and "Characters"   lix
    The Printer's Copy   lx
    Editorial Policy   lxvii

The Sources
    The Question of Accessibility   lxviii
    Thomas May and Edmund Bolton's Academ Roial   lxxxvi
    The Influence of Classical Literature   xciii

THE REIGNE OF KING HENRY THE SECOND   1

The first booke   3
The second booke   19
The third booke   31

The fourth booke   47
The fift booke   67
The sixt booke   89
The seauenth booke   103
The Description of King Henry the Second   115
The Single, and Comparative Characters of Henry the Sonne,
    and Richard   120

Textual Notes   123

Explanatory Notes   135

Genealogical Tables   227

Appendices: Excerpts from Source Texts
    The Coronation of Young Henry   229
    The Fleas Banished by St. Nannan   233
    King Henry's Penitential Walk to Canterbury   233
    The Capture of King William of Scotland   235
    King Henry's Death   236
    The Character of King Henry   241

Bibliography
    Manuscripts   245
    Editions, Sources, and Analogues   246
    Studies and Reference Works   253

List of Illustrations

Frontispiece: Renold Elstrack, *Henry II of England*, Rosenwald Collection, © 1997 Board of Trustees, National Gallery of Art, Washington.

1 Title page of the fair copy of *King Henry the Second* (Royal MS 18.C.XII, fol. 1v). Reproduced by permission of the British Library. xiv

2 *Cleopatra* entry in the Whitehall inventory (MS Smith 34, p. 107). Reproduced by permission of the Bodleian Library. xix

3 *King Henry* entry in the Whitehall inventory (MS Smith 34, p. 10). Reproduced by permission of the Bodleian Library. xx

4 Sample page from the fair copy of *King Henry the Second* (Royal MS 18.C.XII, fol. 2v). Reproduced by permission of the British Library. xxii

5 A transcript of May's inscription to Daniel Heinsius in the copy of his *Supplementum Lucani* (1640). xxxiii

6 Royal MS 18.C.XII, fol. 21v (p. 40), lines 3–4. Reproduced by permission of the British Library. xxxv

7 Royal MS 18.C.VII, fol. 4r, lines 14–19. Reproduced by permission of the British Library. xxxv

8 Royal MS 18.C.XII, fol. 2v, lines 23–24. Reproduced by permission of the British Library. xxxv

9 Title page of the 1633 edition of *King Henry the Second* (Folger Shakespeare Library, STC 17715 copy 1, the Cole/Mitford copy). Reproduced by permission of the Folger Shakespeare Library. xliii

10   Huntington Library copy of the 1633 edition of *King Henry the Second* (RB 62625); back cover with center- and cornerpiece stamps. Reproduced by permission of The Huntington Library, San Marino, California.   lv

11   Frontispiece from the 1633 edition of *King Henry the Second* with Robert Vaughan's portrait of the king (Folger Shakespeare Library, STC 17715 copy 2, Harmsworth copy). Reproduced by permission of the Folger Shakespeare Library.   136

12   Plantagenet shield from the Vaughan frontispiece (enlarged detail from the Harmsworth copy of the 1633 edition). Reproduced by permission of the Folger Shakespeare Library.   139

13   Plantagenet badge from William Segar's "The Variation of the Arms, and Badges of the Kings of England," MS Harley 6085, fol. 15v. Reproduced by permission of the British Library.   139

14   Great Seal of King Henry II; from John Speed's *Historie of Great Britain* (1632), IX, 6 [1], p. 484; reproduced from the British Library copy, shelf-mark 505.h.14, by permission of the British Library   142

Genealogical Tables

Diagrams redrawn from the "Genealogicall Table" (1682) in MS Lansdowne 884; reproduced by permission of the British Library

I   Saxons and Normans   227

II   Tudors and Stuarts   228

Acknowledgements

When I first approached the RETS with the project of an edition of Thomas May's *The Reigne of King Henry the Second* about fifteen years ago I lived under the illusion that this would mean little more than reproducing Augustine Mathewes' print of 1633. It was only after I had read the printed text into my computer that I came across a reference hidden in Denzell Smith's edition of May's *Tragœdy of Cleopatra* that a Royal Manuscript of the epic existed which even at a glance looked close enough to the author to qualify, according to a rationale by then rarely questioned, as copy-text for a second edition. This prompted not only another transcription, this time of the manuscript, but also an epic quest for the provenance of that manuscript which took me first into the interiors of its holder, the British Museum with its North Library, Students' Room and Old Bindery (all of them renamed and relocated by now), and then further and further afield, always goaded by intimations of its earliest location in one of the Old Royal Libraries. A generous grant from the Deutsche Forschungsgemeinschaft enabled me to follow its traces to some of the major libraries in the New World, in particular the Folger Shakespeare Library and the Huntington Library, and to gather evidence that one of the copies of the printed edition went back to this earliest location, too.

It is to the keepers of these libraries and their staff that I owe my greatest debts. I can name but a few: Janet Backhouse, Michelle Brown, Philippa Marks and Hilton Kelliher of the British Library, Peter Blayney and Georgianna Ziegler of the Folger Shakespeare Library, Thomas Lange and Mary Robertson of the Huntington Library, and the late Martin Boghardt of the Herzog August Bibliothek, Wolfenbüttel. Of experts from outside the libraries I am greatly obliged to Peter Beal of the Department of Manuscripts and Printed Books at Sotheby's and Kevin Sharpe of the Department of History at the University of Southampton, though I met them, too, on library grounds in London and San Marino.

For permission to reproduce the text and illustrative material I should like

---

to acknowledge my gratitude to the trustees of the Bodleian Library, Oxford, the British Library, London, the Folger Shakespeare Library, Washington, the Huntington Library, San Marino, and the National Gallery, Washington.

Of the many colleagues I am indebted to for criticism and encouragement I would like to name only two, again as representatives: Dennis Danielson of the University of British Columbia, and Burkhard Niederhoff of the University of Bonn. Special thanks are due to the board members of the RETS, in particular Karl Josef Höltgen and Arthur Kinney, for their trust and patience, and above all to Tom Berger who accompanied this edition through all its stages with unfailing good eye, good sense, and good humour.

January 2000
G.S.

18 C XII. p. 280

The reigne of King Henry
the Second

Written

in Seauen bookes

by Tho: May.

Invalidas vires Rex excitat, et iuuat idem.
Qui iubet; obsequium sufficit esse meum.

Auson:

Title page of the fair copy of *King Henry the Second*.

Introduction

THE MANUSCRIPT COPY OF *KING HENRY THE SECOND*

Description and Collation

The manuscript of *The Reigne of King Henry the Second*, British Library Royal Manuscript 18.C.XII, is an exceptionally well prepared and preserved fair copy written in an italic book hand of the seventeenth century.[1] It is bound in vellum, and all edges are gilt. The front cover of the binding bears the gold-tooled initials B.M.; the spine has the following gold-tooled letters and marks between raised bands: THO. MAY. / REIGN. / OF. / HENRY. II. // COD.   SEC. / XVII / BIBL.   REG.   MUS.   BRIT. // 18.C.XII / P. 280. / PLUT. XXIII.D. The mark XXIII.D. has later been stamped over to read XII.D. The tooling on the spine indicates that it is a Museum Binding (M.B. = Museum Britannicum) made after 1734, the year in which David Casley's *Catalogue of the Manuscripts of the King's Library* appeared, for the mark "P. 280" refers to the page in that catalogue where the manuscript is listed. "PLUT. XXIII. D." or "PLUT. XII.D." are old British Museum pressmarks.

The text of the manuscript is written on paper and contains eighty-six folio leaves, sized 12.5 x 8.5 inches (31.6 x 21.4 cm). The paper is strong

---

[1] Cf. the description in Julius P. Gilson and George F. Warner, *Catalogue of Western Manuscripts in the Old Royal and King's Collections in the British Museum* (London, 1921), II, 303, which the following description will extend and qualify.

and well preserved; the watermark, as revealed in a beta-radiograph, is that of a peacock closely resembling mark 174 in Edward Heawood's inventory.[2] According to Heawood this points to Venice as the place of production where it was used for a 1628 edition of Della Valle's *Re Abbas*.

The manuscript has a concurrent foliation (leaves 1–86) and pagination (pages 1–169, starting with the Argument of Book I on fol. 2r) in the top outer corner of the leaf or page; the pagination is written in ink, by a contemporary hand, probably that of the scribe, the foliation is a later addition in pencil. There are catchwords throughout, but no signatures. The front leaves once formed a quire of six leaves; now leaf one is lacking (the stub of six runs under two, i.e., under the pastedown). Folios 2–81 are regular quires of four leaves. Folios 82–84 formed a quire of four leaves, of which the fourth leaf has been excised, for reasons unknown, perhaps because of errors or damage. The final quire has four leaves, comprising folios 85–86 and two blanks (flyleaf and pastedown).[3] The title page shows a number of additions: the name of the author has been extended from *T.M.* to *Th: May*, the motto has been identified by an added *Auson:*, and a comma has been inserted between *excitat* and *et*. These additions are written in a contemporary hand of a slightly less set appearance. At the top of the page a mark has been added in a florid eighteenth-century script, "18 C XII. P. 280."

Provenance

Casley's *Catalogue* of 1734, to which the marks "P. 280" on the spine and title page refer, contains the first printed record of Royal MS 18.C.XII. The standard catalogue of manuscripts in the old royal libraries, published by Gilson and Warner in 1921, says that it was "not in the old catalogues."[4] This presumably means that the *King Henry* manuscript is not listed in the oldest handwritten catalogues of the royal libraries, seven of which have been preserved in the Department of Printed Books at the British Museum (BL C.120.h.6 [1–7]). The last two of these lists date from the early eighteenth century and deal with Queen Caroline's books (mostly French); the others

---

[2] Edward Heawood, *Watermarks Mainly of the 17th and 18th Centuries* (Hilversum, 1950).

[3] I am grateful to Michelle Brown and Scot McKendrick of the British Library for their help in collating the tightly-bound volume.

[4] Gilson and Warner, *Catalogue of Western Manuscripts*, II, 303.

were compiled in the Commonwealth and Restoration periods. Strictly speaking, therefore, only the early ones should be referred to as catalogues of the Old Royal Library. If Gilson and Warner had these lists in mind, their qualification "not in the old catalogues" would imply that the *King Henry* manuscript found its way into the Royal Library not before the eighteenth century, an implication of obvious importance for the textual history of a poem which, as its dedication states, was written by command of Charles I and is preserved in a royal manuscript.

The qualification in Gilson and Warner's catalogue, however, holds true only if it is taken to refer to the oldest of the early lists, shelf marks C.120.h.6 (1–3), which date back to 1650 when the Royal Librarian Patrick Young, who had been dismissed after the death of King Charles I, was reappointed to make an inventory of the Royal Library at St. James's by a Parliamentary commission headed by Bulstrode Whitelocke. The *King Henry* manuscript is not listed in any of these three, but it is entered in one of the later catalogues, BL C.120.h.6 (5), together with its companion piece, a fair copy of May's *Tragædy of Cleopatra* (MS Royal 18.C.VII). This later inventory lists both manuscripts and printed books in the Royal Library at St. James's Palace and was compiled towards the end of the seventeenth century.[5] The references to May's works appear in a section headed "English MSS.":

1531 The Tragedy of Cleopatra.

1532 The Reign of K. Henry ye 2. an heroick Poem by Tho. May.[6]

Towards the end of this section, which shows signs of extensive revision, a number of manuscripts with royal associations are registered, some of which had been presented to members of the royal family on various occasions, for example "The Masque of Queens, by Ben Johnson," probably the annotated copy Jonson wrote at Prince Henry's bidding (now Royal MS 18.A.XLV),

---

[5] See Sears Jayne and F. R. Johnson, *The Lumley Library: The Catalogue of 1609* (London, 1956), 21, n. 2. The editors give the following short description of this inventory, "Morocco of about 1660, with Royal Arms. Shelf list of St James about 1694" in a note on the hand-written catalogues kept in the British Library (p. 288). There are, however, some later entries, perhaps acquisitions, the most recent item being dated 1703. The introduction to the edition of the Lumley catalogue contains a very helpful short history of the old royal libraries at Whitehall and St. James's; appendix B supplements it with a useful chart of names and dates.

[6] BL C.120.h.6(5).

"Daniells Panegericke to his Matie verse foll" (now BL MS Royal 18.A. LXXII), or "A Description of ffire Works," an illustrated programme for the fireworks designed for the Palatine marriage by the King's gunners, John Nodes and Thomas Butler (now Royal MS 17.C.XXXV).[7] Like the May manuscripts, these presentation copies are not mentioned in the inventories made of the St. James Library shortly after the death of King Charles I.

A possible explanation for this omission is to be found in another inventory hidden in a composite seventeenth-century manuscript now kept in the Bodleian Library, MS Smith 34.[8] The manuscript consists of papers (mostly letters in Latin and Greek) that belonged to Patrick Young, the Royal Librarian from c. 1605–1649. It was given to Thomas Smith (1638–1710), the compiler of a catalogue of Cotton manuscripts and fellow of Magdalen College, Oxford, by Young's grandson, William (?) Atwood.[9] Smith passed it on to Thomas Hearne, the antiquary, who added a title page and an index. Bound up with the papers of this composite manuscript is a list of "Books and Manuscripts of King Charles" which, according to Madan, was "made soon after 1641, not by Young." The Royal Librarian must have taken it with him into retirement, as he did with the catalogue of the Lumley Library, when he was dismissed after the execution of King Charles in 1649.[10] The date given by Madan is accepted by Sears Jayne, who adds that it "is a fragment of some larger catalogue."[11] The list fills seven and one-half pages (MS Smith 34, 105–112) and records 226 manuscripts in a first section inscribed "1) Whitehall. These Following are Manu-

---

[7] BL C.120.h.6(5), Nr 1794, p. 130; Nr 1807, p. 130; Nr. 1621, p. 125.

[8] See the description in Falconer Madan, *A Summary Catalogue of Western Manuscripts in the Bodleian Library at Oxford*, Vol. 3 (Oxford: Clarendon, 1895), Nr 15641, 457–8.

[9] See Madan's description of the manuscript and Johannes Kemke's short biography of Patrick Young in the introduction to his collection of Young's letters, *Patricius Junius (Patrick Young). Bibliothekar der Könige Jacob I. und Carl I. von England. Mitteilungen aus seinem Briefwechsel*, Sammlung bibliothekswissenschaftlicher Arbeiten, 12. Heft (Leipzig, 1898).

[10] See Jayne, Introduction to *Lumley Library*, 19. Young had compiled a catalogue of the Lumley Library shortly after it was incorporated into Prince Henry's collections in 1609.

[11] Jayne, *Lumley Library*, 293. The *terminus post quem* is set by an entry in the list of printed books: "L[ondon] 1641 Roberts Answ[er] to Ford." Mirjam Foot accepts Madan's date, too, in her article on "Some Bindings for Charles I," *Studies in Seventeenth-Century English Literature, History and Bibliography*, Festschrift for Professor T. A. Birrell on the Occasion of his Sixtieth Birthday, ed. G. A. M. Janssens and F. G. A. M. Aarts (Amsterdam, 1984), 106, n. 45.

scripts"[12] (105–110), and 92 printed books in a second section inscribed "2) Whytehall. English bookes printed" (111–12). The list looks like an inventory rather than an index; there are, for instance, no subject divisions or press marks as in some of the early catalogues of the old Royal Library. The entries are short, usually giving title and format only, with place and date of publication added to the titles of printed books. The contents of the list point to an early Stuart taste, in particular that of King James I. Theology and church politics prevail, with an admixture of titles on history, geography, and genealogy. A great number of the items listed are associated with members of the royal family, for instance the "Catalogue of Q Eliz Jewells foll," "K James Instruct to P Hen Italian 4°" (probably the *Basilicon Doron*), or the "Triumphs at ye Princes Ret fr Sp fren 4°" (all on p. 109). The following entries, which are listed in the manuscript section, have some bearing on the present discussion:

Tragœdy of Cleopatra foll (p. 107)

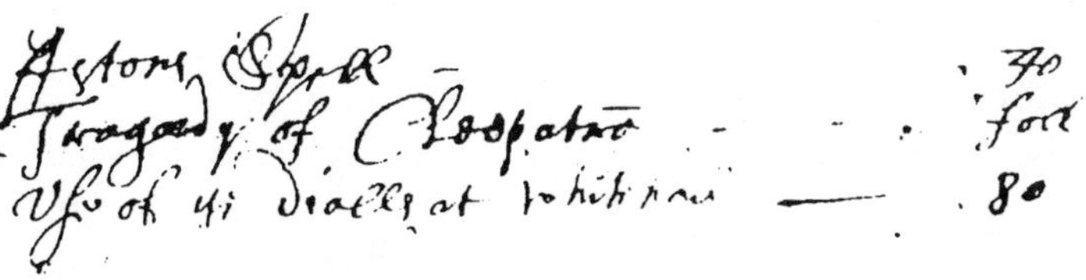

Figure 2. *Cleopatra* entry in the Whitehall inventory.

and

---

[12] To this subscription is added, in a different script and hand, "in the floare."

ye Reigne of Hen 7th verse p[er] May. foll (p. 110)

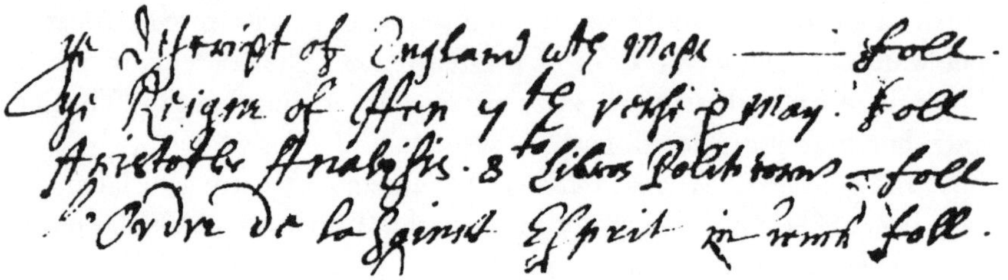
ye Discript of England wth Mapps —— foll.
ye Reigne of Hen 7th verse p[er] May. foll
Aristotles Analisis . 8to Liber Politicorum — foll
l'Ordre de la Sainct Esprit in french foll.

Figure 3. *King Henry* entry in the Whitehall inventory.

There can be little doubt that the first of these entries refers to May's play as none of the other candidates (the Cleopatra plays by Mary Sidney, Daniel, Brandon, Shakespeare, or Fletcher) has exactly this title or is preserved in an early manuscript. Thus this appears to be the fair copy of the play, now BL MS Royal 18.C.VII.

The second entry raises a number of questions; the ordinal "7th" in particular causes problems. There were two roughly contemporary lives of King Henry VII, one, *The Historie of the Raigne of King Henry the Seventh* by Francis Bacon (STC 1159, printed in 1622 and 1629), the other, *The Historie of that Wise Prince, Henrie the Seventh* by May's friend and fellow student Charles Aleyn (STC 353, printed 1638). Bacon's *Historie* is in prose, which Aleyn versified in his poem; neither of these works has survived in manuscript form. The specification "p[er] May" raises some paleographical questions. The mixed-language expression "per May" is rather unusual in itself; the compiler uses the looped abbreviated form here as a separate word (elsewhere in the list it is employed in its usual function in vernacular texts, namely as a sign of contraction in words like "*per*fection" or "*par*ts," both on p. 105). Also, the phrase "p[er] May" looks somewhat reduced in scale compared with the rest of the line. Another oddity is that the title of May's poem is given before the name of its author. Usually, if authors are named at all in this list (which is by no means the rule), the name precedes the title, as in "Daniells Panegerick to his Matie verse foll" or "Burtons praise of Vertue a poem 4o" (105). Another exception to this rule is "A Booke in fren[ch] verse by Cecill 4o" (107), but this is to distinguish it from "A Booke in French verse 4°" listed on page 105 and another "Booke in french Verse" on page 107, which the compiler had specified in a crammed-in addition as being "on seu[er] Noble P[or]tr [aits ?]." This last entry suggests that the scribe added the abbreviated specification as an afterthought, when the next line had already been filled. It could well be that he was in similar straits with the *King Henry* entry and that "p[er] May" is an addition. The compiler probably made his entries intermittently after looking at one or two volumes on the shelf (or on the floor, if the additional headnote to the manuscript section of the list, "in the floare," refers to being on the ground rather than on the storey); this would explain why many entries, in particular the French and Latin ones, give paraphrases rather than proper titles.[13] In the case of the *King Henry* entry, he may have become uncertain about the exact title of the volume (perhaps confusing it with Bacon's *Historie*, or Aleyn's versification of it)[14] and therefore squeezed in the author's name without bothering to go back to the volume itself. The wrong ordinal could also have been prompted by the latter part of the full title of the poem, which refers to the number of its books: *The Reigne of King Henry the Second Written in Seauen Bookes by Tho: May*. Whatever the explanation, there is reason to assume that the entry describes Royal MS 18.C.XII, that both the *Cleopatra* and the *King Henry* manuscripts were kept at Whitehall in the 1640s, and that the entry in the Gilson and Warner *Catalogue of Royal Manuscripts* needs to be corrected.

The fact that neither of the two May manuscripts entered in the Smith Inventory in the early 1640s appears in the lists compiled at St. James's immediately after the death of King Charles could be an indication that they were more closely linked with the king himself than most of the items listed in these early inventories. It is well known that both King James and King Charles, though they were no great book-collectors, were fond of association

---

[13] Storage of books was not as careful as it is today; a heading in Young's catalogue reads: "Between the Chimney and the Dore in folio 4to & lesser vollumes. Next to ye floure on ye lower shelues of folio bookes in great vollumes" (BL C.120.h.6 [1]).

[14] Thomas May and Charles Aleyn were fellow students at Sidney Sussex College, Cambridge, and kept up their acquaintance. May wrote complimentary verses for Aleyn's historical poem *The Battailes of Crescey and Poictiers* (1631; 2d ed. 1633). Collectors apparently considered them to be kindred spirits, because the printed editions of their historical poems are often bound together; the Bodleian copy of *The Reigne of King Henry the Second*, for instance, is bound up with Aleyn's *Historie of Henrie the Seventh* (Wood 90 [7,8.]).

Booke 1.

How his great vertues were too sadly try'de
By rebell subiects, by the Papall pride,
And his owne childrens strange impiety.
By opposition to ecclipse his high
And great renowne, or higher to aduance
The fame of his vndaunted puissance.
 Vouchsafe, dread Soueraigne Charles, with that most cleare
And gratious eye, with which you vse to cheare
Poore suppliants, while destinyes attend
Your royall doome, to view these lines, and lend
Your favoures mfluence, which can infuse
Vertue alone into an English Muse.
Shee else would tremble to approach too nigh
So pure a mynde, so great a Maiesty.
Vouchsafe to read the actions of a King
Your noble ancestour; and what wee sing
In Henry's reigne, that may bee true renowne,
Accept it, Sr. as Prologue to your owne,
Vntill this Muse, or some more happy straine
May sing your vertues, and vnæquall'd reigne.
 Those ciuill swords, that did so lately stayne
The land with slaughter, now were sheath'd againe.
The rents of State were clos'd, the wounds were cur'de;
Peace by victorious Henry was secur'de,
And justice waited on his awfull throne
Without controll; all feares, all faction,
                          That

Figure 4. Sample page from the fair copy of *King Henry the Second*.

copies.[15] Both lists refer to "Whitehall" books, but a distinction needs to be made here. Shortly after the death of Prince Henry, most of the books in the royal library at Whitehall were joined with the prince's extensive library in St. James's Palace. These books were, however, kept apart from Prince Henry's;[16] they are listed as "Whitehall" books in the early handwritten catalogues preserved in the British Library (BL C.120.h.6 [1–3]) and are thus separated from "St. James" items. The Whitehall books listed in the Bodleian manuscript, on the other hand, must refer to a different lot altogether. None of these are listed in the early, that is, pre-1694 handwritten catalogues of the St. James Library; they are mostly manuscripts, and many of them are association or dedication copies. The most likely explanation for this is that King James kept the more private section of his library at hand when the bulk of it was moved from Whitehall to St. James's, and that Charles kept and added to this personal library when he succeeded to the throne. At some point soon after 1641, the Smith inventory preserved in the Bodleian was made of this small library; "Whitehall" books in this inventory would then refer to books actually kept in Whitehall Palace in the early 1640s.[17] These books rejoined those kept in the St. James's Library only towards the end of the century when some of the association copies mentioned above, Daniel's *Panegyrick* and the *Description of Fireworks* by Nodes and Butler, turn up in the 1694 catalogue of the St. James Library, BL C.120.h.6 (5). All this would explain why these manuscripts, as well as those of Thomas May's poems, are not listed among the Whitehall books in Young's inventories of the St. James library of 1650 or in the subject catalogue of St. James's books drawn up by Thomas Ross, the keeper appointed by Charles II in 1661.[18] The eventual merger of what was left of the private Whitehall library with the bulk of the royal libraries at St. James's around 1694 may well be connected with another household move, from the house of Stuart to that of Orange, or with the appointment of Richard Bentley as Royal Librarian in 1693. If they hibernated at Whitehall, it was a lucky move, for they might well have perished in the fire that largely destroyed the palace in January 1698.

---

[15] See T. A. Birrell, *English Monarchs and their Books* (London, 1987), 24.

[16] See Jayne, Introduction to *Lumley Library*, 21, n. 2.

[17] This date would suggest a connection with the removal of the royal household in January 1642.

[18] This catalogue is now in the Huntington Library, MS HM 180.

Scripts and Scribes

MS Royal 18.C.XII is an exceptionally well-prepared manuscript. There are, normally, twenty-six lines to the page; the ruling is clearly, almost obtrusively, visible, with vertical lines to the right and the left and horizontal ones (at intervals of 10 mm) for every line of text. The lineator knew exactly what the layout of each page would be; this is obvious from the exact grids of guidelines on pages with chapter-endings and beginnings. When the end of a book occurs in the middle of a page, only the exact number of lines needed for the text of the ending are drawn out (though there usually are prick marks from top to bottom). At the beginning of books there are two extra vertical lines for the indented verse Argument, and an exact number of shorter and more closely spaced supporting lines (at 8 mm intervals) needed for the text of the Argument. There is no lineation in the gaps between the Arguments and the main text. On the whole, the exactness of the guidelines suggests that the scribe worked from a fair copy rather than from foul papers.

The script of MS Royal 18.C.XII looks like a hybrid form between cursive italic and sloped roman. It resembles most closely the *cancellaresca romana bastarda* as developed by Italian writing masters in the sixteenth century, but it contains also elements of the set *formata* and the fluent *corsiva*.[19] These humanist scripts were still being taught and practised in the first half of the seventeenth century, especially in aristocratic circles.[20] Since the poem was written by command of King Charles I, it is tempting to think that the manuscript has close royal associations, in particular if the hypothesis is correct that the king kept it in his private library. If it had been submitted to the king himself, one would expect it to carry a dedication similar to the one published in the printed edition. No such dedication is preserved; there is room for speculation, however, that it may have been on the leaf that is lacking in the first quire of six leaves. Whoever the recipient of the manuscript was, it seems plausible to assume that it was handed in for inspection by some person close to the king. The dedication in the printed edition suggests as much when it says: "BORNE BY HIS COMMAND;

---

[19] The development and distinction of these scripts is best described in James Wardrop's article on Giovanbattista Palatino, the sixteenth-century Italian writing master, "Civis Romanus svm: Giovanbattista Palatino and his Circle," *Signature*, N.S. 14 (1952): 3–39.

[20] See Anthony G. Petti, *English Literary Hands from Chaucer to Dryden* (London, 1977), 19.

AND NOT TO LIVE BVT BY HIS GRATIOVS ACCEPTATION."[21]
This could mean that the king ordered the composition of the poem but made its publication subject to his approval. If this was indeed the case, the dedication would yield a more precise date for the production of the manuscript than the evidence from the script allows, namely not long before the title of the poem was entered in the Stationers' Register in November 1632.[22]

The uncommon regularity of the script looks as if the scribe had tried to give his reader a foretaste of what the poem would look like in print. He certainly achieves a maximum degree of legibility; the overall effect, however, is too rigid to be altogether pleasing to the eye. The slope of the letters is only slight, and there are hardly any joinings, not even in the ligatures. This gives the words and lines an almost Roman stiffness; the model in the scribe's mind may have been books and manuscripts in the Italian humanist tradition, the italic type of Aldus Manutius, or the *cancellaresca* scripts of Giovanbattista Palatino, but the result looks rather strained. What has been said of Palatino, that he tended "to adjust and refine his material by just that scruple too much, whence spontaneous charm in a script may be lost, and its title, as handwriting, forfeited," is certainly true of this scribe.[23] The wide spaces between letters, words, and lines give the page a much less compact look than it would have in a printed book, which again irritates the eye. One is left with the impression that the scribe has labored for a mistaken aim and that he missed in the end both the elegance of a manuscript and the evenness of a printed text. The awkwardness of the exercise soon leads to doubts of what one tends to take for granted at first sight: that this is the work of a professional scribe. Such doubts are nourished by the thought of its costs. Fair copies, even if only meant to serve as printer's copy, were expensive. Peter Beal mentions the example of Davenant who was satirized for paying £ 10 to have his poem neatly transcribed for the printer: " 'Twas hop'd in time thou woulldst despaire / To give ten pounds to write it faire."[24] An expense like that would have been even more desperate for the

---

[21] *The Reigne of King Henry the Second*, London, 1633, A4r.

[22] Gilson and Warner give only the date "XVII cent." in their *Catalogue of Western Manuscripts*, II, 303.

[23] Wardrop, "Civis Romanus svm," *Signature*, N.S. 14 (1952): 19.

[24] Peter Beal, *Index of English Literary Manuscripts*, (London, 1987), II, Part 1, 311. The couplet is in *Certain Verses Written by Severall of the Author's Friends* (London, 1653), here quoted from *Sir William Davenant's Gondibert*, ed. David Gladish (Oxford, 1971), 277.

impecunious May than it was for Davenant, his rival for the laureateship.
For economic as well as paleographical considerations, then, the question
of whether May himself could have written the fair copy of *The Reigne of
King Henry the Second* should not be ruled out entirely. The lettering is, on
the whole, fairly consistent. There are only the usual variations, for instance
in the undiscriminating use of long or short *s* and of round or angular *E*.
The *p* has a prominent *formata* terminating serif, a stock calligraphic fea-
ture,[25] and the *l* is usually spurred at medium height. Only a few traces of
nonitalic scripts creep in: the *w* is written in a formal secretary throughout
and the *d* alternates between an almost Roman angularity (with vertical stem
and serif head) and the French form, as Palatino called it,[26] a hybrid secre-
tary with an arched back ending in a wide, almost closed backward loop (of-
ten used in *nd*-lettergroups). The *h* is similarly varied; there is an upright,
serifed form, but usually the stem is curved to an open forward lobe ap-
proaching the curled finials of its *piacevole* pendant.[27] The adverse, back-
ward and forward slopes of the hybrid *d* and this French *h* often disrupt the
movement of a line, and their flourishes counteract the otherwise set appear-
ance of the script and add to its slightly awkward look.[28] In later practice,
a script like this was usually reserved for Latin texts or to set off proper
names in a differently written context; Sir John Harington, an excellent cal-
ligrapher, switches to a similar script when inserting a Latin piece in his col-
lection of epigrams (BL Add. MS 12049) or in the marginal notes, which
often refer to Latin parallels, in his largely autograph copy of the English
Orlando furioso (BL Add. MS 12049).[29] An italic book hand was seldom
used for longer passages of vernacular text outside aristocratic circles; a rare

---

[25] See Peter J. Croft, *Autograph Poetry in the English Language*, (London, 1973), I, 43.

[26] He criticized its use in an italic script; see Wardrop, "Giovanbattista Palatino," 29.

[27] The *h* shows the greatest number of variations within the cancellaresca skeleton
form. Besides the two with straight and looped stems there is a *testeggiata* form with a
clubbed head, and one with an elegant, though not quite joining, *formata* link in liga-
tures. All these forms are visible in the specimen page, Figure 4, p. xxii.

[28] To this list of variations on the basic script a number of cases might be added
where the scribe slips up the calligraphic register and employs the *cancellaresca formata*
script he uses for his titles. The more formal *g*, for example, with its lower bowl hanging
from the upper one like a noose, is used alternately with the more fluent *g* with a simple
drop-like descender in the Argument to Book VI.

[29] Philip Gaskell gives a specimen page from the *Orlando* manuscript that has a short
shoulder note in the italic hand in his article on "Harington, Ariosto's *Orlando furioso*,
1591," *From Writer to Reader: Studies in Editorial Method* (Oxford, 1978), 18.

example is a transcript of the fifth book of Richard Hooker's *Lawes of Eccle-siastical Politie*, which served as printer's copy to John Windet in 1597 (Bod-leian MS Add. C. 165). Percy Simpson, who reproduces a page of this tran-script in facsimile, calls the scribe "a scholarly calligrapher," a distinction for which writers such as Thomas May or his friend Ben Jonson may well have striven.[30]

The same hand that wrote the main text of *The Reigne of King Henry the Second* added a number of marginal notes in the manuscript that usually re-fer to chronicles used by the author as sources; these notes are written in the same script as the main text but in a smaller size. There are also a number of mostly interlinear corrections. By necessity, these are small-sized again, but they are also in a different script, a cursive italic that shows greater fa-cility and a greater amount of secretary elements. Most conspicuous is the consistent use of the Greek *e* in these corrections,[31] but many of the con-sonants betray secretary influence, too. In III, 8, for instance, a cursive "two" written with a secretary *t* replaces an illegible cancellation; on the facing page "weare" (with two Greek *e*s) is inserted over an inferior caret in line 47; similarly, "winde" in IV, 752 is written with secretary *d* and Greek *e*.[32] The difference in scripts does not necessarily point to different hands, as the example of Harington has already indicated;[33] it is only for convenience, therefore, that the writer of the set italic hand who wrote the main text will be called the scribe and the writer of the corrections in cursive italic the corrector in the following analysis.

The interlinear corrections are of particular importance for the authority and transmission of the manuscript and hence the choice of a copy-text for this edition. Many of these corrections are of a minor character and affect the text only marginally. Thus, in Book III, a dropped word, "weare," is in-serted in line 47, a dittographic "the" is cancelled in 133, a lacking *y* is added to "the" in 143, "had" is inserted in 216, the orthography of "insep-

---

[30] Percy Simpson, *Proof-Reading in the Sixteenth, Seventeenth and Eighteenth Centuries* (1935; rpt. Oxford 1970), 41; facsimile page on plate X.

[31] A single epsilon *e* has crept in at VII, 392 of the *King Henry* manuscript in "dayes."

[32] Two pages of the manuscript showing revisions in Book I and II are reproduced in Denzell Smith's edition of one of Thomas May's plays, "*The Tragoedy of Cleopatra Queene of Aegypt* by Thomas May: A Critical Edition" (Ph.D. diss., Minnesota, 1965; rpt. New York, 1979), xxxvi, xxxvii, figures 4 and 5.

[33] Anthony Petti, who gives a short assessment of the penmanship in courtly circles around 1600 in his *English Literary Hands*, says that "most educated men in the period were able to write both scripts [i.e., italic and secretary] with equal facility" (p. 19).

arable" is corrected in 254, a forgotten "em" is added in 257. With alter-
ations like these it is sometimes hard to say whether they come from the
scribe or the corrector. Since the corrector wrote in a mixed hand, only the
cursive slope of the italic letters helps to assign some of the corrections to
the corrector rather than the scribe. In addition, the unusually wide spacing
of words and letters in the manuscript made insertions fairly easy (in partic-
ular between words), and we find letters squeezed in which, in a manuscript
written in a cursive hand, would have been interlined. Crammed in like this,
an italic letter's slope may be lost and identification made impossible. Book
I, line 202 provides two examples of such circumstances concurring, with an
italic *s* added to "hill" and an *i* inserted in "theire."

   With punctuation marks it is sometimes hard to decide whether they were
added or not, and if they were, whether by the scribe or the corrector. The
generous spacing between words facilitated additions at any time, but there
are indications that the punctuation was checked by a corrector at a later
stage. In particular, a considerable number of commas appear to have been
inserted after the completion of the manuscript, and in a less careful man-
ner: the ink looks bolder, and the inserted marks are placed below the base
line (usually they sit right on the line). While their outward appearance is
somewhat slapdash, the function of these additions betrays an uncommon
concern for clarity. A full range of marks is employed and used mostly ac-
cording to modern practice. For an example, see the attempt at distinguish-
ing between question and exclamation marks in Book V, lines 359–92 (a
passage with an unusually intrusive narrator), and the use of both commas
and brackets for parenthetical remarks (V, 373–4, 387). This kind of heavy
pointing is more than accidental, and it has obviously been employed with
an eye to sense and effect. The additional marks suggest that the punctua-
tion has been revised by the author himself; perhaps Thomas May was influ-
enced in this respect by Ben Jonson, whose fastidiousness in points of orth-
ography and punctuation is well known from the pains he took over the
preparation of the folio edition of his *Workes* in 1616.[34]

   Apart from punctuation marks, there are altogether more than ninety cor-
rections to the manuscript. The more substantive of them are interlinear in-

---

   [34] For W. W. Greg, such careful supervision of semisubstantials constitutes a reason
for choosing a revised reprint as copy-text (*The Editorial Problem in Shakespeare*, Oxford,
1941, xx). Denzell S. Smith transfers this argument to the equally carefully corrected
manuscript of Thomas May's *Cleopatra; A Critical Edition*, xxiii.

sertions.[35] Since these insertions comprise either a group of letters or a whole word (in line IV, 694, two words, "by night"), it is usually possible to say whether they are in the set or the more cursive italic script. There are altogether five interlinear insertions that are definitely written in the set italic script: III, 216, 407; IV, 694; V, 299; VI, 507 (II, 274 is a doubtful case). All but one of these additions are corrections of omissions or obvious mistakes that the scribe detected shortly after working on his copy; to correct them no editorial decision needed to be taken. The exception is V, 299, where the scribe corrected the number of the Yorkshire knights who captured King Malcolm near Alnwick from "sixe" to "fiue." This is the only instance of a substantive variant originating from the scribe, but he probably had the marginal note giving the names of five knights to prompt him. As will be explained later, the author was faced with conflicting accounts in his sources, and this may have caused the confusion about numbers which the scribe noted and tried to correct.[36] Another explanation would be that the marginal note giving the names of the knights has been added at a later stage in the preparation of the manuscript, and the scribe realized only then that the numeral given in V, 299 did not correspond with the number of names in the note.

On the whole, the scribe worked carefully and overlooked only a few of his own errors or omissions. When he did, the corrector stepped in, and some of the latter's additions fill up the gaps undetected by the scribe, for example I, 34, 532 (the same error in II, 253); II, 274, 378; III, 47, 257; IV, 754. The restricted number and strictly subordinate quality of the scribe's corrections may have implications for the question of who wrote the text and who made the corrections. The conclusion, however, that scribe and corrector were different persons is not as self-evident as it may appear at first sight. There was a long tradition of scribes changing their script from text to commentary. Eventually this led to the formation of a hierarchy of scripts; the interlinear corrections in the less learned script could well be a remnant of this tradition, and instead of making a distinction between scribe and corrector one could also distinguish between glossarial and textura hands.[37]

---

[35] Possible exceptions are line IV, 146, where "gett," and line VI, 388, where "a way" appear to have been appended to the end of the line.

[36] For the question of conflicting authorities see the section on Sources, below, and the explanatory note to V, 299.

[37] For the establishment of this hierarchy see M. B. Parkes, *English Cursive Book Hands 1250–1500* (1969; rpt. with rev. London, 1979), xxiv, and the paragraph "Hands"

While it is thus conceivable that a scribe, or, indeed, the author, changed scripts from writing a set italic in the main text to a more fluent cursive italic with secretary elements in his corrections, it seems improbable that he did so from one correction to the next; one would expect him to avoid inter-linear corrections altogether (for instance by erasing) or, if unavoidable, to write them in the more prestigious script—unless one assumes him to have added some of the corrections after the manuscript had been inspected and had been returned to him, for instance, to serve as exemplar for another copy.

This raises the question of the identity of either scribe or corrector with increased urgency. Normally, one would assume that a fair copy of this length was prepared by a professional scribe, and that the author added a few unavoidable corrections. Writing with the regularity of the main script would certainly have taken more schooling and discipline than an author was normally prepared to invest. The willingness to undergo such an exacting task increases, however, the nearer one gets to the court. Ben Jonson could afford to approach it in comparatively cavalier fashion; the fair copy of *The Masque of Queenes* which he wrote for Prince Henry in 1609 is apt to set off the somewhat laboured exactitude of the *King Henry* manuscript by comparison. Nevertheless, Jonson's autograph, written in a set mixed hand, has been described as a "delicate example of literary calligraphy."[38] Other presentation manuscripts, some of them autograph, come closer to the print-like formality of the *King Henry the Second* manuscript. The copy, for instance, that Henry Peacham made of his Book of Emblems, based on the *Basilikon Doron*, for presentation to Prince Henry around 1610 (it is listed in the inventory that Patrick Young was asked to make after the death of King Charles in 1650) has a similarly stylized, though, owing to the illuminations, rather sumptuous appearance as the *King Henry* manuscript.[39] The script, too, looks even more elaborate than May's and shows two distinctly different italic hands. Each page contains an emblem with motto, verse sub-

---

in Harold Love's *Scribal Publication in Seventeenth-Century England* (Oxford, 1993), 108–16. James Wardrop points to the fact that the *cancellaresca corsiva* (like italic type) had its origin in the humanists' glosses; see "Giovanbattista Palatino," 18.

[38] See Edward Maunde Thompson, "Handwriting," *Shakespeare's England*, eds. Sidney Lee and C. T. Onions (Oxford, 1916) I, 293; Anthony Petti analyses and reproduces fol. 19v. of Jonson's presentation copy (British Library MS Royal 18.A.XLV) in his *Literary Hands*, 46.

[39] Nr 29 in *The 4.ᵗʰ Catalogue of Bookes belonging to yᵉ Liberarie att Sᵗ Jameses*, BL C.120.h.6 (1), p. 17, now Royal MS 16.E.XXXVIII.

scription, a quotation from King James's *Basilikon Doron*, and frequently an additional learned reference in the form of a footnote. The motti and Latin verse subscriptions are written in a set *cancelleresca testaggiata* with print-like, mostly unconnected letters (though not as uncomfortably wide apart as those in May's *The Reigne of King Henry the Second*); the mostly English quotations and the footnotes (Latin, English, and Greek) are written in a slightly more facile *cancellaresca* leaning towards the *piacevole*. The manuscript was probably produced in several stages, as can be deduced from the different shades of the ink: first the motto and *subscriptio* were written, then the quotations from the *Basilikon Doron*, and lastly the footnotes. As noted above, there are indications in the manuscript of *The Reigne of King Henry the Second* that some of the marginal notes were added after the main text had been written, though this does not constitute a separate stage in the production but rather a process of revision.

The John Marston manuscript mentioned above as listed in the 1694 catalogue of the library at St. James's provides another, surprisingly close, parallel to some of the scribal idiosyncrasies in the *King Henry* manuscript. It contains the speeches of a short pageant presented on the occasion of the King of Denmark's visit to England, in particular his passage through the city of London on 31 July 1606: "The Argument of the Spectacle presented to the Sacred Maiestys of great Britain, and Denmark, as they Passed through London" (BL Royal MS 18.A.XXXI). There is a speech of the Recorder, Sir Henry Montagu, in Latin prose, and there are Latin verses spoken by characters of the pageant; the whole is signed, with a subscription, by Marston. The speeches are written in a clumsily formal italic hand which in many respects shows even more obvious signs of strain than does the text in the *King Henry* manuscript. There are several corrections (a superscription on fol. 4v, and a marginal one on 5r), and there is a marginal note on 4v, all of them probably authorial.[40] In these corrections there is some effort to approach the formality of the original text, but Marston falls back into some of the habits of his (apparently more natural) secretary hand, most notably by using the Greek instead of the italic *e*—very much like the corrections in MS Royal 18.C.XII. As in the case of May's *The Reigne of King Henry the*

---

[40] For evidence see W. W. Greg's note in his *English Literary Autographs*, Part I, "Dramatists" (London, 1925), No XVIII. The manuscript is edited in Arnold Davenport, *The Poems of John Marston* (Liverpool, 1961), 183–8; and in an article by R. E. Brettle, "Notes on John Marston" in *Review of English Studies*, N.S. 13 (1962): 390–3.

Second the question arises of who was responsible for writing the main text of the manuscript.[41]

A further parallel of an autograph written for dedication is provided by Daniel's "Panegyrick congratulatorie to his sacred maiestie," one of the manuscripts listed in the Smith 34 inventory (now BL Royal 18.A.LXXII). It is a fair copy of the poem in fifty-eight stanzas which was presented to King James at Burley-on-the Hill, Rutland, on or shortly after 23 April 1603. It is written in a very delicate fluent italic script, widely spaced, but with long and finely drawn strokes connecting the small letters which give a generous appearance to the page. It shares some orthographical and paleographical features with the *King Henry* manuscript. The punctuation is unusually full and precise,[42] and different forms of particular letters are used. Basically the script is a neat *cancellaresca corsiva* with a tendency towards *testeggiata*; as in the *King Henry* manuscript, the most striking variation is in the different kinds of *d* employed: an italic one with a straight stem, the other French, with a wide, open loop leaning to the left. Daniel prefers the French type in an initial position (but not consistently), whereas it is used almost consistently in *nd* combinations, which means mainly in final positions, in MS Royal 18.C.XII. He seems more at ease than the scribe of the *King Henry* manuscript; in spite of an occasional insecurity in the layout of the page his manuscript looks more elegant than May's rigidly ruled copy.

The Autograph Copy of May's Tragœdy of Cleopatra

With these parallels in mind it seems less unlikely that the author himself sat down to copy *The Reigne of King Henry the Second* in a rigorously set italic hand. May would probably not have shunned the exertion it entailed, as is attested by the companion piece of MS Royal 18.C.XII, MS Royal 18.C.VII. This fair copy of May's *Tragœdy of Cleopatra* can now be proven to be an autograph. The key to the identification lies in a presentation copy of May's *Supplementum Lucani* (Leyden, 1640) with an autograph fourteen-

---

[41] P. J. Croft describes similar features in his analysis of Marston's autograph copy of the verses spoken in honour of the Dowager Countess of Derby when she visited Ashby House in 1607. The manuscript shows the strained effect that an amateur like Marston is likely to produce when aiming at calligraphic effects in a presentation copy; *Autograph Poetry in the English Language* (London, 1973), I, 28.

[42] Usually, Daniel is more casual in this respect; cf. the pointing in his autograph copy of the lyrics to his masque *Hymen's Triumph* (Edinburgh University Library MS De.3.69) as analyzed by P. J. Croft in his *Autograph Poetry*, I, 21.

Nobilissimo viro, omni doctri=
narum genere clarissimo, et
honoratissimo in perpetuum inter
literatos nomini
D Danieli Hensio, illustrissini [sic]
ordinis Sᵗⁱ Marci apud Venetos
Equiti.

hunc libellum suum mittit

obseruantissimus

Tho: May.

tur
Pagina iudiciũ docti subitura moue=
Hensiadæ, ut Clario missa legenda
Deo.
Ouid:

Figure 5. A transcript of May's inscription to Daniel Heinsius in the
copy of his *Supplementum Lucani* (1640), which was sold at auction by
Sotheby's on 19 July 1990. The auction catalogue (*English Literature
and History*) carries a reproduction of the original on page 17. Unfor-
tunately, the present owner of the volume refused permission to repro-
duce a facsimile of the inscription in this edition.

line inscription by the author to the Dutch humanist Daniel Heinsius, which has recently come to light. The book was auctioned by Sotheby's and went to Maggs, who sold it to a private collector.[43] Although the inscription is written in Latin, a detailed comparison makes it virtually certain that Denzell Smith, who edited *The Tragœdy of Cleopatra* from the manuscript, was right in suspecting that this fair copy had been prepared by the author himself.[44]

Furthermore, a comparison between the fair copy of *Cleopatra* and the corrector's insertion in the *King Henry* manuscript confirms the suggestion of Gilson and Warner that the hand that copied *Cleopatra* is also the correcting hand of *The Reigne of King Henry the Second*.[45] Owing to the infrequency of corrections in the *King Henry* manuscript this identification is somewhat harder to prove than the one between the autograph dedication of the *Supplementum Lucani* and the *Cleopatra* manuscript. MS Royal 18.C.VII is written in an easily legible cursive italic hand with secretary elements (in particular the consistently used Greek *e*) that closely resembles the *King Henry* corrections. The basis for comparison is rather small; in sum, however, the similarities furnish close to conclusive evidence. Hilton Kelliher has pointed out to me "that there are definite resemblances between, for example, the interlined 'take' of fol. 21b, l. 4 [i.e., II, 378 of the poem] and that found in *Cleopatra*, fol. 4, l. 18, and between the lower-case *d*s and *w*s of the corrections here and on fols. 31b and 75 [i.e., "badd" and "weake" on p. 60, lines III, 425–6, and "a way" on p. 147, line VI, 388] and those found in the play text."[46]

---

[43] The sale was held on 19 July 1990. The sales catalogue points out that "examples of Thomas May's handwriting are of the utmost rarity" (p. 17). Hilton Kelliher, who drew my attention to the autograph inscription, knows of only one other (allegedly autograph) letter dated 1647 which was sold from the collection of John Young F. S. A. at Sotheby's on 14 April 1875, and has since disappeared (letter of 18 April 1990). The note in another copy of May's *Supplementum Lucani*, "Ex ipsius Authoris dono, Hagæ Comitis," is not autograph (Folger Library, PR2709 M3 C6 L3 1640 Cage).

[44] Denzell Smith had no opportunity to make comparisons with a specimen of May's handwriting.

[45] Gilson and Warner, *Catalogue of Western Manuscripts in the Royal and King's Collections*, II, 303.

[46] Letter of 25 July 1990.

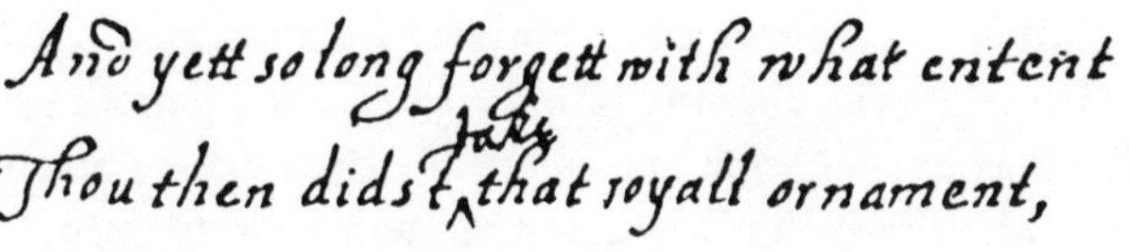

And yett so long forgett with what entent
Thou then didst that *royall ornament,*

Figure 6. Royal MS 18.C.XII, fol. 21v, p. 40, lines 3–4.

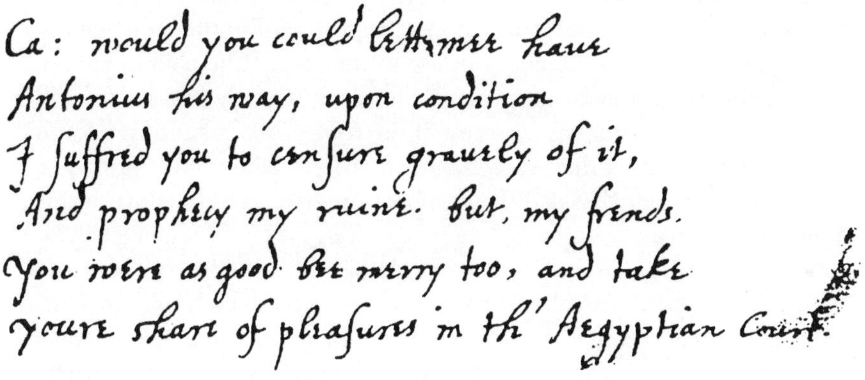

Ca: would you could lettymer haue
Antonius his way, upon condition
I suffred you to consure grauely of it,
And prophecy my ruine. But, my frinds.
You were as good bee mirry too, and take
youre share of pleasures in th' Aegyptian Court.

Figure 7. Royal MS 18.C.VII, fol. 4r, lines 14–19.

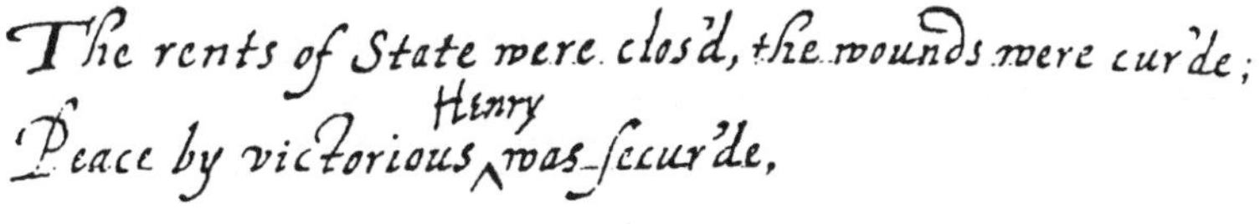

The rents of State were clos'd, the wounds were cur'de;
Peace by victorious Henry *was secur'de,*

Figure 8. Royal MS 18.C.XII, fol. 2v, lines 23–24.

On the other hand, the corrector of *The Reigne of King Henry the Second* prefers an initial secretary *b* with indented bowl to the italic one with a straight shaft written by May himself; but this small difference is overridden by the otherwise similar duct. Peter Beal, Sotheby's manuscript expert and compiler of the *Index of English Literary Manuscripts* for the period, gave the two manuscripts a short examination and noted the discrepancy but saw no reason to doubt the identity of both hands. One will have to make allowances because the print-like appearance of the main text has apparently induced the corrector to give his script a more set appearance. This becomes obvious if one compares the interlined "Henry" on fol. 2v (I, 34) of the *King Henry* manuscript (see Figure 8) with the autograph "Hensio" and "Hensiadæ" in May's inscription (Figure 5, p. xxxiii): the slightly detached characters of the correction do not obscure the close similarity of the hands. Moreover, on the title page of the *Cleopatra* manuscript, where May gives his script a more set appearance, the "He" in "Hesperios" corresponds almost exactly with that in the interlinear "Henry," down to a foot serif in the right column of the capital "H," which he does not use in the text of the manuscript.

It is paleographical evidence, then, that argues strongly and in the end convincingly for the author as corrector of the *King Henry* manuscript. With the *King Henry* manuscript, such evidence is less telling. The print-like quality of the script makes it difficult, if not impossible, to identify an individual, be he writer or scribe. There is, however, evidence of an equally, if not more, compelling kind. The very long copies of the *Cleopatra* play and the *King Henry* poem provide plenty of evidence from which to draw conclusions about their writers' spelling habits. In an age that had no generally accepted system of "right writing," this evidence amounts to a kind of orthographic fingerprint of the copyists, and in the case of these two texts it is hard to escape the conclusion that they were written by one and the same person who would, of course, again be Thomas May himself.[47] This conclusion is the more compelling because both manuscripts show a number of

---

[47] It is mistaken, I think, to assume that the absence of hard-and-fast spelling rules led to loose habits in every single writer. Thomas May provides another example of the well-known fact that learned people in particular wrote with a considerable degree of consistency. As Denzell Smith has noticed in his edition of *Cleopatra* (Introduction, p. 1), the scribe of Royal MS 18.C.VII is much more consistent in his spelling than the compositor of the 1639 printed edition; it seems probable, therefore, that May cared about orthography. This does not preclude, of course, the possibility that even with an educated person like May spelling habits could be highly idiosyncratic.

unusual orthographic features. The *Cleopatra* manuscript literally shares these features to a tittle with the text of the *King Henry* manuscript. The doubling of the vowels in words like "hee" and "wee," "whoo" and "doo," the doubling of consonants at the end of a syllable, as in "fitt" or "spiritt,"[48] the older spelling of "fower" instead of "four,"[49] the use of lowercase after a period in midline, and the apostrophising of mute *e* in the past tense and past participle are cases in point, but there are many more.[50] A comparison of the very different treatment of accidentals in the *printed* text of *King Henry*, or of the manuscript and printed versions of *Cleopatra*, shows at a glance how close the correspondence is.[51] It was not uncommon for writers of the seventeenth century to use more archaic spellings and pointings than their printers,[52] but a concordance as steady as that between the two manuscripts can not be explained by a common tendency to retain conservative habits of orthography. It seems just as unlikely that May supervised the transcribing of *King Henry the Second* so closely that the scribe adhered to even the minutest accidental detail of his copy. It is hard to escape the conclusion that the author was also the scribe of the manuscript.

This last assumption is connected with the question of what purpose the fair copy of *The Reigne of King Henry the Second* was supposed to serve. Apparently, May did not always feel compelled to produce as careful copies as he did in the case of the *King Henry* manuscript. MS Royal 18.C.VII, his fair copy of *The Tragœdy of Cleopatra*, is written in a much more facile hand than MS Royal 18.C.XII. The care with which the latter manuscript was prepared and the high quality of the paper on which it was written suggest that it was indeed produced for presentation or inspection at court, if not for the king himself.[53] It is worth mentioning that King Charles took some interest in the art of calligraphy. He was taught by a writing master, Martin

---

[48] For instances see the pages reproduced in facsimile in Denzell Smith's edition of *Cleopatra*, pp. 31, 34, figures 1, 3.

[49] See *Cleopatra*, I, ii, 103, and cf. *King Henry*, IV, 214, 231, 312.

[50] For a list of idiosyncrasies see p. lxii.

[51] Sometimes the scribal spelling has, apparently, spilled over into print, for instance in I, 268–75, where we find "greisly," "feirce," and "Feind" instead of the usual "ie" forms.

[52] Percy Simpson provides a number of examples, mainly from Harington's translation of *Orlando furioso* (1591) and William Wake's *Preparation for Death* (1687), in his *Proof-Reading*, 38–9, 52, 74, 98.

[53] Janet Backhouse, Curator of Manuscripts at the British Library, thinks it reasonable to suppose that the fair copy was made for the king himself (letter of 23 March 1990); W. H. Kelliher thinks it possible (letter of 18 April 1990).

Billingsley, and wrote, as William Massey put it, "a fair open Italian hand and more correctly perhaps than any prince we ever had."[54] Like his father and brother, Charles also cared about presentation and association copies and kept several of them in his library; as argued above, this may well have saved the manuscript for posterity.[55]

Like his addressee, May was an amateur calligrapher, and the stately script of the manuscript was not his everyday medium. The reason why May chose the set italic, almost roman, script was probably to convey a rough idea of what the poem would look like in print, the sort of print associated with classical texts. Seeing his poem in print may well have been the ultimate ambition of its author, for the printed medium carried a great deal of prestige, at least in the humanist circles to which May aspired.[56] This would allow for the fact that some of the features of the manuscript are not easily compatible with the idea of a presentation copy, a copy that was meant to be the final form in which the poem was to be read and kept. There are, in particular, a great number of rather crude corrections in the manuscript. In addition to the two kinds of corrections mentioned above— those inserted in the set italic hand and those written in a more cursive italic hand—there are quite a few less substantial corrections with an ink that looks different from that used in either of these. It is darker and on close inspection radiates a kind of metallic luster. Many of the added commas have this luster; some of the more substantive corrections are also executed so carelessly that they stand out in marked contrast to the otherwise neat appearance of the manuscript. All this argues for several different processes of correction, the latest of which (the one executed with the metallic ink) was brought off with very little respect to the outward appearance of the manu-

---

[54] Quoted from Ambrose Heal, *The English Writing-Masters and their Copy-Books 1570–1800: A Biographical Dictionary and a Bibliography.* Introduction by Stanley Morison (London, 1931; rpt. Hildesheim, 1962), 18. Martin Billingsley dedicated one of his copybooks, *The Pen's Excellencie* (1618) to Prince Charles. Cf. Charles Carlton who mentions that John Beauchesne taught Prince Charles his "distinctively beautiful italic handwriting" (*Charles I: The Personal Monarch* [London, 1983], 16).

[55] See T. A. Birrell, *English Monarchs and their Books: From Henry VII to Charles II,* The Panizzi Lectures 1986 (London, 1987), 24, 43–54.

[56] This may have been different in the coteries where manuscript lyrical poetry circulated, as Arthur F. Marotti has argued in his *Manuscript, Print, and the English Renaissance Lyric* (Ithaca, NY, 1995). May is often represented in the miscellanies which constitute these coteries, but their commonplace appearance and contents seem to assign these manuscripts to a completely different plane altogether.

script as a whole. Since these corrections affect mostly the pointing only, it is not impossible that they were added by a different hand altogether.[57] Whether there was a third hand involved in correcting the manuscript or not, there is little doubt that the corrections made in the more cursive script are authorial. Some of them affect the sense of lines which did not of themselves demand correction. Minor cases of this kind are to be found in Book II, where in line 417 "hee" was altered to "bee," and "hee" is, at least grammatically, more plausible than the subjunctive "bee" (in this case the author would have reinstated the *lectio difficilior*), and in line 446, where "waken'd" was probably changed from a grammatically possible, though less plausible, "weaken'd" (the letter struck out between the "w" and the "a" is illegible). More substantive are two cases in which the cancelled words have remained legible. In III, 425–6 the adjectives "badd" and "weake" have been exchanged. The original wording, which describes the frail position of King Stephen, was: "Nor durst that King, that had so weake a cause, / So badd a title, to maintain those lawes." The terms "weake" and "badd" were then struck out and overwritten with "badd" and "weake." The interlinear words are in a darker ink, and the differences in script recorded above are clearly visible, in particular the secretary elements, the Greek *e*, the uncial *d*, and the *b* with indented bowl. The verbal variation does little to change the sense of the line; it may have been undertaken with euphony rather than clarity in mind: it opts for the conventional phrase, the "weak title" and the "bad cause," and it avoids the clattering effect of consecutive *k* sounds in "so weak a cause." Still, it is an alteration unlikely to have been made by a copyist, and aiming at smoothness of sound and sense is in keeping with May's classicist style as a whole.

With similar ends in view, the epithet "bounteous" (applied to Venus) is changed to the more conventional "beauteous" in II, 90, and with a more daring author like Ben Jonson or John Donne such standardising would argue for nonauthorial influence, this is different in the case of Thomas May: his revisions not only for the manuscript copy but also for the printed version of *The Reigne of King Henry the Second* prove him to be striving above all for "correctness."[58] Another example of this tendency is the revi-

---

[57] Kevin Sharpe has pointed out to me that King Charles himself was not above correcting the punctuation of manuscripts that came to his attention (letter of 4 October 1996).

[58] In this respect he differs from John Milton, who in his proofreading corrected accidentals for stylistic reasons. As Helen Darbishire has shown, Milton used archaic spell-

sion of line I, 244, where Enyo, the goddess of war, complains of the peace reigning in Henry's realm, and paints a bucolic (or rather georgic) scene with, among other rustics, shepherds tending their sheep. Originally, the line ran "And theire owne feilds the fearelesse shepheards know"; "feilds" was then struck out and "flockes" brought in—the author again apparently deciding in favor of the more appropriate term against the more obtrusive alliteration plus assonance.

If these revisions were inserted with an eye to correctness it is the more puzzling that they were added with a decreasing respect for calligraphic decorum. This leads back to the question of what the writer of the manuscript aimed at. The answer could well be that it mainly served a practical purpose: it was handed in at court for inspection, to be sent back to the author in order to be prepared for the printer. The fact that the latest layer of corrections was added without regard to the outer appearance of the manuscript would then be explainable by the fact that May expected it to remain with himself, or to serve as copy for the printer. Both these courses would probably have led to the loss of the manuscript, but things turned out differently. The manuscript did not serve as a printer's copy, as a comparison with the printed version shows. Someone may have thought better of it—hardly the author himself who seems to have been indifferent to the appearance of the manuscript once it had served its purpose and who must have been weary of copying by then—more probably someone at court, and possibly the king himself, who reclaimed the manuscript and sent May back to prepare another copy for the printer.

---

ings for emphasis and punctuation marks for rhythmic effects, whereas the accidental corrections in the *King Henry* manuscript strive mostly for consistency and smoothness. See Helen Darbishire's edition of *The Manuscript of Paradise Lost. Book I* (Oxford, 1931).

THE PRINTED EDITION (1633)

Description and Collation

The title of Thomas May's *The Reigne of King Henry the Second* was entered
in the Stationers' Register on 30 November 1632: "30°. Nouembris 1632.
Beniamin ffisher Entred for his copy vnder the hands of Master BUCK-
NER and master *Aspley* warden a booke called **The raigne of King
HENRY the SECOND** written in **Seaven bookes** by Master THOMAS
MAY. vj d." It was published in an octavo volume in 1633 (STC 17715).
The size is approximately 4 in. x 6 in. (10 cm x 16 cm), the collation is
[A]4, B–O8, adding up to a total of 108 unnumbered pages. In extension of
the poem as preserved in the manuscript, the printed addition has a portrait
of King Henry, engraved by Robert Vaughan (size 12.4 cm x 8.3 cm [sub-
ject] + 1.9 cm margin), a dedication to King Charles, and two prose charac-
ters of King Henry and his sons, Henry and Richard. The contents of a
complete copy are: [A1] blank; [A2] recto [blank], verso [portrait]; [A3]
recto [title], "THE / REIGNE / OF KING / HENRY / THE SECOND,
Written in Seaven Bookes. [single rule] / By his Majesties Command. [single
rule] / [motto, two lines] *Invalidas vires Rex excitat, & juvat idem / Qui jubet;
obsequium solicit esse meum.* Auson: [single rule] / *LONDON,* / Printed by
A.M. for *Benjamin Fisher,* / dwelling in Aldersgate-streete at the / signe of
the *Talbot.* 1633.", verso [blank]; [A4] recto [dedication], "TO / THE
SACRED / MAIESTIE / OF / CHARLES" [etc., signed] "THO. MAY.",
verso [blank]; B1 recto–M7 verso [text, with heading], "THE REIGNE
OF / KING HENRY the Second"; M8 [blank]; N1 recto–O1 verso,
"THE / DESCRIPTION / OF KING HENRY / THE SECOND, WITH A
SHORT SURVEY / of the Changes in his / REIGNE"; O2 [blank, sig-
nature lacking;] O3 recto–7 recto "THE / SINGLE, AND / COMPARA-
TIVE / CHARACTERS OF / HENRY the Sonne, / and RICHARD"; O7
verso–8 verso [blank]. There are ornamental initials at the beginning of each
book and the additional "Characters" and conventional headpieces at the
start of the "Characters" on N1 recto and O3 recto. This, the only printed
edition of the poem, must have had considerable circulation, if the number
of preserved copies is a figure to go by: most of the major libraries in Britain
and the United States have one; the British Library and the Folger Library
own two each.[59]

---

[59] Eleven copies have been inspected in the original: in the United States those in the

The Printers

The Revised Short Title Catalogue adds to the imprint of the 1633 edition by naming John Beale besides Augustine Mathewes as second printer of May's *King Henry II* (RSTC 17715). Recent investigations have shown that sharing a printing job was much more common in the hand-press period than has hitherto been supposed; this is reflected, for instance, in the much greater number of double ascriptions in the A–H volume of the Revised STC than in the earlier-published volume I–Z.[60] In the case of *The Reigne of King Henry the Second*, evidence for a division of labour is not hard to find. There are several clear indications that a break occurred in the printing of the volume between quires K and L. In a well-preserved copy like that in the Huntington Library it is evident at first sight that the quality of the printing changes for the worse from K8v to L1r. This becomes particularly evident in the appended "Characters." The hyphenation in these prose additions is rather erratic, the spacing uneven, and there is a considerable amount of turned or wrong-font letters, damaged types, and rising spaces left standing.[61] Some of the uneven impression left by the "Characters" may be due to the generally rougher appearance of the type used in these appendices (which is larger than that in the verse parts). Together with the faults and errors an overall air of ineptitude prevails in these appendices which makes them look like apprentice work or a rush job.

A closer look reveals differences between the layout of preliminary mate-

Folger Shakespeare Library (STC 17715 copy 1, the William Cole/John Mitford copy, and STC 17715 copy 2, the Harmsworth copy), the Houghton Library (14454.49*), the Huntington Library (RB 62625), the Library of Congress (PR.2709.M3A.76. 1633), the Newberry Library (Case Y.185.M.45), and the Regenstein Library (PR.2709.M3R4 1633 Rare); in Great Britain those in the Bodleian Library (Wood 90 [7.]), the British Library (two copies, Casebook 1076.h.15[1.] and the Grenville copy G11413) and in the Cambridge University Library (Syn. 8.63.157). In addition, three copies have been consulted on microfilm: those in the Dulwich College Library, the Durham Cathedral Library, and the Lincoln Cathedral Library. The copies in the Folger Library have been collated with a Hinman collator; those in the British Library with a Marshall Smith collator. A xerox of the Huntington Library copy has been used for a transcript and as a working copy of the printed edition.

[60] A good number of these ascriptions were suggested by Peter Blayney on the basis of his collection of ornamental typographical material.

[61] A sample of these is to be found on N7r: damaged type in "Normandy" and "strength," filled lobes in "Scotland" and "English," no space between "English" and "Peers," a rising space between "of" and "Norfolk," roman instead of italic 'R' in "*Richard.*" See also the list of printer's errors in footnote 77.

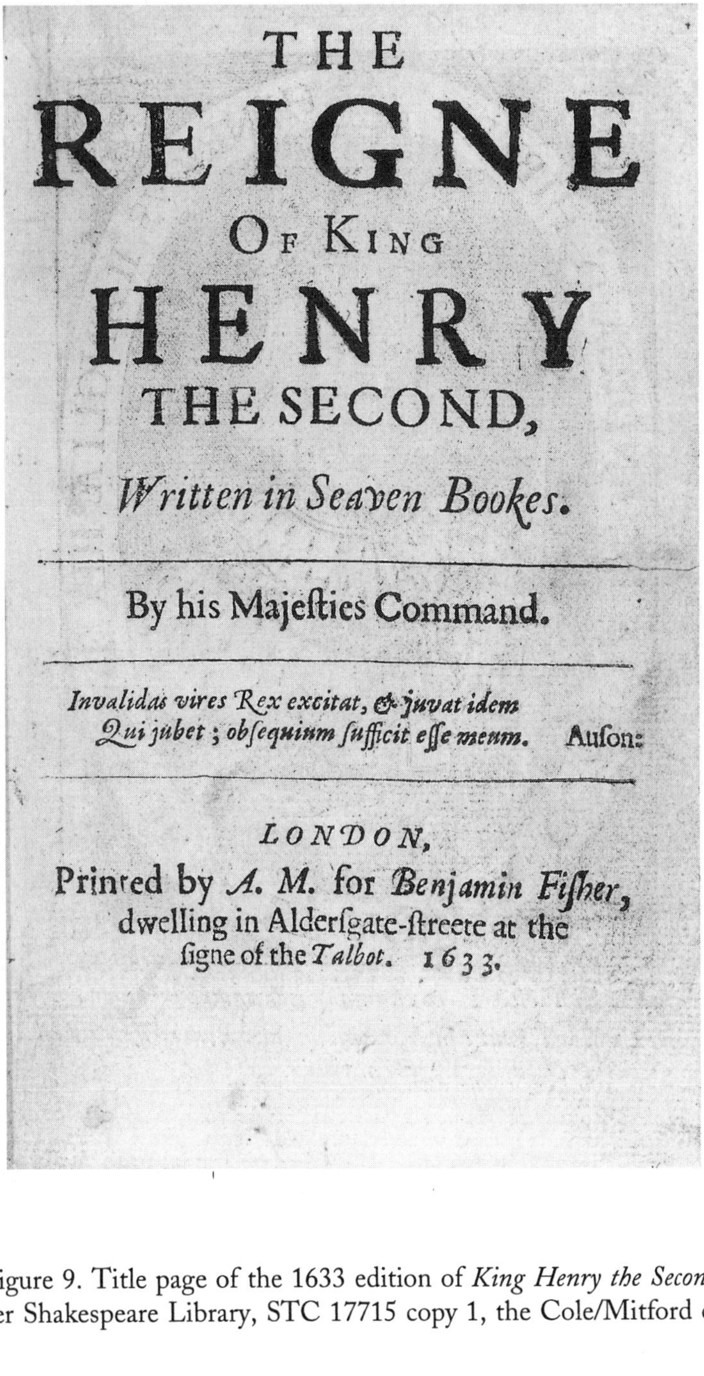

THE
REIGNE

OF KING

HENRY

THE SECOND,

Written in Seaven Bookes.

By his Majesties Command.

Invalidas vires Rex excitat, & juvat idem
Qui jubet; obsequium sufficit esse meum. Auson:

LONDON,
Printed by *A. M.* for *Benjamin Fisher,*
dwelling in Aldersgate-streete at the
signe of the *Talbot.* 1633.

Figure 9. Title page of the 1633 edition of *King Henry the Second* (Folger Shakespeare Library, STC 17715 copy 1, the Cole/Mitford copy).

rial in Books I–VI and in Book VII of *King Henry.* The beginning of Books I–VI is marked by a three-line subtitle, "The Reigne of / King Henry the Second. / The [x]th Booke.", followed by a headline above the Argument that is set between single rules, "The Argument of the [x]th Booke." At the beginning of Book VII (L7r) this changes; there is no subtitle, only the usual running title, "Lib.7. Henry the Second," followed by the headline "The Argument of the seventh Booke." The arguments at the head of each book are printed in italics (except for proper names). Usually, these italics are smaller and look slimmer than the roman type of the main text. At the beginning of Book VII, however, the italic type is slightly larger than the roman type of the text, and the roman type used for proper names in the argument is visibly larger than that used in the main text. Also, the ornamental initials in Book VII and in the additional "Characters" differ in size and type from those used in Books I–VI; the ornamental *T*, for instance, used at the beginning of Book VII is considerably larger than that at the beginning of Book I. All of this argues for a break somewhere between Books VI and VII.

The material used in the skeletons further shows that the boundary between the different sections lies between quire K and quire L (after line VI, 238). The upper and lower rules used to set off the headlines and the bottom rule that separates text from direction line in the verse parts of the poem help to locate this break. Several of these rules have individual features; since all the verse parts of the book were set by forms, and the skeletons were used repeatedly, these rules recur regularly according to their position in the inner or outer form. None of these individual rules are used, however, before *and* after the break between quires K and L. The rule under the headline on B5r, for instance, which has a marked hook at its right end, recurs on C4v, E3v, F5r, G6r, H5r, I6r and K5r, but not thereafter. On the other hand, a rule having a break about 2.6 cm from its right end is first used under the headline of L6r and recurs in L7r, M5r, M6r, N6r, N7r and O1r (the last page of the "Description of King Henry the Second," after which the sequence may have been interrupted).

Supporting evidence comes from the type employed in printing the verse parts. Both printers used type of the same style and size in setting the verse parts of the poem. Some of the types used in the second section, however, apart from looking more worn altogether, differ in nuances from their counterparts used in the earlier section. The lowercase *w* of the roman font used for the lines of verse, for instance, appears to have a slight slope in the earlier part of the book. This is due to the fact that the second *v* of this *w* does not take ink as well as the first; the *w* in the latter part is bold and slightly larger. In the lowercase *k*, the angle between stem and arm is narrower in the latter part than in the earlier.

That John Beale, who is not named in the imprint, was Mathewes' partner in the printing of *King Henry* can be proved by comparing the ornaments (including ornamental initials) and display types employed on titles and other preliminary pages. They help to establish bibliographical links between *King Henry* and other books printed by Mathewes and Beale in and around 1633. The most conspicuous ornament in the book (apart from the frontispiece, Robert Vaughan's engraving of King Henry II) is a headpiece at the beginning of "The Single, and Comparative Characters of Henry the Sonne and Richard" (O3r). It measures 3 cm x 6.4 cm and shows a Jehovah with tetragrammaton enthroned in the empyreum, with trumpet-blowing putti hovering around him and under his feet an altar with a pair of scales, a woman kneeling in prayer in front of it, and a satyr-footed Father Time (with scythe and skull) approaching her from behind. This same ornament is also used in the second edition of John Preston's *Sins Overthrow*, London: Printed by J. Beale, for Andrew Crooke, 1633, page 159 (X4r; STC 20276).[62] Beale apparently put it in as an alternative for an ornament of similar size, a crowned rose flanked by serpents, apples, and leaves, which he used at the head of the same page in the first edition of *Sins Overthrow* and in several other of Beale's books of this period.

Several other pieces of ornamental equipment are clearly associated with Beale. A headpiece showing Aeolus or some other windgod flanked by ornamental floral designs (measurement 1.7 cm x 6.2 cm), which is used at the beginning of "The Description of King Henry" (N1r), was definitely in Beale's possession.[63] A large factotum initial (size 3.2 cm x 3.3 cm) containing an "I" at the beginning of "The Description of King Henry" (N1r) originally belonged to Valentine Simmes and reached John Beale via William Hall; it is also used at the beginning of the section "A Short genealogi-

---

[62] Cf. R. B. McKerrow and K. F. S. Ferguson, *Title Page Borders Used in England and Scotland* (London, 1932), Nrs 271–273.

[63] Peter Blayney has traced it back to Beale's predecessors Robert Robinson, Richard Bradock, and William Hall; it is described in J. A. Lavin's "John Danter's Ornament Stock," *Studies in Bibliography* 23 (1970): 21–44, as Ornament 4 (Danter apparently only borrowed it for a time). I am very grateful to Peter Blayney for these references and for searching his archive for information on the blocks used by Beale in the *King Henry* volume.

call Dedvction of the Pedigree and *Progenie* of *Sveden* and Polonia" (Elr) of *The Genealogie and Pedigree of the most illustrious and most mighty Kings in Sveden* which Beale printed in 1632 (STC 13458).[64] It seems fair to assume from these links that John Beale printed the latter parts of *King Henry*.

If Mathewes' name were not named in the imprint, it would be harder to prove him as the main printer because the ornaments used in the first section of *King Henry* are much less conspicuous and therefore harder to trace than those used by Beale. Each of the first six books has a small ornamental initial (sized approximately 1 cm x 1 cm) at the beginning of the text set in roman. The initial "T," which is made to look like a tree by added floral ornaments, seems to be particularly revealing. It is used at the beginning of Book I (B1r) and appears to be identical with the same initial used in three other books printed by Mathewes around 1633. It is used at the beginning of Book III (D4r) of the second edition of *Lucan's Pharsalia*, 1631 (STC 16888), at the beginning of Act I, Scene i of Shakerley Marmion's *A Fine Companion*, 1633 (STC 17442, A4r), and at the beginning of the Prologue of "Antonio's Revenge," the second play in *The Workes of Mr. Iohn Marston*, 1633 (STC 17471, E8r). In the Newberry copies of *Pharsalia* and *Companion* and in the Huntington copy of *Antonio's Revenge* there are six clearly visible hair-like "roots" at the bottom of the tree-shaped "T" initial, and it looks as if this set these ornamental initials apart from the one used in *King Henry* which has only five, very thin, roots left. The Newberry copy of *King Henry* suggests, however, that one of the middle roots had broken away in the process of printing *King Henry*: a small part of its base and a dot of its stem remain visible. These root-like lines could well be leftovers from ornamental leaves that were sheared off by being repeatedly fitted into their place at the beginning of a line. Evidence for this is provided by the initial "S" at the begining of Book III of *King Henry* (D7r) and its correspondent, another initial "S" set upside down at the beginning of Book VII of the *Pharsalia*. What clearly are leaves at the bottom of the "S" in *King Henry* appear to be hairs in *Pharsalia* because the tips of the leaves have been shorn off. A slight difference in height between these two initials (the *Pharsalia* "S" is almost 1 mm shorter) would support this conclusion. The Huntington copy of *King Henry* probably shows the latest state in this development; its initial "T" is similar to the Newberry one, but looks more

---

[64] It is described as Factotum 1 in W. Craig Ferguson's *Valentine Simmes* (Charlottesville, 1968).

worn: only four of the hair-like roots are clearly visible; a magnifying glass reveals tiny specks left over from the second and third hair from the right. Further evidence comes from an investigation of the titling types used in the preliminary parts of *King Henry* and in other books printed by Mathewes around 1633. The large-sized types used in these parts come from a roman font with serifed capitals and a characteristic forked-head "A" which stands out, for instance, in lines 2 ("SACRED") and 5 ("CHARLES") of the dedication page of *King Henry* (A4r). Mathewes had used these large types in the first line of the title page (a2r) of *Lucan's Pharsalia* ('LVCANS') which he printed for Thomas Jones in 1631 (STC 16888). In fact, the "A"s in "LVCANS" and in "SACRED" correspond exactly in appearance, height, and breadth (8 mm x 8 mm). Another "A" of that font occurs in the first line of the subtitle to the first book, "LUCANS / Pharsalia" of that edition (A1r); this subtitle is taken over at the beginning of the succeeding nine books on B6r, D4r, F1r, G8r, I7r, L6r, N5r, P5r, and R8r. A similar "A" (apparently from the same font, but not identical with the one found in STC 16888) had already been used in the subtitles at the beginning of each book in an earlier edition of *Lucan's Pharsalia* which Mathewes printed for Thomas Jones and John Marriott in 1627 (STC 16887). The "A" of "MAIESTIE" in the third line of the dedication of *King Henry*, which lacks the forked head and seems to lift its left foot, occurs in line 2 on the title page of *The New Artificiall Gavging Line*, printed by Mathewes in 1633, except that it seems to have taken more ink in *King Henry* and looks somewhat bolder.

While these correspondences in the typographical equipment of Mathewes and Beale suffice to prove that these printers shared the work on *The Reigne of King Henry the Second*, it should be made clear that the differences are not obtrusive in the body of the text. In fact, the break between gathering K and L is much less conspicuous than the change in type size between the poem, including subtitles and running titles where both printers used types of almost identical fonts, and the prose appendices. It takes close inspection to notice that some of the types used in Beale's section of the poem, apart from looking slightly coarser altogether, differ in nuances from their counterparts used in the earlier section. The lowercase *w* of the roman font used for the lines of verse, for instance, appears to have a slight slope in the earlier part of the book. In the lowercase *k* the angle between stem and arm is narrower in the latter part than in the earlier. So there is no question of Mathewes and Beale sharing their equipment, but they may well have bought their stock from the same foundry.

It is hard to tell exactly what prompted a cooperation like that between Mathewes and Beale in this particular case. Perhaps Mathewes took on a more important job while still working on this book; perhaps he ran into trouble of some kind, as he did several times in the course of his career. Whatever the reason for the cooperation, the need to rush this particular job was, in all probability, not one of them. Rather, the asymmetrical sharing pattern (Mathewes produced nine and one-half, Beale only four sheets) suggests that the decision to share was not taken beforehand, as might have been the case if there had been a need to shorten the production period. The book was printed serially; concurrent printing would have resulted in equal shares.

Augustine Mathewes was not a master printer and he only rented his shop from White, and the Company of Stationers reminded him from time to time of his precarious position. In the company's census of July 1623 he was allowed only one press and had to be asked to take his second press down. He was also told that only if he complied with this order would the company consider his petition to become a master printer.[65] Mathewes had to be commanded repeatedly (1622, 1627, 1630) to dismiss apprentices whom he employed against the regulations of the company (that is because he was not a master). A typical record is that of 1627:

> This day Augustine Mathewes had warning to put away 3. boyes that he keepes disorderlye in his house within Eight dayes vpon the pen-altye of 40^s. for eu'ye eight [dayes] he keepes them or any of them Contrary to the order.[66]

Clearly, working conditions must have been strained from time to time in Mathewes' shop. The busiest year in his career was 1633, when he managed to print about forty books, some of them as substantial as the collection of Marston plays mentioned above.[67] This will have meant a very tight schedule and little room for manoeuvre. If, for instance, Thomas May handed in the extra copy for the "Characters" in *King Henry* while the text of the poem

---

[65] William A. Jackson, *Records of the Court of the Stationers' Company, 1602 to 1640*, (London, 1957), 158–9.

[66] Jackson, *Records*, 194. Mathewes never attained recognition as a master printer and was eventually deprived of his press in 1637.

[67] By far the most massive assignment that year was William Prynne's thousand-page pamphlet against the theatre, *Histrio-mastix*, but Mathewes printed only the first part of it (gatherings B–M).

was already in the press, this may well have induced Mathewes to call in a colleague.

This colleague, John Beale, was the more respectable printer of the two; in the year following the publication of *King Henry* he was elected Assistant to the Stationers' Company. As the somewhat slipshod appearance of the parts printed in his shop, however, may indicate, respectability alone does not make for better workmanship.[68] Beale, being a master printer, could have left the job to be finished by one of his apprentices. He did this sometimes regardless of his reputation. On one occasion he was fined by the Court of the Stationers' Company for a particularly bad job on the *Pueriles confabulatiunculae*:

> Mr Beale haueing printed Puerilis in such ill manner that they are not fitt to be sould. The Co^{rt}. taking the same into Consideracōn haue thought fitt & so ordered that Mr Beale shall pay for all the paper imployed in the printing of the said Booke & shall not be allowed anything for his workmanship thereof.[69]

Whatever caused the somewhat coarse appearance of the pages in the latter parts of the book (factors like worn type or uneven inking may have contributed), it was not occasioned, as might be supposed, by the use of different paper. Wherever an inspection was possible, a crown watermark (resembling mark 1031 listed by Heawood) appeared to run through the whole of the volume. This would mean that the usual practice was followed: the master who took on the printing of a book bought enough paper for the whole job; if, as in the case of *King Henry*, he decided to hand on part of the work to a partner, he would also hand on the paper necessary to finish it. Among this heap of paper were a number of sheets of superior quality. This seems clear from the Huntington copy of the book which, for this and other reasons, deserves special attention.

The Huntington Library Copy

The Huntington Library copy of *The Reigne of King Henry the Second* is the best-preserved and most lavishly produced of the extant copies of the book,

---

[68] Nor did it prevent him from running into trouble: in 1639 he was suspended for several months because he printed Bacon's *Essays* against an injunction of the Company's; see Jackson, *Records*, 327, 334.

[69] Jackson, *Records*, 324.

and there are strong indications that it is of courtly, if not royal, provenance. The copy is complete with all the genuine blanks, A1, M8, O2, O8, some of which are lacking in several of the other copies, and the size of the leaves is slightly larger than average (6 3/8 x 4 1/16 in. or 16.3 x 10.3 cm). It is bound in morocco leather with the Stuart royal arms on both covers. Henry E. Huntington acquired the volume from the collection of Beverly Chew (probably in the private *en bloc* purchase of Chew's English poetry collection in 1912). Little can be established about its provenance. The back of the front cover bears Beverly Chew's ex libris.[70] The royal arms on the covers have, apparently, encouraged at least one auctioneer or antiquarian book-seller to assume that this is the copy presented to the king and afterwards kept in his library: an unidentified catalogue slip pasted into the Huntington copy (fol. A1r) claims as much in no uncertain terms:

THE DEDICATION COPY: UNIQUE:
MAY (T.) The REIGNE of KING HENRY the SECOND, written in Seaven Bookes, portrait of the King by VAUGHAN, small 8vo. old olive morocco,[71] covered with gold tooling, WITH THE ARMS OF CHARLES I. ON SIDES, gt. edges, RARE, 1633.
At the end of the above (which is in verse) is the author's Description of K. Henry *in prose,* not mentioned by Lowndes. The book was written at the request of Charles I. and the above is the DEDICA-TION COPY to him.[72]

---

[70] Chew must have had the volume restored, because the ex libris is pasted onto marbled endpapers that clearly are not contemporary with the covers. Incidentally, the catalogue card in the Huntington Library mentions two more tokens of former owner-ship, the bookplates of Edward Hale Bierstadt and Edwin B. Holden. These refer to a different copy altogether, the so-called Bierstadt volume, which had a modern morocco binding by Salvador David. It was bought by Holden in the Bierstadt sale of 1897 and sold in the Holden sale of 1920. At some time this copy formed part of the Huntington collection but was sold as a duplicate; its catalogue card was subsequently adapted to the Chew copy, but the references to the Bierstadt and Holden bookplates were left standing; for descriptions of the Bierstadt/Holden copy see *Catalogue of the Library of the Late Edward Hale Bierstadt* (New York, 1897), item Nr 1470, and *Illustrated Catalogue of Early English and Later Literature* (New York, 1920), item Nr 1062.

[71] If, as seems likely, this entry refers to the Huntington copy, the description of the leather's color is odd. It looks brown or maroon rather than olive, but this may be due to use and age. In any case it shows one of the quiet colors preferred for morocco bindings of the period (see Cyril Davenport, *English Heraldic Book-Stamps* [London, 1909], 248).

[72] The slip most probably describes the Huntington copy since no other copy of the book is recorded as bearing the royal arms on its covers. It comes from an antiquarian

Claims like these have to be treated with suspicion; the royal arms were popular motifs for blind-stamping since the early days of printing. Even if used for clients connected with the court, they might be stamped on books given away by a member of the royal family or on books presented to the monarch. In the case of the Huntington copy, however, there is additional evidence to support the claim that it is closely connected with the court. Morocco leather bindings are rare in books of this period and point to a prominent owner. All of the other copies of *King Henry the Second* in original bindings that have been inspected or have come up for auction are or were bound in calf (or vellum).[73] The center- and cornerpiece pattern, the heavy decoration of the covers, moreover, arabesque cornerpieces and fleur-de-lis semis, point to the style prevalent around the early Stuart court.[74] In addition, the paper of the Huntington copy is of superior quality. Its watermark (a bunch of grapes similar to, but not identical with, the watermarks reproduced by Heawood as Nrs 2344 and 2347) is different from the crown watermark in all of the copies listed above. This argues for a kind of fine paper edition and thus supports the assumption that the Huntington copy was indeed connected with a high-ranking owner. It is also of more than antiquarian importance, for fine or thick paper copies required special attention in the printing process. The special sheets might have been printed before or after the ordinary ones, depending on what the printer rated higher, a better text or less worn type. As shown above, the ornamental initials in the Huntington copy represent a slightly more impaired state than, for instance, those in the Newberry copy. This could mean that the special-paper copies were printed at the end of a run when the type and other printing

---

rather than an auction catalogue, for a price is given in Sterling (the figures have been cancelled, but the signs for pounds and shillings can be discerned). The catalogue must have been printed after 1886 because a copy of Montagu Burrows' *The Family of Blocks of Beaurepaire and Roche Court* (London, 1886) is offered on the reverse side of the slip. I have been unable to identify the dealer who issued this catalogue. Another slip from an auction (or antiquarian book) catalogue describing a copy of May's *King Henry* is pasted onto the last page of the Huntington copy (O8v); this is of a later date, does not mention covers and, because damage to the Vaughan portrait is stated in the description, must refer to a different copy.

[73] In the past hundred years about thirty copies are recorded in the American Book-Prices Current and Auction Records series; about one third of these are described as being covered in "original calf" or "original vellum." For a detailed analysis of the binding see below, pp. liv–lix.

[74] See Davenport, *English Heraldic Book-Stamps*, 104, 247–8.

material would be more worn but presswork would have improved.[75] Most stop-press corrections would then have been made before the better-quality paper was printed, and this is obviously of weight for editorial decisions, in particular if there is reason to believe that the author himself made these corrections. There are, however, few such corrections, and the evidence they yield is not very satisfactory. They are all to be found in the Huntington copy, except for a wrong number that was left standing with the skeleton work. The figure "Lib. 1." in the headlines should change to "Lib. 2." from C5v but is retained throughout gathering C in the Huntington copy. Apparently the headlines were left standing with the skeleton work, and the printer forgot to change the numbers before he transferred the furniture and headlines to a new form. This has been corrected in some of the other extant copies (for instance the Grenville copy in the British Library and the Cole/Mitford and Harmsworth copies in the Folger Shakespeare Library), though only in the outer form (that is in the headlines to O6v, 7r, 8v), but not in the Huntington copy. The other stop-press corrections are two corrected misprints, "Descrirtion" for "Description" in the headline of N5v, and "stir-ning" for "stir-ring" (the word is hyphenated and runs over from O3r to O3v; the second syllable "-ring" serves, therefore, as catchword in the direction line of O3r and is correct in all the copies). The stop-press corrections mentioned so far occur in the vicinity of the skeleton frame. They might, therefore, be the work of a printer; compositors in particular are always more likely to spot an error in the skeleton work than in the main text.[76] Another stop-press correction, a turned letter on O1v ("Those troubles tha*t*"), which has been set right in the Huntington copy but not all the others, falls in the same category. Three commas added during the presswork might be ascribed to the author and would then provide further

---

[75] See Philip Gaskell, *A New Introduction to Bibliography* (Oxford, 1972), 136.

[76] They failed to spot, however, major damage on C5v, where in about half the inspected copies, including the Huntington copy, the upper five lines are in striking disarray. The damage was probably caused by two of the blocks between headline and text which were, apparently, not properly locked up and may have been shaken loose or pulled out by a sticky inking pad. The pressure from the quoins at the sides of the quarter containing page C5v pushed the types under the blocks towards the top of the page, creating a delta-shaped area of deranged lines and threatening to collapse a whole quarter of the form. A similar, though less dramatic, oversight occurs on N8v, where the first three characters at the beginning of some lines in midpage begin to slide in the Harmsworth and Huntington copies and seem to be on the point of falling out in the Cole and Houghton copies.

evidence of the author's concern with punctuation: a comma was added on G1v ("Even he, to whom" V, 285), and two commas were introduced on O7r ("Which notwithstanding was many wayes, after the death of old King *Henry*, testified by *Richard*"). The small number of corrections, however, makes it unlikely that the author attended the printing process. He would probably have stopped the press more often, for a great number of mistakes were left standing and none of them is corrected in any of the copies.[77] The number of uncorrected errors raises doubts that the author read proofs at all. This doubt is nourished by a small pen correction in the Huntington copy, "suc=" for "ex" in "exceed" on the margin of N4r, which is probably authorial.[78] The note corrects a substantial error, whereas all the other mistakes are accidental; it would, therefore, attest to the special attention given to this copy. The author did not want to see it disfigured with too many corrections, but he stopped short of letting it pass with a serious mistake.

Special-paper copies of a book were not unusual in the early seventeenth century. Several such copies may have been produced to fetch a higher price or to serve for presentation. The fact that the Huntington copy was printed on better paper is therefore not sufficient proof that it was printed for presentation to the dedicatee, King Charles. Additional evidence for a close connection with the court comes, however, from the tooling of the covers.

---

[77] These are "Hirst" for "First" in the half-title at the beginning of the poem (B1r); "must" for "much" in I, 153 (B4r); "all the worl'd" in I, 474 (C2v); "*Becket*, who these five yeares ha's beene fled" in I, 589 (C4v); uppercase after semicolon in "Bold *Lycence*" in II, 153 (C8r); lowercase at the beginning of line III, 268 ("in power," E4v); "Of *Beckt's* safety" (IV, 256, G1r); uppercase instead of lower, "in Pensive wise" (V, 256, I1r); "thy" instead of "they" in V, 629 (I8r); "Hing" for "King" in V, 616 (I8r); a missing round bracket in VI, 317 ("So then"), the first line of L2v (the catchword at the bottom of L2r has it); "Riihard" for "Richard" in VI, 352 (L3r); the doubling of "By by" for "But by" in VI, 395 (the first line on L4r, the catchword on L3v gives "But"); "sucst" for "such" on M1v (VII, 121), the turned letter in "yonnger" on M5v (VII, 302) and "disobedieuce" (O5r); and the wrong font "R"s in *Richard* on O1v, O4r, O6v, and O7r.

[78] Three letters are too small a basis for a confident identification of the hand that wrote this correction, but there is nothing to contradict such an identification. No difference visible between the same combination of long *s*, *u*, and *c* in this marginal note and in May's autograph *Cleopatra* manuscript or in the combinations of long *s* and *u* in his dedication to Heinsius of a copy of the *Supplementum Lucani* which are both written in the same cursive italic script. See, for instance, "successour" and "succeeded" in the *Cleopatra* manuscript, fol. 4v, lines 12 and 13, and "suum" and "subitura" in lines 8 and 11 of the *Supplementum* dedication.

The Binding of the Huntington Copy

The Huntington volume has an elaborate contemporary morocco binding. The covers measure about 16.8 cm x 10.3 cm; they are both gold stamped with center and corner blocks on a semis of ermine; the sides are gold tooled with a border of small triangular stamps. All edges are gilt; the spine has seven bands and eight compartments gold tooled with a repeated small flower-head design. The centerpieces show the Royal Stuart Arms within the Garter; the volume has been rebound with the original boards and spine; only the silk ties have been renewed, and marbled endpapers have been added in the restoration.

The Centerpiece

Both covers of the Huntington volume of *The Reigne of King Henry the Second* have centerpieces sized 7.2 cm x 4.1 cm with the royal coat of arms in a round field encircled by the Garter. The arms are those used by James I and Charles I, a shield with the three fleurs-de-lis of France and the three lions passant guardant for England in the first and fourth quarters, the lion rampant within a treasure for Scotland in the second quarter, and the stringed harp for Ireland in the third quarter, imperially crowned and encircled with the Garter belt and buckle.[79] Books stamped with the royal arms were not as exclusive as one might suppose. These stamps were used not only for members of the royal family or other owners with close court connections but also in trade bindings for books which were written by royal authors or dealt with royalty in some way.[80] Unless a book is very elaborately decorated or was listed in one of the catalogues of the Old Royal Library, the armorial stamp does not prove royal ownership. Different blocks were used in several binderies catering for courtly circles in London. The Binder's Office (now part of the Department of Collections and Preservation) at the British Library keeps a large number of photocopies and rubbings made from bindings with similar stamps. Mirjam Foot gives a fivefold classifica-

---

[79] For detailed descriptions of bookstamps with the Stuart arms see Davenport, *English Heraldic Book-Stamps*, 103, 239–44. The armorial stamp on the Huntington copy of *King Henry* most closely resembles the coat of arms shown on p. 243; it lacks, however, the ornaments around the Garter ribbon.

[80] See Howard M. Nixon, *Royal English Bookbindings in the British Museum* (London, 1957), 6.

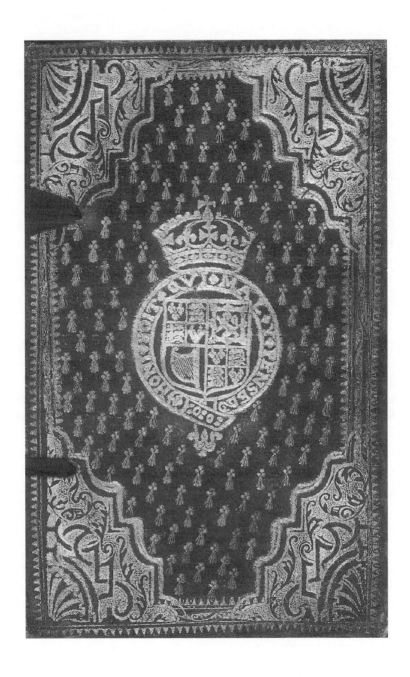

Figure 10. Huntington Library copy of the 1633 edition of *King Henry the Second* (RB 62625); back cover with center- and cornerpiece stamps.

tion of the Stuart Royal Arms blocks used for tooling in "Some Bindings for Charles I."[81] In this article she deals with the most common of these types, a large armorial stamp with mask and claw handles of which many variants are known. The block used for the Huntington copy of *King Henry* would fit in with the fifth category, "a round block without handles or supporters" which comes "in roughly two sizes, the smaller of which is often found on small books in vellum bindings,"[82] though this copy has a morocco binding. Blocks of a similar description were used already in the reign of James I. A slightly larger specimen (7.7 cm x 4.3 cm) is used on the volume of Thomas Lansius, *Fr: Achillis, Ducis Würtemberg. Consultatio de principatu inter provincias Europæ habita Tubingæ in Illustri. Collegio*, Tübingen: Eberhard Wildius, 1620 (BL C.79.b.16), a slightly smaller one (3.7 cm instead of 4.1 cm wide) is on the binding that covers a 1623 edition of the *Romanae Historiae Anthologia* (Oxford: Iohn Lichfield and Iames Short, for Henry Crypps, 1623; BL C.183.d.9). Several rubbings of the smaller variety are collected in the bindery files of the British Library; many of these were taken from books printed in the 1630s, and some of them have royal associations, for instance: Venceslaus Clemens, *Viola*, (Leyden, 1636, 4° C.78.b.1, presented to the king); King James, trl. *The Psalmes of King David* (London[?]: Thomas Harper[?], 1637, 8°, G 20090; the translation is said to have been prompted by Prince Charles); Charles Louis, Count Palatine, *The Manifest Concerning the Right of his Succession* (Given at London, 12.1.1636; trl. 1637: Anne Griffin for John Norton and R. Whitaker, 1637, 4° C.81.b.18); William Parks, *The Rose and the Lily* (Four Sermons on the Song of Solomon ii, 1, delivered at the lecture, in Ashby de-la-Zouch, London: J. Norton for G. Wilne, 1639, 4°, C.82.a.17; a slip, dated Feb. 17, 1858, and pasted in by "S.M. Magd. Coll." has a handwritten note saying: "This copy of the Rose & the Lily belonged to the library of King Charles the first, whose arms are impressed on the binding"). Mirjam Foot assigns the cover of the Count Palatine's *Manifest* to the Lord Herbert/Squirrel bindery, one of the shops known to have worked for King Charles.[83] The triangle tool used to line the edges of the cover and to separate the panels on the spine of the Huntington copy of *The Reigne of King Henry the Second*

---

[81] Foot, "Some Bindings for Charles I," *Studies in Seventeenth-Century English Literature, History and Bibliography*, 95–106.
[82] Foot, "Bindings for Charles I," 96.
[83] Foot, "Bindings for Charles I," 104.

appears to have also been used for the binding of the *Manifest* and the *Rose and Lily* volumes. Since they all have decorative gilt borders formed by small triangles of exactly the same size and distribution (five per cm), there appears to be a link between the Huntington volume and this bindery.[84]

None of the stamps mentioned so far matches the one on the Huntington *King Henry* exactly, so it must have been less common than the smaller one. There are, however, two rubbings in the files of British Library bindery which were made from armorial stamps of exactly the same size:[85]

1)   A composite volume containing *The Book of Common Prayer, The Genealogies Recorded in the Sacred Scriptures, The Holy Bible*, and *The Whole Book of Psalmes*, London, 1629, C.130.bb.5 (1–4), of which only *The Holy Bible* names the printer, "IMPRINTED AT LONDON by *Bonham Norton* and *Iohn Bill* Printers to the Kings most *Excellent Maiestie*." The volume has been rebound, with the original gold tooled calf covers preserved. The armorial centerpiece stamp on the front cover measures 7.2 x 4 cm, that on the back 7.2 x 4.1 cm.

2)   Pr. la Barre, *DES SAINCTS, OEVVRE VTILE A TOVS FIDELLES CATHOLIQVE ET Chrestiens qui desirent sçauoir les bonnes parties & qualitez de ceux que L'Eglise appelle Saincts Et de quel honneur ils sont à respecter, & comment ils se doiuent prier, seruir, & reclamer.* Paris: Chez Lavrent Sonnivs, 1619, 2 vols. (C.73.a.18, part of the Old Royal Library). The volumes are uniformly bound in brown calf. The decoration is less elaborate than on the Huntington volume; the gilt centerpieces are framed with a single gilt fillet. The spines have five raised bands and six compartments. The second compartment is lettered in gilt, the other compartments are gilt tooled alternately with a crown and a Tudor rose; the bottom compartment has a crown and the initials of King James, I.R. The centerpieces are more deeply impressed than in the Bible volume, and all measure 7.2 x 4.1 cm.

The centerpieces of these three volumes match those on the cover of the Huntington volume exactly in type and, allowing for a certain amount of

---

[84] See Mirjam Foot's chapter on this bindery in her catalogue *The Henry Davis Gift. A Collection of Bookbindings* (London, 1983), I, 50–8; in her article on "Bindings for Charles I" she mentions triangle tools from the Herbert/Squirrel bindery which were used on a 1630 London *Book of Common Prayer* (p. 105).

[85] I am grateful to Philippa Marks of the British Library Department of Collections and Preservation for allowing me to search these files.

shrinkage, in size. They were in all probability made from the same block that was used in decorating bindings for the Royal Library.

The Cornerpieces

The binding of the Huntington copy of *The Reigne of King Henry the Second* has gilt cornerpieces made from large ornamental blocks engraved with a shell and interlacing ribbons amid foliage. Mirjam Foot describes a binding with similar impressions covering a volume of Guillaume Saluste du Bartas, *Divine Weekes and Workes*, translated by Joshua Sylvester, *The History of Judith, in Forme of a Poeme*, Englished by Tho. Hudson (sm 4°, London, Humfrey Lownes, 1613), STC 21652.[86] The type of ornament on the blocks used for these cornerpieces must have been fairly common at the time. There are dozens of examples in the files and folders of the British Library's Binder's Office. Mirjam Foot lists six bindings with similar cornerpieces in her description of the Du Bartas volume; of these, only the last, covering a French translation of the Book of Common Prayer, *La Litvrgie Angloise. Ov le Livre des Prieres Publiques, de l'Administration des Sacremens, & autres Ordres & Ceremonies de l'Eglise d'Angleterre. Nouuellement traduit en François par l'Ordonnance de sa Maiesté de la Grande Bretaigne* (A Londres, par Iehan Bill, Imprimeur du Roy. M.D.C.XVI. Auec priuilege de sa Majesté, 4°, STC 16431) has exactly the same cornerstamps as the Huntington copy of Thomas May's *King Henry the Second*; although the covers on the *Liturgie Angloise* are much larger (22 cm x 15.3 cm), the measures of the cornerpieces are exactly the same. The centerpiece of the *Liturgie* binding, however, a Stuart coat of arms as described by Davenport (but with additional scrolls bearing the initials of King James, I.R., attached to the Garter), is larger than the one on the Huntington volume and is stamped on a semis of fleurs-de-lis.

A Semis of Ermine

Decorative bindings of the center-and-corner pattern with a semis background, that is a sprinkling of small ornaments, were in fashion in England during the reign of James I and remained in use under Charles I.[87] In the Huntington copy of *King Henry the Second* the armorial block is stamped on

---

[86] Foot, *The Henry Davis Gift*, II, 100, with illustration. The Davis collection, now in the British Library, is kept confined; I am grateful for permission to inspect the Du Bartas volume.

[87] See Davenport, *English Heraldic Book-Stamps*, 104.

a semis of ermine. A similar ornament, but with the stamps slightly larger and more widely spread, is found on the gold tooled vellum binding which covers a 12° volume, Alexander Gil's ΠΑΡΕΡΓΑ! *sive Poetici Conatvs* (London: 1632; BL C.46.a.34). It was printed shortly before *King Henry* by Augustine Mathewes and bound for King Charles. The center design of the cover also corresponds to the Huntington volume with a similar, but much smaller, coat of arms within the Garter for a centerpiece.[88]

To sum up, nearly all the elements that make up the binding of the Huntington copy of *The Reigne of King Henry the Second* can be linked with bindings made for the royal household, perhaps by the so-called Lord Herbert/Squirrel bindery which is known to have worked for the Royal Library. Even though neither the shop nor the provenance can be positively identified, it seems safe to say that the evidence from the binding supports the assumption that the Huntington volume was produced for presentation to a person very closely connected with the Stuart court. Whether it was destined for the king's own use it is hard to determine; the very absence of a presentation inscription might be taken as a sign that it was: if it was meant for the king, there was no need for an inscription since the book carried a printed dedication.

Additions to the Printed Edition: Frontispiece, Motto, and "Characters"

This dedication "TO THE SACRED MAIESTIE" of King Charles is one of the additions Thomas May made in the preliminaries of the printed edition. The other is Robert Vaughan's engraved portrait of King Henry.[89] These additions, in conjunction with the motto on the title page, give the book a somewhat Byzantine air. The motto is taken from Ausonius and was originally addressed to Theodosius, the East Roman emperor, and Henry is presented in Vaughan's engraving with very prominent regalia.[90] Also the prose characters of King Henry and his sons, which May attached to the poem in the printed edition, might be said to add to the imperial aspect of

---

[88] See Cyril Davenport's *Royal English Bookbindings* (London, 1896), 65 and plate 7 after p. 68.

[89] The portrait is described by Margery Corbett and Michael Norton in their *Engraving in England in the Sixteenth & Seventeenth Centuries: A Descriptive Catalogue with Introductions*, Part III, "The Reign of Charles I" (Cambridge, 1964), 55–6, a reproduction and an analysis of its contents are given below, pp. 135–44.

[90] See the description of this portrait on pp. 141–4.

the book: they are, at least partly, inspired by Tacitus, whose terse characters of imperial Rome had come to influence historiography in the early seventeenth century.[91] All this was in line with classicist tendencies in both King James's and King Charles's court, and to judge from the number of ordinary printed copies that have been preserved of May's *Reigne of King Henry the Second*, this taste must have appealed to readers well beyond the inner court circle. In spite of its early success, however, the book has never been reprinted.[92] May's classicism soon took a republican turn, and the outwardly regal aspect of the book may have become an embarassment to him and a cause for bitterness among those of his friends who stayed in the monarchist camp. After the Protectorate, during which May had served as Secretary of Parliament, its dedication to King Charles would have looked like instant proof of a turncoat, and reflections on his character like that in Marvell's lampoon "Tom May's Death" virtually damned this work, if not its author, to oblivion.[93] The poem itself hardly supports this view of May as opportunist, but this will be dealt with later on. First, the relation of the text of the poem in the printed edition to that in the manuscript will have to be considered in detail.

The Printer's Copy

The text in MS Royal 18.C.XII is, on the whole, remarkably close to the text in the printed version of *The Reigne of King Henry the Second*. It seemed close enough for the compilers of the Royal Library Catalogue to state sim-

---

[91] See F. Smith Fussner, *The Historical Revolution: English Historical Writing and Thought. 1580–1640* (London, 1962), 157–60.

[92] After Benjamin Fisher's death in 1637 the copyright for his books passed to Robert Young, Printer to the City of London and to the King; among the 80 items listed in the Stationers' Register is "23. *The raigne of king* HENRY *the* SECOND by Master THOMAS MAY" (ed. Arber, IV, 351–2). Apparently Young made no use of his right to print another edition of the book.

[93] Extracts from *The Reigne of King Henry the Second* were published in two anthologies of the early nineteenth century: Sir Egerton Brydges, *Censura Literaria: Containing Titles, Abstracts, and Opinions of Old English Books*, Vol. X (London, 1809), 40–6. ("Description of Henry the Second's Coronation of his Son at Westminster" *King Henry* II, 25–250), and Henry Kett, ed., *Henry Headley's Select Beauties of Ancient English Poetry: A New Edition, To which Are Added his Original Poems*, Vol. I (London, 1810), 69–72, 150–6 ("The Den of Vices"; *King Henry* I, 465–560, "The Death of Rosamond"; *King Henry*, V, 455–644).

ply that the manuscript agrees with the printed edition.[94] The correspon-
dences are particularly striking in the case of proper names, which are uni-
form even in idiosyncratic spellings, such as "Vercingentorix" (II, 409), or in
the forms of foreign names, where variations would most likely have occur-
red if the manuscript submitted to the printer had been at more than one
remove from the author. More examples of this conformity are to be found
in Book IV, where neither the catalogue of heroes from Roman history (26–
36) nor the list of submissive Irish chiefs (423–46) show any significant vari-
ations between the Royal Manuscript and the printed text.[95] If a scribe was
employed to prepare the printer's copy, he must have been very conscien-
tious in this respect or very closely supervised by the author. Usually, vari-
ants are bound to creep in if a text studded with exotic names is transmitted
over more than one stage.

Such close conformity between printed text and manuscript, at least with
respect to names, would normally suggest that the manuscript served as
copy-text for the printer. There are even several errors common to both ver-
sions to support the assumption: the unwarranted capitalization in V, 256
("Pensive"), the excess parenthesis in IV, 181 ["thought)"], and the single
parenthesis in VII, 344 ["foes,)"]. But there are no compositor's (or printing
house corrector's) marks in the pages of the manuscript, and there are other
indications that rule out the possibility the Royal Manuscript has served as
printer's copy. The least of these are the accidental variations between the
manuscript and the printed version of *The Reigne of King Henry the Second*.
The most prominent feature to distinguish the printed text from the manu-
script is the use of italics for proper names and the frequent use of capitals
for nouns. The scribe of the manuscript changes scripts for emphasis only
once by using a kind of *antiqua romana* to highlight the allegorical names of
the courtiers in Book II, "loose Lycence," "Bold Theft," etc. (lines 153–6),
whereas the compositor uses italics freely and fairly consistently throughout
the poem for the names of persons.[96] Scribe and printer agree in using

---

[94] Gilson and Warner, *Catalogue of Western Manuscripts in the British Museum*, II,
303.

[95] One of the very few exceptions is again connected with the names of the five
Yorkshire knights listed on the margin in V, 299–300; this may be due to the last-minute
consultation of additional source material and will be discussed below; see pp. lxxviii–lxxix
and the explanatory note to V, 299.

[96] The Arguments to the seven books and most of the notes are also set in italics.
The compositor of the Beale section of the poem italicizes all names, personal and
topographical, as in line VI, 278, "*Saladine* had tane *Ierusalem*."

lowercase letters after a full stop in midline,[97] but this is about the only archaic orthographical feature they have in common; otherwise, regarding capitalization, the compositor is more modern in that he uses capitals more liberally than the scribe of the manuscript. In general, the printed text is much closer to modern spelling habits than the manuscript which looks decidedly old-fashioned, mainly because of the scribe's habit of doubling both vowels and consonants in final positions and of keeping the otiose end-*e* ("Yett did one deede with sadd injustice blott" against "Yet did one deed with sad injustice blot" in the printed version, I, 151). Other regular preferences of the scribe's are for "frend," "togither," "feild," "theire," "only," and "engage" against the compositor's "friend," "together," "field," "their," "onely," and "ingage." On the whole, the printed text may be taken as an example for the influence of printinghouse practice on the development of modern spelling.[98]

With regard to these marked differences in spelling habits, it is surprising to see that the punctuation of the printed text corresponds very closely with that in the manuscript, even in cases where habits varied widely, as for instance in the use of colons or semicolons. A good example is furnished by a passage taken almost at random from the beginning of the poem:

> Now like bright *Phœbus* to the longing sight
> Of all the People did young *Henry* rise;
> Before whose rayes all past calamities
> Like mists did vanish: no sadd clouds accloy
> The aire of England; with loud showtes of joy
> The People flock, the Peeres their wealth display
> To grace his wish'd-for Coronation day. (I, 46–52)

The punctuation matches exactly the manuscript; in fact, the compositor, perhaps warned to follow the rather idiosyncratic punctuation of his copy carefully, seems to have kept so close to his copy that he adopted some of its spellings, too, and set "sadd" where he usually prefers "sad." Were it not for

---

[97] This applies to Mathewes only; Beale capitalizes after a full stop.

[98] There are inconsistencies, though. As mentioned above, Beale is closer to modern practice by capitalizing after full stops. On the other hand, the compositor at work in the prose "Characters" retains the older spellings of "hee," "shee," "mee," and "bee" where Mathewes has "he," "she," "me," and "be." With regard to "yield," Mathewes is inconsistent—influenced, perhaps, by his copy (23 times "yeild," 6 times "yield"; the manuscript has "yeeld" consistently), whereas Beale sets "yeeld" in his section.

the physical evidence, these close correspondences in matters of punctuation would again argue that the manuscript served as printer's copy. The lack of compositor's marks, however, contradicts this argument, and the punctuation marks added in the manuscript also present contrary evidence since they did not always find their way into print. Of the three commas, for example, that were inserted in lines III, 397–8 of the manuscript, the printed text has taken over only the second one.[99] A possible explanation is that some of the marks had been inserted in the manuscript by someone other than the author and were ignored in the preparation of the printer's copy. This would be supported by the fact that part of the added marks come from a cruder hand than others, and that only commas were added in this hand, whereas the text as a whole gives evidence of a sophisticated punctuation which, as in the passage quoted above, makes use of a full range of marks.[100]

Whatever the conclusions to be drawn from the punctuation of manuscript and printed text, the more substantial corrections to the manuscript clarify at least its relation to the printed copy. Nearly all of the over ninety corrections in the manuscript found their way into the printed version, for instance the change from "bounteous" to "beauteous" in II, 90 (the printed version reads "beautious," but this is the spelling of the compositor who has distinctive orthographic habits of his own), and the "two" written over an illegible cancellation in III, 8. There are only two exceptions. In one the original reading of the manuscript was allowed to stand: the exchange of "bad" for "weak" and vice versa in III, 425–6, was not taken over into print. This can hardly be a compositor's error; apparently the author himself had second thoughts on his earlier correction. In the other, the case of the "fearlesse shepheards" in Book I, matters are more complicated: in line 244 the printed text has neither "feilds," the original reading, nor "flockes," the revision in the manuscript, but "folds." It looks as if the author knew he had

---

[99] In a similar grammatical context, a pair of commas was inserted on the last page of the *Characters of Henry and Richard* (O7r) in a stop-press correction. This might argue for the author's attending the printing process, but there are too few such corrections to be sure of this.

[100] The process as a whole would be similar to that of Harington's translation of *Orlando furioso*. According to Gaskell, the mainly autograph manuscript of that translation "was at first lightly punctuated, then somebody (probably Harington) went over it after it was copied out and added a much heavier punctuation which was later refined and the spelling, capitalization, and contraction were normalized" (From *Writer to Reader*, 12). In that case the manuscript served as printer's copy.

made an alteration at this point but could not quite remember which. In both these cases the explanation could be that the author was present during the printing process and read proofs but without consulting his or the printer's copy.

While it is conceivable that such variants between the printed version and the manuscript could have been introduced when the Royal Manuscript was in the shop and served as printer's copy, a number of substantial revisions in the printed text virtually exclude this possibility. Some of these revisions are so extensive that it is unlikely they were introduced at the proofreading stage. There are, in particular, a number of rearranged or newly phrased lines and, most important, a number of cuts in Books II–V that had been made in an extra copy prepared for the printer. They thus belong to a different process of revision than the one that produced the heavier punctuation and the interlinear corrections in the manuscript. The cuts amount to sixteen lines altogether; the rearrangements and altered phrasings affect about a dozen more.[101] These revisions deserve closer attention since they are of importance not only in themselves but also for the process of transmission and the choice of a copy-text for this edition.

The changes were made for various reasons; a few of the more weighty examples will serve to establish the fact that they were most probably the result of an authorial revision. To begin with, May was very particular about the metrical regularity of his poems. This is almost painfully obvious in the blank verse of his *Tragœdy of Cleopatra*: Denzell Smith notes only three irregular lines in the whole of the five-act play.[102] Compared to this "metronome-like regularity"[103] the heroic couplets in *The Reigne of King Henry the Second* are remarkably lively and fluent, not least because of the frequent use of midline pauses and *enjambements*. Still, May seems concerned to a remarkable degree about the regularity not only of the meter but also of the rhythm and sound in his lines, and a number of changes made from manuscript to print are meant to smooth out rough spots. Some of them are minute; for example, the substitution of the lighter "King" for "braue" in I, 93, "Nor did braue Henry vindicate alone," which helps to avoid both a level

---

[101] Two lines are cut in Book II (after line 238), six in Book III (two each after 41, after 77, and after 328), two in Book IV (after 491) and six in Book V (two in the Argument, two each after 381 and 398). The rearrangements are in III, 499–500; IV, 151–2; V, 33–7, 435–7.

[102] See the introduction to his edition of the play, pp. xxiii–xxv.

[103] *Cleopatra. A Critical Edition*, xxiv.

stress and a sequence of *vs* too close for May's ear; or the replacement of the clearly bisyllabic "prudent" for an almost trisyllable "glorious" in I, 136. An inversion is avoided in I, 208 ("And leaves" for "Leauing"), and a clashing of [æ] and [e] sounds in I, 450 by the substitution of "those foes that threaten *Palæstine*" for "the threats of dreadfull Saladine"; a more regular rhythm is achieved in II, 61 by replacing "And from the Regall power and office free" with "That from the burden of a King art free," and so on. Striving for metrical smoothness is probably the reason, too, behind the shortened version of the address to Erato (III, 77–80), which also avoids an ellipsis ("tell" has no object in the manuscript version) and an awkward repetition ("to tell [. . .] Declare").

Again, the rhythm is improved in the line "King *Lewis* of France assists his sonne in Law" (V, 33), which supplants "Lewis king of France first plotted that designe," but the placidity of the phrase also disguises the active role of the king in the beginning of the Civil War. Such deference towards royal personages can be suspected behind a number of other changes. Two of the revisions in the printed edition of the poem may come under that heading in that they help to eliminate references to Henry's love sickness that may have looked too disparaging for the heroic king (II, 238; III, 38–41). The symptoms of *amor hereos*, which are thus suppressed, look conventional enough; they certainly would not have worried Daniel or Drayton in their poems on King Henry's love affairs, the *Complaint of Rosamond* and the *Heroical Epistles*, but times had changed from the liberal 1590s to the Halcyon 1630s, and May is anxious to stress that King Charles, the patron of his poem, refrains from "All the licentious pleasures of a throne" (II, 440). Similarly, the cut after IV, 491, which eliminates a reference to the antiquities of Ireland, could be due to an even more topical case of deference to King Charles if it is to be linked with the antiquarian movement, which King Charles had quelled,[104] and in particular with the royal displeasure that fell on the antiquarian Sir Robert Cotton and was extended, after Cotton's death in 1631, to his son Thomas.

These observations on the manuscript and the printed version of May's *Reigne of King Henry the Second* do not add up to a clear course of text transmission from author to printer since there are missing links and crossing lines. A plausible explanation for the different revisions of manuscript

---

[104] For May's personal contact with the antiquaries see below, pp. lxxxvi–xciii, and explanatory note to IV, 58.

and printed text could be that after May had finished a rough draft of his poem, an inspection copy was written in a set italic script. The very close correspondences with May's own spelling habits suggest that he did this himself. He checked this fair copy before sending it to court, adding a few verbal changes in his more fluent italic hand. The corrections in a cruder hand and with different ink, which mainly affect spelling and punctuation, were added at court or after the manuscript came back with the royal imprimatur. They could be the work of a different person; this would explain why the one substantial correction written with the metallic ink uses a "b" that is markedly different from the author's hand. It could also explain why not all these corrections, in particular not all the additional punctuation marks, were taken over into the printer's copy. The inspection manuscript probably served as exemplar for the copy that was prepared for the printer; otherwise it is hard to explain the unusual errors shared by manuscript and printed text in V, 256 and VII, 344. The manuscript then went back to court where it was preserved as MS Royal 18. C. XII. May either supervised the preparation of the printer's copy very closely or, as seems more likely, wrote it out himself and introduced a number of substantial changes. He also added the prose "Characters" and the preliminary material. He then sent this revised and enlarged second copy to the printers. The compositors in both Mathewes' and Beale's shops adapted the accidentals of the text to their own habits or the style of their shops but kept remarkably close to their copy in matters of substance, including punctuation and the spelling of proper names. May read proofs, probably without recourse to the manuscript that had served as printer's copy and is now lost. At least one copy was printed on special paper, probably at the end of the run.[105] The special copy now kept in the Huntington Library underwent another cursory inspection, which resulted in the manuscript correction on page N4r; it was bound in a morocco cover with the Stuart coat of arms, probably for the library of King Charles.

---

[105] The Pforzheimer Catalogue of early printed books mentions in its description of May's *The Reigne of King Henry the Second* that "copies are known on thick paper." Apparently, the Pforzheimer copy is not one of them, but no further specification is given (*The Carl H. Pforzheimer Library. English Literature, 1475–1700* [New York, 1940], item 686).

Editorial Policy

On the basis of this hypothetical transmission, the following editorial procedure has been chosen: the manuscript is used as copy-text and has been followed closely, except for the few cases where the printed version has corrected obvious errors or omissions. Substantive revisions in the printed edition, however, are accepted as authorial; the original readings, like any other variants of substance, are recorded in the Textual Notes. In revised passages taken over from the printed text italicised names are silently rectified and thus brought into line with the manuscript practice. In the appended "Characters," however, for which there is no manuscript text, the printing house style has been allowed to stand.

In view of the unusually careful preparation of the manuscript, a conservative policy has been chosen with respect to accidentals. The old-fashioned spelling is preserved since it provides the rare example of a long text which, if it is not autograph, follows closely and consistently the spelling habits of an author who observed clearly-defined rules of orthography against the changing habits of his time. Since there are indications that the author took similar care over his pointing, the punctuation in the manuscript has also been taken over. The numerous differences in spelling and punctuation between manuscript and printed text are not registered. Exceptions are made where a punctuation mark (usually a comma) has been added in the manuscript but is lacking in the printed text. This rather meticulous procedure seems justified because the additional marks are probably authorial and may be of use to the student of both textual transmission and the process of modernization or standardization. With respect to such considerations, the Renaissance English Text Society's style has been overruled in favor of a more conservative policy, and modernization has been kept to a minimum. The positional use of *u* / *v*, *j* / *i* has not been changed, and the use of lower-case after periods has been retained. Only the use of long *s* has been discarded. Since the digraphs *æ* and *œ* are hard to distinguish in the manuscript, the spelling of the printed version has been adopted.

THE SOURCES

The Question of Accessibility

In his "Description of King Henry II," a prose tract that was added to the printed edition of his verse history of *The Reigne of King Henry the Second*, Thomas May gives ample praise to the king's erudition in historical matters: "Eloquent he was by nature, and (which was rare then) very learned. The best histories, which in those dark times could be gotten in Christendome, he had perused with diligence, and by the benefit of an extraordinary memorie did retaine them perfectly" (18–22). The praise could be applied to May's own practice. There are numerous passages in *The Reigne of King Henry the Second*, the one above included, that are taken almost verbatim from works of history, and May took some pains to choose the best histories available at the time. Carew Hazlitt, who edited May's comedy *The old Couple*, has called him "a great borrower,"[106] but he also was a scrupulous borrower; a positivist critic said of May's dealing with classical sources in his *Tragœdy of Julia Agrippina* that "going against the historical tradition must have seemed sacrilegious to him."[107] In his verse history as in his tragedy, May followed classical models, and he might have taken much more poetic license than he allowed himself. Moreover, he was a poet associated with a Renaissance court and might have shown more clearly the patronizing attitude with which many of his contemporaries viewed the dark age in which his subject had to act. He also might have shown more deference to the patron for whom he wrote and who had very definite ideas about the uses of learning and history. All these factors—poetical precedent, contemporary prejudice, and political pressure—came to bear on May's poem, and they will be dealt with later; the first element to take into account, however, is the diligence with which he sought out sources for his medieval subject.

In composing his *Reigne of King Henry the Second* May was not content to go to one of the printed collections of chronicles compiled by Tudor historiographers or one of the ready-made Stuart royal histories in verse or prose. That is what a fellow student at Sidney Sussex College, Cambridge,

---

[106] In W. C. Hazlitt, ea., *Select Collection of Old English Plays*, 4th ed. Vol. XII (London, 1875), 4, n. 1.

[107] F. Ernst Schmid, *Thomas Mays "Tragedy of Julia Agrippina, Empresse of Rome" nebst einem Anhang: Die Tragödie "Nero" und Thomas May*, Materialien zur Kunde des älteren englischen Dramas, vol. 43, Louvain, 1914 (quote in my translation).

and lifelong friend, Charles Aleyn, did in his verse chronicles. Aleyn had written a poem on *The Battailes of Crescey and Poictiers* in 1631 (second edition in 1633; May contributed complimentary verses to both editions) and went on to write a *Historie of King Henry the Seventh* (1638) which J. L. Lievsay characterised in an article as "Bacon Versified."[108] May did, in fact, use several of the Elizabethan and Jacobean compilations, in particular John Speed's *Historie of Great Britain* and Holinshed's *Chronicles*, but he conflates them and goes to more authentic source material from time to time. Whether he did this for reasons of accuracy or affectation is sometimes hard to decide. Before speculating on his motives, the question of what sources were at his disposal will have to be considered.

One should, of course, be wary of confusing the situation of an author in early Stuart London with that of a modern historian. Though there was no British Library yet, there were the two cornerstones on which that institution was to be founded, the Old Royal Library and the Cotton Library, and an author like Thomas May, with connections to the court (if not a royal command to show) and a number of antiquarian friends, was in as privileged a position as any historian at the time could be. The largest library containing source material for a writer of medieval history clearly was Sir Robert Cotton's, and it served as a sort of research library for students of that period. Sir Robert had made this "magazine of history" readily available to his antiquarian and political friends.[109] Thomas May, however, is not one of the many borrowers named in numerous lists preserved among Cotton's papers. Ben Jonson, who shared many of May's interests, is mentioned as "Mr Johson. [sic] Beniam" in one such list, and so are several of his antiquarian friends, most notably John Selden, who worked closely with Cotton, but also Edmund Bolton, John Speed, and Henry Spelman.[110] Neither is May's name among Sir Robert's correspondents; but if he had his lodgings

---

[108] Lievsay, John L., "Bacon Versified," *Huntington Library Quarterly*, 14 (1951): 223–38.

[109] See Chapter 2 "Jacobean England's 'Magazine of History': The Library of Sir Robert Cotton," in Kevin Sharpe's *Sir Robert Cotton 1586–1631: History and Politics in Early Modern England* (Oxford, 1979), 49–110.

[110] BL MS Harley 6018; Jonson is mentioned on fol. 149v. The manuscript contains an inventory (fols. 3r–145v) with an additional list of books lent out or received, mainly from the days of Sir Robert Cotton, who died in 1631. There is a list of books out on loan to John Selden (fol. 147r) and a list of other borrowers dated 23 April 1621 ("The names of such as I have lent books too," fol. 151r). Only the last part of the list of books on loan extends to the period of Sir Robert's son Thomas (fols. 152v–190r).

in Cannon Row, as Aubrey mentions in his *Brief Lives*,[111] he lived very close to the Cotton home and library in Westminster and might have looked in as casually as his friend Ben Jonson did.[112] A collection of letters addressed to Robert Cotton (BL Cotton MS Julius.C.III.) shows not only the wide range of his correspondence (which extends to the Continent—one of the more prominent names is Gruter, the librarian of the Palatine Library at Heidelberg; others are Heinsius, Grotius, and Vossius in the Netherlands), it also proves his library to be a rallying point for the scholarship of the day.[113] Apparently May, who was befriended by Ben Jonson and also corresponded with scholars on the continent (it will be remembered that he sent a dedication copy of his *Supplementum Lucani* to Heinsius), did not belong to this circle, though he sought the favor of some of the antiquaries of the day, in particular Sir Kenelm Digby and Endymion Porter, both of whom figure on Edmund Bolton's list of prospective members for the *Academy Royal* he hoped to establish.[114] Sir Robert Cotton was dead by the time *The Reigne of King Henry the Second* was composed, but Sir Thomas continued his father's policy of giving scholars free access to his library, though in a more cautious way.[115] This fairly liberal practice, however, was a reason why the Cottons themselves were temporarily shut out from their library. The state papers and medieval manuscripts in the collection provided material not only for antiquaries but also for politicians who looked for legal precedents, in particular on the debate on royal prerogatives. In November 1629 the library was sealed up by Privy Council order, and Sir Robert was sent to the tower because of his support of the parliamentarian cause. In spite of several petitions to King and Council by Cotton father and

---

[111] For May's private life see Allan Griffith Chester, *Thomas May: Man of Letters 1595–1650* (Philadelphia, 1932), 32–9.

[112] *Ben Jonson: The Man and His Work*, ed. C. H. Herford and Percy Simpson, Vol. I (Oxford, 1925), 242.

[113] See Chapter 3, " 'The Famous Antiquarie of Europe': Sir Robert Cotton and the Historical Scholarship of Western Europe," in Sharpe's *Sir Robert Cotton*, 84–110.

[114] See also below, pp. lxxxvi–xciii; Ethel M. Portal gives an account of the failure of Edmund Bolton's plans for a Royal Academy of Antiquaries in his article "The Academ Roial of King James I," *Proceedings of the British Academy, 1915–1916*, 189–208. The works of John Speed, one of May's major contemporary authorities, belong to this second phase of the antiquarian movement.

[115] For this, and the following, see Colin G. C. Tite's Panizzi Lectures 1993, printed as *The Manuscript Library of Sir Robert Cotton* (London, 1993), Lecture I, "The Development of the Manuscript Collection, 1588–1753," in particular pp. 20–9.

son, the library was not restored to Sir Thomas until 1633, long after Sir Robert's death.[116] Although the Cottonian library remained accessible for authorised writers (Edward Herbert, first Baron Herbert of Cherbury, was admitted by royal command to collect material for his *Life and Raigne of King Henry the Eighth* at about the same time May was working on *The Reigne of King Henry the Second*), it would have seemed tainted in loyal eyes, and this may well have scared off a poet with courtly ambitions.[117] There had been the cases of Sir John Hayward, who ran into trouble with his *First Part of the Life and Raigne of King Henry IIII* (1599) and never published the second; of Ben Jonson, who was accused of "popperie and treason" after a royal command performance of *Sejanus his Fall* (1603);[118] of Sir Francis Bacon who made use of Cotton's library for his *Historie of the Raigne of King Henry VII* but failed to mend his reputation with its publication in 1622; and of Sir Robert himself, whose *Short View of the Long Life and Raigne of Henry the Third* had been published without his consent in 1627. Clearly, writing history with Cotton material (and in particular writing on Henrys) had its pitfalls.[119]

The pride of Cotton's library (and its use for precedent hunters on both the Royalist and the Parliamentarian sides) was its historical records. Thomas May, who was neither a historian nor an antiquary in the stricter sense but a poet working in a classical tradition and on the king's command, would have found the facilities of the Royal Library at St. James's more con-

---

[116] Cotton was accused of having appropriated state papers; in the course of the investigation the king ordered a catalogue of his library to be compiled before he was willing to reconsider the closure; in a petition to the council (*Calendar of State Papers*, 1633–34, 370) Sir Thomas Cotton mentions this catalogue as finished; a copy is preserved as BL Add. MS 36789.

[117] Herbert's research may have taken a turn unsympathetic to the Stuart king; his repeated appeals for support in the mid-thirties went unanswered (see *Calendar of State Papers Domestic*, 1634–35, 468; 1640, 388, 351). The *Life and Raigne of King Henry VIII* was finished only in the mid-1640s and published after its author's death in 1649; see D. R. Woolf, *The Idea of History in Early Stuart England: Erudition, Ideology, and "The Light of Truth" from the Accession of James I to the Civil War* (Toronto, 1990), 137–8. The early years of the reign of King Charles saw a tightening of censorship which affected several private libraries besides that of Cotton; see Kevin Sharpe's Chapter on "The control of private papers and archives" in *The Personal Rule of Charles I*, 655–8.

[118] Quoted from David Riggs, *Ben Jonson; A Life* (Cambridge, MA, 1989), 105.

[119] The name had become programmatic ever since King James had his first son christened Henry to placate the more militant Protestants; see Riggs, *Ben Jonson*, 164–5 and below, p. lxxxv.

venient for his purpose.[120] In addition to a sizable collection of medieval chronicles, this library held a large number of printed books.[121] One of May's principal authorities, John Speed's *Historie*, is not even mentioned in the numerous extant Cotton lists,[122] whereas all of the printed compendia of chronicles consulted for *The Reigne of King Henry the Second* (Polydore Vergil, Holinshed, Speed, Camden, Savile, etc.) are listed in the Old Royal catalogues. Another attraction of the Royal Library for a man of May's inclinations must have been the much more pronounced classical and Latin emphasis in the Royal Library, which still showed the predilections of Lumley on the one hand and King James on the other. A look into the old catalogues of the Royal libraries (British Library C.120.h.6. [1–5]) makes this abundantly clear. Both the Royal and the Lumley collections had their basis in Latin writings, with a bias towards classical authorities, whereas Cotton's collection concentrated on medieval and vernacular sources.[123] It seems plausible, then, that Thomas May, as protégé of the king and proven classicist, went to St. James's for his source material.

There is proof to suggest that May made good use of whatever material he consulted for his poem on Henry II. In several instances, he must have worked from more than one source text dealing with the same events. He not only exchanged one authority for another as he moved from one episode to the next, but he wove details from different sources into his own version of a particular episode. A good example of both these methods is found to-

---

[120] As has been pointed out above (pp. xxiii), there were two collections at St. James's Palace, the Old Royal and Prince Henry's Library, which had been combined (but kept separate) after the prince's death. Prince Henry had been given the Lumley Library with its great store of printed books; see the Introduction to Sears Jayne and F. R. Johnson, *The Lumley Library: The Catalogue of 1609* (London, 1956), in particular p. 21.

[121] The total number of books, most of them printed, that are listed in the 1650 inventories of the library at St. James's is over 4000 (see Sears Jayne, Introduction to *The Lumley Library*, 21, n. 2). The number of printed books in the Cottonian Library is likely to be in the hundreds rather than thousands. So far, bibliographers working on Cotton's or the Royal collections have concentrated on the manuscripts; T. A. Birrell and Colin Tite, however, have recently done some valuable work on lists and catalogues of printed books in the Cottonian and Old Royal Libraries; see Birrell's Panizzi Lectures of 1986, published as *English Monarchs and Their Books: From Henry VII to Charles II* (London, 1987) and Tite's article "A Catalogue of Sir Robert Cotton's Printed Books?" *British Library Journal* 17 (1991): 1–11.

[122] See Sharpe, *Sir Robert Cotton*, pp. 56/7; these lists, however, usually refer to manuscripts.

[123] Sears Jayne calculates that 88 percent of the Lumley books were in Latin, Greek, or Hebrew (Jaynce, Introduction to *The Lumley Library*, 11).

wards the end of Book IV of *The Reigne of King Henry the Second*, where May switches from the *Topographia Hibernica* of Giraldus Cambrensis to the same author's *Expugnatio Hibernica* as he cuts short the description of the island and returns to political events on the Continent (the turning point is in line 712). He then moves on to Holinshed as he follows his hero across the Irish Channel into Wales (751–3), thereafter to William of Newburgh to weave in a piece of information about Henry's submission to the pontifical legates in Normandy (754–7), and finally back to Holinshed to record Henry's clenched-teeth acceptance of the pope's penance (761–2). May repeatedly conflates facts and phrases from different sources, mainly English translations, but goes back to medieval chronicles if necessary. His praise of Henry's achievements near the beginning of Book VI is another case in point: he conflates Holinshed with Speed but goes back to Hoveden for the Christian names of the potentates who sued King Henry for a settlement of their differences (IV, 186–94). In his account of Henry's last meeting, when he had to do homage to the French king, this preference paradoxically leads him into error. May mistakes the name of the town where the humiliating meeting took place as "Turwin" (Thérouanne in Artois, ironically the site of one of Henry VIII's greatest military victories over the French in 1513). He probably mistranslated (or misread, if he made use of a manuscript) "Turonim" (acc. of "Turonis," Latin for Tours), as it is called in Roger of Hoveden's chronicle.[124]

In cases of doubt, May appears to prefer a Latin source to its vernacular equivalent or a translation. His account of the civil war in England in 1174, for instance, is based on Roger of Hoveden, not on Holinshed who also uses Hoveden's *Annales*; this is indicated by the fact that May says, like Hoveden, that Norwich was burned, which is not mentioned in either Holinshed or Speed (see V, 204 and explanatory note).

If, however, a translation offers additional information, as in the case of certain passages in Speed's *Historie* or Hooker's translation of the *Expugnatio* of Giraldus in Holinshed's *Chronicles*, May uses it. Hooker added explanatory notes to his translation, and May sometimes profits from them, as in the case of the first invasion of Ireland. May says that the expedition corps under Fitz Stephen landed near Waterford at the mouth of the river Banne, which was "scarcely nam'de" before. This is taken from a footnote in Hook-

---

[124] Roger has "colloquium inter Turonim & Arasie" (*Annales*, ed. Savile, 653,49). See explanatory note to VII, 369 and Appendix 5 for more details.

er's translation explaining that the river (no more than a creek) was named after one of the ships that brought the English over (see IV, 50-6, and explanatory note).

May's preference for Latin sources may be due to the prestige these enjoyed simply because they were written in a more scholarly language. In fact, May never mentions English authors such as Holinshed or Speed, whose compilations he certainly knew and used, although he gives a number of references to his Latin sources in both the manuscript and the printed version of his poem.[125] These references (marginal notes in BL Royal MS 18.C.XII, footnotes in the 1633 edition) are of special interest not only for the question of sources used in *The Reigne of King Henry the Second*. Here is a complete list with the lines they are keyed to in the printed version and the material they refer to:

II, 118   Polydore Virgill in H.2.
           [Young King Henry's boast about his descent]

III, 380   The Monke of Nuborough lib: 2. has all this
           [The case of the criminal clerks]

III, 408   The Monke of Nuborough ibidem
           [The hundred murders ascribed to clerics]

III, 494   Houeden
           Chronicon de passione et miraculis Thomæ
           [Opposition to the election of Becket as archbishop]

III, 564   Math: Paris
           [The "parliament" of Northampton]

III, 566   Geruaise of Douer
           [The bishop of Chichester accuses Becket of treason]

---

[125] In this respect May's documentation, though not his practice, differs from that of Samuel Daniel who names (besides Polydore Vergil) several English chroniclers (Fabyan, Grafton, Holinshed, Stowe, and Speed) at the beginning of his *History of England,* but also relies on manuscript sources. See May McKisack "Samuel Daniel as Historian," *Review of English Studies* 23 (1947): 226–43.

IV, 294   Aurea Legenda in vita Thomæ
          [The legend of a bird being rescued by the saint]

IV, 593   Sylus: Giraldus Cambr: relates all these wonders
          [The marvels of Ireland]

V, 262   Houeden
          [Henry's penitential walk to Canterbury]

V, 291   Willi: Paruus
          [The capture of King William of Scotland]

V, 299   Stouteuile, Glanuille, Vrsy, Ballioll, Vmfreuille
          [The names of the knights who captured King William]

V, 329   Will: Paruus
          [King William's army of 80,000 men]

VII, 86   William, Archbishop of Try
          [The legate appointed by the pope to propagate a crusade
          in the west]

The notes are almost identical in the manuscript and the printed version,
except that the last reference to the Archbishop of Tyre is lacking in the
manuscript. They are also fairly accurate as far as the identification of au-
thors and titles is concerned. Even the note at III, 494, which, if read as
referring to a single source, might be taken to ascribe to Hoveden a chron-
icle he did not write, is correct if read as pointing to two different sources,
Hoveden and an anonymous "Chronicon de passione et miraculis Thomae"
(see explanatory note on III, 494).

As will be evident from the explanatory notes in this edition, these anno-
tations are far from exhaustive. Only a tiny fraction of the passages bor-
rowed from historical sources are indicated by marginal references (or foot-
notes in the printed edition), and not all of them are reliable. John Speed
was much more conscientious in his notes; he sometimes even gives page
references, so it is easy to identify the exact edition he quotes from. When
quoting from Roger of Hoveden, for instance, Speed goes to Sir Henry
Savile's collection of chronicles, *Rervm Anglicarvm scriptores post Bedam
præcipui*. The page references in his sidenotes reveal that he used the edition

of 1596; he points to "Houe. f. 359," for instance, as source for the knight-ing of Prince John at Windsor. This refers to the 1596 edition of Savile's collection; the edition of 1602 has a different pagination. Thomas May is never that accurate; at best, he gives title and chapter of a source. Some of his references to Latin authorities are simply taken over from one of his English compilations. This secondary source is sometimes given away by the form of the reference. Holinshed and Speed, May's major English authorities, have different ways of referring to their medieval sources. Both compilers use, in more or less abbreviated forms, Latin or half-Latin names, Speed preferring the more latinized forms. Thus William of Newburgh, the author of the *Historia rerum Anglicarum*, is usually called Gulielmus Nubrigensis in Speed's *Historie* but William Parvus in Hol-inshed's *Chronicles*. When May, therefore, refers to the "Monk of Nubor-ough" (as in III, 380 and 408), this is an indication that he relies on Speed; when he refers to William Parvus (as in V, 291 and 299), it is likely that he worked from Holinshed.

The aim of May's notes cannot have been that of documentation, not even to the limited extent that Elizabethan and Jacobean chroniclers found necessary; nor was he pressed to add "protective" notes as Ben Jonson did in the published version of his *Sejanus*.[126] May felt obliged, however, to veri-fy some of the more controversial anecdotes or episodes in his poem, such as the hundred murders allegedly committed by clerks in the first nine years of Henry's reign, the fantastic legends about Ireland, or the capture of the Scottish king from the midst of a huge army. They also lend an aura of prestige to an enterprise that otherwise would have incurred the risk of being considered lightweight in comparison with serious works on similar subjects. Works of history usually take pride of place in the Old Royal Cata-logues, second only to theological treatises. Thomas May was not the first to guard his poem against an unfavorable comparison by giving it a scholarly touch. Daniel and Drayton had done the same with their historical epics on medieval civil wars. The annotation in these poems is much lighter than in a work of history, but this need not mean that their aspirations are lower. May's personal ambition may well have been to prove poet, scholar, and

---

[126] This is how Blair Worden interprets, convincingly, the profusion of marginal notes in the 1605 edition of *Sejanus his Fall* in "Ben Jonson among the Historians," *Cul-ture and Politics in Early Stuart England*, ed. Kevin Sharpe and Peter Lake (London, 1994), 79.

mentor all in one, and to improve on a classical model such as Lucan, whose unfinished *Civil Wars* he had taken on to complete a couple of years before. He would, of course, not stretch the comparison with a work of history cut short by a tyrant, but his *Continuation of Lucan* was, like the original, aimed at a prince. If the verse was meant to entertain, the notes stressed its instructional value.[127]

The notes added to the *Continuation of Lucan* (as well as those attached to May's second historical epic on a medieval subject, *The Victorious Reigne of King Edward the Third*, 1635), are extensive, explanatory, and sometimes critical. In *The Reigne of King Henry the Second* the scholarly apparatus is little more than a gesture. Nevertheless, the few notes scattered over the poem add up to an almost comprehensive list of the medieval authorities May consulted. Even priorities can be deduced. Top of the list, with four references, is William of Newburgh (also known as William Parvus), followed by Roger of Hoveden with two references and Gerald of Wales and Matthew Paris with one each. Again, this does not mirror the exact amount of material taken from these authorities; Gerald, in particular, whom May exploited not only for the Irish episodes but also for his character sketches of Henry and his sons, seems underrated—May probably knew that Gerald was by no means an impartial witness. May's emphasis on Newburgh and Hoveden would confirm his judicious approach. Newburgh in particular is rated high even by modern historians: Austin Poole says of his *Historia* that "it is of great value for the period it covers owing to the literary merit and discriminating judgment of the writer,"[128] and Antonia Gransden calls

---

[127] The *Continuation of Lucan's Historicall Poem till the death of Iulius Caesar* (1630) is the first work that May was allowed to dedicate to King Charles. In his address to the king May compares himself in all humility to Lucan but avoids mentioning Nero. His reserve paid off, as a contemporary noted in 1640: "Thou hast got Charles his love, he Nero's hate" (*Wits Recreations*, 1640, quoted from Chester, *Thomas May*, 47). When William Prynne drew a comparison between the courts of Charles and Nero in his *Histriomastix* (1633), this cost him his ears.

[128] Austin Lane Poole, *From Domesday Book to Magna Carta*, Oxford History of England, vol. III (Oxford, 2d ed. 1955), 496. Poole's own presentation of the life of Henry II, incidentally, gives proof of the accuracy and the lasting impression of Thomas May's portrait of the king and his contemporaries. Poole comes close to May in his judgment, and sometimes even in his phrasing; see, for instance, his assessment of the position of Pope Alexander III (p. 204; cf. *The Reigne of King Henry the Second*, III, 507–12), or the title he gives the "Amazon wife" of the Earl of Leicester (p. 336; cf. May's "Amazonian Countesse," *King Henry*, V, 179).

him simply "a man of outstanding ability."[129] It is no mean proof of May's critical sense, then, that he chose this most accurate source and the most discerning chronicler of the period as his chief authority.

Not all of the notes in *The Reigne of King Henry the Second*, however, point out medieval sources; two of them are explanatory and give names of historical persons not mentioned in the text: the names of the five Yorkshire knights who captured King William (V, 299) and the name of the legate from Jerusalem who persuaded the French and English kings to take the cross (VII, 86). These explanatory notes are of special interest in offering a glimpse at May's handling of specific source material. They are keyed to passages that even in their phrasing betray a certain insecurity on the author's hand. In the case of the Yorkshire knights, May appears to have been confused even about their number: the manuscript first read "sixe" but was then corrected to "five" (V, 299). With the Archbishop of Tyre the awkward paraphrase "one of greatest name / . . . that Prelate was" (VII, 86–8) speaks of a similar uncertainty. It looks as if the notes were meant to fill the gaps or stop the doubts left by these phrases, and they may have been added in a process of revision, with new or different source material at hand. Concerning the prelate the main Latin sources yielded only his title, Archbishop of Tyre, but May could have found his full name in Speed's *Historie* (see explanatory note to VII, 86).[130] The addition was probably made shortly before a copy of the text was sent to the printer; it is lacking in the fair copy preserved in the British Library, Royal MS 18. C. XII, which may have been at court at the time. In the case of the "five [or six] gallant Yorkshire knights," the erroneous spelling of one of the names "Ursy" for "Vesci" points to Holinshed's *Chronicles* as the most likely source for the list of names given in the additional note. May's account of the episode, however, comes mainly from Roger of Hoveden, as he himself indicates in his note to V, 291. Hoveden may, in fact, have caused the confusion about the number in both Holinshed and May (he names six knights as defenders of Prudhoe

---

[129] Antonia Gransden, *Historical Writing in England: I. c. 550 to c. 1307* (London, 1974), 264.

[130] It is interesting to see that one of the manuscripts which may have been accessible to Thomas May (Bodl. MS Laud 582, which complements BL MS Royal 14.C.II) leaves a blank at precisely the point where May added the Christian name of the Archbishop of Tyre in the latter of the two explanatory notes. See the textual note in William Stubbs's edition of Roger of Hoveden: "*archiepiscopus Tyri*] [. . .] blank in A. for the Christian name. It is questionable whether this was William of Tyre the historian, as commonly supposed" (*Chronica magistri Rogeri de Houedene*, Vol. II, London, 1869, 335, n. 1).

castle, the gallant knights among them; see explanatory note to V, 299–300), and the resulting uncertainty may have kept him from including the names of the knights in the poem. Historians and antiquaries had to be careful with names, as the example of Camden shows.[131] They owed at least part of their esteem to the fact that the nobility cared for the reputation of their ancestors. Whatever the exact reason was, May apparently revised his original manuscript, probably with Holinshed or Speed on his desk, and added the names of the knights in both the fair copy, which later went to the Royal Library, and the manuscript he sent to the printer.[132]

Another reference to a nonmedieval source, which is keyed to an incident at the coronation of young King Henry, is revealing in several ways. It not only allows a glimpse at May's cut-and-paste method of composition but also at the aims he pursued in redacting his source material. May refers to Polydore Vergil as his source ("Polydore Virgill in H.2.", II, 118 marg.) for the well-known anecdote about Henry playing butler to his son, when Henry junior comments on his father's services as being quite appropriate because he himself is of royal blood from both his parents' side, whereas his father is only from his mother's side (II, 99–129). Vergil does indeed report this incident in his *Anglicae Historiae libri*.[133] The reference is slightly misleading, nevertheless, because May did not go to his declared source but to an English translation, probably Speed's, whose sidenote runs "*Polydor. Virg. in H.2.*" whereas Holinshed's refers only to "Polydor."[134] Like Speed, May gives the episode a lighter touch than Holinshed. He says of the Archbishop of York that "the Prelate gently smyl'd" (I, 117); Speed has him speaking "in pleasance to the young King." Holinshed leaves Polydore Vergil's "ioci

---

[131] Rudolph B. Gottfried has shown how scrupulously Camden dealt with the Anglo-Irish nobility in his revisions of the *Britannia*; "The Early Development of the Section on Ireland in Camden's *Britannia*," *Journal of English Literary History* 10 (1943): 119–20.

[132] Something similar seems to have happened in Book V, where May added the Christian name of the Earl of Flanders to his list of conspirators against King Henry; see explanatory note to V, 35.

[133] *Polydori Vergilii Urbinatis anglicae historiae libri vigintiseptem. Ab ipso autore postremùm iam regogniti, ádque amussim, salua tamen historiæ veritate, expoliti* (Basle, 1570), lib. XIII, fol. t1r–v, 215–16. The anecdote goes back to Matthew Paris, *Historia Minor* (ed. Frederic Madden, I, 352–3).

[134] On the other hand, May's use of the technical terms for Henry's mock office could indicate that he also made use of Holinshed's account of the episode. Like Speed, May calls the king a "servitour" (*King Henry*, II, 116), but like Holinshed he also uses the more precise term "sewer" (*King Henry*, II, 105); Polydore Vergil has "administer," Matthew Paris "dapifer."

causa" untranslated but keeps the Italian's stern comment: "Thus the yoong man of an euill and peruerse nature, was puffed vp in pride by his fathers vnseemelie dooings."[135] The different comments on this episode are revealing, both in terms of narrative technique and of the morals drawn from the incident. Vergil allows Henry a clear foreknowledge of the evils that will proceed from the presumption of his son: "Iam inde prospexit futurū, vt filius sibi adversaretur" (*Historiae*, 216). May gives him no more than an ill feeling, "and gan even then to feare / What after might ensue from such a pride" (*King Henry*, II, 126–7). This points to May's generally more dramatic technique. Although he casts himself in the role of the traditional Olympian narrator and has, of course, a complete view over the action, May stands back and comments as a sympathetic bystander rather than a stern preceptor. The episode is turned into a dramatic scene in which the narrator is anxious not to intrude. Apart from this dramatizing effect, May's reticence seems to allow his characters more freedom of movement, judgment, and moral growth. They are treated with tact and respect.

Thomas May is equally patient with other legendary material that had been regarded with raised eyebrows in his sources, for instance the Irish *mirabilia* which he inserts in his relation of the conquest of Ireland in Book IV of *The Reigne of King Henry the Second*. These legends are taken from Gerald of Wales's *Topographia Hibernica*. As will be evident from the explanatory notes below, May went to his main source directly, though he must have known the extracts (translated by John Hooker alias Vowell) that were added to Holinshed's *Chronicles* in 1587.[136] Hooker treats the miraculous elements of Gerald's description with a great deal of skepticism, and this ultimately undermines their credibility. Typical of his attitude are comments like this on the life-preserving qualities of the *Insula viventium*: "For my part, I haue beene verie inquisitiue of this Iland, but I could neuer find this estrange propertie soothed by anie man of credit in the whole countrie. Neither trulie would I wish anie to be so light, as to lend his credit to anie such feined gloses, as are neither verefied by experience, nor warranted by

---

[135] Speed, *Historie*, IX, 6 [43], 493; Holinshed, *Chronicles*, II, 130. For a full text of Polydore Vergil's version see below, explanatory note to II, 99–127.

[136] See Annabel Patterson, *Reading Holinshed's "Chronicles"* (Chicago, 1994) on this compilation and its contributors.

anie colourable reason."[137] May's dramatic device (which he adopted from Lucan's *De belle civili*)[138] of having a venerable inhabitant relate the Irish *mirabilia* enables him to let them stand unqualified. A sense of wonder is thus preserved.

These instances indicate that May was careful with matters of style and tone, and less than ardent in following his material to its sources or testing its accuracy. In the case of Young Henry's coronation, he might have gone to Matthew Paris, who was well represented in the Old Royal Libraries. Matthew is even sterner than Holinshed in his condemnation of the young king. In the *Historia Minor*, its ultimate source, the episode is inscribed "De Coronatione regis Henrici III. Junioris nimis detestanda," and Henry's revulsion from his son is given biblical overtones: "Poenitet me fecisse hominem."[139] May was apparently anxious not to look too censorious, as is borne out by his treatment of the miracles said to have been worked around the tomb of Thomas Becket. In Book IV of his poem May reports some of these miracles, once more giving his actual source away in a sidenote to the most extravagant of them, which tells of a small bird who called on the saint when faced with a hawk and was saved. The reference, "Aurea Legenda in vita Thomæ," is the latinized version of a note in Speed's *Historie*, "The printed golden Legend, in vit. Tho."[140] John Speed, always a cautious commentator, treats such material, which provoked earlier Protestant readers of manuscripts into acts of vandalism, with a comparatively lenient irony by inserting a "belike," for instance, when closing his version of the miraculously saved bird, "*her enemie fell presently dead, and she escaped*, and (belike) reported it."[141] This interjection is a far cry from the harsh comments Foxe or Holinshed insert in similar contexts. Thomas May follows Speed and puts in an extra example that is neither in Speed nor in the equally accessible Foxe but apparently taken from the *Miracula* collected by Benedict of Peterborough. His tone resembles that of Speed, again, although he achieves his effect not by a piece of condescending comment but by questioning the miraculous effect of one of Thomas's relics in an apostrophe: "How much

---

[137] See Holinshed, *Chronicles*, VI, 38; for details cf. explanatory notes to IV, 553–704.

[138] See below, explanatory note on IV, 488.

[139] Paris, *Historia Minor*, ed. Frederic Madden, I, 353; cf. Gen. 6:6.

[140] *The Reigne of King Henry the Second*, IV, 294, marg.; Speed, *Historie*, IX, 6 [43], 495, marg. For details see below, notes to IV, 273–96.

[141] *Ibid.*; for a longer quotation and further comment see below, explanatory note to IV, 294–6.

did every fatall circumstance / In this abhorred act of theires, advance / Thy name, oh Beckett?" He thus draws the saint into a tacit acknowledgement of how improperly his martyrdom was exploited by followers who believed that not only his "nobler parts" worked miracles but also his "ridiculously-holy shoo" (IV, 273–5, 292).

Apparently Speed and his friends, the early Stuart historians, were less loath to follow chronicles from the age of "fatall darkenesse" than their Tudor forerunners such as Foxe and Holinshed; at least they were ready to distinguish between the collectors of legends (such as those springing up around the tomb of Thomas Becket—see Book IV) and more trustworthy chroniclers. Chief of their medieval authorities are Matthew Paris, William of Newburgh, and Roger of Hoveden, all favorably mentioned by Speed. His judgment is vindicated by later historians.[142] May, who closely follows Speed, would thus have imbibed a more tolerant attitude towards the Dark Ages than some of his contemporaries and friends, such as Ben Jonson and Francis Bacon, and his lenity is even more pronounced than that of Speed, who soon loses patience with the Canterbury legends: "Many of which kinde of follies, (if that word be sharpe enough) might be here inserted, were not our present argument more serious, and these forgeries fit onely for Monkes to endite, children to reade, and fooles to beleeue" (Speed, *Historie*, IX, 6 [43], 495).

The life of Thomas Becket was a sensitive issue throughout the Renaissance. Becket had become the most revered English martyr in the course of the later Middle Ages, but by the early sixteenth century the mass of legendary material that had accreted to his shrine became offensive to both Humanists and Protestants. The process left its traces in the early printed editions of the *Legenda Aurea*, which contains the most popular version of his legend. In many of the early editions of this legendry, the parts containing Becket's life and miracles are more or less mutilated; most of the copies preserved of editions printed by Wynkyn de Worde and Julyan Notary between 1493 and 1527 now in the British Library have these parts cut out or inked over.[143] Tudor historians used less drastic means of obliterating Becket's memory. His stalwartness was interpreted as ingratitude and stub-

---

[142] See William Stubbs, ed., Roger of Hoveden, *Chronica*, vol. I (London, 1868), lxx, and Poole, *Domesday Book to Magna Carta*, 203. On Speed's method see Woolf, *Idea of History*, 64–72.

[143] Wynkyn de Worde, 1493, shelf-mark IB.55161; 1498 mark C.11.c.16; 1527, mark C.15.c.7; Julyan Notary, 1503.

bornness, and the miracles around his shrine were treated with derision or contempt. For obvious reasons, John Foxe felt compelled to tarnish his image in the interest of his Protestant martyrs. He goes to great pains to discredit not only Becket's claim to being a martyr but also his reputation as antagonist of the king in the dispute between crown and miter. Most of the chronicles of the sixteenth and early seventeenth century reflect Foxe's strictures to a greater or lesser degree. In the light of this tradition, Thomas May's attempt at treating the saint (if not the cult that sprung up after his death) in all fairness and to allow him a certain aura of greatness attests to his tolerant attitude.

John Speed may have encouraged May's comparatively sympathetic treatment of medieval material; they both strive for detachment and have a sense not only of distance from the world of their medieval witnesses but also of the futility of polemicizing against this world from their own advanced position. The means, however, they choose to distance themselves are different. Speed makes use of an ironic method to throw a medieval legend into relief; sometimes simply quoting from a source makes the excesses of medieval credulity obvious. May keeps his distance by epic and dramatic means; he rarely introduces comments in his own voice, rather he assumes the role of a well-meaning witness or he hides behind a *persona*. By introducing fantastic elements and dramatic episodes he creates an epic world on the borderline between history and fiction. It is a world in which the epic machinery works quite naturally, and references to this machinery do not necessarily raise the question of belief.

An example should serve to explain the difference between Speed's ironic and May's epic mode. Shortly after his penitential pilgrimage to Canterbury, news is brought to Henry that one of his worst enemies, King William of Scotland, has been captured. This is one of the turning points in the civil war that had seriously threatened Henry's rule. Medieval chroniclers did not fail to interpret this happy turn as a sign that Henry's penitence had found grace in the eyes of God. William of Newburgh clearly attributes it to heavenly providence, "quia Deus sic voluit, ut voluntati magis divinæ, quam potentiæ prudentiæve humanæ, ascriberetur eventus" (Newburgh, *Historia*, II, xxxiii, 184); Speed says that "some Monkes" attributed the reversal in Henry's fortunes to his penitence (Speed, *Historie*, IX, 6 [76], 503), with an ironic reference to those monks whom he has just castigated for having displayed a diabolical joy in lashing the barebacked king. May attributes the zeal of the monks to the zeitgeist of their era ("but lett the sage / Nor censure them, nor Henry, but the age," V, 283–4); the epic mode enables him to dispense with the question of providence altogether by resorting to the most neutral device of epic machinery available ("as if chang'de Fortune meant / To recompense him for her threats of late, / And now on all sides make him fortunate," V, 286–8). Even when he clearly refers to the hand of God, as he does a little later ("And twas the hand of heauen, not Henry, fought," IV, 372), May is taking recourse to that machinery, not advancing an argument in a religious debate.

May's concern, then, in shaping his material, is less with the historical aspect of his subject and its political or religious implications but with molding it into an epic that can compete with classical models in theme and structure. Another instance of this intention is provided by his treatment of Prince Richard's submission to his father at Gisors (V, 727–86). The ultimate source for the incident is Hoveden's *Annales*, which gives facts and basic feelings but little interpretation. Polydore Vergil expands and adds a wry comment insinuating that Richard's contrition may have been insincere. Holinshed is careful and bland as always, leaving room for interpretation and retaining a faint hint of Polydore Vergil's insinuation, but he refrains from giving a clear judgment himself. May, again, dramatizes the incident, stresses his main thematic point, filial piety, and creates an intimate, pathetic scene. Basic family values always rank high in his poem, in spite of its epic aspirations. This seems to be in concordance with the attitude at the court of Charles, with its yearning for heroism on the one hand and stress on clean living on the other. It is also in line with historical writing and thinking modelled on classical "analytic" authors such as Polybios or Tacitus (taken up by Cotton, Jonson, and Bacon), which sees the causes of historical events in the vacillations of human passions rather than the workings of providence or of institutions, and therefore the aim of history writing in the knowledge of man.[144]

May's striving for epic but not martial effects is not without topical relevance. The stress laid on family virtues was a preoccupation of King Charles, who was anxious to dispel the reputation of dissolute living that had hung over his father's court; his obsession with heroism was inherited from his father and was just as theoretical as that of King James. When *The Reigne of King Henry the Second* was written, the disastrous outcome of his Spanish

---

[144] See R. Malcolm Smuts, *Court Culture and the Origins of a Royalist Tradition in Early Stuart England* (Philadelphia, 1987), in particular his chapter on "The Halcyon Reign," 245–83.

and French adventures had certainly dulled Charles's appetite for military adventures, and he was entering the Halcyon phase of his reign. It is interesting to note that King Henry in May's poem is not a martial hero and that the imperial theme, though obviously central to an epic poem on the classical scale, is sounded in a strangely muted way. An example is the treatment of the Irish question, one of the imperial strands that is woven into the poem. As befits both epic and romance, King Henry has to be roused from his infatuation with a paramour; Minerva herself calls him to his imperial duties and gives a prophetic preview of the future of the English empire (II, 381–454). Anticipating the loss of the French provinces, she calls Ireland the one lasting possession of the English crown (which implicitly belittles the gains and losses of the Hundred Years' War). This might be compared to the treatment Ben Jonson gives the same theme in his "Speeches at Prince Henries Barriers" where the tenor is "that ciuill arts the martiall must precede" (line 212) and the pacific King James is praised for uniting the crowns of England and Scotland and peacefully subduing Ireland. This last achievement is set off against the exploits of his more militant forbears: "*Ireland* that more in title, then in fact / Before was conquer'd, is his *Lawrels* act" (347–8).[145] Jonson repeatedly sets James's peaceful heroism against the triumphs of the more contentious Tudors (James joining the rose and the thistle, for example, is said to be a more lasting, and less bloody, achievement than Henry joining the white and red roses); Jonson tries, in effect, to keep Prince Henry from joining the warrior line of Henrys as advocated by more militant advisers of the Elizabethan (or Tudor) revival. Similarly, Thomas May commends the diplomatic and civil achievements of King Henry over his military victories.[146] The conquest of Ireland is accomplished without bloodshed, the "Halcyon dayes of . . . happy peace" (VI, 110) are praised in a long encomium on King Henry as a Solomon on the throne that begins with an invocation of Calliope to sound the achievements of King Henry in Book VI: "But now, my faire Calliope, relate / How high, how glorious was old Henry's state / In this so happy and establish'd peace!" (151–3). This replaces a Christian reflection in Speed: "Let the greatnesse

---

[145] *Ben Jonson*, ed. C. H. Herford and Percy Simpson, Vol. VII (Oxford, 1941), 329, 333.

[146] This may reflect the diplomatic activities of King Charles that led to the peace treaties with France and Spain in 1629/30; see Kevin Sharpe's chapter on "Pax Carolina: Peace and Diplomacy" in *The Personal Rule of Charles I* (New Haven, CT, 1992), 65–104. I am grateful to Kevin Sharpe for pointing out this parallel to me.

and felicitie of this King be now but sleightly looked vpon, and it will appeare, that no Prince of those times was hitherto so much bound to God for manifold fauours as hee." (X, 6 [78], 503). May thus formally embellishes and aggrandizes the merits of the king, but these merits are of a civil order: Henry holds court in London, receiving ambassadors from the Continent (including the divided Roman Empires of East and West) and settling their disputes by arbitration; he consolidates both church and state by calling synods and parliaments ("in which, according to his mind, hee was furnished with treasure");[147] he reforms the legal system by introducing itinerant judges, and he pursues a successful marriage policy. Wars are always seen as disruptions of such peaceful activities, and Henry is always reluctant to take up the sword. The ideal proclaimed in such lines is in a way opposed to that of the traditional epic; the epic style is employed not to propagate new frontiers (or a specific policy like that of a Protestant crusade, for which purpose the Arthurian epic had been revived two decades before), but to praise peaceful reforms. The encomium in Book VI rather pointedly ends with the arrival in London of an ambassador from the Holy Land who offers King Henry the crown of Jerusalem. Henry, however, is not a crusader: "For hee too much perplex'd about his owne / Affaires at home, refus'd that sacred crowne" (263–4).

Thomas May and Edmund Bolton's Academ Roial

It is true that the narrator deplores King Henry's refusal to enter on a crusade (which, after all, robs him of an opportunity of playing Tasso to another Godfrey); it would have appealed to King Charles, however. The scene may have reminded Charles of his brother-in-law, Palsgrave Frederick, who accepted the crown of Bohemia and thus triggered off the war that was devastating the Continent. The phrase "Affaires at home," moreover, may allude to Charles's trouble with his parliament, which urged him to intervene on the Continent but refused him the means to do so effectively. It is hard to determine May's position in political questions like these. From his later career it is tempting to identify his attitude with that of his narrator

---

[147] This is one of the few allusions to political problems in Charles's reign; it is in the prose "Description of King Henry the Second," which was added in the printed edition (lines 157–8); there may be a similar allusion in a corresponding passage in Book VI, when King Henry is said to possess "Without controll those stately Provinces / Of France" and Ireland is praised for "quietly" obeying "His powerfull scepter" (VI, 158–61).

and to translate it into political terms by associating him with the survivors
of Prince Henry's academy, with Spenserian poets and historians such as
Michael Drayton or Sir John Hayward who tried to revive medieval chivalry
and Tudor triumphs in the interest of the Protestant cause. Their hopes
were shattered by Henry's death, and even Hayward had taken a turn to-
wards the "politique" stance of Jonson or Camden. The society of antiquar-
ies, which in its Elizabethan phase supported the Protestant cause of the
Netherlands, had also taken a turn towards King James's irenic views, but it
barely survived Prince Henry's death and met for the last time in 1614. The
later years of King James, however, saw a kind of revival, launched by Ed-
mund Bolton, who managed to overcome the initial reluctance of King
James to finance his ambitious plans. Bolton's proposal was for the estab-
lishment of an Academ Roial, (an alternative name was College and Senate
of Honor), something much grander than the Society of Antiquaries. Both
these associations were dedicated to the study of history but with more or
less political purpose. Crown and Court had become wary of the way mem-
bers of the Society of Antiquaries went about their studies of medieval pre-
cedents, which they feared might serve seditious purposes. In 1600, Hay-
ward was imprisoned because the Queen's councillors suspected his *Life of
King Henry IV* of containing subversive comparisons between the usurper
king and the reigning queen.[148] King James observed, with increasing irri-
tation, that the antiquaries supplied his parliamentarian opponents, who
fought against royal perogatives, with ammunition from medieval docu-
ments. When Edmund Bolton campaigned between 1617 and 1630 with
petitions and proposals to erect an academy he was anxious, therefore, to
play down its scholarly activities. His Royal Academy was not meant to be
a research institute; there were no plans to set up a library, for instance. In
a draft for an intended book, to be titled *Agon historicus*, Bolton had noted:

That it is more profitable for virtue among us, to found a College for
the Studies of Honor, and Antiquitie of Britainn, then to erect a li-
brarie, as bigg as K. Ptolemies.[149]

He may have been thinking of Sir Robert Cotton and his "magazine of his-

---

[148] See Margaret Dowling, "Sir John Hayward's Troubles over his Life of Henry IV,"
The Library, 4th Series (1931): 212–24. For a sketch of his career see the paragraph
"Sovereignty, Civil Law, and History" in Woolf's *Idea of History*, 106–115.
[149] Quoted from Bethel M. Portal's paper read on November 24, 1915, "The Academ
Roial of King James I," *Proceedings of the British Academy 1915–16*, 206.

tory." There would, apparently, be no need to send Bolton to the tower like Hayward or Selden. Bolton secured the favor of the king's favorite, Buckingham (Bolton's Pseudonym was Philanactophil, Friend of the King's Friend), and eventually of King James himself, but he failed to obtain the necessary funds before the king's death. James had suggested that the academy should act as a censor's office, "it should be theirs to authorize all books and writings which were to go forth in print which did not *ex professo* handle theological arguments; and to give to the vulgar people indexes expurgatory and expunctory upon all books of secular learning printed in English never otherwise to be public again."[150] In a proposal inscribed "The Cabanet Royal" and addressed to King Charles (which is preserved as BL Royal MS 18.A.LXXI) Bolton agrees that the academicians would strive "to knit together for the rights of monarchy,"[151] —he is obviously moving even further away from the idea of disinterested pursuit of historical knowledge than such antiquaries as Camden, Cotton, or Selden, who became increasingly attached to the Parliamentarian cause.[152] He knew perfectly well that, unlike his father, King Charles was less interested in scholarship than in standards of taste, and that he collected ancient medals and modern paintings, not medieval manuscripts. "The Cabanet Roial," Bolton's final proposal, takes this into account and implores the king not to forget that there are things that "marble and metal cannot give, but writing only" and he calls his enterprise "a proposition very heroicall."[153]

Wrapped as it is in so much adulation, one might find this final proposal slavish rather than heroic, but it can also be seen as a last, almost desperate, attempt at rescuing an originally grand design. If the ending looks like a debasement of Elizabethan ideals, the beginning was just the reverse. One of

---

[150] See Portal, "Academ Roial," 196. This policy was put into effect by Charles I. Thomas May's second historical epic, *The Victorious Reigne of King Edward the Third* (1635), though dedicated to the king again, underwent such censorship and was licensed by Sir John Coke, Principal Secretary of State, at Whitehall, 17 November 1634, in anticipation of the Star Chambers Decree governing printing in 1637. On the question of censorship in the 1630s see Chapter XI, " 'Itching Ears to Hear Anything against the Commonwealth'? Censorship, Criticism and Constitutionalism" in Kevin Sharpe's *The Personal Rule of Charles I*, 644–730.

[151] Quoted from Linda Van Norden's doctoral thesis, which gives a detailed account of Bolton's endeavors, "The Elizabethan College of Antiquaries" (Ph.D. Diss., University of California at Los Angeles, 1946), 471.

[152] On the increasing political impact of the antiquarian movement see Kevin Sharpe, *Sir Robert Cotton*, 27–32.

[153] Quoted from Portal, "Academ Roial," 197.

Bolton's pet ideas, and the first duty he assigned to the members of his Academ Roial, was the "supervision of translations of secular works: that good books might be sincerely turned out of foreign tongues into ours."[154] He had advocated this duty before in an essay on history writing, "Hypercritica; or A Rule of Judgment for writing, or reading our History's,"[155] which he wrote, according to Anthony à Wood, as early as 1610. The essay is a critical reflection on Henry Savile's edition of medieval Latin chroniclers, *Rerum Anglicarum Scriptores*, as its lengthy subtitle declares:

> Deliver'd in four Supercensorian Addresses, by occasion of a Censorian Epistle, prefix'd by Sir *Henry Savile*, Knight, to his Edition of some of our oldest Historians in Latin dedicated to the late Queen *Elizabeth*. That according therunto, a compleat Body of our Affairs, a *Corpus Rerum Anglicarum*, may at last, and from among ourselves, come happily forth, in either of the Tongues. A Felicity wanting to our nation, now when even the name therof is as it were at an End.

The slightly depreciative allusion to the new style, Great Britain instead of England, which had been introduced by King James, betrays some sympathy with the Elizabethan revival associated with the Academy, as it has been called, that had assembled at the court of Henry, Prince of Wales, around 1610. Henry and his followers were bent on making, not only calling, Britain great, and there were plans for setting up a formal Academy to which, as Sir John Holles wrote in a letter prompted by the Prince's death, Henry "had given his stables, and other helps for the better 'address' of our youth."[156] Sir John Hayward was apparently meant to play an important role in that academy; Henry "stipended Hayward at 200 l. per annum to write the universal history of this kingdom."[157] This plan may have been

---

[154] See Portal, "Academ Roial," 196.

[155] Bolton's *Hypercritica*; first published by Anthony Hall in Oxford, 1722; rpt. in J. E. Spingarn, *Critical Essays of the 17th Century* (Oxford, 1908), Vol. I, 1605–1650, 82–115.

[156] Quoted from Roy Strong, *Henry, Prince of Wales, and England's Lost Renaissance* (London, 1986), 8.

[157] Strong, *Henry, Prince of Wales*. Hayward was already a member of King James's Chelsea College when Prince Henry won him over for his project of a universal English history. Roy Strong suggests that Henry intended to set him up as a rival for William Camden, the scholar-king's historian (*ibid*, p. 148). The first fruits of Hayward's labours, among them *The Lives of the iii Normans, Kings of England*, were published after the Prince's death (1613) and dedicated to Prince Charles.

at the back of Bolton's mind when he proposed his academy, but he was forced to adjust it to the changing political situation; therefore Great Britain was used instead of England, and it was called a senate instead of a society. That in the beginning Bolton was anxious to uphold rather than debase Elizabethan values becomes quite clear in the fourth of the addresses delivered in *Hypocritica*, which demands that good works of history be "Prime Gardens for gathering English: according to the true Gage or Standard of the Tongue, about 15 or 16 years ago."[158] Such purification of the language has two aims: to cleanse history writing from foreign influence and to bring it up to classical standards. The first aim is taken up again in the proposal for a Royal Academy when Bolton speaks of the second duty of an academician:

> II. To celebrate the memory of the secularly noble of Great Britain that the history of our country may rescue itself from the shears and stealths of Tailors, and obtain at last a grave and free authentic text, not only in our mother tongue, but also in the Latin also, therby to correct the errors and repress the ignorance and insolencies of Italian Polidores, Hollandish Meterans, Rhapsodical Gallo-Belgici and the like, wherein Mr. Camden hath gone before us, to his everlasting praise.[159]

What he pleads for, moreover, is an orderly style and a well-founded exposition; the model for such presentation is to be found, if his metaphors are to be trusted, in classical art:

> The vast vulgar Tomes procured for the most part by the husbandry of Printers, and not by appointment of the Prince, or Authority of the Commonweal, in their tumultuary, and centonical Writings, do seem to resemble some huge disproportionable Temple, whose Architect was not his Arts Master, but in which, store of rich Marble, and many most goodly Statues, Columns, Arks, and antique Peices, re-

---

[158] The "chief Point or Summ" of Address IV (Bolton, *Hypercritica*, in Spingarn, ed., *Essays*, I, 82).

[159] Portal, "Academ Roial," 196. The sartorial quip is directed against less erudite historians such as John Stow and John Speed, both members of the Merchant Taylors' Company; cf. Bolton's somewhat ambiguous praise of Speed in the following quotation. "Meterans" refers to Emanuel van Meteren, the Dutch merchant and historian who lived in London and corresponded with Cotton and Camden; I am grateful to Kevin Sharpe for giving me this reference.

cover'd from out of innumerable Ruins, are here, and there in greater
Number, then commendable order erected, with no Dispraise to their
Excellency, however they were not happy in the Restorer. In Mr
Speed's Stories publish'd since that Knights [i.e., Savile's] Epistle,
besides all common Helps, there are for the later times, the Collec-
tions, Notes, and Extracts out of the Compositions of Ld Vicount St
Alban, of the Ld *Carew*, of Sr *Rob. Cotton*, of Sr *Hen. Spel*[man] of
Doctor *Bar*[cham], of Mr *Edmund B*[olton]. &c. *Speeds* own Part is
such therein for style, and industry, that for one who (as *Martial*
speaks) hath neither a *Græcum* Χαῖρε, nor an *Ave latinum*, is perhaps
without many Fellows in Europe. So much also have I understood of
him by sure Information, that he had no Meaning in that labour to
prevent great practick Learnedness, but to furnish it for the common
Service of *England*'s Glory.[160]

What it all should lead up to is a history of Great Britain that can vie with
the great works of ancient history, written by historians who can compete
with their classical forebears, even in the face of learned sceptics such as
Henry Savile:

> Many great Volumes carry among us the Titles of History's. But
> Learned men, and *Sr Henry Savil* one of them, absolutely deny
> that any of ours discharge that Office which the *Titles* promise.
> For my part I think that the most of them have their Praises, and
> all of them their uses towards the composition of an universal his-
> tory for *England*.[161]

I have quoted at length from Bolton's various proposals because they appear
to illustrate a change in style and taste which gradually, and not only moti-
vated by political pressure or opportunism, changed the way historical sub-
jects were treated under the Stuarts. The key term is "classical" or, as the
contemporaries preferred to call it, "heroical." Bolton uses it several times in
his proposals; at one point he calls on King James

> to found an Academ Roial or College of Honor where lectures &
> exercises of heroick matter & of the antiquities of Great Britainn may

---

[160] Bolton, *Hypercritica*, ed. Anthony Hall, 1722, 220–1; Ee2v–3r.
[161] Bolton, *Hypercritica*, in Spingarn, ed., *Essays*, I, 83.

be had & holden for ever ... although to many it will appear little more than a glorious dream.[162]

May's poem is called "an heroick Poem," as will be remembered, in one of the early catalogues of the Royal Library. The constant heightening of character, the harping on classical virtues, and, not least, the striving for purity of language in *The Reigne of King Henry the Second* immediately strike one as falling in with this new style and the ethos it sets out to propound. Thomas May was not on the list of prospective members for the Academ Roial, but he had connections with some of them, for instance with Endymion Porter and, somewhat surprisingly, Sir Kenelm Digby, a professed Catholic.[163] His choice of subject brings him into even closer connection with some of the names bandied about by Bolton. He makes use of Savile's compilation of medieval chronicles, which he brings into classical shape. His main source is, as we have seen, John Speed's *Historie*, the pioneer work singled out by Bolton which May, "his Arts Master," sets out to restore in "commendable order." May's choice of King Henry II as the hero of an English historical epic brings him even closer to Bolton, who had been asked by Speed to write the life of Henry II for his *Historie*. As it fell out, Bolton, another Catholic, gave too favorable an account of Thomas Becket, and John Barkham, a chaplain to Archbishop Bancroft, stepped in. Bolton retained, however, some sort of advisory position, for Speed acknowledges his help (see his note on the Pendergasts, quoted in explanatory note to IV, 58). It seems not altogether unwarranted to assume that some such cooperation went into *The Reigne of King Henry the Second*, though May was probably solely responsible for the poetical and classical adornment. It may even be permitted to assume that May's poem was part of a concerted effort to realise Bolton's glorious dream. He had stressed the heroical aspect of his *Continuation of Lucan* and toned down its republican spirit by raising its style, "the happie conceits, and high raptures of that Noble LVCAN," said to be in concordance with the king, "your Majesties renowned worth, and Heroicall vertues (the perfection of minde meeting in you with the height of

---

[162] Portal, "Academ Roial," 192.

[163] He dedicated the 1631 edition of his *Tragedy of Antigone, The Theban Princesse* to Porter, and the joint edition of his *Cleopatra, Queene of Egypt* and *Julia Agrippina, Empresse of Rome* (1639) to Digby. See Chester, *Thomas May*, 49–50. Digby wrote an essay on Spenser at May's instigation; see Digby, "Concerning Spenser," in *Spenser, The Critical Heritage*, ed. R. M. Cummings (London, 1971), 148–9.

Fortune) may make you securely delighted in the reading of great actions"
(with a stress on "reading," perhaps, to adapt it to King Charles's by then
more peaceful disposition).[164] Later on, May wrote another historical epic
poem on Edward III, "which is there ended," as he explains in his dedi-
cation to King Charles, "where his fortune beganne to decline" because his
later years "may affoord fitter observations for an acute Historian in Prose,
than straines of height for an Heroike Poem."[165] Others had striven for
similar aims, most notably May's friend Charles Aleyn, who had published
an epic poem on the Hundred Years' War, *The Battailes of Crescey and Poic-
tiers*, in 1631 and went on to write another one on *The Historie of that Wise
Prince, Henrie the Seventh* (1638). If these works did not add up to the
universal history planned by Bolton, it was not entirely the authors' fault; the
last we know of Bolton is that he was sent to prison for his debts and died
in poverty. Thomas May fared somewhat better; at least he was allowed to
dedicate the first of his historical epics to King Charles, but he, too, may
have felt disappointed that the king failed to live up to the glorious role they
had designed for him.

The Influence of Classical Literature

Thomas May's preoccupation with honour and the heroic ideal corresponds
with similar concerns in the works of not only the antiquaries but the most
eminent historians of the time. With someone like Sir Francis Bacon, this

---

[164] May, *A Continvation of Lucan's Historicall Poem till the death of Ivlivs Cæsar* (Lon-
don, 1630), A5r–v. It is worth noting that Bolton, being a client of the duke of Bucking-
ham, argued against the republican view of history often attached to poets and historians
such as Lucan and Tacitus; see David Norbrook, "Lucan, Thomas May, and the Creation
of a Republican Literary Culture," *Culture and Politics*, ed. Kevin Sharpe and Peter Lake
(London, 1994), 56. As Norbrook points out, May shifted towards this position between
the time when he published his translation of Lucan's *De bello civili* (first part 1626,
second 1627), to which he added an anti-Caesar ending and which he dedicated to such
staunch critics of the Stuarts as the earls of Essex and Lincoln, and his *Continuation of
Lucan* (1630, 2d ed. 1633), which presents Caesar as a martyred monarch and is dedi-
cated to King Charles ("Lucan, Thomas May," 58–61). With his historical poems on
English subjects May moved further in the direction of Bolton's position. On the later
development of the republicanism inspired by Roman writers see Blair Worden, "Classical
Republicanism and the Puritan Revolution," *History and Imagination: Essays in Honour of
H. R. Trevor-Roper*, ed. Hugh Lloyd-Jones, Valerie Pearl, & Blair Worden (London,
1981), 182–200. Again I am grateful to Kevin Sharpe for alerting me to these devel-
opments.

[165] May, *The Reigne of King Edward the Third*, fol. A3v.

seems due to a common interest in classical historiographers, in particular
Tacitus. Sir Robert Cotton combines this interest with a nostalgia for the
heroic past of his own nation. Thomas May adds to this his interest in clas-
sical epic and elegiac poetry.

It is not surprising, therefore, that May, in addition to the historical ma-
terial he borrowed from various medieval chronicles, made use of a great
number of classical models in his poem. He was an accomplished Latinist;
before entering on historical poems such as *The Reigne of King Henry the
Second* he had translated not only Lucan's *De bello civili* (1626–7) but also
Virgil's *Georgica* (two editions in 1628), *Selected Epigrams of Martiall* (1629),
and two of John Barclay's neo-Latin works, *Argenis* (verse parts only, 1629)
and *Icon Animorum* (as *The Mirrovr of Mindes*, 1633). In 1640 he published
a Latin tanslation of the *Continuation of Lucan's Historicall Poem* (Leyden,
1640) which, in the words of Anthony à Wood, was "written in so lofty and
happy Latin hexameter that he hath attained to much more reputation
abroad than he hath lost at home."[166] It is no wonder, then, that May's
knowledge of classical literature exerted a considerable influence on his
handling of an English subject. The influence affects his history on several
levels, but it is not historiographic in a stricter sense. Apart from a few
references to Caesar's *De bello gallico* (see explanatory notes to *The Reigne of
King Henry the Second*, II, 405–11), there is barely a trace of ancient histor-
ians in his poem.[167] Some of the features that might be thought to point
in the direction of Tacitus or Livy, such as the character sketches of leading
personalities and the speeches prefixed to crucial events, had already become
elements of medieval and Tudor historiography. Most of the classical ma-
terial in *The Reigne of King Henry the Second* comes from works of poetry
and serves mainly decorative purposes. There are, for instance, plenty of
mythological allusions that are hard to trace to a particular author. When-
ever a specific source can be identified, as in the descriptions of various fes-
tive occasions such as the coronation of Young King Henry in Westminster
(II, 128–78) or the marriage of Strongbow in Ireland (IV, 83–108), which
are embroidered with mythological material from Claudian's *Epithalamium*,
this is indicated in the explanatory notes.

---

[166] Wood, *Athenae Oxonienses*, III, 810. The *Supplementum Lucani* continued to be re-
printed all over Europe well into the nineteenth century.

[167] This is, of course, mainly due to the medieval subject matter. May was well read
in ancient historiography, as is evident, for instance, from the notes to his *Cleopatra* and
his annotations to the *Continuation of Lucan*.

There is, however, an undercurrent of classicism in May's poem that runs deeper than the superficialities of style and affects both the theme and structure of the poem. This undercurrent can be devided into an epic strain that is mainly centered on King Henry's role as statesman and conqueror, and an elegiac strain that is mainly concerned with Henry's role as husband and lover. The epic strain is pervasive and never far from the surface. It affects the style of the poem and becomes visible in epic features such as apostrophes to the several Muses, extended similes of an appropriately heroic mold, and pieces of epic machinery like Jove descending from Olympus or Enyo descending into Hell. Two main models emerge behind these surface appearances. One is *De bello civili*, Lucan's unfinished epic on the struggle between Pompey the Great and Julius Caesar, which May must have known almost by heart. The poem influenced not only the style of *The Reigne of King Henry the Second* (in particular, May tries to imitate Lucan's laconic, sometimes paradoxical sentiments), it also provided him with a number of characters and situations that he employed, for example, in his presentation of the marvels of Ireland. These marvels are related by an ancient bishop as part of a Christmas banquet in Dublin that is closely modelled on an Egyptian episode in Lucan's *De bello civili*, where after a sumptuous meal an aged priest unfolds the mysteries of Egypt (see IV, 488 and explanatory note; cf. *De bello civili*, X, 172). The description of Ireland in *The Reigne of King Henry the Second* is colored to a surprising extent by the African episodes in Lucan's *De bello civili*, the common factor being the obscurity of these countries, which is exploited for exotic effects.

The African scenery provides, of course, no more than a backdrop to the predominantly Roman concerns in Lucan's epic; its main theme is domestic, the "more than civil war" that threatens to disrupt not only the Roman empire but every single family in the realm. The affinity of this theme to a poem on Henry II is obvious: there were civil wars at the beginning, middle, and end of his reign. Medieval historians such as William of Newburgh and Gerald of Wales had adapted the opening line of *De bello civili*, "Bella per Emathios plus quam civilia campos," to French and English battlefields before Thomas May did the same at the beginning of Book V in his *Reigne of King Henry the Second*. In a way, Henry's wars are even more aptly called "plus quam civile" than those of Lucan's hero because they were not only fought between in-laws, as in the case of Pompey and Caesar, but between fathers and sons and husbands and wives. The feuds that tore Henry's family apart had provoked strong remonstrances in medieval chronicles; William of Newburgh, for example, generally a very sober historian, calls it "inexecrabilis et foeda dissensio" (*Historia*, II, 169–70). Some of the chroniclers had laid most of the blame at Henry's feet, be it for his part in the murder of Thomas Becket or for his private conduct towards his wife, Eleanor of Aquitaine. May, however, finds the motivating force behind the wars not in Henry himself but in his sons whom he repeatedly blames for their impiety.

Impiety becomes the main motive in May's poem, and this seems to be May's own doing, for he found it neither in Lucan's epic nor in the chronicles he used. He raises this motive to epic proportions; it becomes the propelling force behind Henry's fall, and he invests it with a nemesis-like inexorability that lifts the poem to a level high above the flat moralization of the chronicles. This is made apparent from the very start of the poem, when in Book I Enyo, the goddess of discord, descends into Hell and asks Satan to help her disturb the peace that Henry has brought about at the beginning of his reign. Satan complies; he stirs up Impiety and implants her in the ambitious breasts of Henry's sons, who eventually work the destruction of the realm. May's frequent references to the impiety of these sons invests his hero, by force of contrast, with the image of a pious ruler. In connection with the many classical allusions, this calls to mind the best-known pious hero of antiquity, Aeneas, and this association is underlined by a number of references to Virgil's *Aeneid*. In the course of the poem these references establish the impression that May aims at creating a national epic not far from the Virgilian scale. An important indication of this aim is how May links the subject of his poem with its patron, King Charles. He repeatedly stresses the Scottish ties of his hero, and at one time stops his narrative to establish a genealogical link between the houses of Plantagenet and Stuart (I, 109–34). Genealogical lists, a favorite item in epic poetry at all times, had already been present in some of the medieval chronicles, but these looked backward rather than forward. Matthew Paris, for example, has a chapter "De genealogia Henrici regis" in his *Chronica majora*, which goes back to Noah and the flood.[168] In the Elizabethan epic, in particular in Spenser's *Faerie Queene*, the device had been turned into an instrument of propaganda for the Protestant Tudor cause. By stressing the Scottish connection, May takes up the themes of dynastic union, so dear to the early

---

[168] Paris introduces it on the occasion of young Henry's birth (*Chronica majora*, II, 209–10). Genealogy was another of the preoccupations of the antiquaries; in 1603 Sir Robert Cotton had written a treatise that proved King James's descent from the Anglo-Saxon kings (see Fussner, *Revolution*, 128).

Stuarts, and of the creation of a British, rather than English, empire. On a more domestic level he contrasts the impiety of Henry's sons, which eventually disrupts the house of Plantagenet, with the piety of Charles, "Th'admir'd example of true piety" (V, 56), who will be revered by his equally pious son, thus securing the Halcyon reign of the House of Stuart, "a King in vertue as in royalty" (II, 442).

Following his epic themes along these dynastic lines, May is anxious to lift not only his subject, King Henry, but also most of his antagonists to heroic heights. This is most obvious in the case of William of Scotland and Thomas Becket. King William is treated with much more, and Becket with scarcely less, respect than they were in May's medieval sources. The ignominy of King William's capture is softened in several ways. The outrages of his army, much maligned in the chronicles, are no more than hinted at. William is given a brave fight before surrendering to the Yorkshiremen ("the King [...] / Did not forgett hee was a King" V, 317–19), and he is spared the humiliation of being led to London with his feet bound under his horse, as in May's source, Roger of Hoveden's *Annales* (see V, 356–8 and explanatory note). Similarly, Becket is allowed an impressive struggle and (as far as possible for a martyr) a heroic end. May expressly attests him the virtue traditionally assigned to an epic or a tragic hero, "fatall magnanimity" (IV, 260). He censures the cult that springs up around Becket's tomb, but he ascribes it to the mistaken motives of a blind age; May does not question the martyr's dignity as some of his colleagues and even some of Becket's contemporaries did (see IV, 273–96 and notes).

Some of the ennobling effects in May's epic treatment of almost all the contestants in *The Reigne of King Henry the Second* may, of course, be due to the deference of a poet with courtly ambitions. There were plenty of political pitfalls hidden in the field of historical literature, as attested by the examples of Sir Robert Cotton and Sir John Hayward, whose lives of Henry III and Henry IV had brought them into royal disfavor. The Court and the Privy Council had become particularly sensitive to questions of historical precedents. In addition, the more personal background of the royal family, King Charles's Scottish and Queen Henrietta's French connections, as well as both their Catholic leanings, called for caution in directions where the writers of a former age had been allowed to vent their prejudices. The general impression is, however, not sycophantic. Thomas May deals with his subject in a conscientious way. Keeping in mind that the poem was ordered by the king himself, the passages that are directed at this patron are advisory as much as flattering; May's friend Ben Jonson, for instance, was much more exuberant in similar circumstances; in fact, the comparison is apt to cast some doubts on May's later reputation as a turncoat.[169]

May's prime concern in *The Reigne of King Henry the Second* was probably poetical rather than political, and writing his poem along Virgilian lines may have helped him to avoid its being read along partisan lines. This is confirmed by his handling of the imperial mission of his hero, which points back, of course, to Virgil's epic and its romance descendants. May's Henry is roused to the task of conquering Ireland in much the same way that Aeneas is called to his duty of conquering Italy in the *Aeneid*, and like Aeneas he has to contend with the rival force of imperial love. This struggle between public and private claims is at the center of the poem, and it is the main shaping factor in its structure. In Virgil's *Aeneid* the hero's love for Dido, the Queen of Carthage, is prominent only in Books I and IV, and Dido makes a short last appearance in Book VI; most of the first and nearly all of the second half of the twelve-book epic is filled with the struggles of the hero and his men. The heroine is allowed no more than a marginal role; the poem moves away from her and builds up to a triumphant end with the imperial mission about to be fulfilled in spite of her pathetic appeal. May's poem culminates in the center, with the carefully interwoven four major strands of action, Henry's conquest of Ireland, the struggle with Becket, the rebellion of his sons, and his love affair with Rosamond Clifford, all coming to a climax in Books III–V. This gives the seven-book poem a dramatic structure. May himself draws attention to this point in his recapitulation of the main events in his "Description of King Henry the Second": "consider it divided as it were into five Acts; for as one says, *Tanquam fabula est vita hominis*" (lines 67–8). With respect to May's constant endeavor to ennoble his hero, it comes as a surprise how much weight he gives to Henry's concubine Fair Rosamond. This seems warranted neither by medieval nor by classical precedent. Rosamond can hardly be called a historical figure; she is barely mentioned in the medieval chronicles on which May relied for the political facts about Henry's reign. But Rosamond had played an increasingly important part in Tudor popular and poetic historiography, with Samuel Daniel and Michael Drayton as her foremost champions. She is the repen-

---

[169] For some of the more extravagant congratulatory verses presented to King Charles see Percy Simpson, *Proof Reading*, 227–32, and T. A. Birrell, *English Monarchs and Their Books*, 47–8. See Chester, *Thomas May*, 46, on the comparatively moderate degree of flattery in May's dedications.

tant heroine, if that term is appropriate, of Daniel's semidramatic *Complaint of Rosamond* (1592), and she is one of the letter writers in Drayton's *English Heroical Epistles* (1597). Both these poems proved very popular; they quickly went through several editions and helped to establish an elegiac mode in the literature of the 1590s that can be traced back to Ovid's handling of legendary material in his *Fasti* and *Heroides*. This elegiac poetry rivalled the epic tradition and questioned its values to such an extent that after the turn of the century a backlash set in with poems that presented historical heroines, both classical and medieval ones, as protagonists deserving of that title. An interesting example of this backlash is the epic *Sophonisba* (1611), written by Sir David Murray, who came to London with King James and had a considerable influence on the cultural climate at his court.[170]

It is another sign of Thomas May's independence of mind that he struck a balance between these rival literary traditions. With his Rosamond he tried to create a pathetic heroine who is neither as fury-like as Virgil's Dido (the hellish part is played by Eleanor in his poem), nor as conscience stricken as the weeper in the Ovidian tradition. Since Daniel's and Drayton's poems were written in an appropriately humble style, this amounted to a lifting of the concubine's status, at least stylistically. An example of this is May's handling of a descriptive set piece that he takes over from the elegiac tradition. The heroines in this tradition, from Ovid's *Heroides* onwards, are usually shown in domestic surroundings where they complain about their unhappy fate. Their situation is private in a double sense: they are deprived of their lovers, and they defend their private feelings against the heroic aspirations of their mates. From their domestic point of view even the Olympian gods take on an all too human aspect, and epic descriptions shrink to epyllion size. In the case of Fair Rosamond, a casket Henry was said to have filled with jewels to win her favor had become the subject of such descriptions that usually dealt with the amours of the Olympians. A decorated chest is first mentioned in Ranulph Higden's *Polychronicon*, in Daniel's *Complaint of Rosamond* and Drayton's epistle of "Rosamond to Henry the Second" the decoration is described as a series of mythological scenes depicting the falls of Io and Amymone to Jupiter and Neptune.[171] Both these de-

---

[170] I have dealt at length with these developments in my study of *The Fall of Women in Early English Narrative Verse* (Cambridge, 1990).

[171] Ranulph Higden, *Polychronicon*, ed. Joseph Rawson Lumby, Rolls Series 41, (London, 1882), VIII, 54; Samuel Daniel, *The Complaint of Rosamond*, lines 379–420, in *The Complete Works in Verse and prose*, ed. by A. B. Grosart (1885; rpt. New York, 1963), I,

scriptions serve moralistic purposes: Rosamond fails to interpret the mytho-
logical scenes as forebodings of her own fate. To underline the lesson, Dray-
ton, the more morally-minded of the two, adds a reference to a picture
gallery at Woodstock in which a servant asks Rosamond a question about a
painting of the chaste Lucrece which Rosamond, for shame, can hardly
answer. To Thomas May the casket and the moral it carries (suggesting that
Rosamond allowed herself to be bought with a set of jewels) must have
seemed petty and out of keeping with his epic poem. He takes up Drayton's
hint of a picture gallery and projects the mythological subjects from the
casket onto the paintings there, dropping, by the way, the all too obvious
and embarrassing subject of Lucrece. Like Drayton, May creates an indoor
scene, but he enlarges it to royal size (III, 197–248). The ornaments on the
casket are blown up to paintings in the heroic style, and the gallery, being
part of the palace at Woodstock which Henry built for his love, becomes a
fitting emblem of the greatness of a king whose advances Rosamond could
not resist, with a hint, perhaps, at the treasures in King Charles's Whitehall
gallery. The whole scene is a telling instance of the skill with which Thomas
May integrated medieval, classical, and contemporary elements in his histo-
rical epic.

94–6; Michael Drayton, "Rosamond to Henry the Second," lines 93–101, 153–74, in *The
Works*, ed. J. William Hebel (Oxford, 1932), II, 135–7.

The reigne of King Henry

the Second

Written

in Seauen bookes

by Tho: May.

Invalidas vires Rex excitat, et iuuat idem
Qui iubet; obsequium sufficit esse meum.

Auson:

TO

THE SACRED

MAIESTIE

OF

CHARLES,

BY THE GRACE OF

GOD, KING OF GREAT

BRITTAINE, FRANCE,

AND IRELAND, DEFEN-

DER OF THE

FAITH, &c.

THIS HISTORICALL

POEM, BORNE BY HIS

COMMAND, AND NOT

TO LIVE BVT BY HIS

GRATIOVS ACCEPTA-

TION, IS HVMBLY

DEDICATED BY

THE AVTHOR,

His Majesties most obedient

Subject and Servant

THO. MAY.

[1]

The first booke

Argument

The happy part of Henry's reigne is showne.
His first triumphant yeares and high renowne.
His peace and power Enyo greiues to see;
And to disturbe his long tranquillity
5   Descending downe to Lucifer below
Shee craues some Vices aide, to overthrow
The causes of it. there those tragike times
Of Stephens reigne, and Englands ciuill crimes
So lately past, Enyo dooes relate;
10   And shewes with greife King Henry's present state.
The fiend foretells what suddaine change shall bee
Of Englands peace and his felicity.

The Second Henry, first Plantagenet,
The first of Englands royall Kings, that sett
Victorious footing on the Irish shore,
And taught that warrelike nation to adore
5   A forreine scepter, sound yee Muses forth.
Declare how much his high heroike worth
By stormes of spitefull fortune oft assail'd,
As oft 'gainst fortunes spitefull stormes prevail'd.
His glorious reigne, but wrapt in various fate,
10   And, though triumphant, yett vnfortunate.
How his great vertues were too saddly try'de   [2]
By rebell subiects, by the Papall pride,
And his owne childrens strange impiety.
By opposition to ecclipse his high
15   And great renowne, or higher to aduance
The fame of his vndaunted puissance.
       Vouchsafe, dread Soueraigne Charles, with that most cleare
And gratious eye, with which you vse to cheare
Poore suppliants, while destinyes attend
20   Your royall doome, to view these lines, and lend
Your favoures influence, which can infuse

Vertue alone into an English Muse.
Shee else would tremble to approach too nigh
So pure a mynde, so great a Maiesty.
25 Vouchsafe to read the actions of a King
Your noble ancestour; and what wee sing
In Henry's reigne, that may bee true renowne,
Accept it, S^r, as Prologue to your owne,
Vntill this Muse, or some more happy straine
30 May sing your vertues, and vnæquall'd reigne.
        Those ciuill swords, that did so lately stayne
The land with slaughter, now were sheath'd againe.
The rents of State were clos'd, the wounds were cur'de;
Peace by victorious Henry was secur'de,
35 And justice waited on his awfull throne
Without controll; all feares, all faction,
That tooke beginning with King Stephen's reigne,   [3]
With him descended to the graue agayne.
Stephen deceas'd, the crowne of England now
40 Came by accord t'empale young Henry's brow,
Which was before by right of birth his due.
But hee, least England too too long should rue
In blood and slaughter theire ambitious strife,
Came to accords of peace, and during life
45 Of Stephen, respited his royall right.
Now like bright Phœbus to the longing sight
Of all the people did young Henry rise;
Before whose rayes all past calamities
Like mists did vanish: no sadd clouds accloy
50 The aire of England; with loud shoutes of ioy
The people flock, the Peeres their wealth display
To grace his wish'd-for coronation day.
His braue atcheiuements, and that early fame
Which hee in France had gain'd, had made his name
55 Already lou'd in England and admir'd.
Him all the people for their Lord desir'd,
And now possest of him, take faire presage
Such youth would end in a triumphant age.
        Then, as when once the charriot of the Sunn
60 Had beene misguided by bold Phaëton,

Ioue walk'd the round, and veiw'd with carefull eye
If heauen were safe; then from the starry sky
Descending downe, suruey'd the scorched ground,   [4]
And there repair'd the ruines that hee found;
65   To theire dry channells hee call'd backe the floods,
And with fresh verdure cloath'd the seinged woods,
Renew'd the herbage, and redresse ordain'd
For all that wronged nature hadd sustein'd:
So Henry stablish'd in the Regall throne
70   Ioue-like surueyes his large dominion,
To see what parts of state might be decay'd,
What rents so long a civill warre had made.
With phisicke fitt hee purges from the state
Those humors that did stirre and swell so late,
75   Digests the reliques, and by Princely arts,
And policy, corroborates the parts.
        And first of all, those troopes of forreiners,
That from all parts, during the ciuill warres
Resorted hither to seeke spoyle and prey,
80   Hee banishes, that at th'appoynted day
Within the coasts no strangers did remaine,
Restoring England to it selfe agayne.
        And least the crowne should want for that expense,
That must support the high magnificence
85   Of such a Monarchy, into his hands
Hee boldly seizes all the royall lands,
Which either greatest men did vncontroll'd
In those tumultuous tymes vniustly hold;
Or else King Stephen to support so badd   [5]
90   And weake a title, as (they knew) hee had,
Had giuen freely, as rewards to ty
Theire truth to him against theire loyalty.
        Nor did King Henry vindicate alone
The state and wealth of his imperiall crowne,
95   But the iust power, and with a puissant hand
Settled that sure obedience through the land,
That to his awfull scepter did belong.
The greatest Peeres, that were before too strong
To bee commanded, hee by force compell'd

100 To yeild to him the castles that they held.
     And all the Midd-land forts hee rased downe
     (The strength of nothing but rebellion.)
     Nor, though as yett presumptuous Mortimer
     Had not forgott the late licentious warre,
105 But stroue to guard against his soueraigne
     By lawlesse armes the strengths that hee had tane,
     Could hee resist the king, enforc'd to yeild
     To him those three strong Castles that hee held.
         Well did this reformation suite the thought
110 Of such a great Heroike King, whoo brought
     Besides his persons worth, and true esteeme,
     So lou'de a title to the crowne with him.
     Not from the Norman Conquerour did hee
     Deduce alone his royall pedegree:
115 But from the ancient Saxon Kings beside,   [6]
     As lineall heire to Edmund Ironside;
     And in his happy birth did so conioyne
     The conquering Norman and old Saxon line.
     Which hearty loue and reverence to his throne
120 From all the English people justly wonne.
     Whoo now forgate, pleas'd with his lawfull power,
     That they were seruants to a Conquerour.
     Great Grandchilde, by the Femall side, was hee
     To Margaret the Queene of Scotland; shee
125 Daughter to Edward, sonne to Ironside;
     Whose royall birth and blood was dignify'd
     By twenty faire descents of Saxon Kings.
     All which the happy birth of Henry brings
     The more to England to endeare his reigne.
130 And heere your selfe most Gratious Soueraigne,
     Your ancient right to Englands crowne may see.
     In Scotlands royall blood your pedegree
     Is farther drawne; and no knowne King, as you,
     So long a title to two crownes can show.
135   Then to the North with puissant armes hee makes
     A prudent voyage, and by conquests takes
     (To keepe entire his kingdomes ancient bounds)
     From Malcolme king of Scotland, all those grounds

That to the crowne of England did belong.
140   No cityes could withstand, no forts so strong
      But yeild to Henryes force. there with the rest   [7]
      Newcastle, Carleill hee againe possest.
      But least iniustice any staine should bee
      To his great deedes, in thankfull memory
145   Of what king Malcolme in the warres had done
      For th'Empresse Mawde, hee giues him Huntingdon
      A midd-land county, rich, and fitter farre
      For the behoofe of both; from whence no warre
      Nor troubles could arise, and which before
150   Had beene possess'd by Malcolmes ancestor.
            Yett did one deede with sadd iniustice blott
      The reputation hee before had gott;
      Whilest too much thirsting for encrease of lands,
      He seiz'd out of his brother Geoffrey's hands
155   The Earldome of Aniou; forgetting both
      The sacred tyes of nature and of Oath;
      That Oath which once so solemnly he swore.
      His Father Geoffrey Anious Earle, before
      Knowing that Henry was, by birth, to bee
160   Both Englands King, and Duke of Normandy,
      Had giuen that Earldome to his second sonne
      Geoffrey, and putt him in possession
      Of three the strongest castles in the land.
      But falling sick, when deaths approaching hand
165   He felt, mistrusting that his eldest sonne
      The potent Henry might, when hee was gone,
      Disseize young Geoffrey, made his Barons sweare   [8]
      (For at his death Prince Henry was not there)
      That his dead corps should not enterred bee
170   Till Henry had beene sworne to ratify
      His will. Prince Henry, though vnwillingly,
      Yett rather then his fathers hearse should ly
      Vnbury'd still, that oath before them tooke.
      Which afterward, when Englands king, hee broke;
175   And, though possessed of so many lands
      And large estates, out of his brother's hands
      That Earldome tooke by force of armes away;

And did in lieu, a yearly pension pay.
But though the King could for that oath obtaine
180   A dispensation from Pope Adrian,
A higher power (it seem'd) would not dispense;
But afterward in kinde did recompence
That foule misdeede. for when King Henry meant
To Iohn his youngest sonne the gouernment
185   Of those three castles; thence his eldest sonne
Tooke first pretence for that rebellion
Against his father. so what iniury
Impiety had wrought, Impiety
Reveng'd; and scourg'd by an vnnaturall sonne
190   What was 'gainst nature by a brother done.
    Yett could not Henry's deedes of highest fame
Teach stubborne Wales to tremble at his name,
Or feare t'offend him by rebellious warre,   [9]
Till shee had felt him there a Conquerer,
195   And beene herselfe enforced to implore
His grace and favour, with one triumph more
T'enrich his conquering head; not all her great
Rough woods could yeild her soldiers safe retreat;
Nor could those high and craggy mountaines bee
200   Of proofe 'gainst Henry's magnanimity.
Although the Welsh rely'd not on the aide
Of hills and woods: theire Prince was not afraide
To ioyne in battell with the English strength;
Where, though stout Owen and his powers at length
205   Subdu'de, did yeild themselues, yett so they fought,
That they true fame to Henry's conquest brought.
Whoo now triumphant backe to England goes,
And leaues strong forts to aw rebellious foes,
To guard the coasts and marches, and appeare
210   The lasting trophees of his conquests there.
    Those large dominions, which hee held in France,
The fame alone of his great puissance
Preseru'd from tumults, from rebellions free,
Or feare of any forreine enemy.
215   King Lewis himselfe was there to weake a foe
To doo him damage, or his power orethrow

Beyond the seas; yett though each neighbouring state
With envy trembled at the prosperous fate
Of Englands King; such moderation hee   [10]
220   Had shew'd, so rul'd his power with equity,
Seeking no lawlesse and vniust encrease,
That Europe then possest a happy peace.
This peace when feirce Enyo had beheld,
And saw all seedes of warre and faction quel'd,
225   She sigh'd and wept; for nought could pleasing bee
To that dire mayde but warres calamity;
Nought but dissention did to her seeme good;
No sights but feilds and rivers stain'd with blood
Were her delightsome prospects. into aire
230   Shee mounts, and fill'd with fury and despaire
Shakes as shee flyes, her now-extinguish'd brand,
Which giues no blaze at all, then taking stand
Aboue the shore of fruitfull Normandy
Vpon a lofty cliffe veiwes from on high
235   Great Henry's large dominions, that extend
From Scotland Northward to the Southerne end
Of spatious France, which those high mountaines bound
Nam'd from Pyrenes death. ore all that ground
Shee sees, and gnashes for disdaine to see,
240   No streaming Ensignes, no hostility;
The murdrous swords to sythes were turn'd agayne,
And cheerefull plowmen till the fertile plaine;
The heardsmen heare theire bullocks gently lough,
And theire owne folds the fearelesse shepheards know.
245   Am I then banish'd quite? shall peace (quoth shee)   [11]
Boast through these lands so great a victory
Ouer Enyo? will no power orethrow
These nations quiett rest? if heauen allow
This Lethargy, and still would haue it so:
250   I will descend, and see what hell can doo.
        A Spatious cave there was (not oft before
Descry'd by mortall eye) within that shore
Which wealthy France doth to the North display,
And Brittaines Ocean bounds. thither, they say,
255   The wise Dulychian Heroe, by advise

Of beautious Circe, came to sacrifice,
And there restor'd, by blood of bullocks slaine,
To silent ghosts the vse of speech againe.
Through that darke vault did Phœbus nere shoot ray,
260   Nor ever glided beame of cheerefull day.
The groue of Proserpine oreshadow'd quite
That dismall shore, and dampes of drery night
Condens'd the aire; no birds those boughs did grace,
Nor with sweete musicke cheer'd the balefull place;
265   No Tritons play'd, nor did blew Proteus feede
His scaly flocke, nor faire Halcyon breede
Beneath the shelter of so sadd a shore:
But greisly feinds and furies evermore
In hideous shapes did to the cave repaire,
270   And ghosts sadd murmurs did affright the aire,   [12]
Whoo in vnnumber'd companyes attend.
Thither the feirce Enyo did descend,
And all her strongest arts and charmings bring
To hold converse with Hells infernall king.
275   The Fiend himselfe was busy farre below,
And ranne with gnashing envy too and fro
To finde out plotts of ruyne, and suruey
His Master-vices, whoo fast chained lay
In adamantine cavernes; and from thence
280   (So pleas'd the great Creators providence
To curbe theire might for mankindes sake, least all
The world should in a quick confusion fall)
With all theire force at once, and licens'd power
They cannot goe; for soone they would devoure
285   All states all lands, and worke more tragike woe
Then earthquakes, fires, or pestilence can doo.
Within their severall denns the Vices lay;
And ore the doores proud pictures did display
What severall feates and conquests they had wrought,
290   What states, what kingdomes they to ruine brought.
For of destroying houshoulds, or the fall
Of private men they made no boast at all.
And as sterne Aeolus is forc'd to locke
The boistrous windes in caves of strongest rocke

295   By Ioue's command, least if they wholly goe,
      They should all woods, all cityes ouerthrow,
      And beare downe all that did before them stand,   [13]
      Confounding Neptune's kingdome with the land.
      Yett haue those windes still leaue in some degree
300   (Though they disdayne such petty liberty)
      To range abroade, to make theire natures knowne,
      To shake some weakely founded houses downe,
      Oreturne some aged Oakes, and now and than
      To cause a shipwrack on the Ocean.
305   Even so these hellish monsters, though great Ioue
      Permitt them not in theire full strength to moove,
      Are acting mischeife every day, and goe
      Contriving heere and there designes of woe,
      And worke (though they almost such worke despise)
310   The wrack of priuate men and familyes;
      But to effect a great and publike woe
      Without a speciall license cannot goe.
      Hither, while Lucifer did thus suruey
      His Master-vices as they chained lay,
315   Hee bad them bring Enyo downe below,
      For then to th'vpper cave hee would not goe.
      What would'st thou crave (quoth hee) what blacke designe,
      What stratagem t'enlarge thy power or myne
      Hath made Enyo hither take her flight?
320   The furious mayde replies; great Prince of night,
      Tis not my cause alone that makes mee come
      (As fearing generall peace in Christendome.)
      Thy cause is ioyn'd; I feare if that peace bee,   [14]
      Such warres as more will hurt thy Monarchy.
325   Then breifely thus; full fifteene yeares are gone
      Since potent Henry wore the English crowne,
      Possest besydes, in wealthy France of more
      Strong lands, then doo the crowne of France adore,
      Blest with a numerous issue, and by none
330   Annoy'd, disturb'd by no rebellion,
      Nor forreine foes; and least French Lewis should bee
      His foe (though too too weake;) affinity
      Ioines them; faire Margaret is by wedlocke ty'de

To young Prince Henry; Brittaines heire's affy'de
335   To Geoffry his third sonne, whoo comes to add
That Dutchy too, to what before hee had
In France; it did not seeme enough that hee
Before possest Maine, Aniou, Normandy,
Nor that hee did by Eleanor obtaine
340   Poictou besydes, and fertile Aquitaine.
What warre dares menace such strong power as hee
Possesses now? what fortune (woe is mee)
Has chang'de the tymes? with what delight could I
(If now not crost by this tranquillity)
345   Remember Stephen's reigne, and tragicke tymes?
O heauens what slaughters then, what civill crymes
Did England see, when on her frighted Coast
The Empresse Mawde was landed with her hoast?
And came by armes to claime her royall right?   [15]
350   What suddaine tumults rose, and did affright
The wretched people? different passions then
Made sadd divisions in the hearts of men.
Some wept, some fear'd, some saddly tooke theire armes,
And with entent to cure theire countryes harmes
355   Prepar'd to wound her more; some did not know
What syde to take, or where they might bestow
Theire rage or loue. before each mourning eye
Did formes of fire, of blood, and slaughter flye.
Within themselues theire passions made arise
360   Such things as they imagin'd prodigyes;
With thoughts confus'd the people rush'd to armes;
No noyse in England but my loud alarmes
Was heard; the warre long carryed to and fro
At Lincolne wholly mett at last, and now
365   All hop'd one battell would the right decide.
No feild was ever with more fury try'de,
Nor rage ere mett more æquall rage, as they
That saw the slaughters of that dismall day,
Could iustly tell; till great Augustaes right,
370   Whose powers renowned Gloster ledd in fight,
Prevail'd at last; there after hee in vayne
Had shew'd rare valour, was king Stephen tane,

And to the conquering Empresse captiue brought.
Then turn'd the state. who would not then haue thought
375   All ciuill warres had ended quite, when shee   [16]
Had on her syde both right and victory?
The people all congratulate her state;
But soone beginne to pitty Stephen's fate,
And too hard durance. whoo a king had beene,
380   Then pinch'd in irons lay. his weeping Queene
For her deare Lord did to the Empresse sue,
But all in vayne. the warres from thence renew;
Againe the discontented people rise
In aide of Stephen's faction, and surprise
385   Glosters braue Earle, Augustaes Generall.
Then seem'd the like calamityes to fall
On both the parties, and in æquall payne
Of durance did the king and Earle remaine.
Accord was made, but not an end to make
390   Of ciuill warre, nor for theire countreyes sake,
But to release theire owne captivity,
And in exchange they sett each other free.
From this accord with greater fury farre
Through all the kingdome rose the ciuill warre.
395   For those sadd changes had not pacify'de
But more incens'd the Cheifes of either side.
Whose wrath the people felt; all kindes of woe
The wretched Realme was forc'd to vndergoe.
The countreys pillag'de, castles lost and wonne,
400   Rich cloysters rob'd, the fairest cityes downe
Or ras'd or burned, in rude heapes did ly;   [17]
As Wiltons pityed sacke could testify
By Glosters furious army burn'd with fire.
Nor thee faire Worster, in king Stephens ire
405   Could all thy beautious structure saue from wracke;
In fatall flames thy walles and houses cracke.
Through what great hazards did both Princes runn?
How hardly oft escape destruction!
What neede I tell how Stephan forc'de to flye
410   From Gloster's powers, forsooke his treasury
At Wilton Abbey? how the Empresse fledd

When least shee seem'd to fly (supposed dead)
And like a corse was carryed through her foes
So to escape? what neede I now disclose
415   How after shee, when shee in Oxford lay
Straightly beseig'd by Stephan, gott away?
No strength of frends at all, no parleyes there
Could free her person; Winter rescu'de her,
And the cold season stroue to mock the foe.
420   December rag'de, the Northern windes did blow,
And by theire power had glaz'd the siluer flood
Of neere-adioyning Thames, whose waters stood
Congealed still; ore which the snow around
Had fall'n, and with white fleeces cloath'd the ground;
425   When the wise Empresse cloath'd a like in white
Forsooke the towne, and past a long by night,
Deluding so the watches carefull eyes.   [18]
They thought the snow had moou'de, or did surmise
Theire opticke spiritts had disturbed beene,
430   Not cleare, and they tumultuously had seene.
Fixt obiects oft doe seeme in motion so.
Thus then securely did the Empresse goe,
And was receiv'd with ioy to Wallingford.
Nor then did England bleede alone; her Lord
435   Anious great Earle by feirce and bloody warre
Was winning Normandy in right of her.
Those, those were tymes; but now, ah woe is mee
Great Lucifer, if this tranquillity
Without disturbance hold in Christendome,
440   I feare for thee a farre worse warre will come.
Thy Saracens shall rue the Christians peace,
And feele theire conquering swords. what large encrease
Of territories, honour and of fame
Through farthest Asia will the Christian name
445   Acquire? what bounds, alas, would Salem know
If potent Henry to this warre should goe?
If hee should there the English crosse advance?
His aide they all will seeke; his puissance
Will Salems feeble king implore to ioyne
450   Against those foes that threaten Palæstine.

Therefore in tyme this peacefull knott diuide.
Enyo ceas'd; when Lucifer reply'de;
Thy iust complaint, heroike Maide, I heare;   [19]
But doo not doubt the power of Lucifer.
455   Those instruments, that I from hence shall bring,
Will soone divert it all, and make this king,
Whose strength the world so much admires, and feares,
Whome now they deeme so blest, ere many yeares
Into themselues revolue agayne, to bee
460   The pity of his foes; nature for mee
Against herselfe is working. come and veiw
My champions heere that shall with speede pursue
What I designe. with that hee leads her by
The denns, where all along his vices lye.
465   There in her denn lay pompous Luxury
Stretch'd out at length; no Vice could boast such high
And generall victories as shee had wonne.
Of which proud trophees there at large were showne.
Besydes small states and kingdomes ruined,
470   Those mighty Monarchies, that had orespread
The spatious earth, and stretch'd theire conquering armes
From Pole to Pole, by her ensnaring charmes
Were quite consum'de. there lay imperiall Rome,
That vanquish'd all the world, by her orecome.
475   Fetter'd was th'old Assyrian Lion there,
The Græcian Leopard, and the Persian beare,
With others numberlesse lamenting by
Examples of the power of Luxury.
        Next with erected lookes Ambition stood,   [20]
480   Whose trophees all were pourtray'd forth in blood.
Vnder his feete law and religion
Hee trampled downe; sack'd cityes there were showne,
Riuers and feilds with slaughter overspread,
And stain'd with blood which his wilde sonnes had shedd.
485   There Ninus image stood, whoo first of all
By lawlesse armes and slaughter did enthrall
The quiet nations, that liu'de free till then,
And first tooke pride to triumph ouer men.
There was Sesostres figur'd; there the sonn

490   Of Philip lay, whose dire ambition
       Not all the spatious earth could satisfy.
       Swift as the lightning did his conquests fly
       From Greece to farthest Easterne lands, and like
       Some dire contagion, through the world did strike
495   Death and destruction; purple were the floods
       Of every region with theire natiues bloods.
       Next him that Roman lay, whoo first of all
       Captiu'de his countrey; there were figur'd all
       His warres and mischeifes, and what ever woes
500   Through all the world by dire ambition rose.
              Next to that Fiend lay pale Reuenge; with gore
       His ghastly visage was all sprinckled ore.
       The hate hee bore to others had quite reft
       Him of all loue vnto himselfe, and left
505   No place for nature. ore his denn were showne   [21]
       Such tragedyes and sadd destruction
       As would dissolue true human hearts to heare,
       And from the furies selues enforce a teare.
       Those bloody slaughters there to veiw were brought,
510   Which Iacobs cruell sonnes in Shechem wrought,
       When all the Males but newly circumcis'de
       To theire revengefull rage were sacrific'de.
       There the slayne youth of Alexandria ly
       By Caracalla's vengefull butchery.
515   The captiu'de fate of Spaine was there display'de,
       Which wrathfull Iulian in revenge betray'de
       To Pagan Moores, and ruin'd so his owne
       Sadd house, his country and religion.
       Not all these sacred bonds with him prevaile,
520   When hee beholds his ravish'd daughter waile,
       Wring her white hands, and that faire bosome strike,
       That too much pleas'd the lustfull Roderike.
              The next Sedition lay; not like the rest
       Was hee attir'de, nor in his lookes exprest
525   Hatred to heauen and vertues lawes; but hee
       Pretends religion, lawe, or liberty,
       Seeming t'adore, what hee did most orethrow,
       And would persuade vertue to bee a foe

To peace and lawfull power. aboue his denn
530   For boasting trophees hung such robes, as when
Old Sparta stood, her Ephori did weare,   [22]
And Romes bold tribunes. storyes carued there
Of his atcheiuements numberlesse were seene,
Such as the Gracchis factious stirres had beene
535   In ancient Rome, and such as were the crymes,
That oft wrack'd Greece in her most potent tymes,
Such as learn'd Athens, and bold Sparta knew,
And from theire ablest soldiers oft did rue.
        Next to that Vice lay foule Impiety
540   At large display'de, the cursed enemy
Of natures best and holyest lawes; through all
Her loathsome denn vnthankefull vipers crawle.
Aboue those storyes were display'd, which show
How much the Monarchy of Hell did ow
545   For peoples wracke to that abhorred Vice.
There were Mycenæ's balefull tragœdies,
And all the woes that fatall Thebes had wrought.
There false Medea, when away shee brought
Her owne betrayed countryes spoiles, before
550   Her weeping father Aeta, peicemeale tore
Her brother's limmes, and strew'de them ore the feild.
There with the same impiety shee kill'd
Her owne two sonnes, and through the aire a pace
By dragons drawne shee fledd from Iasons face.
555   There strong Alcathoë, king Nisus towne
By Scyllaes impious treason was orethrowne,
And sack'd with fire and sword; the wretched maide   [23]
Had from her lofty sounding tower suruey'd
King Minos hoast, and doating on her faire
560   Foes face, cutt off her fathers purple haire.
        This, this is shee, this is the Vice must goe
(Quoth Lucifer) to worke the ouerthrow
Of Englands peace; Impiety shall doo
What ever thy designes can reach vnto.
565   Shee shall ascend to England, and possesse
The breasts of Henry's sonns; with what successe
Enyo feare not; I haue seene the boyes.

Though yett but young; I marke, to swell my ioyes,
Such forward signes of theire ambition,
570   They soone will by Impiety bee blowne
Vpp into such attempts, as that thy brand
Shall quickly blaze againe through every land
That Henry rules. this is the cause that hee
Continues yet in his prosperity,
575   His sonnes are not of age. they, they must grow
Theire fathers only ruine, th'overthrow
Of all his weale. besydes to further oure
Designe in this, and lend vs present power,
The king himselfe consents; who govern'd by
580   Strong dotage and disastrous policy
Dooes now entend to crowne his eldest sonne.
Soone as his feasts at windsore shall bee done,
Where now, with William Scotlands king, hee lyes,   [24]
Shall Westminster see these solemnityes.
585   There see how soone Impiety shall fire
The young kings breast, and make him more aspire
The more his father giues. and though of late
Sedition well haue wrought vpon the state
By Becket, whoo these five yeares has beene fledd,
590   And yet that strife is not extinguished;
No warres from thence grow, nor has thy desire
Enyo, beene fullfill'd; that factious fire
Has burnt no cityes, nor has blood at all
Beene drawne in that; be sure in this there shall.
595   Impiety shall doo't. the Fiend heere ends,
And pleas'd Enyo from the cave ascends.

[25]

The second booke

Argument

King Henry crownes at Westminster, his sonne:
But soone beginns to feare what hee had done.
Hee feasts the King of Scotland at his court.
Among the tempting beautyes, that resort
5   To that great festivall, hee falls in loue
With Rosamund. arm'd Pallas from aboue
Appeares to Henry's sleepe: chydes him, as slow
In his affaires of Ireland; and dooes show
What lasting honour that great Ile shall bee
10 To him and his victorius progeny.

Now had great Henry his designe declar'd
To crowne his sonne, and all that state prepar'd
That might befitt the great solemnity.
The Peeres and people all approue what hee
5   Rashly decrees, and in the triumph ioyne.
With glittering pompe the streetes of London shine.
Theire wealth the greatest citizens display
To grace young Henry's coronation day.
But most of all, though least discerning why,
10 Vnusuall ioy the vulgar testify.
Not good but new things please the peoples eyes.
Nor dooes king Henry in his loue surmise
That all the face of England, all the state   [26]
Were witnesses enow to celebrate
15 His sonn's high honour; but king William too
Arriu'de from Scotland, must bee brought to doo
His homage to him as to Englands King,
And with him must his brother Dauid bring.
The sacred oyle, in banish'd Becket's stead,
20 Is by Yorkes Prelate pour'd vpon his head;
The diadem, which was possess'd before,
Empales his brow; whilest all the Peeres adore
Two Sunns at once, and, ill presaging, see

(What after proou'd) a fatall prodigy.
25   How ill Imperiall Maiesty can brooke
A sharer, seeke not farre; nor neede you looke
Storyes, whose creditt tyme has ruin'd quite;
Nor neede you read what old tragœdians write
Of this sadd theame, or cast your pitying eyes
30   Vpon the Theban brothers tragœdyes,
Or brothers blood that Romes first walls did stayne.
The spatious heavens (as Poets wisely faine)
Brook'd not old Saturne and his Iupiter.
By every age and dire examples neere
35   To vs, how oft has this sadd truth beene proou'd?
How many sonnes and fathers haue beene moou'd
To parricide, to sett themselues but free
From that which Henry makes himselfe to bee,
Rivall'd in reigne? but if hee still retayne   [27]
40   Full regall power, what more doost thou obtaine
By this thy father's kinde donation,
Young king, then title and a fruitlesse throne?
How vayne thy scepter is, when thou shalt see
The power divided from the dignity?
45   Yett doe not so mistake thy fate; no lesse,
Nay greater farre esteeme thy happinesse
Then if thou now wert seiz'd of all alone.
The cares and dangers waiting on a crowne
Haue made some feare the burden, or despise
50   That sacred iewell of vnvalewed price.
A prudent King, when hee a while survey'd
The glittering splendour, that his crowne display'd,
Was sighing heard to say, if those that view
Farre-off thy flattering gloryes only, knew
55   How many cares and greifes in thee are found,
They would bee loath to take thee vpp from ground.
This wisest Monarch, if hee now should see
Thy royall state, young king, would envy thee,
And count thee happy sure, that doost alone
60   Weare, without cares, the gloryes of a crowne,
That from the burden of a King art free,
Invested only with the dignity.

Yett this prerogatiue brings no content
To thee that seem'st to want th'accomplishment
65   Of royalty, the power and Regall sway.   [28]
Nothing (alas) this coronation day
Has brought thee to, but to a nearer sight
Of what thou hast not, nor is yett thy right.
Thy stirring minde meetes torture with a throne,
70   But Tantalized in dominion.
The cause (alas) of woes that must ensue,
And thy great father too too soone shall rue.
That dayes solemnity in truest state
The court of England strove to celebrate,
75   And with such great magnificence, as might
The Maiesty of that high presence fitt;
Where all at once three Kings, two Queenes were mett,
Besydes so many high-borne Princes, great
In fame and wealth. the feasting boords were fill'd
80   With what this Iland or rich France could yeild.
Such cates as those, with which old Poets fain'd
In Thessaly the Gods were entertain'd
At siluer-footed Thetis bridall feast,
Where Ioue himselfe vouchsaf'd to bee a guest.
85   Where aged Chiron waited at the boord,
And brought what aire, earth, waters could afford,
When all rich Tempe, and th'adioyning seas
Were search'd, besides what then the Naiades,
What young Palæmon, Glaucus, and the greene
90   Sea-nymphs had brought to grace theire beauteous Queene.
The choisest wines that France or Spayne could yeild   [29]
In cupps of gold studded with gemms were fill'd,
And antique gobletts, where the caruer strove
To æquall natures skill; beasts seem'd to moove,
95   And pretious birds theire glistering wings display'd.
The faire and massy vessels, that convey'd
The feast to them, did farre in their high rates
Exceede the valew of those sumptuous cates.
King Henry wanton with excesse of ioy,
100   Which now hee thought no fortune could destroy
(How soone deceiu'd! how soone enforc'de to finde

The errour in his ill-presaging minde)
To testify a great affection,
And grace the state of his young-crowned sonne,
105   Himself, as sewer will vouchsafe to waite
Vpon his sonne, whoo sitts in Regall state,
And to his table the first dish present.
The Lords and Princes all with one consent
Applaud the Kings great loue, but secretly
110   Are strooke with wonder these strange rites to see.
Some seeke examples for it; some within
Themselues, doo saddly from that sight divine;
When Yorkes Archbishopp the young King bespake;
Reioyce, my Princely sonne, and freely take
115   The comfort of your state; no Monarch (know)
On earth, has such a servitour as you.
With that the Prelate gently smyl'd; but hee   [30]
With a proud looke replyes; why wonder yee?   Polydore
Or think these rites so strange my father dooes?   Virgill
120   My birth is farre more royall (well hee knowes)   in H.2.
Then his. hee only by the mothers side
With high imperiall blood was dignify'de;
His father was but Anious Earle; but I
Derive from both my parents royalty,
125   A King and Queene. they all with wonder heare;
King Henry sigh'd, and gan even then to feare
What after might ensue from such a pride.
But at that triumph hee resolu'd to hide
His feares or greifes. instead of which, the court
130   Was fill'd with revells, with all royall sport,
All showes that high magnificence could giue.
There art in strange varietyes did strive
Both to perplexe and pleas the eyes of all,
But nature more. for to the festivall
135   From every part the choisest beauties came.
There like a fire ætheriall, every Dame
Did blaze, more bright then Elements could make.
While from the countrys they all flock'd to take
Survey of kingly gloryes, while they sought
140   To view the lustre of a court, they brought

The lustre with them, and might seeme to bee
Themselues that splendour, that they came to see.
Amidd'st those sparkling beautyes Cupid sate   [31]
Loues powerfull God, and rul'd in highest state
145   Arm'd with his fires and shafts, resolu'd to bee
In Henry's court a greater King then hee,
Whose yoake the King must suffer. on the state
Of Cupid there the little Loues did waite.
Throughout the Court they tooke theire wanton flight
150   With wings vnseene, and when they list, would light
Vpon the Ladyes shoulders or theire breasts,
Theire ruffes or tires; they feele not those light guests,
Which they giue harbour to; **bold Lycence** there,
Sweete reconciled **Anger, blushing Feare,**
155   **Vnsafe Delight,** did with **pale Watching** fly,
Desiring teares with **Wanton periury,**
And all the rest. They say the beautious Queene
Of Loue herselfe vpon that day was seene
Approaching London; vp cleare Thames his streame
160   Borne on a sounding Triton's backe shee came.
The river smooth'd his face to entertaine
The Queene of Loue with her light-footed traine.
The siluer Swanns ador'de her all the way,
And churking did theire snow-white wings display.
165   The river-nymphes, that saw her coming, thought
Some sweete atcheiuement now was to bee wrought,
That Cupid sure had promis'd her to see
Some high exploit, some royall victory,
As that when once hee made imperiall Ioue   [32]
170   Lough like a Bull for faire Europaes loue,
Or when hee made rough Neptune feele his fire,
Or warm'd chast Cynthiaes bosome with desire,
And made her court the Shepheard. such a one
Loues Queene now look'd for from her conquering sonne.
175   Nor was her expectation voyd; shee found
As much as shee could hope, a royall wound.
No lesse then Henry's noble breast must bee
The trophee of her Cupid's victory.
Henry's pleas'd eyes now wander'd every where

180   Among those starres, that made his court theire sphære,
       (For such they seem'd, and no lesse bright they shew'd,
       Although of different light and magnitude.)
       Oft could hee change the obiects of his eye
       With fresh delight, praise the variety
185   Without distracted thoughts, till like the Queene
       Of light, faire Cinthya, Rosamund was seene.
       There did hee fixe; there his amazed eye
       Forgott all pleasure of variety,
       And gaz'd alone vpon her matchlesse hew.
190   False Cupid laugh'd, and thence in triumph flew.
       Too much (alas) found Henry's wounded brest
       How much her beauty did outshine the rest.
       So golden Venus 'mongst the Sea-nymphs, so
       Did Deidamia 'mongst her sisters show,
195   When shee enflam'd the young Achilles heart,   [33]
       As Rosamund appear'd. each single part
       Of Loues rich dower, which shee alone possest,
       Had beene enough to fire a vulgar breast,
       And in another raise high beauties fame.
200   Into her forme all severall Cupids came,
       And all the Graces theire perfection show'd.
       Nature confest shee had too much bestow'd
       On one rich mixture, which alone must weare
       All her faire liveries; pure whitenesse there,
205   Nor redd alone must beauties colours show.
       Blew pleads a title, since her veines are so;
       Even black it selfe, plac'd in her eye, is bright,
       And seemes to bee the colour of the light.
       As they are hers, all formes, all colours please.
210   Henry, the more hee lookes, does more encrease
       His flame; and whither hee should check desire,
       And goe about to quench so sweete a fire;
       Or feede the flame, hee cannot yet resolue.
       A thousand thoughts dooes his sick breast revolue,
215   Sometymes hee seekes to cure the wound, and cast
       Out Cupids fatall shaft; but still more fast
       The arrow sticks, and goes more deepe into
       His wounded heart; ensnared fishes so

When they haue once receiu'd the baited hooke,
220 The more they plunge, the deeper still are strooke.
So when by chance the stately stagg is shott,   [34]
In vaine hee strives 'gainst fate; it bootes him not
Through all the forrests, lawnes, and feilds to take
His speedy course; no force, no flight can shake
225 The mortall shaft out of his wounded side.
It bootes not Henry to survey the pride
Of other beauties now; converse with all
The Princes mett at his great festivall,
Or fixe himselfe on the solemnities,
230 The sports and revells of his court. His eyes
Can recompense him with no sight at all,
Nor yeild him pleasure æquall to the thrall
They brought him to by sight of Rosamund.
No thoughts of state haue power t'allay his wound.
235 Sometymes hee yeilds to Loues imperiall flame;
Resolues to court her favour straight; but shame
Restraines that thought. His seruants all discerne
A change; but are afraide the cause to learne.
Tis not the crowning (Henry) of thy sonne
240 (Though that shall breede a sadd confusion)
Can make thee lesse then king, or disinthrone
Thee halfe so much, as loue of her has done.
That makes thee humbly sue: makes thee become
Thy selfe a subiect, forc'de t'abide the doome
245 That soueraigne beauty shall be pleas'd to give.   [35]
Thou, mighty Prince, whose high prerogatiue
Æquall to fate it selfe, vs'd to bestow
Or death or life on suppliants, art now
Thy selfe an humble suppliant, and bound
250 To sue for health to beautious Rosamund.
While thus the Princes mett do celebrate
In feasts and Revells young king Henryes state,
And London's fill'd with severall jollityes;
Swift-winged fame from thence to Paris flyes,
255 Where then the French king Lewis kept his court,
And fills his iealous eares with this report;
Young Henry on the royall throne is sett

Without his wife the Princesse Margarett
(Though Lewis his daughter.) iealousy can finde
260 A reason quickly to torment his mynde.
That reason flattering Courtiers aggrauate,
And those that loue the troubles of a state,
The factious spiritts, that seeke from thence theire prey.
What other reason can there bee (say they)
265 Vnlesse contemptuous scorne of thee and France,
That Henry singly should his sonne advance
Without his wife, nor lett young Margarett bee
A sharer in her husbands dignity?
What end of his, or what designe had beene
270 Made frustrate else, had shee beene crowned Queene?
These slight surmises are too soone approou'de,   [36]
And for iust reasons tane; the King is moou'de
To ground a warre on these, resolu'de (although
No hopes invite him) to bee Henry's foe;
275 Forc'de by miscalled honour to pursue
What most of all he would himselfe eschew.
        Honour is to a man a tyrant then
When honours lawes hee seekes from other men,
Not findes them in himself; when hee attends
280 Not reall truth but fame, which still depends
On others breaths; yett makes a man to goe
'Gainst his owne passions and his reason too.
        Nor must king Lewis his fury stay so long
As fairely to expostulate the wrong,
285 To send his greivance first, then to defy,
And bee a just and royall enemy.
Those fiery spiritts, that too much feare a peace,
That discontents betwixt the Kings would cease,
And no swords drawne at all, if that were done,
290 Still vrge king Lewis; with speede, say they, goe on.
There's no advantage in a course so slow;
Tis best to bee, before you seeme, a foe.
Before the newes to Henry's eare can fly,
With fire and sword invade his Normandy.
295   Meane tyme king Henry, fearelesse of the blow
Of warre, was master'd by a greater foe,

Enforc'de to yeild to Cupids powerfull bow.   [37]
The triumphs all were done; King William now
Had with Prince Dauid tane theire leaves, and from
300   The court of England were retourning home,
By English Lords attended on theire way.
The court seem'de nak'de, robb'd of that bright array,
And beautious splendour it so lately wore;
How much vnlike the place it was before!
305   How solitary now! but Henry's minde
That change, which others thinke of, cannot fynde.
No other absence can hee feele but one:
His dearest life faire Rosamund was gone
To grace the countrey with her presence now.
310   The wounded louer did by this tyme know
Her birth and countrey. thither flyes his heart,
And from his palace, nay himselfe would part.
Or else contrives to bring a gemme so bright
To court, and place her nearer to his sight.
315   No kingly pleasures, no magnificence
Can tast; no musick's sweete, while shee is thence.
So when the faire Calisto did remayne
In woods, a huntresse of Dianaes trayne,
And wore her quiver, when enamour'd Ioue
320   Beheld her matchlesse beauty from aboue,
The woods before heavens palace please his eye;
Before the starry regions of the sky
Hee loves th'Arcadian forrests to suruey.   [38]
Not those bright houses, nor the milky way
325   All pav'de with silver starres, doe seeme so cleare.
The woods are heauen while faire Calisto's there.
Iune then begann, and roses grac'de the spring.
Into his garden walkes the Loue-sick King
To seeke a sweete retreat, with her alone
330   To feast his pleas'd imagination.
There while he view'd the Queene of flowers, his flame
Encreas'd, and tooke fresh fuell from the name;
For her the blushing rose must praised bee,
And scorn'd agayne because it is not shee.
335   No roses can (quoth hee) be fragrant else;

There is no spring but where Lord Clifford dwells.
Thus vainely runne his thoughts vpon the flower,
While gentle birds about his shady bower
Tune theire soft notes, and by degrees sweete sleepe
340   Through all his wearyed senses 'gan to creepe;
As if faire Venus pitying his sadd plight
Would send him now by dreame some short delight,
And what his waking eye could not haue found,
Present in sleepe, the shape of Rosamund.
345   But heauen was more propitious to his fame,
And for loue-dreames, a nobler vision came.
Honours bright Goddesse, that heröike majde,
That issu'de from the braine of Ioue, array'de
In all her radiant gloryes came, before   [39]
350   Whose face the Cupids fledd; her right hand bore
The warrlike lance, her left Medusaes head;
Her golden plumed helme, both full of dread
And maiesty, such rayes of splendour yeilds
As rising Phœbus, when farre off he guilds
355   The Easterne cloudes; her eyes wore starry light,
But fixt, not twinckling like weake humane sight.
Nor did shee seeme by stepps at all to goe,
Or stirring severall limmes, as mortalls doe,
But one sole motion through the ayre to make.
360   Thus shee appear'd and thus the king bespake;
Forgettfull Henry wake; the fates provide
While thou art sleeping, fame for thee, and chide
Thy dull delayes. how long to thee in vayne
Shall Ireland yeild herselfe, and court thy raigne?
365   Ireland, that must hereafter bring a style
So great to thy posterity; that Ile,
The most enduring part of thy renowne,
And best addition to faire Englands crowne?
Ten yeares haue turn'd into themselues agayne
370   Since that late Pope deceased Adrian
Did freely send by Iohn of Salisbury
The grant of Irelands soveraignty to thee,
And with it sent that ring, to be a sure
And lasting signe of thy investiture
375   Into that sacred honour. canst thou weare   [40]

The pretious Emrauld on thy finger there,
And yett so long forgett with what entent
Thou then didst take that royall ornament,
That mariage token? wilt thou now refuse
380   The spouse, thou did'st with such affection chuse?
        Lett not the thoughts of factious Beckett now,
Nor what church-threats or censures thence may grow
Divert thee from this happy enterprise.
Thinke not that troubles may in France arise
385   Through thy short absence; since no stirres at home,
No losse that to those provinces can come,
Can counteruaile such great and lasting gaine.
That Westerne Iland, as the fates ordayne,
To thy victorious seede, through every age,
390   Shall be, a great, and constant heritage,
And flourish then, when all those Provinces,
All those rich lands thou doo'st in France possesse,
Shall from the English crowne divided bee.
When thy most ancient right, faire Normandy
395   It selfe is gone, togither with rich Maine,
With Brettaine, Aniou, Poictou, Aquitaine;
Although how oft shall France, before those dayes,
Bee scourg'd? what trophees shall the English raise
In every part and province, which no power
400   Shall ere extinguish, nor strong tyme devoure?
When all amazed christendome shall see   [41]
The Armes of England twice with victory
To graspe great France, and once to seize her crowne,
And wear't in vncontroll'd possession;
405   When Cæsar's deeds against the ancient Gaules
Shall bee outdone by English Generalls;
And three fam'd battells shall exceede what hee
Atchieu'd against his strongest enemy
Stout Vercingentorix; that Princes fall,
410   Arvaricum's fam'd sacke, and th'end of all
Alexia taken, to each severall feild
Of Cressy, Poictiers, Agincourt shall yeild.
But Ireland, which by easy victory
Without a warre almost shall yeild to thee,
415   Shall to thy royall heires remaine; although

Before that Kingdome to perfection grow,
And bee establish'd in a quiet reigne,
Oft horrid warres, and bloody feilds shall stayne
Her face in future tymes, and loud alarmes
420 Oft to the world shall fame the English armes,
And raise the glory of Elisaes name.
A virgin Queene shall all rebellion tame,
And to her rule, in spight of Spaines proud fate,
That spatious Iland wholly vindicate.
425 There wise king Iames shall spread the English law,
And by divinest skill (like Orpheus) draw
Those ruder people to a civile life,   [42]
And well establish'd peace; all iarres and strife
Shall fly before his most auspicious reigne.
430 This is that Prince, by whome highe heauens ordeine
The long wish'd marriage of two royall lands.
Britaines vnited Ile to his comands
And sacred scepter shall obedient bee.
Who after long and blest tranquility
435 Shall leaue those States to his heroik sonne
Renowned Charles; in whose pure breast alone
All regall vertues shall inhabite, ioin'd
With those that make a spotlesse private mynde,
Who shall refraine, pleas'd with just power alone,
440 All the licentious pleasures of a throne,
And by example governe, pleas'd to bee
A King in vertue as in royalty.
     The troubles now, that threaten Normandy,
Are sent to wake thee from this Lethargy,
445 And bring thee nobler thoughts; and now was rest
Quite banished from waken'd Henry's breast.
Hee with amazed thoughts look'd vp and downe;
But when his eyes were ope, the sight was gone;
And yett on Ireland wholly ranne his thought.
450 When suddaine tidings to his eare were brought
Of what king Lewis of France, beyond the Seas
Had then attempted 'gainst his Prouinces;
At which moou'd Henry armes; and crosses ore   [43]
As swift as thought, vnto the Norman shore.

The third booke

Argument.

> The Kings of France and England at Vendome
> Without a battell, to agreement come.
> Henry return'd to England, meetes againe
> With beautious Rosamund, and dooes obtaine
> 5   His wanton suit. hee builds for her a rare,
> And sumptuous bower. Stout Becket's famous iarre
> This booke declares, and dooes at large relate
> By what degrees it had disturb'd the state.
> His soueraignes pardon Becket dooes obtaine,
> 10   And to his See returnes in peace agayne.

Soone were those stormes, that threaten'd Normandy,
Blowne ore agayne; and that hostility
That Lewis of France in vnaduised ire
Had rashly harbour'd, did as soone expire
5   Before that any dire effects it wrought.
A peace King Henryes armed presence brought,
Whoo now in France arrived. at Vendosme   [44]
To enterview the two great Kings doo come.
There Lewis declares his cause; that wrong was done
10   To him and France, when Henry crown'd his sonne,
And with like state (befitting) had not sett
That crowne vpon the head of Margarett
His princely spouse. but this, which first did seeme
A cause of just hostility to him,
15   Was there controll'd by all; and iudg'de to bee
On sound advise, a lighter iniury
Then that the hand of warre should it decide.
For such a wrong a promise satisfy'de;
Which Henry freely gaue, and did maintaine;
20   That hee, ere long, would crowne his sonne againe;
And then young Margaret should full sharer bee
In all her husbands state and dignity.
Then to performe what hee had promis'd there,
Since these late-raised stormes allayed were,

25   Back into England Henry crost agayne;
And in his noble breast 'gann entertaine
The thought of Irelands conquest now; although
He yett in person did not meane to goe;
But vnto Dermot th'Irish Prince he gaue
30   Free leaue from any of his realmes to haue
What voluntaryes hee could cary ore,
That might hereafter to the Irish shore
Prepare his passage, and beginne the warres   [45]
On fitter tearmes. but not those high affaires
35   Of warre and fame could keepe imperious Loue
From tyrannizing, nor much lesse remooue
His force, that had before found entrance there.
Againe to him did Rosamund appeare.
And what ensu'd, declare my Muse, resound
40   The love of Henry and faire Rosamund;
Thou knowest it Erato, thou, that to give
My pen a true intelligence, did'st dive
So lately downe into th'Elizian groves,
And there beheld'st the seat of tragicke Loues,
45   That farre renowned shade of Mirtles, where
The beautious troope of Loue-slayne dames appeare,
And weare the markes of theire sadd ruines yett.
Vpon those gloomy grounds no flowers are sett
But such alone, which (as old Poets sing)
50   Did from wail'd deaths, and tragike changes spring;
Such as the pale-fac'de Daffadill, that from
That too too beautious boy's selfe-loue did come,
And purple Hyacinth, that first tooke growth
From that so much lamented Spartan youth,
55   Adonis short-liu'd flower of crimson hew,
That from faire Venus sprinckled Nectar grew
Dooes there appeare, by whome is saddly sett   [46]
The pining Clyties pale-leau'd violett.
Thou Erato, within that Mirtle grove
60   Saw'st those fam'd ladyes, whome theire owne sadd loue
Or others loue had ruin'd, wandring there;
Thou saw'st the Theban Semele appeare,
Whoo too too late complain'd of amorous Ioue,

And now condemn'd her owne ambitious loue.
65 There with the fatall shaft did Procris stand,
Whoo yett forgaue her Lord's mistaking hand;
Faire Dido too, of life and crowne bereft,
By whome the periur'd Troian's sword was left;
And there by Aspes destroy'd, sent from aboue
70 In all her gloryes to th'Elysian groue
Great Cleopatra walk'd; there thou did'st see
The Lesbian Sappho, sadd Eryphile,
The wailing Phædra, sham'd Pasiphaë,
Chast Thisbe, and incestuous Canace;
75 With them the much lamented Sestian Maide,
And thousands moe; whome whilest thyne eyes survey'd
Thou saw'st the second Henry's Paramour
Faire Rosamund within that gloomy bower
Among the rest, and, now return'd relate
80 The circumstances of her love and fate.
        While those late stirres detain'd the King in France,   [47]
By power of Cupid's godhead, or by chance
To Court the beautious Rosamund had beene
Brought vpp, to waite on Elianor the Queene.
85 There did the longing eyes of Henry finde
Theire brightest blisse; the wishes of his mynde
There mett their bound, and her at court, to whome
Hee had resolu'd the Court it selfe should come.
Twas then too late for him to checke desire,
90 Or to suppresse so strong and sweet a fyre
When hee had seene his loue agayne so soone.
A longer absence might perchance haue done
That cure on him; short absence hurt him more,
And made his wound farre greater then before.
95 Absence not long enough to roote out quite
All loue, encreases loue at second sight.
So fares it now with Henry, who pursues
His amorous wishes, taught by Loue to vse
All those rich aides that nature could allow,
100 That birth and height of Fortune could bestow.
For him his persons worth, his deedes of glory,
His royall guifts the strongest oratory

Doo proudly plead. all subiect-witts must mooue
(As second causes serue the will of Ioue)
105   For him, that hee may his desires enioy;
And great enough are his desires t'employ
All aides. in this faire suite you might descry   [48]
The charmes of beauty, power of Maiesty,
And all that ancient Poëts sung of Loue,
110   When they ascrib'd it to Imperiall Ioue.
When hee a bull would for Europa bee,
A showre of gold for beautious Danaë,
A Swann for Leda, with a thousand moe
Such shapes to woo and winne faire dames. why so
115   Could hee change shapes, and gaine in them so much?
Because hee was great Ioue, his power was such.
But why should Ioue himselfe vouchsafe to take
Such humble formes as these? why should hee make
Himselfe a bull, a swann, a golden shower?
120   Because so great was Loues commanding power.
And nothing else was shadow'd in those things
But power of beauty, and the power of Kings.
        How oft in Court the Royall Henry stroue
By secret favours to endeare his loue
125   To Rosamund, yett to delude the eyes
Of Elianor, and her officious spyes!
How many spyes a iealous Queene may finde!
Some bounty makes: some Dames an envious minde
Workes to that cruell office, to betray
130   And ruine her that is more grac'd then they.
Faire Rosamund, so young and innocent,
Shee could not fully sound the kings entent,
Yett loues the grace hee dooes her, loues the thought   [49]
Of that effect which her owne beauty wrought;
135   And, though shee feele no flames reciprocall,
Nor Cupid's golden shaft 'gainst her at all
Had beene discharg'd, shee loues king Henry's flame
As her owne trophee. there's no beautious Dame
But in that kinde's vniust. they often strive
140   To gaine loue there where they refuse to giue;
And spread theire proudly charming netts t'enthrall

All hearts, but cherrish few or none at all.
They ioy that men are forc'de to make the suite,
Yett too much grudge that men should reape the fruite
145 Of theire desires; and wish those hearts to haue,
Which they resolue to ruine, not to saue.
But Cupid oft is iust, and by degrees
(While they foresee not) workes his seruants ease,
Making those beauties, while they boast the fame
150 Of firing hearts, approach too neere the flame,
And bee themselues at last, the selfe-same way,
By which they meant to triumph, made a prey.
    The open Court in Henry's owne surmise
Was thought a place too full of eares and eyes,
155 Too full of eminence, to woo and winn
A mayde so coy, so young and bashfull, in.
That loue that hee to her had then declar'd
By graces at the Court, had but prepar'd
Her minde, and taught her how to entertaine   [50]
160 That parley, that must his full suite obtaine.
A faire retreat of greater privacy
Remoou'd from London, then was sought, where hee
Might lodge that iewell which hee meant t'enioy,
With other agents fitting to employ.
165 An ancient Dame skill'd in those arts, was found
To aide the Kings desires; of most profound
And subtle witt, of winning speech was shee;
And such in all, shee might bee thought to bee
No Beldame, but wise Venus lurking in
170 A Beldames shape, faire Rosamund to winne.
False Venus, for her ends, has oft done so;
And once, as Homer's wisest Muse did show,
Shee tooke the shape of an old Spartan Dame,
In Hellens breast to blow Loues powerfull flame,
175 And subtly winne her to the Troian's bedd.
Perchance this Dame was Venus, or else bredd
In all her arts, and subtle sure as shee;
Whoo now by Henry was employ'd to bee
The cheifest agent in his amorous ends;
180 Vpon whose skill his sweetest hope depends.

No farther distance then, at ease, a day
Might reach from London, stoode the place, which they
Had chose for beautious Rosamund to bide,
Within a forrest, rarely beautify'de
185   Without, by all that nature could afford;   [51]
Within the house it selfe was richly stor'd
(As guesse you may) with what a bounteous King
To please his dearest mistres eye would bring.
The place it selfe did seeme his suite to mooue,
190   And intimate a silent plea for loue.
Such was that bower, where oft the Paphian Queene
With young Anchises was on Ida seene.
About this house such groues, springs, gardens were
As Poëts placed in Loues region, where
195   The Westwindes ever blow, faire youth doth stay,
And keepes from thence old age and care away.
       To this delicious countrey house is shee
Conducted by a trusty company
Appoynted by the King on her to waite,
200   And doo her seruice in the highest state;
While Henry's loue is in such guifts exprest
As might haue power to tempt the chastest breast,
And each day courts her with a richer shower
Then rain'd on Danaë in the brazen tower.
205   The subtle Dame that waited on her there,
On all occasions fill'd her tender eare
With Henry's praise and fame, striving t'endeare
His bounty and vnæquall'd loue to her.
Into a spatious gallery they went,
210   Where well-wrought pictures did to life present
Those things, which ancient tales or storyes told;   [52]
Which whilest faire Rosamund did pleas'd behold,
And, entertain'd with fresh variety,
To severall pictures oft remoou'd her eye,
215   The cunning Dame pick'd some; nor would shee name
Those beauties, that had beene of loosest fame;
But chose the coyest out. behold (quoth shee)
My noble daughter, the seuerity
Of Dian' there, by which Actæon dy'd,

220   Cause vnawares her naked limmes hee spy'de.
       Yett this (forsooth) sower Goddesse (turne your eye
       The tother way) by Pan of Arcady
       Is caught, and with a toy of no esteeme
       A white-fleec'de Ramme. see how shee followes him
225   Into the grove, and dooes not there disdayne
       In kindest sort to ease a lovers payne.
       See Atalanta the swift-running mayde,
       Whose cruell beauty to sadd death betray'd
       So many noble youths, at last by one
230   For three gold apples willingly is wonne,
       And yeilds her beauty to Hippomenes.
       Oh godds; what pretious guifts indeed are these!
       What is a white-fleec'de Ram, or golden ball
       Compar'd to what the greatest Lord of all
235   This Westerne world great Henry can bestow!
       Nay blush not faire one; this conceit iust now
       Runne crosse my brest; nor was it in my thought   [53]
       That guifts could meritt, or true loue bee bought.
       But where true loue doth reigne, guifts may expresse;
240   And that alone is great mens happinesse,
       That by so braue a way as guifts can show
       That love, that poore ones are enforc'd to doo
       By sighs and teares, and many tymes too late
       By pining death. behold that cruell fate
245   In Iphis there, that hangs himselfe; and see
       The faire but scornefull Anaxarete,
       Whoo with dry eyes beholds poore Iphis death,
       Whome only loue of her had reft of breath.
       The godds themselues were moou'd her spite to see,
250   And in revenge of such a cruelty
       Turn'd her to stone. replyes faire Rosamund,
       If loue haue power to make so deepe a wound,
       Has hee not iustice too? those two should bee
       Inseparable in a Deity.
255   Why fitts hee not his shafts to both the parts,
       And wounds reciprocally Louers hearts?
       That sure were iustice. I remember, I
       Once read, and pity'd Iphis tragœdy,

And wonder'd that her cruelty was such
260 To kill a heart to whome shee ow'd so much,
And thought what I in such a case should doo.
The subtle Dame straight answeres; and would'st thou
Be iuster faire one? since wee heere are free,   [54]
Ile boldly speake; a Monarch pines for thee.
265 And what the difference is 'twixt slighting him
And vulgar loues, weigh in a iust esteeme.
I doo not speake it only 'cause a King
In power a greater recompence can bring
For loue then others: iuster reasons farre
270 And truer, fairest Rosamund, there are.
As kings haue greater soules, so they in loue
Doo feele farre stronger passions then can mooue
A priuate breast; besydes those spiritts that reigne
Ore other people, lesse can brooke disdaine.
275 It therefore double cruelty must proue
To giue a sterne repulse to those, whose loue
Is both in nature strongest, and beside
Lesse patient a denyall to abyde.
But most of all consider at how great
280 And high a value Monarchs liues are sett;
If they should dye for loue, that sway the fate
Of nations, borne to change the worlds estate,
Or settle it; to judge of peace and warre;
Oh what respects of private honour are
285 To bee in ballance putt with these. but lett
Mee speake in more particular; as great,
As high a fortune would from Henry's loue
Accrew to Rosamund, should death remoue
Queene Elianor away, as Englands throne   [55]
290 And royall title. nor can death alone
Divide her from him; a divorce may doo it,
And her vnkindenesses may moove him to it.
Shee was divorc'd before from Lewis of France;
He brook'd her not; great Henry did advance
295 Her lessen'd state agayne to royalty
By leave obtein'd from Rome: and may not hee
Agayne reiect her? may not Rome bee wonne?

And that for Henry which for Lewis was done?
. Oh could'st thou fortunes gratious proffers vse?
300 While thus alone they were discoursing, newes
Was brought them vpp the King was lighted there.
Faire Rosamund was strooke with suddain feare,
Yett such a feare as did containe a kinde
Of ioy, and twixt the two perplex'd her minde;
305 Nor had shee leisure to dispute the case,
The King himself so soone appear'd in place.
Whoo with so sweete a kisse salutes his loue,
That in his lipps his soule did seeme to moove,
And meete the obiect it desir'd so much.
310 His powerfull language Cupid aides; and such
His whole deportment was, as most might mooue,
And seeme to challenge, by desert, a loue.
    Oh what beseidged chastity could long
Hold out against so many and so strong
315 Assaults? such cruell snares, as there were lay'd,   [56]
What beauty could escape? the noble Mayde
At last (alas) is wonne to his delight.
Within whose armes he spends the wanton night.
Th'vnlawfull fruite of his desires hee tasts,
320 And by that action with dishonour blasts
The pity'd sweetnesse of so fresh a Rose.
Yett thence when tyme maturely shall disclose
Her burden'd wombe, (the fates had so decree'd)
A braue and noble offspring must proceede
325 William surnamed Long-sword, after by
His right of marriage Earle of Salisbury,
And made the happy father of a faire
And Noble issue, by that Earledomes heire.
    Great Henry now possest of that bright gemme,
330 Which almost æquall to his Diadem
His longing fancy oft had priz'd before,
In this sweete trance could slumber evermore;
Heere could hee dwell, arrived at the height
Of his desires, and ravish'd with delight,
335 Contemning fame, could bee a while content
To lay a syde the cares of gouernement,

And only feast on Loues transporting ioyes.
But soone a weighty businesse destroyes
His short delight. the Pope is discontent   [57]
340   That Becket suffers so long banishment;
And, intermixing threats, requires an end
Of this debate. King Lewis of France, a frend
To Becket's side, and other Princes too
Are forward, for their owne respects to show
345   Themselues complyers to the Popes desire.
Hence Henry's wisedome feares some raging fire
Of warre, while hee is absent, might breake forth
Beyond the seas, and thinkes it therefore worth
His passage ore; assured that the sight
350   Of him in armes would those weake Princes fright.
        But yet before the king from hence depart,
For thee the dearest jewell of his heart
Faire Rosamund (as fearing where to hyde
So sweete a pledge) his loving cares provide.
355   A sumptuous bower did hee at Woodstock build,
Whos structure by Dædalian art was fill'd
With winding mazes, and perplexed wayes;
Which whoo so enters, still deceived strayes
Vnlesse by guidance of a clew of thread
360   Through those obscure Mæanders hee bee ledd.
There with all obiects that delight might lend,
And with such chosen seruants to attend
And guard her, as had still beene faithfull knowne
Dooes Henry leaue this beautious Paragon;
365   And swiftly passing into Normandy   [58]
Findes there no stirres. in peace and amity
King Lewis and th'Earle of Bloys neere Ambois were
Both mett, to parley with king Henry there,
And mediate with him for Becket's peace,
370   That all dissention now at last might cease.
Sixe yeares in exile had the Prelate liu'de
By France supported, since hee first had striu'de
Against his King, and for the clergy cause
Oppos'de himselfe against the royall lawes.
375   Which made the name of Beckett sound so farre.

Declare, my Muse, from whence this fatall iarre
Arose; and from th'originall relate
By what degrees it had disturb'd the state.
The English Clergy (if wee trust record
380 Of Monkes then living) at that tyme was stor'd   The Monke
With all the blessings temporall; they flow'd   of Nuborough
In wealth; with strange immunityes endow'd;   lib: 2.
And wanted nought, but what they ought to haue,   has all this
Knowledge and piety; which essence gaue
385 First to that sacred stile of Clergymen.
Whoo dooes not know what fatall darkenesse then
The mourning face of Europe had orespread?
How all the arts and sciences were fledd,
And learnings Sunn, to these darke regions sett,
390 Was not recouer'd from Arabia yett.
As much did wisest writers of those tymes   [59]
Complayne of theire licentious clergyes crymes.
The powerfull Prelates stroue not to correct
The vices of theire clerkes, but to protect
395 Theire persons 'gainst the iustice of the state,
And to affront the civill Magistrate;
And, pleading priviledge, oppos'd to stand
Not 'gainst the vice, but iustice of the land.
The meaner clerkes by this impunity
400 With greater boldnesse durst offend. that high
And sacred order (so it ought to bee)
Was growne a refuge for impiety,
And not a burden but an ease to men,
Which worst of people sought; and thither then
405 As to a place of safety vices fledd,
And justice only thence was banished.
    An hundred murders done by Clergymen
And more, in those nine yeares that Henry then   The Monke of
Had reign'd ore England, were before him proou'de;   Nuborough
410 At which King Henry was in iustice moou'd;   ibidem
Since it appear'd no punishments at all,
Or those too vnproportionably small,
Too slight for that abhorr'd and crying sinne
On the delinquents had inflicted beene

415   By those that claim'd the power to punish them.
        King Henry weighing in a iust esteeme
        How much the land and state was wronged then   [60]
        By this pretended power of Cleargymen,
        Strove to reviue those ancient lawes, which were
420   Establish'd by his royall grandfather
        Wise Henry Beauclerke to secure the state,
        And from the Papal claymes to vindicate
        The royall power. those lawes, while Stephen kept
        Vniustly Englands crowne, a while had slept;
425   Nor durst that King, that had so badd a cause,
        So weake a title, to maintaine those lawes
        In contestation 'gainst the power of Rome.
        Then is the tyme for Papall claymes to come,
        When Kings estates are in distresse, and stand
430   On doubtfull tearmes, as almost every land
        Of Christendome has beene too sadly taught.
        King Stephen knew not against whome hee fought.
        Hee thought the Empresse Maude alone had beene
        The foe to his estate; but Rome stept in.
435   So in the age that follow'd, when king Iohn
        Vniustly did ascend the regall throne,
        And Englands Peeres in armes against him rose,
        King Iohn suppos'd hee had no other foes
        But only them; 'gainst them his strength hee bent,
440   But found a sterner foe Pope Innocent.
        Twas hee that watch'd theire tryalls, and his prey
        That syde was sure to bee, that lost the day,
        (So crowes on armyes waite.) because King Iohn   [61]
        Could not 'gainst them guard his vsurped crowne
445   The Pope claymes that; which when the king resignes,
        His holynesse straight to the King enclines,
        Whome hee before had curst. the right was try'de,
        When the Popes power and ends were ratify'd.
        To Arthur and the realme the wrong was done;
450   To Innocent the satisfaction.
            Those wholesome lawes the noble Henry striu'de
        To haue by act of Parliament reviu'de,
        Which hee had therefore call'd at Westminster.

The Prelates there and Peeres assembled were.
455 The Peeres and Com̃ons all approu'de the lawes;
Some Prelates only judging that the cause
Of holy church would bee impeach'd thereby,
Refus'd by theire assent to ratifie
The Kings desire; others more moderate,
460 Whoo weigh'd how great a proffit to the state
Losse of a shadow from the church would bee,
Would gladly yeild. 'mongst those that did deny
Becket was stoutest in resolue, as hee
Was highest farre in place and dignity.
465 Hee was the stay of all, and kept the rest
From then assenting to the Kings request.
      But how this famous Becket grew in state,
And whence hee sprung, Calliope, relate.
A London citizen by birth hee was,   [62]
470 But of an actiue spiritt, and for place
Of high employments ever seem'd to bee
By nature moulded, borne for dignity.
The gratious fortunes of his youth had brought
Him first to court attendance, and there taught
475 Him all those wily garbes; from thence the warre
Receiu'd him as an able souldier;
In which he came to be implanted high
In Henryes grace, then Duke of Normandy.
Whoo when hee first gain'd Englands royall power,
480 Created Becket his Lord Chancellour.
      Oh haddst thou there great Henry, stay'd thy grace,
And not advanc'd him to that higher place,
More happy farre (perchance) had Becket liu'de,
Nor on those termes had King and Clergy striu'de.
485 Thou had'st not then that sadd example beene
Of pœnitence, nor had religion seene
Those fooleryes that heathens may deryde,
When Becket was so strangely Deify'de.
      But Canturburyes Prelate Theobald dead,
490 The King promoted Becket in his stead,
Though the wise Empresse (whose direction
In other things was followed by her sonn)
Mislik'de the choyse; so all the Clergy did,

As then theire speeche and writings testify'de,
That hee a Courtier and a souldier
Not learn'd enough, was farre vnfitt to weare
So high a Mitre. but the Kings sole grace
Was strength enough to lift him to the place.
Which by those factious stirres that must ensue,
Shall both the King himselfe, and Becket rue.
    But now when hee deny'd to giue assent
Vnto those lawes propos'de in Parliament,
The King was moou'de; the other Bishops all
Fearing his wrath, from Becket's party fall.
Hee stiffely stands alone, although to gayne
Him to his syde, the King had striu'de in vayne.
Pope Alexander, though hee knew the cause
To bee his owne, and greatly fear'd those lawes,
Yett since his Papall diadem did stand
On doubtfull termes, and th'Emperours strong hand
Did then support the Antipope, hee stroue
In every thing to keepe king Henryes loue.
Hee therefore wrote to Becket to assent
Without all clauses to the Kings entent.
Becket repaires to Woodstock to the King,
Humbly submitts himself, and promising
That hee now freely without any clause
Of reseruation, would accept the lawes,
Is by the King receiu'd to grace agayne;
Whoo much reioyces, thinking that the mayne
Opposer of him, now was growne his owne.
A Councell straight hee calls at Clarendon
Assur'd that all the bishopps now would signe
What hee proposd to them; the rest encline
To his desire; Becket revolts agayne,
Seemes to repent his promise, to complaine
That hee in that had rashly sinn'd before,
And in that kinde resolues to sinne no more.
    The King deluded and enrag'de at this
So vnexpected a revolt of his
Threatens th'Archbishopp; but a Princes threats
Cannot prevaile with him; nor all th'entreats
Of th'other bishopps, and those Peeres that loue

Houeden
Chronicon [63]
de passione
et miraculis
Thomæ

[64]

The quiett of the state, haue power to moove
535   His resolution. now the fatall wound
Was growne past cure; nor must this kingdome bound
The maladyes of such a spreading sore.
King Henry's fill'd with greife and scorne; the more
His great soule weighs the meannesse of his foe,
540   The more his wrath fedd by disdaine doth grow.
Hee greiues yet scornes to greiue. so when a nett,
Which treacherous hunters in the woods haue sett,
To bee a snare for smaller beasts, doth stay
(By chance) a noble Lyon in his way,
545   The royall beast with greater shame then greife
Teares his base bonds, and almost scornes releife.
The more King Henry calls to mynde, how hee   [65]
Had rais'd this Becket from a low degree
Against the wills of all, hee still doth finde
550   More fuell for his wrath-enflamed mynde.
At last resolu'de hee cites him to appeare
Before his judges, and to answere there
Vpon accompt for such large summes, as hee,
When Chancellour of England formerly,
555   Had from the King detain'd, for seignioryes
Vniustly held, for proud enormityes,
And disobedience in a high degree
Vnto the King, his state and dignity.
To these will Beckett scarse vouchsafe replyes;
560   But (being no layman) at theire courts denyes
At all to answere, or obey theire doome,
From thence appealing to the court of Rome.
But that discharg'd him not; the Parliament
(Then at Northampton) did with one consent   Math:
565   Confiscate all his goods; the Bishopps there   Paris
Pronounc'de him by the mouth of Chichester   Geruaise
To bee a periur'd and a factious man;   of Douer
Disclaim'd him for theire Metropolitan,
And all obedience to him. Becket now
570   Weary'd with these calamityes that grow,
And fearing worse disgraces every day,
Findes secrett meanes at last to scape away,
And from the kingdome in disguise is gone   [66]

To plead his cause before the Papall throne.
575   Oh what vnwearied Muse at large can tell
Each seuerall iarre that from that day befell?
How Becket to the Pope resign'd his Pall?
How in his wrath king Henry banish'd all
Becket's allyes and kinn? how oft 'gainst Rome
580   In contestation hee was forc'd to come,
The Papall power against the royall right?
How oft it was debated in the sight
Of Christendome? how Henry by entreats
Sometymes, and sometymes, like a king, with threats
585   Maintain'd his cause? how oft the dreadfull doome
And interdicting thunderbolt of Rome
Was fear'd in England? and for Becketts iarre
Whole nations likely to bee drawne to warre?
How oft did forreine Princes interpose,
590   Some to encrease the wound, and some to close?
How many vaine commissions had beene spent?
How many fruitlesse Legacies were sent?
How many dayes of bootlesse parleys sett?
How oft with him the King in person mett?
595   Seaven yeares had past, since this debate beganne;
Sixe yeares had Becket as a banish'd man,
At Pointinew, and St Columba liu'de,
Maintain'd by Lewis of France, whoo oft had striu'de
Or seem'd to strive (and so had Flanders Lord)   [67]
600   In vayne (till now) in making this accord.
But now accord (although in vayne) is made.
For though King Lewis and Bloyses Earle persuade
King Henry all offences to forgett
That past before, and Beckett to submitt;
605   Though both agreement make, and Becket bee
With Henry's leaue returned to his See,
The church from thence no lasting concord findes:
Seldome is factious fire in haughty myndes
Extinguish'd but by death. it oft like fire
610   Supprest, breakes forth agayne, and blazes higher.
This end ends not the strife, nor drawes more nigh
The churches peace, but Becketts tragœdy.

[68]
The fourth booke

Argument

Th'occasion heere, and noble deeds are showne
That first brought Ireland to the English crowne.
From Wales Earle Strongbow and Fitz-Stephans bring
(In aide of Dermot Leinsters banish'd King)
5   Theire forces ore. Archbishop Becket slayne
Dooes with his blood his owne Cathedrall stayne.
King Henry sends to plead his innocence
Before the Pope; to England goes; from thence
Himselfe in person into Ireland sailes;
10   In which his power without a warre preuailes,
And gaines that land without the aide of swords.
In royall state hee feasts the Irish Lords;
And heares the wonders of that Ile. thence hee
To England sailes, and thence to Normandy.

Faire Floraes pride into the earth agayne
Was sunke; cold winter had begunn his reigne,
And summon'd beautious daylight to restore
To night those howers which hee had stol'n before.
5   King Henry then in Normandy resolu'de
To make abode, and in his thoughts revolu'de
Th'affaires of Ireland. tydings daily came
From thence, and spread his valiant seruants fame,
What noble actions they had there atcheiu'd,   [69]
10   How many townes already were receiu'd
By that small strength which they transported ore
From Southerne Wales vnto the Irish shore.
Fame had already fill'd his Princely eare
With what Fitz-Stephens, what Fitz-Girald there
15   What noble Raimond had with handfulls wonne,
And private men against a land had done;
Besydes what great Earle Strongbow's actions were,
Whoo was already growne the Ilands feare.
Fame is not onely due (though louder farre

20   She needes must speake of those) to deedes that are
      By potent Monarchs or huge armies done,
      That change the worlds estate, and overrunne
      With speede the farthest-spreading Emperyes.
      No deedes of worth can fame at all despise,
25   Though done by few and those the meanest men;
      Nor did shee only sound Romes gloryes then
      When Pompey's laurell'd charriot show'd at once
      The vanquish'd West and Easterne nations:
      Nor when great Cæsar's triumphs did extend
30   From farthest Thule to Cyrenes end:
      She did record Romes infant honours too;
      What poore Quirinus could 'gainst Tatius doo:
      What Tullus then 'gainst Alba wrought; and now
      Whoo does not Numa and Aegeria know?
35   How king Porsenna did for Tarquin come?   [70]
      How Cocles kept the bridge? how Clœlia swumme?
      The worthy deedes of her beginning age
      Gaue to her after greatnesse faire presage:
      Her greatnesse after gaue this age renowne,
40   And made her infant honours clearly knowne.
      Theire noble deedes in Ireland gaue presage
      Of her full conquest in this later age:
      Her conquest now shall theire first deedes renowne
      As long as Ireland serues the English crowne.
45   The yeare before, when first the Westerne windes
      Blew on the waters, when all various kindes
      Of flowers begann to beautifie the spring,
      (In aide of Dermot, Leinsters banish'd king,
      To whome that promise was engag'de before)
50   The braue Fitz-Stephens launching from the shore
      Of Wales, with three tall shipps, accompany'd
      With his stout brother by the mothers syde
      (Fitz-Girald) safely crost the Ocean,
      And with theire souldiers landed at the Banne,
55   A little Creeke neere Wexford, then scarce nam'de,
      But ever since by his arrivall fam'de.
      The next day after on the selfe same shore
      Maurice de Pendergast with two shipps more

(Part of Fitz-Stephans company) arryu'de,
60   And there by ioyfull Dermot were receiu'de;
     Whoo by that Prince his guidance, and his aide   [71]
     With th'English colours and theire armes displai'd
     With dauntlesse courage, able to supply
     The want of number in theire company
65   To Wexford march'd; which by assault they wonne.
     The country neere, togither with the towne,
     Dermot Mac Morough, for such valour show'd,
     Vpon Fitz-Stephans thankefully bestow'd.
     There planted they; that towne of all the rest
70   Was first by English victory possest,
     And has a lasting colony remayn'd;
     Which through all changes ever has retain'd
     The English manners, theire attire, and (though
     With Irish somewhat mixt) theire language too.
75   When famous Strongbow had in Wales receiu'de
     The newes of what Fitz-Stephans had atcheiu'de,
     With fresh supplyes vnto the Irish shore
     Hee sends his frend the valiant Reimond ore,
     And shortly after with farre greater bands
80   The noble Earle himselfe in Ireland lands
     Within the bay of Waterford; which towne
     The next day after by assault hee wonne.
     Thither King Dermot came, and brought with him
     His beautious daughter Eua, Irelands Gemm,
85   The pretious cause which drew the Earle so farre,
     The faire reward of his victorious warre.
     This beautious Lady, when her father fledd   [72]
     For aide to England, then was promised
     To noble Strongbow, and with her for dower
90   Th'inheritance of Leinsters regall power.
     Which heere the King performes, and with as high
     A state, as might befitt theire dignity,
     The marriage rites are celebrated now.
     Mars smooth's the horrours of his wrinckled brow,
95   And folds his bloody colours vpp a while:
     The Paphian Queene in that delicious smile,
     With which shee charmes the Thracian God, appeares;

His purple roabe the pleased Hymen weares,
While Dermot giues (with right of all those lands)
100   His beautious daughter into Strongbow's hands.
Nor was this marriage managed alone
By those two deityes; but from his throne
Great Ioue look'd downe, and made that knott to bee
A worke belonging to his deity
105   By which himselfe did into vnion bring
Two spatious lands; and by that marriage ring,
Which noble Strongbow to his bride combind,
To Englands crowne the Realme of Ireland ioyn'd.
      A Ladyes loue, when Dermot was decay'd
110   In state and power, first brought this forreine aide,
And to his native land did him restore.
A Ladyes loue had banish'd him before,
And of his crowne and countrey him bereft.   [73]
The King of Meth had in an Iland left
115   (While hee farre of into the land remoou'd)
His faire but wanton Queene, whoo long had lou'd
This Dermot Leinsters King with flames vnchast.
His loue on her, as hers on him, was plac'de.
Her Lords departure from herselfe or fame
120   Had Dermot learn'd, and to the Iland came;
Where soone hee gayn'd his wish; a willing prey
From thence hee tooke the wanton Queene away.
Then, as when once the Troian Paris came,
And stole from Greece that farre renowned Dame,
125   Twas not her husbands strength alone, that sought
Revenge: a cause of that foule nature brought
All Greece in Armes; the Princes ioyn'd in one,
And drew a thousand shipps to Ilion:
So when this Prince his fatall Hellen gain'd,
130   The land was moou'd, her wronged Lord complain'd
T'ambitious Rotherike Connaughts King, whoo claim'd
The style of Irelands Monarch, and had aim'd
At Conquest of the land. hee wondrous gladd
Of such a faire pretence, as now hee hadd,
135   Rais'd his owne Forces, and 'gainst Leinsters King
Did all th'incensed neighbour-Princes bring.

Whose force when Dermot could no way withstand,
Bereft of all his strengths; hee fledd the land,
And to great Henryes royall court, whome fame   [74]
140 Then spake the greatest King in Europe, came.
The King, that then remain'd in Aquitane,
This Irish Prince did gladdly entertaine,
Whome after feasting and magnificent
Rewards bestow'd, hee with free licence sent
145 To England; there to gather without lett
What Voluntaries hee from thence could gett.
In Southerne Wales Earle Strongbow then remain'd,
Fitz-Stephens too; whoose aide the King obtain'd
On faire conditions; to Fitz-Stephans hee
150 (If wonn) did promise Wexfords seignory,
On th'Earle his daughter Eua to bestow,
Which promises were both performed now.
      The marriage feasts of Strongbow now were done,
The revells ended all, and Mars begunne
155 Againe his threatning colours to display.
When th'Earle and old king Dermot gann to weigh
What acts remayned further to bee done,
And leauing there sufficient garrison,
Through Leinster all a long they tooke theire way,
160 For Dublin bent; the countrey open lay
To theire victorius armes on every syde.
No foe durst meete them, or their force abide.
Proud Roderike himselfe swell'd with the style
Of Vniuersall Monarch of the Ile,
165 Was gladd to lurke within his proper bounds,   [75]
And keepe those safe retreats, the boggy grounds
Which in his owne peculiar Connagh lay.
Thus vnresisted Strongbow kept his way,
Till hee at last to Dublin came, which soone
170 By force, and terrour of his name hee wonne.
      Faine would my Muse in this faire feild proceede.
Of Irelands conquest, and each noble deede
Atcheiued there; of trophees rais'd, to fame
The armes of England and great Henryes name
175 Faine would shee sing: but Becket's fatall iarre

Agayne reviues, and from a nobler warre
Drawes back her eager flight and turnes agayne
Her song triumphant to a tragick strayne.
    By this King Henry in his actiue mynde
180 Great deedes and forreine conquests had design'de
Secure from trouble (as in vayne hee thought
Since Beckets peace and reconcilement wrought)
That might twixt state and Clergy rise at home:
When lo from England swift-wing'd fame was come,
185 And to his greiued eare sadd tydings brought
What reakes his stout Archbishopp there had wrought
Since last hee did his dignity obtaine,
And to his See return'd in peace agayne,
That mongst his fellow bishopps, some of late
190 Hee did suspend, some excommunicate
For actions past before (from whence it plaine   [76]
Appear'd old grudges were reviu'd agayne)
As all that were, when Henry crown'd his sonn,
Assistants at the coronation
195 With Yorkes Archbishopp; for that office hee
Claim'd to belong to Canturburyes See.
Nor would hee then absolue them, though in theire
Behalfe, a suitor yong King Henry were.
While this was rumor'd there, to second fame,
200 To old King Henry the wrong'd bishopps came,
And to his eare declar'd theire greivances.
He vext at Beckets wilfull stubbornesse,
Such words (though generall) in his choller spoke,
As in some breasts too deepe impression tooke.
205 Foure knights, that heard by chance, the kings discourse,
As Morvile, Tracy, Britaine, and Fitz-Vrse,
(Vnhappy men) inflam'd with such a rage
And erring zeale, as no succeeding age
Shall ever praise, resolue in heate to doo
210 For Henryes sake, what Henry's selfe must rue,
And theire sadd memoryes, as long as fame
Has wings or tongues, shall feele in lasting shame.
From Normandy without the Kings consent,
These fower vnhappy knights for England went,

215 To execute what they had there design'de,
And fondly thought would please theire soueraignes minde,
Archbishopp Becket's death; but found too soone   [77]
What fatall seruice they to him had done.
How sadd a cure, fond wretches, haue you found?
220 For balme, you powre in poyson to the wound,
And make that death, which then was but a sore.
King Henryes cause is lost for evermore
If Beckett suffer so; your selues are lost,
The King must suffer; all, but Rome are crost.
225 While Becket bleedes, while you beare lasting staine,
While Henry greiues, the Pope alone shall gayne.
Fate seem'd to pity Henry, and decree
That hee meanewhile should breath in Normandy,
And from his England absent should remaine,
230 Whilest England was defil'd with such a stayne.
       To Canturbury the fower knights at last
Arm'd with theire followers came, and freely past
Into the bishop's pallace; theire entent
Vnknowne, had fill'd with feare and wonderment
235 The peoples hearts, whoo flocking vpp and downe
Affrighted all but Becket; hee alone,
Whose head that suddaine danger threaten'd, hee
In lookes and gesture vnappall'd, and free
From all dismay, theire coming did receiue,
240 And fearlesse answeres to theire threatnings giue,
As if his courage stroue not to asswage
At all, but to exasperate theire rage.
Nor could that stoutnesse hasten on his fate   [78]
So soone; but or theire faultring hands forgate
245 To act it then: or else vnhappy they
Not fully yet resolu'd vpon the way,
A while for counsell, did retire from him.
How much the respite of that little tyme
Did afterwards encrease theire monstrous guilt!
250 Else in the Pallace had his blood beene spilt,
And not the sacred temple made to bee
The seat of that inhumaine butchery.
Which on theire crime by circumstance of place,

Must sett a fouler and more horrid face.
255   While thus the knights retire; the Monkes in care
Of Becket's safety, to himselfe declare
How great a danger hee was in; desire
That from the Pallace straight hee would retire,
And to the Church for safeguard fly: but hee
260   Too full of fatall magnanimity
Disdaines to stirre; but there resolues to stay.
By force, at last, they hurry him away,
When words prevaile not, and (in vayne alasse)
Into the temple, as a safer place,
265   Convey his person. but not all the aw
Which so divine a place from men should draw,
Not all the reverend robes that Becket wore,
Nor th'high and sacred office which hee bore
(When once those furious knights were enter'd in)   [79]
270   Kept him from death, nor them from deadly sinne.
In all his roabes the great Archbishopp slayne
Did with his blood his owne Cathedrall stayne.
         How much did every fatall circumstance
In this abhorred act of theires, advance
275   Thy name, oh Beckett? theire vnhallowed rage
Made thee not only pity'd by the age,
But worshipp'd too. for them no infamy
Is thought enough, no dignity for thee.
How ill the people in so blinde an age,
280   Can keepe a meane in reverence, or in rage?
They first pronounce thee innocent to bee,
A Martyr then, and then a deity.
To thee they all will pray; and to thy tombe
Shall greatest Kings in adoration come;
285   Even hee to whome thou living owd'st thy knee,
Before thy shryne shall prostrate worshipp thee.
Whose gorgeous wealth and lustre shall outshine
All other shrines; as reliques most divine,
Not only shall thy nobler parts bee worne
290   In gold and gemms; but men shall strive t'adorne
Thy meanest garments, and obeisance doo
To thy ridiculously-holy shoo.

Thither from farre shall pilgrimms come to pray.
Nay in her danger once a bird (they say)
295 (Could wee beleiue that any bird would bee   [80]
Of such a Christian faith) did pray to thee.   Aurea
        Soone to king Henry, then in Normandy,   Legenda
Did this sad newes of Becket's murder fly,   in vita
And fill'd his pensiue soule with heavinesse.   Thomæ
300 For well hee iudg'de (nor proou'd it any lesse)
Twould bee by all the Christian Princes thought
That that foule deede by his command was wrought.
But more hee greiu'd that hee had rashly spoke
Such words before in chollers heat, as tooke
305 That badd impression in the knights. alas
Hee greiu'd to thinke into how sadd a case
Those wretched men had plung'de themselues to doo
Him seruice as they thought. they durst not now
Appeare at all. into the North they fledd,
310 And there alone theire liues in sorrow ledd;
And all of them (if we may trust to fame)
Within fower yeares to ends vntimely came.
        King Lewis of France, or for the loue hee bore
To slaughtered Becket (show'd so oft before,)
315 Or else for envy at the high renowne
And power of Henry, that ecclips'd his owne,
(Since now religion gaue him faire pretence)
Pursu'd his ends, with all the vehemence
Of words or prayers, to exasperate
320 Pope Alexander 'gainst king Henry's state,   [81]
Beeseeching him hee would avenge with all
The Armes of holy church, th'vnworthy fall
And cruell murder of so deare a sonne.
The like had other neighbouring Princes done.
325 But Henry full of feares dispatch'd from thence
Embassadours to pleade his innocence
Before the Pope, and there to testify
What greife hee tooke for Beckett's tragœdy,
Beseeching him hee would bee pleas'd to send
330 His Legats thither, that might heare, and end
So sadd a cause; for much hee fear'd from Rome

An interdiction 'gainst his Realmes would come.
But soone the matter could not haue an end.
The fates were pleas'd it should a while depend
335 Vntill successes of a fairer kinde
Had given some ease to Henry's greived minde,
And Irelands conquest prosperously gain'd
Allay'd the sorrow hee for this sustain'd.
His thoughts are wholly bent on Ireland now;
340 In person thither hee entends to goe;
And, fearing interruptions, to prevent
What bulls or mischeifes might from Rome be sent
To trouble England, ere hee leaue the land
Of Normandy, hee layes a straight command
345 On th'officers of every port, to see
That no Breife-carrier, without certainty
Of his estate, entent, and businesse   [82]
Should bee permitted thence to crosse the Seas.
      Nor long in England did the King abide;
350 No cause of stay was there, but to prouide
Such force, and fitt retinew, as from thence
Might guard him ore in high magnificence
To Irelands conquest, like himselfe; which soone
Vnto the height of his desires was done.
355   At Milford hauen by the Kings comãnd
His whole retinue mett; a gallant band
Of English gentry waited on the shore
In glittering armes, to follow Henry ore;
Whose lustre might to those rude Irish bring
360 Astonishment, and shew how great a King
Did now arrive to take possession there;
Whose name before they had beene taught to feare
By what Earle Strongbow in that region,
And braue Fitz-Stephans with the rest had done.
365 But oh (too cruell chance) how neere almost
Had all that valour and themselues beene lost
By Henry's former iealousyes? hee heard
Of theire renown'd and prosperous deedes; and fear'd
That so much puissance by them was showne
370 Not to advance his honour but theire owne,

And for themselues that they had conquer'd there.
Some envious spiritts fedd his iealous feare;
For which hee made a proclamation   [83]
No victualls, armour, or munition
375   Should from his kingdomes bee transported ore
For Strongbow's succour to the Irish shore;
And that his subiects, that did there remaine,
Before next Easter should returne agayne;
This proclamation had so much distrest
380   (Not long before) Earle Strongbow and the rest,
That all, which had beene conquer'd in that coast,
And they themselues had vtterly beene lost,
If matchlesse valour had not stroue with fate,
And rescu'de them. what neede I heere relate
385   How Strongbow, Raimond, and Fitz-Girald were
Besieg'd in Dublin, and theire action there?
When two great Kings with all the strength almost
That could bee levy'd in th'adioyning coast
Beguirt these worthyes, how they issu'd out
390   With courages miraculously stout,
And with successe as high; and march'd that day
Through all theire foes with victory away?
Or how Miles Cogan chas'd the King of Meth
Away from Dublin walls, and in the death
395   Of many thousands seal'd his victory?
Or how Fitz-Stephans, with a company
(Too small almost to bee beleeu'd) did guard
His fort neere Wexford towne, besieged hard
By full three thousand Irish, when no strength   [84]
400   No force could make him yeild, vntill at length
A false report the periur'd foes devis'd,
And with the hazard of theire soules, surpris'd
Fitz-Stephans body? these calamityes
Did through king Henry's iealousyes arise
405   'Gainst those that planted first that Irish coast;
And tyme it was, ere all againe were lost,
The King himselfe vpon that shore should land,
Whose force no Irish Princes durst withstand.
       Nouembers cold had rob'd the forrest trees

410   Of all theire dresse; and winter gan to freeze
      Smalle lakes; when not the season of the yeare,
      (Though iudg'd by some vntimely) nor the feare
      Of those rough Irish Seas had power to keepe
      The king from passing ore; into the deepe
415   They putt, and hoised sailes; the Easterne winde
      Blew faire, and further'd what the King design'd.
      By whose auspicious gales hee safely came
      To land at Waterford; when swiftest fame
      Through every part of Ireland flyes, to bring
420   The fear'd arrivall of so great a King.
      And what that fame had wrought, was quickly seene,
      So soone came Irelands greatest Princes in;
      Dermon MacArth the Prince of Corke, while yett
      The King stay'd there, came freely to submitt
425   Himselfe a subiect to him; and the like   [85]
      Did Donold doo, the Prince of Limericke.
      Whoo to procure his peace, swore fealty.
      Both whome great Henry sent away with high
      And rich rewards; and placed in the townes
430   Of Corke, and Limrick English garrisons.
            The King, when this at Waterford was done,
      Leauing Fitz-Barnard to maintaine the towne,
      March'd with his gallant troopes in faire array
      To Dublin ward, where ere hee made his stay,
435   The greatest Lords of all the countryes nigh,
      As Ophelan the King of Ossory,
      And Ororike of Meth, to Henry came;
      With other Princes of the highest name
      As Mac Talewie, O Carell, Ochadese,
440   Othwely, Gillemeholoch. all of these
      In person did submitt themselues; agree
      To bee his vassalls, and sweare fealty.
      But Rotherike, that bore the Monarchs name
      And king of Connaught then, no neerer came
445   Then to that famous river Shenin's side,
      Which his rough Connaught doth from Meth diuide.
      And there was mett by Hugh de Lacy, and
      Fitz-Aldeline sent by the Kings comand

To take his hostages; which freely there
450   Hee did deliver, and allegiance sweare.
       By his example all the greatest Lords   [86]
       Did freely yeild to Henry's name. no swords
       To gaine that land were drawne; no blood was lost;
       No warre so great an Ilands conquest cost.
455   Now Christmas was; which in all heights of state
       The royall Henry strove to celebrate;
       That those rude Irish people there might see,
       And reverence so great a Maiesty.
       Whoo flock in greatest companyes, to gaze
460   At this vnusuall lustre; with amaze
       They see his great attendance, and admire
       His sumptuous plate, his seruants rich attire;
       While plentious Ireland to theire feasting boords
       The Seas provisions and the lands affoords.
465   Downe with the Irish kings great Henry sate.
       So show'd of old Imperiall Cæsars state,
       When barbarous kings great Rome did entertaine;
       Whoo veiw'd with wonder such a Monarch's traine,
       And gorgeous court. such did old Poets strive
470   To make those feasts, which Ioue was pleas'd to giue
       To rurall Deityes, and to admitt
       The Syluans rough, and rusticke Fauns to sitt
       At his cœlestiall boord; while wondring they
       The radiant glories of great Ioue survey;
475   While they behold the beautious Troian stand
       A waiter by; and from his snow white hand
       Giue cupps; and ravish'd with the sound, admire   [87]
       To heare bright Phœbus and the louely quire
       Of his nine daughters to heauens glorious king
480   The Pallenæan triumphs sweetly sing.
           As much as those rude people wondred at
       King Henry's sumptuous court, and royall state:
       As much the English courtiers did admire
       The Irish Princes fashions and attire,
485   Theire different garbes and gestures; while each eye
       Is pleas'd in veiwing such variety,
       And to each other both afford delight.

When wyne and Cates had weakned appetite,
The noble Henry with a smilyng cheare
490 Offers discourses, longing much to heare
More of theire countreys nature, thus at last
To Dublins reverend Prelate, whoo was plac'de
Not farre from him at boord, the King began;
Graue Father, since I know your wisdome can
495 Diue deepe into the qualities, and state
Of things, and search what old records relate
Too much abstruse for vulgar braines to finde;
From your deepe skill enforme our longing minde,
Of what wise nature for this spatious Ile
500 Has wrought, in tempers of the aire and soile,
And those fam'd wonders, where shee dooes display   [88]
Prodigious power, and leaues her vsuall way,
As if shee meant to mocke the purblinde eye
And feeble search of our philosophy.
505 Loud fame has spread them (though obscurely) ore
All parts of this our Westerne world; nor more
Was scorched Affricke fam'd by elder tyme
For breeding wonders, then your Irish clime
Has beene to vs renowned for her rare
510 And strange endowments. to our eare declare
What you graue father by tradition,
Or by experience know. the King had done;
Attentiue silence all the Princes make;
When thus the bishopp humbly bowing, spake.
515 If I relate by Henry's high command
The wondrous treasures of my natiue land,
Lett him bee pleased with a gratious eare
To censure all; if I endeavour heere
Not, what is smoothly probable, to shew,
520 But that which is (although most strangely) true.
Yett there lett nought seeme strange, where wee vnfold
The workes of him that could doo what hee would;
Nor lett vs say some things 'gainst nature bee,
Because such things as those wee seldome see;
525 Wee know not what is naturall; but call
Those acts, which God dooes often, naturall;

Where if wee weigh'd with a religious eye   [89]
The power of dooing, not the frequency,
All things alike in strangenesse to our thought
530   Would bee, which hee in the creation wrought.
But in those rare and wondrous things may wee
The freedome of that great Creator see;
When hee at first the course of things ordain'd,
And nature within certaine bounds restrain'd,
535   That lawes of seedes and seasons may bee knowne,
Hee did not then at all confine his owne
Almighty power; but, whensoere hee will,
Workes 'gainst the common course of Nature still.
Those workes may wee veiw with a wondring eye,
540   And take delight in that variety.
Such prodigyes the most are seene (as some
Haue thought) in Iles and places farthest from
The center of the world; as heere they may
Behold, that doo this Westerne Ile survay.
545   But ere wee mention those rare wonders heere,
So please great Henry, to his sacred eare
Wee will at first in generall vnfold
What temper, fruits, and wealth the land dooes hold,
Her wholesome aire; her blessings manifold;
550   That you great king, may in that glasse behold
Th'Almighty's loue to you, that gaue so soone
So easily, so much to Englands crowne.
     Ireland is faire, though rudely cladd, although   [90]
Shee want that dresse that other nymphs can show,
555   Whoo by long wealth and art are civiliz'd.
Nor therefore lett this Iland bee despis'd,
As if that nature negligent had beene
In moulding her, or there no care were seene
Of Ioue at all. rare are th'endowments, know
560   That hee at first did on this Ile bestow.
And largely may for humane health suffice.
Although shee want the pompous merchandise
Which Easterne countryes to the world affoord;
Though not with purple nor rich scarlett stor'd;
565   Although the silkewormes pretious toyle shee want,

To cloath for shew her gay inhabitant;
Though from the wounded entrailes of her ground
No gold bee digg'd, no pretious pearles bee found
Within these lakes, nor from the glistering rockes
570   Rich diamonds gather'd: plenteous are her flocks
And graine. shee wants the meanes of those sadd crimes,
That doo infest the gaudy Easterne clymes;
Shee brings no poisons, such as guilty gold,
And cupps of choisest gemms too often hold.
575   Her harmelesse grounds no balefull hearbs doo beare,
Nor Aconite can Steppdames gather here.
Arachnes poison is not vnderstood,
Nor those sadd plagues, which from Medusaes blood
In Affrick grew, and through all lands were spread.   [91]
580   This Ile alone nere felt the Gorgons head.
      Most æquall temper dooes this Iland hold.
When Phœbus sitts in Capricorne, the cold
May well bee suffer'd without Vulcans aide,
And Cancer's heat endur'd without a shade.
585   In winters cold, as summers heat, the feild
Is richly cloath'd, and dooes fresh herbage yeild.
From whence in Iune wee are not forc'd to mow;
Nor doo our cattell stalls in winter know.
Within this aire no sadd contagions breede;
590   Nor dooes this land the aide of Phœbus neede.
Without diseases they enioy their breath,
And know no meane twixt perfect health and death.
      But if those things, that more prodigious are,
You bee desirous in particular
595   To heare related: few 'mongst many take.
In Mounsters Northern part there is a lake,
Within whose bosome two fam'd Ilands stand;
The one farre greater in extent of land
Then tother is; of nature strange; into
600   The greater Ile no woman ere could goe,
Nor any femall creature, but straight dy'd.
Th'experiment in beasts wee oft haue try'd;
And oft obseru'd in birds. from places nigh
Male birds securely to that Iland fly,

Sylus:
Giraldus
Cambr:
relates
all these
wonders

605   And pick the blossomes from each budding stemme.   [92]
        Thither the femalls dare not follow them,
        As if by nature they were taught to fly
        The hidden cause of that mortality.
              But in the lesser Ile none dye at all,
610   Which they the Iland of the living call.
        For in that Iland oft haue many men
        By extreame sicknesse long tormented beene,
        When nature seem'd quite spent, and they in vayne
        Haue wish'd for death, but could not death obtaine,
615   Till that in boates into the Iland by
        They haue beene carried, and there straight they dye.
              Another Ile, which Aren named is,
        Within the Westerne part of Connaught lyes,
        In which mens bodyes dead vnburyed ly
620   In open aire, yet never putrifie.
        Children through many ages, in that place
        Theire fathers, grandsires, and great grandsire's face
        Vnchanged see and know. they neede not carue
        Faire statues, nor draw pictures to preserue
625   The memory of theire dead auncestors;
        By which men know deceased Emperours.
        Instead of statues theire owne bodyes ly
        Discern'd and knowne by theire posterity.
              Another wonder dooes that Iland yeild.
630   All parts of Ireland else with Mice are fill'd;
        But there no Mice breede, nor can live vpon   [93]
        That ground; if thither they be brought, they runn
        With hast, to drowne themselues in water nigh;
        Or if prevented, instantly they dy.
635   A Well there is in Mounster to bee seene;
        Within whose water whosoere hath beene
        Once drench'd, his haire straight takes a hoary dye.
              Another fountaine of quite contrary
        Effect to that, in Vlster springs. for there
640   Those that haue washed once, how old so ere,
        Shall never after haue an hoary haire.
        Thither the beautious women doo repaire;
        And all those curious men, that too much feare

The Ensignes of old age, are bathed there.
645   In Connaught on a mountaines highest ground
Farre from the Sea is a fresh fountaine found;
Whose waters, like the Seas sett tides, each day
Doo twice flow vpp, and twice doo ebb away.
           Not farre from Wexford lies a peice of ground
650   In Leinster Province, where no Ratts are found.
They breede not there, nor brought can liue at all.
If you'll trust fame for the Originall
And cause of this, a curse denounc'd there was
By S[t] Yvorus bishop of the place
655   Against all Ratts (whose bookes by chance they tore)
And they from thence were banish'd evermore.
           A spatious quantity of Meadow ground   [94]
In Connaught lyes; where biting Fleas abound,
And doo so much the happlesse place infest,
660   It lyes forsaken both by man and beast.
The vselesse soile in vayne is fruitfull there.
What lesse then miracle can this appeare?
And shew to vs, that if th'Almighty please,
The least of all his Creatures can disseize
665   Man of a dwelling. so when all that store
Of his most wondrous iudgements heretofore
On sinfull Aegipt hee was pleas'd to bring;
Not all the forces of so great a king
'Gainst lice, flyes, froggs had power to guard the land;
670   Nor theire invasion could at all withstand.
           Some other meadow grounds, quite contrary
To these in nature doo in Leinster ly.
Where the rich soile in pasture so abounds,
If grazing cattell cover all those grounds,
675   They feele no want; what grasse they eate by dayes
The dewy night backe to the land repayes;
And what fam'd Maro of that wealthy feild
In Mantua spake, these meadowes truly yeild.
           But so miraculously temperate
680   Prooues Irelands aire sometymes, wolues haue of late
In middst of bare December whelped beene,
And young-hatch'd crowes at Christmas haue beene seene.
           What neede I speake of that fam'd willow tree   [95]

At Glindelachan; which was knowne to bee
685 Chang'd from his nature (though it yett appeare
In outward forme a willow) and each yeare
Brings forth faire apples, that haue proou'd of strange
And medcinable vertue still? that change
The common people, as divinely rare,
690 Imputed to St Keiwin's powerfull prayer;
Or to your sacred eare relate the story
Of our St Patrick's famous purgatory?
Nine dismall caues there are. in one of those
If any man by night himselfe repose,
695 Such most vnsufferable torments there
(As humane nature scarce has power to beare)
Hee shall endure. the silly folke suppose
The paines of Hell not much exceeding those.
But if that all the prodigyes wee know
700 Of truth in Ireland, or all those that so
Are by the common people thought to bee,
Wee should relate; your sacred Maiesty
Would first bee weary'd: day would first bee done,
Ere through those wonders our discourse could runne.
705   With that the Bishopp his relation ceas'd.
Great Henry gaue him thankes; and highly pleas'd
To heare the nature of his new-gain'd land,
Rewards those Irish with a bounteous hand
That on his royall Court did then attend.   [96]
710 And that this action might to happy end
Bee brought, and Ireland settled in a blest
And sure estate; beginning at the best
Of cares (God's service) hee to Dublin then
A Synod calls of th'Irish Clergymen;
715 With whome were many English Prelats ioin'd;
To sift the state of Irelands church, and finde
What errours had by tyme crept in, to bee
The blemishes of Christian purity.
While thus great Henry labours to secure
720 His new-gain'd realme, to leaue it in a sure
And peacefull state; from these his wish'd affaires
Hee is diverted by more tragicke cares:
Sad newes to him (though secretly) is brought

Of what the fiend Impiety had wrought
725 In his bold sonnes; theire inclinations now
And badd designes beyond concealment grow.
Enough to breake a tender fathers heart.
But of his sorrow this was but a part;
(Although alas, hee were enforc'd to see
730 In this vnnaturall conspiracy
His life and kingly state endanger'd were)
For other tydings to encrease his feare
Came flying ore (as mischeifes ever ioyne,
Not singly come) Albert and Theodine
735 Were by Pope Alexander sent from Rome						[97]
As Legates, and to Normandy were come,
There to examine Becket's murder now,
With power not only to enquire and know,
But punish it, and interdict at once
740 All great king Henry's large dominions,
Vnlesse that hee himselfe in person there
Vppon theire summons did forthwith appeare.
And now the feast of Easter was at hand;
King Henry greiu'd that from his new gain'd land
745 Hee was so soone enforc'd to part away,
Before well settled; yett because delay
On tother side did seeme so dangerous;
Of those affaires hee breifely dooes dispose;
Makes Hugh de Lacy cheife Iusticiar,
750 And to the cheifest Captaines each a share
Of governement hee leaues. then crosses ore,
And with a prosperous winde vpon the shore
Of Wales arriues; but making then no stay
At all in England, sailes with speede away
755 To Normandy, to meete the Legates there.
And dooes before them personally sweare
That hee commanded not that horrid deede;
But for those words, that rashly did proceede
Out of his mouth, and might bee thought to bee
760 The mooving cause of that black tragœdy,
Hee is contented to what pennance fitt						[98]
The Pope or they enioyne him, to submitt.

The fift booke

Argument.

Against theire father Henry's impious Sonns
Raise Warre through all his large dominions
By forreigne Princes back'd. th'old King's successe
On every side, and wondrous happinesse.
5   King Lewis of France is chas'd from Normandy;
And Chesters Earle surpris'd in Brettainy.
At Farneham feild the Earle of Leister's tane,
And almost all his warrelike Flemmings slaine.
The King of Scotland by a little Band
10   Is taken prisoner in Northumberland.
To Becket's Shrine old Henry pensiue goes;   [99]
Then freely pardons all his yeilding foes.
Takes in the forts, that were against him mann'd,
And without bloudshedd quiets all the land.
15   The wofull newes of murder'd Rosamound
Amidd'st these ioyes, his bleeding heart doth wound.
A truce twixt Lewis and him. young Richard getts
Poictou; but, when king Henry comes, submitts,
And by his father is sent forth to winne
20   His yett-offending brothers from theire sinne.

Now did those fatall and vnnaturall iarres
Disclose themselues, and more then ciuill warres
Begann to make afflicted England bleede;
While Henryes foes from Henryes loines proceede.
5   From hell to earth did that accursed fiend
The viper-hair'd Impiety ascend
T'infest the royall houshold; such was shee
As ancient Poets made Megæra bee,
That lou'd no warres, but twixt neere kindred bredd,
10   No blood, but such as sonns or brothers shedd;
Such warres, whose tryalls must bee ever badd,
Whose conquests must bee losse, and triumphs sadd.
Twixt Pelops sonns twas shee that bredd despight,   [100]
Twas shee that made the Theban brothers fight,

15   That made Atrides impiously bee slaine,
        And impiously to bee reveng'd agayne.
        Shee now through France, through England sounds alarmes,
        And Henry's sonns against theire father armes.
        Henry the sonne (too soone crown'd King) on slight
20   Pretences of a wrong, resolues to fight
        'Gainst his deare father. in that black designe
        Richard and Geoffrey with theire brother ioine
        (As then was thought) incensed by the spleene
        And iealousyes of Elianor the Queene.
25   With them the Earles of Chester, Leister too;
        And Bigot Norfolkes Earle, with many moe
        Domesticke rebells ioine. nor did so bad
        So impious a cause as theires (oh sadd
        Crime of the fates) want forreine aiders too;
30   For all the Christian Princes neere, as though
        They vnderstood not what rebellion were,
        Nor treason knew, to th'vniust side adhære.
        King Lewis of France assists his sonne in Law,
        And to that party Scotlands King doth draw;
35   That side does Philip Earle of Flanders take;
        So much old Henry's state now seem'd to shake
        As nothing almost but th'immediate hand
        Of heauen alone had power to make him stand.
                Why doo you Princes such rebellion loue?   [101]
40   Such sadd examples 'gainst your selues approoue,
        You that are kings and fathers? is it hate
        Or envy borne to Henry's prosperous state
        That mooues you thus? alas, you doo not show
        A skillfull hate to him, in arming so.
45   Your arming makes those warres, that were before
        Warres ciuill only, to bee so no more,
        But gives the greived father hope to share
        A glorious triumph from a tragike warre;
        For else the conquest, which great Henry had
50   Ore his owne sonns and subiects, had beene sadd.
        The king of Scotland must a prisoner bee,
        And Lewis with shame oft chas'd from Normandy,
        Least noble Henry should triumph ore none

But only sonns and subiects of his owne.
55   And you, most gratious Soueraigne, borne to bee
Th'admir'd example of true piety
To your deceased father; with an eye
Secure, may read your vertues contrary
In Henry's sonnes. and read it, S^r; true story
60   That brands theire names, will sound your endlesse glory.
King Iames, whilest living, did behold, and blest
Your piety; of what you since exprest
No little part, the wondring people all
Beheld, and honour'd at his funerall;
65   But most of all is, what wee daily see,   [102]
Your pious truth to his deare memory.
So may our princely Hope (lett God aboue
Bee pleas'd) young Charles by your example proue;
And such vnto your selfe hereafter bee
70   As you to blessed Iames in piety.
        The foes in this great combination ty'd,
Invade king Henry's lands on every side.
While Scotlands king falls on Northumberland,
While Chesters Earle and Fulgiers armed stand
75   To seize the townes of Brettaine, Lewis of France
With young king Henry all theire force advance
For Normandy, attempting to surprise
Vernoul, a towne that in the confines lyes.
Thus like a Lyon rowz'd on every syde
80   Old Henry's prudence must at once prouide
For all assaults; and first in person hee
To succour Vernoul marches speedily.
Which Lewis of France by treachery that day
Had tane; but left it straight, and fledd away.
85   The English King pursues, and in his course
Surprises many forts of his by force.
Nor durst the king of France, of all the tyme
That warre endur'd, in feild encounter him,
But making short incursions, as for prey,
90   Would never stand the tryall of a day.
        From thence with winged speede old Henry goes,   [103]
To meete in Brettaine with his rebell foes;

But Chesters Earle and Fulgiers durst not bide
His puissance; but fledd and fortify'd
95   Themselues within the castle Dole; which hee
Straightly besiedg'd, and wonne it speedily.
There Chesters Earle into his hands hee gott,
With fourescore other prisoners of note.
     While thus in France the conquering king proceedes,
100   Heauens potent hand assists theire valiant deedes,
That loyall warres for him in England made.
The Northren parts dooes Scotlands king invade.
To whose resistance, theire most able men
The noble Lucy, Lord cheife Iustice then,
105   And Bohun, Constable of England, bring,
And stay the progresse of that warrelike king.
There whilest with loyall and couragious hearts
They guard the North, in Englands Easterne parts
Arise warres feircer; where with numerous bands
110   Of warrelike Flemmings furious Leister lands.
With him dooes Bigot Earle of Norfolke ioyne.
There theire rebellious forces they combine
To wast theire native soile. the wofull fame
Of which, to braue Bohun and Lucy came.
115   Whoo hearing this, conclude with Scotlands king
A speedy truce, and all theire forces bring
Into the Easterne parts; where fates provide   [104]
Fresh strength to succour iniur'd Henry's side.
The loyall Earles of Gloster, Arundell
120   And Cornewall there are mett, provided well
Of all munition, in theire iust designe
With noble Lucy and Bohun to ioyne.
The Lords all mett, to Farneham march away;
There was the tryall of that bloody day
125   Ordain'd. there Leister with his Flemmish troopes
Comes to encounter them. with different hopes,
Though æquall fury, the two armies fought;
The Flemmings prey, the English freedome sought,
To chase from thence the forreiners away.
130   Long doubtfull stood the tryall of the day.
When thus the loyall Lords theire souldiers cheere;

Now lett your truth and loyalty appeare
Braue Englishmen; nor is it Henry's right
'Gainst rebells armes, for which alone you fight,
135   And to revenge your wronged Prince; (although
That were engagement great and high enough)
You fight least England should bee made a spoile
To vagrant theeues, or (more) your natiue soile
Heere suffer conquest by a forreine sword,
140   And after ages in blacke leaues record
The fatall feild of Farneham. fortune meant
In this to keepe your valours innocent,
Though rebell Leister make a ciuill warre,   [105]
He frees you from it, since his souldiers are
145   All forreiners; in fight you neede not feare
To wound at all your natiue countrey there,
Nor shedd your kindreds blood; the foe frees you
From those foule crimes, which hee entends to doo,
(Fight 'gainst his soueraigne, frends, and natiue land.)
150   What great advantage on our side doth stand!
Our armes are loyall, 'gainst a forreine foe:
His warres both ciuill, and rebellious too.
Such speeches from the lords had raised high
The English vertue; they all wish'd to dy,
155   Rather then see what else they saddly feard.
On one syde Englands wofull state appear'd:
On tother syde the iustice of so braue
A cause, fresh vigour to theire spiritts gaue.
The Flemmings armed with resolue as great,
160   Whose desperate fortunes on that day were sett,
And no hope left beyond, came feircely on,
Breathing out nothing but destruction,
To gaine the price of theire adventures there,
Or to theire foes to leaue a conquest deare.
165   So neere the flockes fight hungry beasts of prey;
So fight braue doggs to chase the wolues away
As then the English and the Flemmings fought.
How many tragœdyes that day were wrought!
How were the feilds with slaughter cover'd ore!   [106]
170   How was th'adioyning river stain'd with gore!

At last bright iustice rose, and by the lawes
Of God and nature ballancing the cause,
Gaue a full conquest to the English syde.
But so the desperate Flemmings fell and dy'de,
175   As in theire deaths it plainely might appeare
With what resolues they had encounter'd there.
Ten thousand of them in the feild were slayne;
Theire great commander Leisters Earle was tane,
With him his Amazonian Countesse too
180   Was taken prisoner, and many moe.
Whoo by the conquering Earles were speedily
Sent out of England into Normandy,
And to old Henry brought, where then hee lay,
With ioyfull news of that victorious day.
185   One of the strongest propps young Henry had,
And bold'st supporter of a warre so badd
Is now remoou'd, ambitious Leister, hee
Whoo most had sooth'd the sonn's impiety,
And 'gainst the father beene most insolent,
190   Is at his mercy now a prisoner sent.
The King forbeares revenge, and dooes disdaine
With any show of cruelty to stayne
The ioy of this successe; but keepes him there
As warre had made him, only prisoner.
195   But Englands wretched state by one successe   [107]
Could not bee rescu'd wholly from distresse,
'Gainst which so great conspiracyes did aime.
For second newes from thence to Henry came
By Richard, then elect of Winchester,
200   That other forces had arrived there
By that rebellious Earle of Norfolke brought;
By whome outragious mischeifes had beene wrought,
And th'Easterne parts of England much annoy'd;
That stately Norwich was with fire destroy'd,
205   That greater woes are feared every day;
That th'Earle of Flanders then at Grauelin lay
With young king Henry, purpos'd to invade
England with all the strength that they had made.
The King is moou'd to heare his countryes woe,

210   And to her rescue straight resolues to goe
      In person. then with his accustom'd speede,
      By which hee found his actions still succeede,
      (For all his acts and marches still did show
      Such speede, that Lewis of France would oft avow
215   Hee thought king Henry did not goe but fly)
      Prepares to crosse the Seas from Normandy.
      And takes aboord, besydes his faithfull men,
      Those Lords with him, that were his prisoners then,
      Leister, and Chesters Earles, with many moe.
220   But when hee hois'd his sailes, crosse windes gan blow,
      The seas grow rough, as if the Seas conspir'd   [108]
      And windes to crosse what hee so much desir'd.
      King Henry sighs, and lifting his sadd eyes
      To heauen, thus speakes; oh God, thou only wise,
225   If my entents in England may succeede,
      If her afflicted state my presence neede,
      And that my safe arrivall there may bee
      Her health, and cure of all her malady,
      Then grant mee passage, thou, whose onely becke
230   Has power the windes and swelling seas to checke:
      But if my presence to her coast may prooue
      More cause of woes, and feircer tumults mooue,
      If my revenging hand may lance the sore
      Too deepe, and make it greater then before,
235   Lett these crosse windes still keepe mee from that shore;
      Oh lett mee never see my England more.
      Rather then these my armes should only gaine
      My right, and not the nations peace maintaine,
      Lett mee loose all; and my vnthankefull sonne
240   Before his tyme, possesse her as his owne.
      Rather then seat a long and tragike warre
      Within her bleeding bosome; farre, oh farre
      Lett my sadd state from thence bee banished.
      Too much already has that Iland bledd
245   For Princes strifes, and soveraigntyes dire loue.
      Oh if my landing may auspicious proue
      For Englands peace, and quench all factious fire,   [109]
      Lett windes and seas consent to my desire.

His pious prayer was heard; the swelling Maine
250   Smooth'd his rough face, the winde turn'd faire agayne,
And gaue presage to his reioycing minde
Of what successe hee should in England finde.
By which his Nauy soone is wafted ore,
And at Southampton safely sett on shore.
255   Departing thence, before hee seeke his foes,
Or realmes sicke parts, in pensiue wise hee goes
Himselfe to visite slaughter'd Becket's shrine;
(Wither the Legates did before inioyne
That pœnitence, or that 'twere voluntary.)
260   At three miles distance off from Canterbury,
The King himselfe, alighting from his horse,
Dooes barefoote thither take his pensiue course,   Houeden
Whilest paines with his humiliation meete,
And ruthlesse stones doo cutt his tender feete,
265   Leauing the peoples wondring eyes, from thence
A bloody tracke of his sharpe pœnitence.
But when hee came to slaughter'd Becket's shrine,
Oh there (could worshipp greater then diuine
Haue beene) hee had perform'd it; on his face
270   Hee prostrate fell, and weeping kist the place,
Which yett of Becket's murder bore the staine.
There with submissiue prayers hee stroue to gayne
Pardon for that which others wrought, and hee   [110]
Was guilty of but accidentally.
275   But yett, as if no teares could expiate,
Nor prayers could clense so foule a crime as that,
(To such esteeme in that blind ages thought
Was this supposed martyr Becket brought)
The pensiue King goes farther; bares his backe,
280   And on his flesh refuses not to take
Rodd-stripes from each blinde Monke, that there did liue.
Which they as freely to theire soueraigne giue.
A strange example sure! but lett the sage
Nor censure them, nor Henry, but the age.
285   But ere great Henry from that city went,
More glorious newes (as if chang'de Fortune meant
To recompense him for her threats of late,

And now on all sides make him fortunate)
Was thither brought to his reioycing eare,
290 That Scotlands King was taken prisoner   Willi:
The warrelike William, whoo had made, almost   Paruus.
Without resistance on the Northren coast
So many inrodes, such rich spoiles had wonne,
And so much wracke in seuerall places done.
295 Huge was his army, but by different wayes
Dispers'd they sought securely for theire preys
Ranging abrode, and pillaging, without
Controll, the townes and Hamletts round about.
Fiue gallant Yorkeshire knights, whome glorious Fame   Stouteuile, [111]
300 Was pleas'd to grace, to Alnwicke Castell came;   Glanuille,
To enter thither secretly they meant.   Vrsy,
The misty weather favourd theire entent;   Ballioll,
Vnseene they came; although the strength were small;   Vmfreuille
(For but foure hundred horse were they in all)
305 Such prize to them did frendly fame ordaine,
As greatest armyes haue beene proud to gaine
A captiue Monarch. from the Castle towers
They veiw'd farre off the scatter'd Scottish powers.
Whose armyes greatest part from thence was gone;
310 And ledd by severall Captaines marched on
To spoile some other parts. the Knights at last,
Whoo in theire actiue thoughts did hourely cast
Some braue designes, by scouts that had descry'd
The Scotts proceedings all, were certify'd
315 Which way King William with small guards abrode
Was gone; and thither with theire troopes they rode,
Oretooke and charg'de him there; the King, although
Amaz'd to meete so suddainely a foe,
Did not forgett hee was a King, but made
320 As braue resistance as the strength hee had
Would giue him leaue. the trumpetts sound in vayne,
To draw to rescue of theire soueraigne
His straggling troopes; whome sweetnesse of the prey
Had carryed thence, and scattered every way.
325 The Knights prevaile, the King's surprised there,   [112]
And to Newcastle borne a prisoner.

(Oh mocke of Fortune!) hee that enter'd late
The English bounds, so strong a Potentate,
Guarded with fourescore thousand souldiers,   Will:
330   As if hee sought to gayne by dreadfull warres   Paruus.
The kingdomes conquest; not a meaner prey,
By this small troope is captiue borne away.
        Pleas'd with this newes triumphant Henry goes
From thence to London; where with all true showes
335   Of ioy and duty they receiue theire king;
And with an army marches thence to bring
The Realmes sicke parts vnto theire former state.
No towne, no fort, how proud so ere of late,
And strongly mann'd, durst now resist, or stay
340   His course; fame opens him a bloodlesse way.
Huntingdon Castle's yeilded to his hands.
Nor durst Earle Bigot with his Flemmish bands,
That lately strooke such terrour through the land,
Resist his Lord; but into Henry's hand
345   Did freely yeild Bungay and Fremingham
His two strong forts, and humbly kneeling came
To sue for mercy, which hee there obtain'd.
The like did Ferrers Darbyes Earle, and gain'd
His pardon too, contented now to yeild
350   Those two strong castles, which hee long had held.
As much stout Mowbray was enforc'de to doo,   [113]
And, with himselfe, resign'd his castle too.
So did the forts then kept in Leisters name;
And to Northampton Duresmes Prelate came
355   To giue three castles freely to the King.
Thither did then the knights of Yorkeshire bring
Theire royall captiue Scotlands king; and there
Presented him as Henry's prisoner.
        Whoo could haue hop'd to finde such blest successe
360   From such a warre? what greater happinesse
Could ore-ioy'd Henry in his largest thought
Haue wish'd to see, or all the starres haue wrought?
So high a conquest gain'd by fame alone!
So many castles without slaughter wonne!
365   No blood in purging of rebellion shedd!

And in three weekes all England quieted
Without the sword! no feilds with slaughter stain'd!
What Prince ore sonns and subiects ever gain'd
So iust and true a triumph? or could see
370   In civill warre a ioyfull victory?
This conquest was ore hearts not bodyes wrought;
And twas the hand of heauen, not Henry, fought.
       But killing greife (as if vnconstant fate
Already 'gann to envy Henry's state)
375   Amidd'st these triumphs comes; and all the ioy
Of this successe must one sadd death destroy.
How deepe (alas) doo Loues disasters wound!   [114]
The wofull newes of murder'd Rosamund
Was now to royall Henry brought. oh what
380   Pathetike tongue can at the height relate
How much hee greiu'd? a starre-crost Louers woe
No living tongue can tell; they only know,
Whome such a cause as that has reau'd of breath.
If those sadd ghosts should from the shades of death
385   Arise, not they themselues could speake that woe,
Which no expression once but death could show.
Yett may the Muse, since Muses are divine,
Vnfold those depths. thou saddest of the nine,
Inspire my thoughts, and lend thy skill to mee.
390   Oh tune thy heaviest notes, Melpomene,
And to the world in fitting accents sound
The tragike fate of fairest Rosamund.
       Whilest old king Henry was beyond the Seas
Detain'd in warre, to guard those provinces,
395   And scattered parts of his dominions
'Gainst Lewis of France, and his vnnaturall sonnes;
Whilest England shaken was with loud alarmes,
And fill'd with forreine and rebellious armes;
Pale Nemesis, that had possest before   [115]
400   The iealous breast of raging Elianor,
In farre more horrid shapes was enter'd now,
And all her wrongs in doubled formes did show;
'Mongst which, (the deepest peircing wrong) shee found
Her bedd despis'd for loue of Rosamund.

405 Then madd, shee raves; tis not the subtlety
     Of that Dædalian Labyrinth (quoth shee)
     Shall hide the strumpett from my vengefull hand;
     Nor can her doating champion Henry stand
     Against mee now to guard his Paramour.
410 If through the winding Mazes of her bower
     No art nor skill can passe: the world shall know
     A Queenes revenge; the house I'le overthrow,
     Levell those lustfull buildings with the ground,
     And in theire ruines tombe his Rosamund.
415 There lett him seeke her mangled limmes. oh draw
     To my assistance, iust Rhamnusia;
     I doo not striue a rivall to remooue;
     Tis now too late to seeke a husband's loue:
     I seeke revenge alone, and in what part
420 I may most deepely wound false Henry's heart.
     The fairer, and the more belou'd, that shee
     Is now: the sweeter my revenge will bee.
     Oh grant that Henry to his Rosamund
     May feele desire, as great as ere was found
425 In man; as great as beauty ere could mooue;   [116]
     To which add all the matrimoniall Loue
     Hee owes to mee; that when his flame is such,
     The death of her may make his greife as much.
     In nothing now but Rosamund alone
430 Can I afflict his heart; what could bee done
     In all his other comforts, has beene try'd.
     I haue already drawne his sonns to syde
     Against theire father in vnnaturall iarre,
     And rais'd him vpp from his owne loines a warre.
435 What could old poets make Medea more
     Against false Iason doe, then Elianor
     'Gainst him has done, when Rosamund is dead?
     Besides Creusaes death, Medea shedd
     Her childrens blood before theire fathers eyes.
440 But I, instead of those madd tragœdyes
     (In which my selfe with him should beare a part)
     Can by his children more torment his heart.
     Theire deaths, perchance, (though murder'd) could not bee

So much his greife as theire impiety,
445 In which they now proceede, theire fathers crowne
Is by theire armes into the hazard throwne.
And to the full revenge I haue begunn
Dooes nothing want but her destruction.
At Oxford then with this revengefull minde
450 The Queene abode, a fitting time to finde
For execution of her blacke entents; [117]
Whilest every day her cruell instruments
Were lurking neere to Woodstocke, to descry
A way to act this balefull tragœdy.
455 Faire Rosamund within her bower of late
(While these sadd stormes had shaken Henry's state,
And hee from England last had absent beene)
Retir'd herselfe; nor had that starre beene seene
To shine abroade, or with her lustre grace
460 The woods, or walkes adioyning to the place.
About those places, while the tymes were free,
Oft with a traine of her attendants, shee
For pleasure walk'd; and, like the huntresse Queene
With her light nymphs, was by the people seene.
465 Thither the countrey Ladds and swaines, that neere
To Woodstocke dwelt, would come to gaze on her.
Theire iolly May-games there would they present,
Theire harmelesse sports, and rusticke merryment
To giue this beautious Paragon delight.
470 Nor that officious seruice would shee slight:
But theire rude pastimes gently entertaine.
When oft some forward, or ambitious swaine,
That durst presume (unhappy Ladd) to looke
Too neere that sparkling beauty, planett-strooke
475 Return'd from thence, and his hard happ did waile.
What now (alas) can Wake or Faire availe
His loue-sick minde? no Whitsunale can please, [118]
No Iingling Morris-dances giue him ease;
The Pipe and Tabor haue no sound at all;
480 Nor to the May-pole can his measures call,
Although invited by the merryest lasses.
How little for those former ioyes hee passes?

But sitts at home with folded armes; or goes
To carue on beeches barkes his peircing woes,
485   And too ambitious Loue. Cupid, they say,
Had stoll'n from Venus then; and lurking lay
About the feilds and villages, that nigh
To Woodstocke were, as once in Arcady
Hee did before, and taught the rurall swaines
490   Loues oratory, and persuasiue straines.
But now faire Rosamund had from the sight
Of all withdrawne; as in a cloud, her light
Envelop'd lay, and shee immured close
Within her bower, since these sadd stirres arose,
495   For feare of cruell foes; relying on
The strength and safeguard of the place alone:
If any place of strength enough could bee
Against a Queenes enraged iealousy.
      Now came that fatall day, ordain'd to see
500   Th'ecclipse of beauty, and for ever bee
Accurst by wofull Louers. all alone
Into her chamber Rosamund was gone;
Where (as if fates into her soule had sent   [119]
A secret notice of theire dire intent)
505   Afflicting thoughts possest her as shee sate.
Shee saddly weigh'd her owne vnhappy state,
Her feared dangers, and how farre (alas)
From her releife engaged Henry was.
But most of all, while pearly dropps distain'd
510   Her rosy cheekes, shee secretly complain'd,
And wail'd her honours losse, wishing in vayne
Shee could recall her virgin state agayne;
When that vnblemish'd forme, so much admir'd,
Was by a thousand noble youths desir'd,
515   And might haue moou'd a Monarch's lawfull flame.
Sometymes shee thought how some more happy dame
By such a beauty, as was hers, had wonne
From meanest birth, the honour of a throne,
And what to some could highest gloryes gaine,
520   To her had purchas'd nothing but a stayne.
There, when shee found her crime, shee check'd agayne

That high aspiring thought, and 'gann complaine
How much (alas) the too too dazeling light
Of royall lustre had misledd her sight;
525   Oh then shee wish'd her beautyes nere had beene
Renown'd: that shee had nere at court beene seene:
Nor too much pleas'd enamour'd Henry's eye.
While thus shee saddly mus'd, a ruthfull cry
Had peirc'd her tender eare, and in the sound   [120]
530   Was nam'd (she thought) vnhappy Rosamund.
(The cry was vtter'd by her greived mayde,
From whome that clew was taken, that betray'd
Her Ladyes life,) and while shee doubting fear'd,
Too soone the fatall certainty appear'd;
535   For with her traine the wrathfull Queene was there.
Oh whoo can tell what cold and killing feare
Through every part of Rosamund was strooke?
The rosy tincture her sweete cheekes forsooke,
And like an Iuory statue did shee show
540   Of life and motion reft. had shee beene so
Transform'd in deede, how kinde the fates had beene?
How pitifull to her? nay, to the Queene?
To free her guilty hand from such a cryme,
So sadd and foule, as no succeeding tyme
545   But shall with greife condemne. yett had shee beene
A statue, and look'd so: the iealous Queene
Perchance on that her cruelty had showne,
Least Henry should haue turn'd Pigmalion,
And for a statues loue her bedd forsooke.
550   The Queenes attendants with remorse are strooke;
Even shee herselfe did seeme to entertaine
Some ruth; but straight Revenge return'd againe,
And fill'd her furious breast. Strumpett (quoth shee)
I neede not speake at all; my sight may bee
555   Enough expression of my wrongs, and what   [121]
The consequence must prooue of such a hate.
Heere take this poison'd cupp, (for in her hand
A poison'd cupp shee had,) and doo not stand
To parley now: but drinke it presently;
560   Or else by tortures bee resolu'd to dy.

Thy doome is sett. pale trembling Rosamound
Receiues the cupp, and kneeling on the ground;
When dull amazement somewhat had forsooke
Her breast, thus humbly to the Queene shee spoke.
565   I dare not hope you should so farre relent
Great Queene, as to forgiue the punishment
That to my foule offence is iustly due.
Nor will I vainely plead excuse, to shew
By what strong arts I was at first betray'd,
570   Or tell how many subtle snares were lay'd
To catch myne honour. these, though nere so true,
Can bring no recompence at all to you,
Nor iust excuse to my abhorred cryme.
Instead of suddaine death, I craue but tyme,
575   Which shall bee stil'de no time of life but death.
In which I may with my condemned breath,
While greife and pennance make mee hourely dy,
Poure out my prayers for your prosperity.
Or take revenge on this offending face,
580   That did procure your wrong, and my disgrace.   [122]
Make poisonous leprosyes orespread my skinne;
And punish that, that made your Henry sinne.
Better content will such a vengeance giue
To you; that hee should loath mee whilest I liue,
585   Then that hee should extend (if thus I dy)
His lasting pity to my memory,
And you bee forc'de to see, when I am dead,
Those teares perchance, which hee for mee will shedd,
For though my worthlesse selfe deserue from him
590   No teares in death: yett when hee weighs my crime,
Of which hee knowes how great a part was his,
And what I suffer as a sacrifice
For that offence; twill greiue his soule to bee
The cause of such a double tragœdy.
595   No more (reply'd the furious Queene) haue done;
Delay no longer, least thy choise bee gone,
And that a sterner death for thee remaine.
No more did Rosamund entreat in vayne;
But forc'd to hard necessity to yeild,

600 Drunke of the fatall potion that shee held;
     And with it enter'd the grimme tyrant Death.
     Yett gaue such respite, that her dying breath
     Might begge forgiuenesse from the heauenly throne,
     And pardon those that her destruction
605 Had doubly wrought. forgiue, oh Lord, sayd shee,
     Him that dishonour'd, her that murder'd mee.
     Yett let mee speake, for truths sake, angry Queene;   [123]
     If you had spar'd my life, I might haue beene
     In tyme to come th'example of your glory;
610 Not of your shame, as now. for when the story
     Of happlesse Rosamund is read, the best
     And holyest people, as they will detest
     My crime, and call it foule: they will abhorre,
     And call vniust the rage of Elianor.
615 And in this act of yours it will bee thought
     King Henry's sorrow, not his loue, you sought.
     And now so farre the venoms force assail'd
     Her vitall parts, that life with language fail'd.
     That well-built palace where the Graces made
620 Theire cheife aboade, where thousand Cupids play'd,
     And cowch'd theire shafts; whose structure did delight
     Even natures selfe, is now demolish'd quite,
     Nere to bee rais'd agayne. th'vntimely stroake
     Of death, that pretious cabinet has broake,
625 That Henry's pleased heart so long had held.
     With suddaine mourning now the house is fill'd;
     Nor can the Queenes attendants, though they feare
     Her wrath, from weeping at that sight forbeare.
     There well they could, while that faire hearse they view,
630 Beleiue the ancient embleme to bee true;
     And thinke pale Death and winged Cupid now
     Theire quivers had mistooke. vntimely so
     By rough North blasts doo blooming roses fade: [124]
     So crushed falls the Lillyes tender blade.
635 Her hearse at Godstow Abbey they enterre.
     Where sadd and lasting monuments of her
     For many yeares did to the world remaine.
     Nought did the Queene by this dire slaughter gayne;

But more her Lord's displeasure aggrauate;
640 And now when hee return'd in prosperous state,
This act was cause, togither with that crime
Of raising his vnnaturall sonns 'gainst him,
That shee so long in prison was detain'd,
And, whilest hee liu'd, her freedome neuer gain'd.
645   But Henry's troubles finde not yett an end,
Whose cares beyond the English shores extend,
As if one kingdomes burden could not bee
Enough for his great magnanimity.
The yett-perplex'd affaires of Normandy
650 Inuite his presence next; where fates decree
Allmost as easy peace shall bee obtain'd
As England late had by his presence gain'd.
Now did King Lewis, and young king Henry ly
Beseidging faithfull Roane in Normandy.
655 To whose releife the braue old Henry goes;
But first with care and prudence dooes dispose
The settled state of England to his minde;
And loath to leaue at liberty behinde
So great a firebrand as his iealous Queene   [125]
660 Feirce Elianor in this late warre had beene,
Comitts her person to close custody;
Then musters all his martiall company,
And, Cæsar-like, transporting all his store
Of great and princely prisoners, crosses ore,
665 As if hee went to triumph, not to fight.
Nor proou'd it lesse indeede; for even the sight
Alone of so renown'd and fear'd a cheife
As old king Henry, was faire Roanes releife.
King Lewis of France no longer meant to stay,
670 Nor on the the tryall of one doubtfull day
To sett his fortunes; yett asham'd that hee
Should seeme to fly before his enemy,
And fearing that disgrace, encamped lay
Himselfe a while; and first convey'd away
675 From thence the sicke and weakest of his men,
And with the rest in order followed then.
For vncontroll'd had Henry enter'd Roane,

Sett ope the gates, and beate the rampiers downe,
Levell'd the trenches all that stopp'd the way,
680 And dar'd the French to tryall of the day.
        But Lewis retir'de, and weighing in sadd thought
What small advantage his designes had wrought
Or for himselfe, or those whome hee entended
To aide, now wish'd this bootelesse warre were ended;
685 And thoughts of peace hee wholly entertain'd.   [126]
And since hee knew a peace might bee obtain'd
(As then it stood) with ease from Englands king,
And loue besides, in labouring to bring
The sonnes in too; and that th'old king would seeme
690 For such a favour much obleidg'd to him;
A reverend bishopp hee to Henry sent,
Whoo signify'd the Christian Kings entent
To worke that pious and religious peace,
That warres so sadd and impious now might cease
695 Twixt sonns and father; nature made the way,
And ioyfull Henry nam'd the meeting day;
Whoo, though successefull ever in that warre,
Was still a father, not a conquerer.
Then to Gisors with ioy hee goes; to whome
700 King Lewis of France, and young king Henry come.
Where though no perfect vnion could be wrought,
(For young prince Richard was not thither brought,
Whoo still was feircely warring in Poictou)
Yett something's done; and as a prologue now
705 To that faire peace, which afterward ensu'd,
A truce both Henryes and king Lewis conclude.
        Fierce Richard, though king Henryes second sonne,
Yett borne to sitt on Englands royall throne,
Had all the tyme of these vnnaturall iarres
710 Against his father made victorious warres
Within Poictou; in which few townes remain'd,   [127]
But that prince Richard the whole land had gain'd.
This is that Heroë, whoo by deedes of fame
Shall gaine through all succeeding tymes the name
715 Of Lions-heart; whose deedes as farre shall sound
As lyes the farthest verge of Christian ground;

Whoo by deserued honours fetch'd from farre
Shall wash the staine of this rebellious warre
From off his sacred memory agayne;
720   And conquests great 'gainst Saracens obtaine.
From him the dreadfull Saladine shall fly.
Philip of France his envious enemy
Shall feare the force of his victorious hand,
And rue it oft. hee in his tyme shall stand
725   Th'ecclipse of other Christian Princes fame,
And only terrour of the Pagan name.
        After the truce concluded at Gisors,
Into Poictou with all his martiall force
The old king Henry marches 'gainst his sonne;
730   At whose arrivall every fort and towne,
Which Richard not by loue, but force, had gain'd,
Straight yeild themselues into his fathers hand;
Whose marches almost no resistance finde.
When young Prince Richard (with perplexed minde)
735   Had heard his fathers comming, and successe,
He stormes, and taxes of perfidiousnesse
King Lewis of France, and young king Henry, that   [128]
Had thus forsaken theire confœderate.
But yett resolues (too proudly) not to yeild
740   At all; but stand the tryall of a feild
Against his father; and with impious hopes
Into the feild drawes all his martiall troopes.
From whence Kings Henry's army was not farre.
And now too neere approach'd the wicked warre.
745   Some pious souldiers 'gann those mischeifes feare
Which they should act, as well as suffer, there.
Richard's great heart began to yeild to shame,
And feele the reverence of a fathers name.
Sometymes his stubborne courage rais'd him high;
750   Sometymes agayne relenting Piety
Check'd those proud thoughts; and in so badd a cause
Told him how great a crime his valour was.
Yett had not Piety alone the power
To curbe his spiritt; his father every hower
755   Encreast in men, and Iustice, with a tide

Of strength, flow'd in, to vindicate her syde.
      Why stood'st thou out (Richard) so long a time?
Tis now too late to free thy selfe from crime
Though thou submitt. the world may iustly say
760 It was not true repentance but dismay.
Thou could'st no longer cheere thy fainting troopes;
And not thy resolution, but thy hopes
Forsake thee heere. that act will termed bee   [129]
Despaire, which had before beene piety.
765 But thanke the weakenesse of thy army now,
That made thee see (though late) and disallow
That horrid guilt, before that liues it cost,
Or blood by thy impiety were lost.
      Struck with remorse at last young Richard throwes
770 His late-rebellious armes a side, and goes
To his offended father, to present
Himselfe a sadd and humble pœnitent.
There on his knees, for that vnkinde offence
Hee pardon craues; no other eloquence
775 But teares and sighs his greife had power to vse.
No other pleas were strong in his excuse.
The royall father meetes with teares of ioy
Those teares; and pardons him the noblest way;
With kinde embraces lifts him from the ground;
780 And in his rich paternall loue had found,
Instead of chiding him for what was done,
A way to praise him by comparison,
That of the brothers hee submitted first;
As if the father had forgott that erst
785 Hee æquall to the rest astray had gone,
Remembring Richard's pœnitence alone.
So much king Henry's wondrous goodnesse wrought
On Richard's noble nature, as it brought
Fresh teares from him; and though it pardon'd, more   [130]
790 Did seeme to aggrauate th'offence before.
Yett such encouragement from thence hee tooke,
As thus, when teares would giue him leaue, hee spoke;
Sʳ, your preventing grace has tane from mee
    So farre the neede of all apology,

795   As I should only speake my thankefullnesse,
      If any language could so much expresse.
      But that my dutious deedes shall better show.
      And for the first true seruice I can doo,
      Vouchsafe mee leaue, great S^r, to goe and winne
800   My yett offending brothers from theire sinne.
      Let mee bee there employ'd; I shall prevaile
      In that, when other advocates will faile,
      When forreine Princes for theire owne close ends
      Shall faintly speake, when false and factious frends
805   In theire misdeedes shall flatter them; shall I
      By true example checke impiety;
      I, that haue sinned happily in this,
      To make them know how good our father is.
      Which (most accurs'd) I had not grace to know,
810   Till by offending I had found it so.
      More had hee vtter'd; but King Henry there
      Cutt off his speach, almost oreioy'd to heare
      That thing propos'd, which was his cheife entent;
      And then with faire and kinde encouragement
815   For that designe dispach'd his sonne away,   [131]
      Himselfe resolu'de in Normandy to stay.
      And thankefull Richard with a ioy as high
      Goes to performe the pious Legacy.

The sixt booke

Argument

Betwixt Ambois and Tours, the Sonns are brought
To meete theire father. perfect peace is wrought;
A peace is made with France and Scotland too.
From Normandy the two king Henryes goe,
5   Great signes of ioy in England every where
Are show'd, to welcome theire arrivall there.
The King his realme of England doth diuide
Into six circuits; and for each prouide
Iudges Itinerant. what great resort
10   Was seene at once in Henry's stately court.
His happinesse, his power, and high renowne,
His daughters royall marriages are showne.
Old Henry dooes refuse the proffred crowne   [132]
Of Palæstine to take. Henry the sonne
15   Rebells againe; and dooes repentant dy.
The third sonne Geoffrey's wofull tragœdy.

Now did victorious Henry's wish succeede.
With such effectuall diligence and speede
Had young prince Richard with his brothers wrought,
That both of them hee to theire father brought
5   Betwixt Ambois and Tours. there first of all
Are discontents and iarres vnnaturall
By old king Henry's prudence made to cease;
There first is wrought a full and finall peace.
The Sonns are taught to hate theire impious crime,
10   And vow obedience for the future tyme.
Nor dooes the father's wisdome thinke hee dooes
Enough, if for the present hee compose
This fatall strife; but carefull to prevent
The causes of all future discontent,
15   Hee lends a gentle eare, while they expresse
In humble sort theire former greivances;
Hee grants theire iust demands, and dooes advance
With liberall hand theire yearely maintenance,

Which had before beene iustly thought to bee [133]
20 Too small for them. and that this enmity
Might not alone bee ended, but forgott
On every side; the lands vniustly gott,
While this sadd warre remain'd, are every where
Restor'd againe, and every prisoner
25 Without a ransome on both sides sett free.
And all theire followers in that state to bee
As when the warre begann. with Henry there
A peace king Lewis, and th'Earle of Flanders sweare;
And that the frendshipp may bee firmely ty'd,
30 Adela Lewis his daughter is affy'de
To princely Richard; to remaine, till shee
Should come of age, in Henry's custody.
There to conclude these sadd dissentions,
Richard and Geoffrey, Henry's younger sonns
35 A personall homage to theire father doo;
Which young king Henry freely offred too;
But that the father suffred not; since hee
Invested was in regall dignity.
        White-winged Concord come from heauen aboue,
40 (Concord, of all estates the ioy and loue,
Whose sacred armes the spatious world enfold,
And that mixt fabricke form dissoluing hold)
On Henry's countreys now was pleasd'd to light.
With her, her lately-banish'd sister, bright
45 As shee, faire Piety, did not disdaine, [134]
Descending downe, to visite earth againe.
Shee that from Englands court had lately fledd,
As once from Argos tragicke towers shee did,
When Atreus feast did her pure soule affright,
50 And made the Sunn obscure his mourning light.
Nor dooes the presence of bright Phœbus more
Comfort earths drooping face, when to restore
Her fragrant Wardrobe, hee returnes in spring,
Then Piety, and blessed Concord bring
55 True ioy to humane hearts. the King in thought
Is recompens'd for what the fates had wrought
So lately 'gainst him. his two younger Sonns

Hee sends away to theire dominions,
And wise men with them; Geoffrey to remaine
60   In Brettaine, Richard in his Aquitaine,
There with theire severall counsells, to advise
The best for theire estates and dignityes.
      The two king Henrys, father and the sonne
Through every part of theire dominion
65   Vpon that side the Sea, a progresse take,
To cure the wounds of that late warre, and make
The rents all whole againe; then from that coast
The Seas for England they togither crost.
But oh what Muse can at the height relate
70   The ioy that Englands long-afflicted state
Exprest, to welcome theire arrivall there?   [135]
Or show how all the waies from Porchmouth, where
They landed first, and thence to London rode,
Were fill'd with people numberlesse, and strow'd
75   With such greene dresse, as then the spring could show,
And Sol from Taurus guilded hornes bestow
Vpon the cheered earth, as if that then
The season had consented with the men.
How did the aire with acclamations sound!
80   When in that ioyous sight the people found
Theire happinesse; they saw two kings as one,
Distracting not the quiet of a throne,
And as a glorious wonder, might descry
Two Sunns at once, and yett a peacefull sky.
85   This sight more ioy'd the hearts of people now,
Then any triumph of a warre could doo.
Nor could the greatest conquest, by the blood
Of slaughter'd nations purchas'd, bee so good.
So did th'Italian youths follow in throngs
90   Theire laurell'd charriots with triumphant songs,
When captiue Kings were brought, when wofull storyes
Of ruin'd lands were made theire envy'd gloryes.
Before this triumph no sadd captiues goe,
To waile in chaynes theire wofull overthrow;
95   No pale deiected lookes, no hearts afraide
Are found, no envy'd Gloryes are display'd;

But gentle peace dooes with a gratious eye   [136]
Appeare, and leade the faire solemnity.
Whose crowne of Oliue dooes more glorious show
100   Then any victor's laurell wreath could doo.
       One court, one table now receiues againe
Whome late this spatious Ile could not containe
(As frends) within blew Neptunes watery armes;
And they whose presence fill'd with warres alarmes
105   So oft of late great France and England too,
Without warres feare are seene togither now;
And promise, like th' Oebalian frendly starres,
Health to the late distressed Marriners.
       Nor dooes king Henry spend in wanton ease
110   The Halcyon dayes of this his happy peace:
But like a wise and noble Potentate,
To cure the sadd diseases of his state,
Hee first beginns (as first it ought to bee)
With holy Church. the sinne of Simony,
115   Which those corrupted tymes too much had fill'd,
A Synod, to that end at London held,
By wholesome lawes and Canons did restraine.
From thence old Henry fully to maintaine
His honour, goes in person, and repaires
120   Some breaches of the late vnhappy warres;
And many Castles of the inner land,
Which had in those rebellious times beene mann'd,
And kept against himselfe, hee rases downe,   [137]
As Leister, Walton, Groby, Huntington.
125   To deedes of Iustice then hee turn'd his minde,
And first of all the English kings did finde
That happy course, applauded till this day,
To giue his subiects by an easer way
The vse of iustice. England hee diuides
130   Into six circuits; and for each prouides
Three reverend Iustices itinerant;
That all his subiects farthest off, whome want
Would not permitt so great a way to come,
Might meete bright Iustice twice a yeare at home;
135   And that offences there, where they were done,

Might bee to Iudges made more clearely knowne.
A glorious act, which shall forever fame
To after tymes the second Henry's name.
Those mighty kings whoo by such specious deedes
140   As founding towers or stately Pyramids
Would raise theire names, and by that vast expence
Doo seeke the fame of high magnificence,
Doo not deserue, by those proud workes they raise,
So true an honour, nor such lasting praise
145   As hee, whose wisdome to good manners drawes
The mindes of men by founding wholesome lawes,
And planting perfect justice in a state.
Those lett the vainer people wonder at;
By those a state showes faire; by this it liues: [138]
150   They outward beauty; this true essence giues.
        But now, my faire Calliope, relate
How high, how glorious was old Henry's state
In this so happy and establish'd peace!
When all dissentions on such termes did cease
155   As hee himselfe could wish! when his command
Was fear'd in Wales: when Englands happy land
Was well assured: Scotlands strength dismay'd:
And conquer'd Ireland quietly obey'd
His powerfull scepter; when hee did possesse
160   Without controll those stately Provinces
Of France, which stretch'd even to the bounds of Spaine,
From Normandy to farthest Aquitaine.
That King of Connaught, Roderike the stout,
Hee that in Ireland had so long stood out
165   'Gainst th'English power, dooes now to England send
Embassadours on Henry to attend,
To yeild himselfe to his protection
A tributary to the English crowne.
And now through Europe the loud voyce of fame
170   So wide had spread this potent Monarch's name,
That from the farthest parts of Christendome
Embassadours of greatest Princes come,
To hold theire leagues and amity with him;
And London saw (so high was his esteeme)

175   In his great court at once th'Embassadours   [139]
       Of the two mighty Christian Emperours
       The East and Westerne Cæsars both, in whome
       The ancient honour of imperiall Rome
       Diuided liues; the Duke of Saxony,
180   The Earle of Flanders, King of Sicily;
       From all these Legates at one tyme resort,
       Togither seene in Henry's stately Court.
           Nor doo the Princes weigh his power alone,
       But wisedome too, and (as to Salomon)
185   Send farre to craue his counsell and advise;
       As two great Kings, when difference did arise
       About the bounds of theire dominion,
       Alphonso then king of Castile was one,
       Tother his vncle Sanctio of Navarre;
190   Whoo loath that the vngentle hand of warre
       Should iudge the cause, to prudent Henry send,
       With power for him to heare and make an end;
       Which hee determines in so braue a way,
       That both the Kings are pleas'd, and both obey.
195   And young Alphonso sends, after the strife
       Had end, to craue of Henry for his wife
       (With full assurance of an ample dower)
       His second daughter louely Elianour.
       Whoo was according to that King's demand,
200   Sent with a rich attendance to his land,
       And there receiu'd with ioy, and highest state;   [140]
       Where they theire wished Nuptialls celebrate.
           His eldest daughter Mawde before had hee
       Bestow'd on Henry Duke of Saxony
205   Surnam'd the Lion, from whose happy wombe
       The fates ordaine great Emperours shall come.
           And in this happy yeare did Henry too
       His third and youngest daughter Ioane bestow
       On noble William King of Sicily;
210   Attended hence with fitt solemnity.
           Nor did it seeme enough to favouring fate
       That Henry's glorious and maiestike state
       Through Europe only should bee honoured;

Even to the farthest bounds of Asia spredd
215 The fame of his great power and happinesse.
The holy land was brought to sadd distresse
By strength of faithlesse Saracens opprest.
Great Saladine the terrour of the East,
That powerfull Soldan that possest the throne
220 And diadem of stately Babylon,
With all that th'old Assyrian Monarchs held,
Whose vnresisted puissance had quell'd
The strength of all those parts, and into thrall
Had brought the other Pagan Princes all,
225 Entitled King of Kings and Lord of Lords,
Against the Christians turn'd his conquering swords,
And now had enter'd, with that proud designe, [141]
Vpon the bounds of fearefull Palæstine;
His dreadfull hoast had past faire Iordans flood,
230 Sack'd townes adioyning, and in Christian blood
Pursu'd the conquest on; great feare of him
Possest the Princes of Ierusalem,
Whoo all consult about theire present state.
Theire king old Baldwine was deceas'd of late,
235 And to his nephew, then a childe (no more
Then five yeares old) had left the regall power.
Too weake his tender age is thought to beare
That weight, when such a threatning warre so neere
Theire Walls is brought. the Princes all consent
240 To offer vpp theire crowne and governement
To some redoubted Christian Monarch's hand,
Whose power might guard theire now-endanger'd land;
And with one voyce agree in Henry's name.
To him, as to the Prince of greatest fame,
245 And best to them for wealth and prowesse knowne,
They meane to tender Salems royall crowne.
And for Embassadour to him they choose
The reverend Patriarch Heraclius,
Whoo beares a long with him (to bee a signe
250 That by the generall vote of Palæstine
This royall tender was to Henry made)
Things of the greatest note that kingdome had;

The keyes of that so much renowned place,   [142]
Which our deare Saviour's happy birth did grace:
255   And of that honour'd tombe, which did containe
His blessed body, till it rose agayne;
The keyes of Dauid's stately Tower: with them
The royall standard of Ierusalem.
Thus fates for absent Henry did ordaine
260   Theire highest graces; but (alas) in vayne,
As afterward it proou'd, when to the King
Those honour'd signes the Patriarch did bring.
For hee too much perplex'd about his owne
Affaires at home, refus'd that sacred crowne;
265   Although the Patriarch did strive to shew
That title was by right of birth his due,
And hee the lawfull heire of Salems throne,
As being Geoffrey Earle of Aniou's sonne,
Whose brother, Fulke Plantagenet, had beene
270   Before anointed King of Palæstine.
And though Pope Lucius had for that entent
Persuasiue letters to great Henry sent,
Hee still refus'd. God, for the Christians sinne,
Was not at that tyme pleased to encline
275   His heart to succour theire afflicted state,
Nor any other Christian Potentate,
Till (all too late) sadd newes was brought to them
That Saladine had tane Ierusalem.
        But long great Henry in that blissefull state   [143]
280   Could not abide; the course of envious fate
Soone wrought a change with him. before the Sunne
Had twice through his cœlestiall Zodiake runne,
Deepe alterations in some mindes appear'd,
And dangers thence the people iustly fear'd.
285   That happy Genius, which of late did guide
Th'affaires of England, now in greife gan hide
His glorious head, lamenting to bee gone;
The date of Henry's prosperous dayes was done;
And nought but troubles from that time ensu'de,
290   And tragike woes. oh sadd vicissitude
Of earthly things! to what vntimely end

Are all the fading gloryes that attend
Vpon the state of greatest Monarchs, brought!
What safety can by policy bee wrought?
295   Or rest bee found on Fortunes restlesse wheele?
Tost humane states are heere enforc'de to feele
Her kingdome such, as floating vessels finde
The stormy Ocean, when each boistrous winde
Lett loose from Aeol's adamantine caues
300   Rush forth, and rowle into impetuous waues
The Seas whole waters; when sometymes on high
The raised Barke dooth seeme to kisse the sky:
Sometymes from that great height descending downe,
Doth seeme to fall as low as Acheron.
305   Such is the fraile condition of mans state;   [144]
Such contrarietyes the turning fate
Of Henry found; to him did fortune seeme
In all her favours and her frownes extreame.
      The former rents, which dire Impiety
310   Had made in Henry's royall family,
Had well beene cur'de againe, and closed all
Without effects so sadd and tragicall
As all the land from thence did iustly feare.
On easyer termes was peace establish'd there
315   Then men could hope; and gentler salues did serue,
Then wounds so fester'd seemed to deserue.
(So then the gratious God was pleas'd) but see
How full of danger all relapses bee.
In humane states how seldome permanent
320   Is perfect health! deserued punishment,
Which heauen is pleas'd to respite for a tyme,
It oft payes home vpon a second crime.
Henry the sonne in heart revolts againe
From his indulgent father. signes too plaine
325   His honest seruants saw, and sigh'd to see.
His aimes on every oportunity
A spiritt so young and hott could not conceale.
And now it seem'd no human skill could heale
Th'inveterate sicknesse of his impious minde.
330   God, for old Henry's sinnes, did iustly finde

Meanes, by his sonns, the father to chastise,   [145]
And yett to punish theire impietyes.
So double woe is to the father sent,
Whoo feeles theire crimes, and then theire punishment.
335   Richard, the second sonne, that held Poictou,
And Aquitaine, for them, refus'd to doo
To young King Henry personall Homage, though
Theire father Henry had commanded so.
Yett Richard soone repents, and tenders it;
340   But his imperious brother with despight
Refuses then to take it from his hands.
A strong desire to seize on Richard's lands
Young Henry had. full well hee knew that all
The Barons of those Provinces would fall
345   Gladdly from Richards sterner gouernement,
Whoo had before declared theire entent.
With him in this his brother Geoffrey ioin'd,
Whoo to his father bore as false a mynde.
With Richard's lands they meane themselues to make
350   Strong 'gainst theire father; and entend to take
Thence the first stepp too theire disloyalty.
Richard in wrath departs from Normandy,
Returning home to fortify and manne
His holds within Poictou and Aquitaine,
355   And by his brothers is pursu'd. hee findes
A great estrangement in the Barons myndes;
And is enforc'de, by theire revolt dismay'd,   [146]
To craue his father old King Henry's aide.
Whoo with an army thither straight repaires,
360   Yett not to make but to compound the warres.
There young king Henry labours to maintaine
The Barons of Poictou and Aquitaine
'Gainst Richard's great complaints, and vnderhand
For his owne ends, persuades them to withstand
365   His fathers force, and not at all submitt.
Old Henry labours by persuasions fitt
To pacifie these new-bred enmityes,
And venturing of himslefe to parleys, twice
Miraculaously scap'd foule treasons hand.

370   Once a true seruant, that did next him stand,
      Instead of him, was with an arrow slaine,
      Nor was the traitour found; and when againe
      Hee made approache, a barbed shaft, that from
      Th'adioyning castle did with fury come,
375   Had peirc'de his royall breast, had not his horse
      Advanc'd his head, and tane the arrowes force,
      By which himselfe, to saue his master, dy'd.
      By these abhorred treasons terrify'd
      The King no more would venture, but prepares
380   To curbe the Barons, and his sonns by warres.
      But that a iuster stronger hand must doo;
      Th'eternall judge of all the world had so
      Decreed, that Henry's sword should spared bee   [147]
      In punishing his sonns impiety.
385   That hee himselfe, whose iust and certaine hand
      No creature can preuent, no force withstand,
      Whose sacred will the elements obey,
      And all the starres doe serue, would take a way
      Without old Henry's aide, or crime at all,
390   Without a warre so much vnnaturall
      To punish guilt; that justice should bee done,
      Yett the old King but loose, not kill a sonne.
            Now young king Henry at Martell prepares
      To meete his father in rebellious warres;
395   But by a Dysentery death assailes
      His youth, and spite of youth or strength prevailes.
      The sharpe malignant humor did corrode
      His gutts; and thence, while there the paine abode,
      A speeding feauer seiz'd his vitall part.
400   Oppressed nature, past the helpe of art,
      Beyond all hope of cure, lay languishing.
      When pœnitence from heauens eternall King
      To saue this dying Prince his soule, is sent,
      And sweeten so his bodyes punishment.
405   Now late alas (though not too late) did hee
      Feele and bewaile his first impiety.
      And to his father humbly sent, to craue
      His pardon now; which hee as freely gaue,

Yett durst not trust himselfe in person there, [148]
410 (The late foule treasons made him iustly feare)
But to declare a true forgiuenesse, sent
His ring to him. which when the pœnitent
And dying Prince receiu'd, hee humbly kist,
While floods of teares his contrite heart exprest.
415 Then hee coniur'd his seruants, that did stand
About him, to fullfill his last command;
Which they in all performed as they swore.
A bedd of ashes on the chamber floore
They strew'd, and thither pensiue sackcloath brought;
420 Then from his royall couch so richly wrought
With various worke, with gold embroider'd ore
They tooke him downe; the kingly roabes hee wore
They stript him of, and putt the sackcloath on,
Then on the bedd of ashes lay'd him downe.
425 This (quoth the dying king) this is the way
To heauens bright pallace; and this sadd array
Is farre more glorious in th'allmighty's eye
Then purple, silkes, or rich embroidery,
And sooner enters heauen; though that bee high,
430 No stepp's so neere it as humility.
Tis not fraile mortalls gorgeous dresse, that there
Can rich at all, or beautifull appeare,
Since twixt the Gloryes of Earths greatest throne,
And blisse of Saints, is no comparison.
435 Waile not my early death; no man is reft [149]
Too soone of breath, to whome a tyme is left
Of pœnitence. I had vntimely dy'd,
Had these late warres in my rebellious pride
Cutt of my youth, and left my name to bee
440 The curs'd example of impiety.
And thou, my wronged father, in this low
And humble state, vouchsafe againe to know
(What impious I had once forgott) thy sonne,
No more thy rivall in the regall throne.
445 Which whilest I sought, I labour'd to destroy
The royall roote, from whence I grew so high.
I craue no interest in thy fortunes now,

But only that that Nature can bestow,
The blessing of a child. seeking thy throne
450 I grew vnworthy to bee call'd a Sonne.
Forbeare you lasting registers of tyme,
To name my title, least you speake my cryme.
Or if the truth of story must doo so,
Bee iust, and publish my repentance too.
455 How ere, when Englands Kings are name'd, lett mee
From that high catalogue excluded bee.
And witnesse you, my frends, when I am gone,
I dy'd no King, but Henry's pensiue sonne.
With that the feauer his strong heart assailes,
460 And 'gainst resisting natures force prevailes.
From his young breast the struggling spiritt flyes,   [150]
And night eternall closes vpp his eyes.
      Soone was the newes to old king Henry brought;
When different sorrow powerfull nature wrought
465 In his great soule. sometymes hee wailes a sonne
In flower of all his youth vntimely gone:
Sometymes hee ioyes to heare that pœnitence,
That wash'd away the staine of his offence.
Yett thence againe flow teares, as cause to prooue
470 His sorrow good, and iustifie his loue.
So Henry wept, in all respects but one,
As holy Dauid did for Absalon.
They both lost sonns, both wail'd theire sonnes offence:
Yett Dauid heard no signes of pœnitence
475 In his slaine Absalon, that could at all
Giue comfort to his greife spirituall.
Had Absalon for his abhorr'd offence
Left markes behinde him of true pœnitence
Instead of that great pillars pride, which hee
480 Had rais'd before to keepe his memory,
Farre lesse (no doubt) in that respect alone,
Had Dauid mourned for his slaughter'd sonne.
      The greife that Henry tooke, though wondrous great,
Yett could not make him his iust wrath forgett
485 Against the Barons of Poictou, from whome
The cause of these rebellions first did come.

Hee drawes his martiall forces vpp, to presse   [151]
With narrow seidge the towne of Limoges.
Which soone was rendred to his powerfull hand,
490   And with that towne and castle, all the land;
The Barons pardon craue; with them his sonne
Prince Geoffrey comes; vpon submission
The King forgiues his sonne; and is content
To take of them an easy punishment.
495   But though a fathers deare affection
Twice freely pardon'd this offending sonne:
Soone after did the hand of God on high
Pursue with vengeance the impiety
Of young Prince Geoffrey. at a turneament
500   In Paris held, to which this Geoffrey went
With other Lords in youthfull brauery
To prooue his actiue strength and cheualry,
Hee fell togither with his horse; the blow
So sorely bruis'd his body, that although
505   Hee presently expir'd not in the place,
(For God in mercy lent him such a space
Of time to breath, hee might repenting call
To him for grace) yett of that fatall fall
(As it appeared plaine) in all the pride
510   Of his fresh youth, hee shortly after dy'd.

[152]

The seauenth booke

Argument

Prince Iohn, king Henry's youngest Sonne is sent
To take the Charge of Irelands gouernement.
Twixt Henry and king Philip seuerall iarres
And quarrells rise, that threaten daily warres.
5 A reverend Prelate by the Pope employ'd
Betwixt the Kings all difference to decide,
Persuades them both an holy warre to make.
Both Kings, with Philip Earle of Flanders, take
The crosse vpon them. but theire good entents
10 Are crost againe by fatall accidents;
And both the Kings against each other bent
To warre againe. Richard in discontent
His father leaues, and takes king Philip's part.
Ensuing losses breake old Henry's heart.

Thus is the King of halfe his store bereft;
Two sonns vntimely dead; two Sonns are left
The seeming comforts of his age; as whoo
Could thinke but living children should bee so?
5 Oh whoo would not suppose that to haue seene [153]
Two youthfull sonns before him dead, had beene
A greivous curse and punishment to him?
But hee, that sees old Henry's end, will deeme
His liuing sonns to bee his curse, and say
10 God pity'd him, in taking two away.
For furious Richard, whoo was eldest now,
And heire apparant to the crowne (as though
His brother's deaths could no examples bee
To show the vengeance of Impiety)
15 Soone after 'gainst his father raises warre
Of worse and sadder consequence by farre
Then all the rest had beene; they caus'd his smart:
But this of Richard breakes his bleeding heart.
  The Realme of Ireland Henry did entend

20   To Iohn his youngest sonne; and to that end
        Had from Pope Vrban gott a grant before
        That hee might freely leaue, as successour,
        Which sonne hee pleas'd, in Irelands gouernement.
        Thither is Iohn with fitt attendance sent
25   (But twelue yeares old) to make him early knowne,
        And lou'd among those people, as his owne.
        To rule among them as theire Governour;
        But not invested in the Regall power.
        Th'example of his eldest sonne, whome hee
30   Before advanc'de to royall dignity
        Too soone (alas,) had made him iustly feare   [154]
        The same from others. but vnhappy there
        This Prince his too too early rule did prooue.
        Instead of gaining that rude nations loue;
35   Which by a sweete demeanour had beene wonne,
        (For they as every barbarous nation,
        Although they know not what is true respect:
        Yett, if respected, wondrously affect.)
        The youthfull gallants of that Prince his court
40   Could not refraine, but in a scornefull sort
        The natiues rude behaviours did deride.
        And so distastfull was theire mocking pride
        To those plaine people; they begann to hate
        Whome else they would haue honour'd, and forgate
45   That loyall loue and reverence, which before
        They to the English King and nation bore.
        From thence sadd warres the Irish Princes moou'd;
        Which by the losse of men and treasure proou'd
        Vnhappy to the English side; till from
50   His governement young Iohn was called home,
        And left it, after an expensiue warre,
        In worse estate then when hee enter'd farre.
            Now daily quarrels twixt the Realme of France,
        And England grow. fresh cause of variance
55   From all occasions dooes the actiue minde
        Of young king Philip 'gainst old Henry finde.
        Sometymes hee claimes Gisors, and other lands   [155]
        By Henry held from him; sometymes demands

The Princesse Adela, his sister (now
60   Of perfect age) to bee deliuer'd to
Her husband Richard, Henry's eldest sonne,
According to the old conclusion,
Which in her father Lewis his tyme was made;
Or else hee is resolued to invade
65   King Henry's Provinces. while hee delayes
His answere; forces on both sides they raise;
While neighbour-Princes kindly enterpose,
And strive these breaches twixt the Kings to close,
Nor perfect peace nor constant warre ensu'd;
70   Theire truces often broke, were oft renew'd:
The sword oft drawne, and oft was sheath'd againe.
While this so iarring concord did remaine,
Betwixt the Kings; sadd newes was brought to them
That Saladine had tane Ierusalem,
75   Discomfited the Noble Christian hoast;
And with theire slaughter had through all that coast
Seized the townes of strength into his hands.
These wofull tydings through all Christian lands
In Europe flew; excitements every where
80   From pulpitts sounded in the peoples eare,
To aide their brother-Christians in the East,
And take revenge on Pagans that opprest
The holy land. for this great purpose some   [156]
Religious Prelates sent through Christendome
85   To seuerall Courts of greatest Princes came,
To draw theire succours. one of greatest name   William,
In that employment; whoo most seem'd t'aduance   Archbishop of Try.
The cause, that Prelate was, whoo then in France
Labour'd to draw these armed Kings from thence,
90   And turne theire swords against the Saracens.
Betwixt Gisors and Try, a day was sett
For enterview; where these two Monarchs mett;
Theire royall armyes stay'd not farre from thence.
No peace was wrought vpon the conference,
95   (Though thither Philip Earle of Flanders came,
A powerfull Prince, and one of honour'd name,
With noble purpose to attone theire iarres,

And to prevent so sadd, and causelesse warres)
Till this graue Prelate to the place was come,
100   And for the generall cause of Christendome
Thus humbly spake; Most puissant Kings, and you
Renowned Earle; lett it in season now
Bee thought to speake, what borne vpon the wings
Of Fame, already through all Europe rings,
105   The tragicke slaughter of our Christian hoast,
And sacred Salem to vile Pagans lost,
Since by those Christians suffrings, God for you
Setts ope the way to highest honour now.
Lett that braue cause engage these armes of yours.   [157]
110   Thither, great Kings, transport your conquering powers;
And for the name of your Redeemer, mooue
A warre more iust then any peace can prooue;
(Much more) a iuster warre then this can bee.
For when the foes of Christianity
115   Doo rage; if peace it selfe, at such a tyme,
May in the Christian world bee judg'd a cryme,
What crime is that when they to warre can goe,
Yett not 'gainst him that ought to bee theire foe?
But for him rather? (lett mee freely speake)
120   When Christian Princes 'gainst each other wreake
Theire wrath at such a tyme; what side so ere
Bee beat, the holy cause must suffer there;
And every death, when your feirce battells ioyne,
A Champion takes from bleeding Palæstine.
125   God (sure) decree'd I should prevaile with you,
Because hee letts mee finde you armed now,
When I am come to speake. your breasts are not
Becalm'd with peace; your actiue spiritts are hott;
And what should hinder you from Salems warre,
130   Since you haue mett a iuster cause by farre
Then that that moou'd this heat, that rais'd these armes.
I doo not seeke to still these loud alarmes;
But to direct them to an obiect right;
Where Godly zeale, not sinfull wrath shall fight;
135   That shall renowne you in all tymes to come,   [158]
And crowne your dying men with martyrdome.

Doo you for honour fight? (as whoo would make
A warre at all, if not for honours sake?)
Behold where truest honour may bee gain'd;
140   When by your armes his cause shall bee maintain'd,
Whoo is the fountaine of it; hee that gaue
To you those royall gloryes that you haue,
And claimes some quitall by your seruice shew'd.
What fame so great as that of Gratitude?
145   Euen Fame it selfe, which in some warres is made
The highest prize, for which great Kings invade
Each others lands, in this more glorious warre
Is a small part of the reward; for farre
More happy recompence ordained is
150   For this religious deede, eternall blisse.
Goe, vindicate that (once most happy) land
So grac'de by heauen, and with victorious hand
Redeeme those sacred monuments, that ly
Detain'd by Pagans in obscurity,
155   Which to the faithfull world would more bee knowne;
And Christian Poets shall hereafter crowne
In deathlesse songs, togither with the fames
Of that lou'd countrey, your victorious names.
If Homers Poëm could so farre renowne
160   That toy, the long-besiedged Phrigian towne:
If hee could giue her very ruines fame,   [159]
And lend each feild, each stone a pleasing name:
What in this sacred subiect may bee done?
A theame, disdaining all comparison?
165   In which for witt they shall not neede to toyle,
The plentuous matter will so stuffe theire style.
Instead of Idaes hill, and famed groue,
Which theire fictitious Gods (they say) did loue,
And oft descended downe from heauen to grace:
170   Theire theame shall bee each truly honour'd place,
Which glorious Angells oft haue hallowed,
Where our blest Lord himselfe vouchsaf'd to tread.
Instead of Priam's pallace, or the caue
Where Paris once his fatall iudgement gaue;
175   Instead of young Anchises bridall wood,

Or that fam'd rocke, where faire Hesion' stood:
Shall they discourse of Dauid's Tower, the caue
Which once vnto that holy Baptist gaue
Aboade on earth; or where Elias stood
180   When lifted vpp; and make faire Iordans flood,
And Kedrons torrent, in true fame surpasse
What Simoïs, or siluer Xanthus was.
But whither has my zeale transported mee?
Or what is this so like an Extasy?
185   Lett mee returne againe. great Kings I see
Your noble thoughts already working bee
In this braue cause. I will presume to add   [160]
No more but this; now lett your goodnesse gladd
All Christian hearts; in frendshipps bands combine;
190   And thinke you haue no foe but Saladine.
With that hee ceas'd; the Princes all are moou'd;
And in theire lookes already had approou'd
The bishopps speeche; when Henry thus begann
T'expresse his thoughts; let it become the man
195   Of greatest age, to show hee dooes forsake
The worlds vaine pompe and honour first, to take
This holy crosse, and fight for Palæstine.
Wee thinke it no dishonour to beginne
To seeke a peace at Philip's hand; nor can
200   Wee feare, for such a cause, that any man
Will thinke distrust in these our warres at home,
And not the loue wee beare to Christendome,
Engages vs; since wee resolue to goe,
And by that souldiers pilgrimage to show
205   No rest from armes is sought, when wee so farre
In person march, to meete a noble warre.
On that shall Henry's thoughts bee wholly sett.
And if king Philip's resolutions meete
With mine in this, and yours braue Earle, to stand
210   Another Champion for the holy land;
Then, Princes, ioyne your armed hands with mine,
And lett our peace bring warre to Saladine.
They both agree to what old Henry spake;   [161]
With that they kindely all embrace, and take

215 The holy crosse before the bishopp there.
    And that a difference plainely might appeare
    Among theire crossed souldiers; they agree
    Those crosses shall in seuerall colours bee
    Worne by the nations; th' English shall bee seene
220 In white: in redd the French: the Flemmings greene.
        And now at home to settle all affaires,
    To theire owne Realmes from thence each Prince repaires,
    To leuy money, and provisions make
    For that great voyage they entend to take.
225 For when they tooke the Crosse, it was agreed
    Betwixt the Kings, and by the Pope decreed
    That all, as well the Clergy as the Lay,
    Within each land should bee enforc'de to pay
    Of theire revenues the tenth part, vnto
230 This warre, vnlesse they would in person goe.
    And for a summe in present to bee made,
    The tenth of all the moueables they had
    Should levy'd bee for preparation.
    In every part of his dominion
235 Beyond the Seas, this order Henry gaue.
    And thence to England crost the Seas, to haue
    The Edict putt in Execution there;
    Choosing his wealthyest subiects every where,
    From whose estates hee might large Summes collect,   [162]
240 Two hundred citizens hee did select
    In London; and in Yorke an hundred moe;
    The like entending in all townes to doo.
    King Philip so; so th'Earle of Flanders did,
    In theire dominions treasure to provide.
245   But what malignant spiritt then did reigne,
    To make so pious an entention vayne?
    How were theire noble preparations crost?
    And that revenge against the Panyms lost?
    Alas, what starres maleuolent aspect
250 Could take such sadd and tragicall effect
    Against king Henry, as to overthrow
    That happinesse, that seem'd so neere him now?
    How true a fame might his last dayes haue wonne!

With what content might those gray haires haue gone
255   Downe to the graue, if in that holy warre
Hee happily had dy'd, though nere so farre
From off his natiue land? hee had not then
With such vnworthy cares, distracted beene
As after must ensue; nor forc'de to see
260   Againe a Sonn's abhorr'd impiety.
But fates to Henry's age had not ordain'd
So great a happinesse; sadd woes remain'd
To vexe his state, and breake his bleeding heart.
Doo thou, Calliope, declare in part
265   What obscure cause produc'de effects so strange,   [163]
And wrought this suddaine, and vnlook'd for change.
        Reimond Tholouses Earle had offer'd wrong
(Although but slight) to some that did belong
To Richard of Poictou, king Henry's sonne.
270   Thence grew so great an alteration.
For feirce young Richard, with his armed bands
(First rais'd for better warre) invades the lands
Of Reimond straight, and wasts his countrey neere
With fire and sword, surprising castles there.
275   At the'Earle's complaint Philip of France was moou'd;
And to king Henry sent; whose answere proou'd
No satisfaction. wrathfull Philip then
Invaded Berry with his choisest men,
And tooke ten townes and castles suddainely
280   From Henry there; whoo straight to Normandy
From England with a mighty army goes;
Now on both sides the warres with fury rose.
The holy voyage is forgott; in vayne
The neighbour-Princes of this iarre complaine:
285   In vayne the Pope entreats or threatens now.
Th'incensed Kings go farther on; although
Young Richard, Henry's Sonne, from whome at first
This breach begann, is by the Legate curst.
        No enterviews, no parleyes can doo good;
290   Though vnder that old famous Elme, that stood
Betwixt Gisors and Try, the Kings twice mett.   [164]
There when the wrongs were thought on both sides great,

Instead of peace, a iarre arose, that more
Deprest king Henry, then all warres before.
295   Philip, for Richard of Poictou, demands
Adela there againe from Henry's hands,
Offers the promis'd dower, requiring that
Th'old King for certainty of Richard's state,
Would now assure him the inheritance
300   Of all his lands in England, and in France.
And to that end that homage should bee done
By all the Lords; that Iohn his younger sonne,
To whome the fathers favour did encline,
Should straight bee sent to warre in Palæstine.
305   To these demands whilest Henry dooes refuse
To yeild assent, a sadder woe ensues;
In indignation Richard straight forsakes
His aged father; and himselfe betakes
Wholly to Philip king of France his side.
310   And firmest frendshipp twixt these two is ty'd.
With Richard many of the Barons goe;
Fortune herselfe forsakes old Henry too.
When now proud Philip, in disdaine that from
This enterveiw no peace at all did come,
315   Fells downe that aged Elme, whose spreading shade
So oft the place of parley had been made
Twixt France and Englands mighty Kings; and swore   [165]
That place should neuer hold a parley more.
          Sadd did the ruines of so fam'd a tree
320   To all the pitying people seeme to bee,
Whose honour'd shade had many ages beene
More then a Royall Court; where oft was seene
Such state, as one Imperiall house (although
Of gorgeous structure) could but seldome show;
325   Nor one whole kingdome at a tyme containe;
Two rivall kings togither to remaine
Beneath the covert of a shady tree,
Where only nature made theire Canopy.
Those old religious trees, that heretofore
330   Great Conquerours spoyles, and boasting trophees bore,
Sacred to Mars, or to Mineruaes name,

Were not more honour'd, or in debt to Fame
Then was this stately Elme; not cause that there
The Druides, when Druides there were
335   Among the ancient Gaules, had pray'd, or done
Theire barbarous rites and superstition;
Nor that the Faunes and Dryades had made
Theire nightly bowers, and sported in the shade:
But cause the peoples pride had lou'd to shew
340   The place, where Kings did stand at enterview.
This Elme was fell'd by Philip in his rage,
Of Henry's following death a sadd presage.
     Now too too weake is old king Henry's side   [166]
For those proud foes, that so vniustly ty'd
345   In combination, threaten his estate;
By his owne sonne and souldiers left of late,
And by those weapons wounded, that should guard
His royall person. while the fates so hard
Opprest his greiued soule, in discontent
350   To his beloued city Mauns hee went,
His place of birth, and high in his esteeme.
But angry Fortune will not leaue to him
That city now; Mauns must bee tane away.
Thither, while hee dooes with small forces stay;
355   (For but seauen hundred souldiers guard theire King)
Philip of France and furious Richard bring
A potent army. for the townes defence
The King too weake, is forc'de to fly from thence,
And to abandon that beloued towne.
360   Hee that had never fledd before, nor knowne
What twas to feare pursuing enemyes,
From his owne sonne and young king Philip flyes.
And, looking backe on that forsaken towne,
Curses the impious prowesse of his sonne.
365   Philip and Richards vnresisted powers
March further vpp, with ease surprising Tours.
Vpon which losse another day is sett
For enterview, and both the Kings are mett
Not farre from Turwyn. where, although that cleare   [167]
370   The sky at theire first meeting did appeare,

Yett on the suddaine from a swelling cloud
The thunder issu'd with report so loud,
It strooke a terrour into every heart
Ore all the feilds; and twice (they say) did part
375 The Kings asunder; once with such a force,
King Henry there had fall'n from off his horse,
Had not his seruants held him vpp. how ere,
It was decreed that Henry's honour there
Should fall farre lower, and hee suffer more
380 Then all his puissant reigne had felt before.
Hee that had giuen conditions still, that nere
Had taken any from what foe so ere,
Yeilds now to all conditions they demand;
Yeilds to deliuer into Philips hand
385 Adela now; and for those Provinces,
Which in that continent hee did possesse,
To doe him homage; letts his Barons sweare
Allegiance to his sonne Prince Richard there;
And yeilds to pay for charges of the warre
390 Two thousand marks to Philip, and so farre
His noble heart, not vs'd to bow, was broke,
That his greiu'd spiritt within three dayes forsooke
The earthly mansion. for a feauer ioyn'd
With the afflicting anguish of his mynde.
395 Whose forces soone dissolu'd that house of clay.   [168]
At Chinon then this dying Monarch lay.
When to encrease the anguish of his thought,
And more disturbe his peace, a scrowle was brought,
And (by ill fate) presented to him there,
400 Containing all theire names, that did adhære
In this conspiracy to Philip's side.
Where first of all his haplesse eye espy'd
The name of Iohn his sonne (whither that hee
Were truly one of that conspiracy,
405 Or some of Richard's followers to remooue
Before king Henry dy'd, that wondrous loue,
Which towards Iohn hee seem'd of late to beare
Aboue the other, falsely wrote him there.)
From thence extremity of passions

410 Surpris'd his soule. hee curst his impious sonnes,
Curst his owne birth; and had despairing dy'd,
Had not diviner counsell come to guide
His greifes aright, and by religions lawes
Direct his wounded conscience to the cause
415 Of those his suffrings, making the disease
The cure, and troubled thoughts the way to peace.
Wailing his sinns, into the temple there
He bidds them his yett-liuing body beare,
Where hee before the holy altar plac'd
420 In humble pœnitence breaths out his last;
And of so great a Monarch now remaines   [169]
No more on earth, then what a tombe containes,
Whoo lately ore so many lands did reigne,
From Scotlands bounds to farthest Aquitaine.
425 A Prince in peace of highest Maiesty;
In warre too great to finde an enemy:
In power aboue his neighbour Princes farre;
Whoo, though his sword were often drawne to warre,
His owne conditions without battells wrought,
430 Liu'd still victorious, though hee seldome fought,
And might haue seem'd aboue the reach of fate,
But that himselfe his greatest foes begate;
Wrong'd by that power which hee had made, and crost
By those of whome hee had deserued most;
435 Blest oft miraculously; oft againe
Beyond beleife deprest; his various reigne
Temper'd with all extremityes of fate;
And though triumphant, yett vnfortunate.

Finis.

THE
DESCRIPTION
OF KING Henry
THE SECOND, WITH
A SHORT SURVEY
of the changes in his
Reigne.

It has beene a custome of old Historians, when they record the actions of great Princes, to deliver also some Characters of their persons [N1v] and peculiar dispositions; that the curiositie of succeeding times, who pry deepely into those men, whose lives were of so great moment in the world, might bee fully satisfied and delighted. It will not therefore bee amisse to deliver a Character of King *Henry* the Second; a Monarch greater in Fame and Territories than any Christian King, that then lived. Hee was a man (as we finde recorded) of a just stature, a strong and healthfull constitution; but somewhat grosse, more by the inclination of Nature, then by any fault either of intemperance or sloth. For besides the sparenesse and sobrietie of his dyet, he vexed his bodie with continuall labour, and to ouercome his naturall [N2] fatnesse, was almost immoderate in all his exercises. Hee was of a ruddy complexion, his head was large, his eyes gray, whose aspect was terrible in his anger; his voyce was hoarse and hollow. Hee was a Prince of great affabilitie, facetious in discourse; and when he was free from anger, or important businesse, hee was most pleasant and Courtly in his whole conversation. Eloquent he was by nature, and (which was rare then) very learned. The best histories, which in those dark times could be gotten in Christendome, he had perused with diligence, and by the benefit of an extraordinary memorie did retaine them perfectly. He was very hardy in enduring either labour, or extremities [N2v] of the seasons; couragious in warre: but not rash, and willing to try all wayes before the chance of a battell; yet when there was occasion, very resolute, and so much feared by those Princes that had to doe with him, that hee

was never put to any great field. Hee was more kinde in honouring
the memories of his souldiers that were slaine, then hee was in re-
warding those that were alive; and never seemed truly to value his
30   best Captains, till after they were dead. Exceeding frugall and parsi-
monious hee was, (almost below the dignity of a King) but it proved
happy to his affaires. Though in private hee were very sparing, yet
abroad hee appeared often in great magnificence; [N3] his bountie
to some poore Princes, and those large summes, which hee disbursed
35   to the holy warre, might teach the world that hee was not covetous,
but wisely provident. The greatest taxe that was laid upon him by
those that lived in the same age, was his too too often breaking of
his promises; a fault that many Princes, great in other vertues, have
beene guilty of. Hee was exceeding fond of all his children, especially
40   in their childish age, before their carriage had deserved either way;
which shewed that Nature onely wrought that strong affection in
him. Yet there, where he most loved; and by those of whom hee had
most deserved, it pleased God, hee tasted the greatest [N3v] crosses;
his Sonnes were his scourges, and the onely instruments that did, or
45   (in likelihood) could shake the felicitie of so puissant a Monarch. So
great a contrarietie there seemed to be betweene his affection to
them, and the returne of theirs to him. Hee appeared in nothing
almost of a tender nature, but in loving them; and might have beene
thought somewhat severe in disposition, if hee had not beene a
50   father, to shew the contrary: they were in generall of a Noble de-
portment, taxed in their times almost of no unjust or bad actions,
but their ingratitude and disobedience to him: and had carried a re-
pute of the Noblest Princes, if they had not at all beene Sonnes. But
[N4] perchance it pleased God by the fruit of his loynes to punish
55   those sinnes of the flesh to which the King was so much addicted.
Hee was noted, more then any Prince of his time, to be given to the
love of women; but especially after the displeasure conceived against
his wife Queene *Elianor* (as a stirrer up of his Sonnes against him)
when hee altogether forbore her bed, hee was growne carelesse of
60   the voyce of Fame, and strove not at all to hide his wanton affec-
tions. All his vertues (which indeed were many) had occasion often
to be knowne by the varieties of his reigne, in which felicitie and
crosses did so often succeed each other, they were not onely tried, but
declared to the world. For very remarkeable [N4v] were the altera-
65   tions of Fortune (if we consider all things) which happened in the

reigne of this great Prince. Of which if you will take a briefe survey, consider it divided as it were into five Acts; for as one sayes, *Tanquam fabula est vita hominis.*

Let the first eight yeares of his reigne (or thereabouts) be count-
70 ed for the first Act. Where the bravery and wisedome of his youth (for but 24. years of age was he) enough appeared in setling the kingdome, and vindicating the rights of his royall Crowne, after so long a confusion, and so many calamities of civill warre. Hee expelled the strangers out of the Realme, which in *Stephans* time had
75 bin the diseases of [N5] it. He providently setled not onely the revenues but the authority of his Crown (as before appeareth) and fitly disposed of all the Castles and strongholds; which he either kept in his owne power, or quite demolished. Hee maintained the ancient bounds & honor of the Realme not onely in the North, but against
80 the Welsh. Beyond the Seas he suffered no damage, but gained upon all occasions. K. *Lewis* & he were sometimes likely to have come to battel; but peace was made, and King *Lewis* content rather to sit downe with some little losse, then contend with so puissant a foe. *Chaumont* he tooke from him, & seized (against his wil) upõ *Nants*
85 in *Britain:* this was indeed the time of K *Henry's* greatest felicity [N5v] in which hee enjoyed his dignitie without any vexations, and the people, that had long beene afflicted with miserable times, did truly rejoyce in their new King. And during these yeares, as a farther blessing to him and securitie to the kingdome, the Queene was fruit-
90 full, and bare him three Sons.

For the second Act, wee may consider his next eleven or twelve yeares; in which time, though hee suffered nothing by the hand of warre, as not molested by rebels at home, nor threatned at all by forraigne enemies: yet by the opposition of one Church-man he found
95 a long and wearisome vexation. For almost all this time did that famous jarre of Archbishop *Becket,* [N6] and at the last his lamentable murther afflict King *Henry,* and exceedingly disturbe the quiet of his minde. The particulars at large have appeared in the foregoing storie, and shall not here trouble the Reader. Yet in this incumbred
100 time, his State and Dignitie had great additions; of which the happiest was that easie accession of the Realme of Ireland unto his Scepter. And another (considering the present occasions of state) of as much importance to him, the gaining of the Dutchy of Britaine to his third Sonne *Geoffrey.* Which hee with great wisedome and

105   industrie obtayned in the nonage of that yong Ladie *Constantia*, the
       daughter and heire of *Coran* Duke of Brittaine, [N6v] then de-
       ceased. Hitherto his happinesse was not at all impaired, nor hee af-
       flicted with any thing but the dissention of Archbishop *Becket*. His
       times of danger, and great sufferings now ensue.
110   Let therefore the three following yeares of his reigne be taken
       for the third Act; in which the Scene is altogether changed, and in-
       stead of a glorious and happy reigne, nothing but afflictions, and the
       extremest dangers that could be feared, threaten not onely his
       Crowne, but life also. This is the time of that great revolt of his
115   three Sons from him; besides so mighty a confederacy ioyned with
       them, as *Lewis* King of France, *William* King of Scotland, *David* his
       brother, *Philip* [N7] Earle of Flanders, *Matthew* Earle of Boloigne,
       Theobald Earle of Bloys, besides so many of the greatest and strong-
       est English Peeres, as the Earls of Leister, Chester, and Norfolke,
120   with the Lord *Mowbray*, and divers others. No part of al his large
       dominions was free from warre; Normandy invaded by *Lewis* of
       France, and young King *Henry*, Aquitaine by his Sonne *Richard*
       possessed against him, as the Dutchy of Brittaine was by *Geoffrey*.
       The Northern parts of England were all wasted by the great strength
125   of *William* K. of Scotland, & the Easterne parts much afflicted by
       those mercenary troops of Flemmings, which the Earle of Leister
       brought over, besides the forces of the Earl of *Norfolk*. [N7v] This
       great Monarch, whose felicitie was so lately the envie of his neigh-
       bour-Princes, is now become the pittie of them all; and the injuries
130   done to his estate and person, are much lamented by some Princes
       too farre off to lend him succour. But behold the turning of Fortune
       againe; it pleased God againe to lift him from this depth of calami-
       tie, to the height of honour. Hee now found the benefit of his fru-
       gality; and that large treasure, which hee before had gathered, was
135   his great assistance in procuring mercenarie souldiers to his side; be-
       sides some faithfull Lords there were, (whom we have named in the
       storie) that were deeply moved at their masters injuries; and so
       Nobly served [N8] him, that within three yeares after the beginning
       of these combustions, King *Henry*, according to his owne wishes,
140   beheld a happy and victorious end of them, as is before expressed.
            Let the fourth Act continue about seven yeares that next ensued,
       a time of honour, and highest happinesse to this great King; after his
       troubles were all ended according to his wish, the King of France

daunted, the martiall King of Scotland his prisoner, all rebels under
145   his feet; his Sonnes brought to acknowlege their duty, and all his
large dominions in great securitie. While the mightiest Monarchs of
the Christian world admired his wisedome and great successe, aston-
ished [N8v] almost at so wonderfull a change as they now beheld.
His sumptuous Court was filled with congratulating Ambassadours;
150   of whom at one time there were moe seene, then ever had beene to-
gether in the Court of England, as namely from the two Christian
Emperours, *Manuel* of Constantinople, and *Frederike* of the Ro-
mans, from the Kings of Navarre, and Aragon, from the Archbishop
of Triers, and the Earle of Flanders. During the time of this happi-
155   nesse, hee marryed his two youngest daughters (for the eldest was
married before to the Duke of Saxony) to the Kings of Sicily and
Arragon. Hee called Parliaments, in which according to his minde,
hee was [O1] furnished with treasure, he wisely setled the estates of
Church and Common-wealth, and besides many other wholsome &
160   happy constitutions, he first appointed Iudges Itinerant for the six
circuits of the Realme of England.

     The last and tragicall Act may be considered in the five follow-
ing yeares, untill the end of his reigne and life. The date of his fe-
licitie was now expired; and nothing followed but trouble and ca-
165   lamitie. The beginning of which was a second revolt of his two
Sonnes, *Henry* and *Geoffrey*, which was soone taken off by the un-
timely death of both the Princes (as it before declared in the Poëm;)
besides the ill successe in the affaires of Ireland under [O1v] the
government of *Iohn* his youngest sonne. Those troubles that arose
170   from *Philip* King of France, and prevailed against *Henry* in his old
age, more then any enemy had beene able to doe before: which had
not fallen so heavily upon him, if *Richard* (then his eldest sonne)
had not unnaturally forsaken his father, and joyned in confederacy
with King *Philip*. That miserable dissention broke the heart of old
175   King *Henry*, and was the end both of his reigne and life.

FINIS:

[O3]

THE

SINGLE, AND

COMPARATIVE

CHARACTERS OF

HENRY the Sonne,

and RICHARD.

Let it not seeme impertinent (if the Reader therby may be informed
or delighted) to deliver the Characters of these two Princes the eld-
est Sonnes of King *Henry* the Second, who bore so great and stir-
ring [O3v] parts in the history of their fathers reigne. They were
5   Princes of greatest eminence in those times, and upon whom the
eyes of Christendome were most set; a large Stage they had to act
upon; and early occasions to discover their worth. They were both
tall of stature beyond the ordinary height of men; of comely visage,
and majesticall presence; for courage and magnanimity they were
10   thought equall; and both admired for royall vertue, though of a na-
ture different. *Henry* was beloved for his sweetnesse: *Richard* hon-
our'd for his gravitie. *Henry* was affable and wondrous liberall: *Rich-
ard* severe and full of constancy. *Henry* was addicted to martiall
sports and pastimes: [O4] *Richard* more inclined to warre it selfe:
15   One was Courtly: the other serious. One beloved for mercy: the
other feared for Iustice. The one a refuge: the other a terror to all
offenders. Two Princes brothers of so great worth; and yet so
diverse, have seldome beene observed. Yet well might they spring
from one root; their father *Henry* in the mixture of his nature was
20   knowne to containe both their different Characters; and iudged to
have a minde (as one speakes of *Augustus Cæsar*) full of varietie.
How much the sweetnesse and lovely carriage of young King
Henry had wonne upon the world, let one observation (which some
of his owne time thought like a miracle) [O4v] teach us to judge.
25   How strange was it, that a young Prince rising in armes against his
father, possessed neither of lands nor treasure, much lesse of a good
or just cause, was followed almost by all the neighbouring world
against a King of so large a territory, and so full of treasure; that in

this great defection from him, hee was able, almost with mercenary
30   souldiers to vindicate his right against all those potent enemies. This
young Prince had gained to his side not onely his brothers *Richard*
and *Geoffrey*, and most of the great Nobility of England, but the
Kings of France and Scotland, the Earle of Flanders, and many
other great forraigne Princes. So many rich gifts of minde and [O5]
35   body were heaped on this young *Henry* (saith a Writer of his time)
that Nature, as it were envying what she had bestowed, soyled it
againe with one staine, the vice of ingratitude, and disobedience to
so good a father. Which sinne of his was thought the cause that
plucked downe Divine vengeance, and untimely cut off that flour-
40   ishing youth which was judged worthy (if God had prolonged it) to
have ruled a greater Empire.

The severity and industrious courage of *Richard* the second
Sonne let this declare; the Earledome of Poictou, and the Dutchy of
Aquitaine, which were the inheritance of his mother *Eleanor*, were
45   committed to his government whilest he was [O5v] very young. Yet
in that tender age (so manly were his vertues, so awefull was the
hand which he carried over the rebellious and stubborne subjects of
those Countryes, that he soone reduced them to a more quiet state,
and setled obedience, then any of their former Princes had ever
50   done. As he was stout in the action of warre; so was hee constant
and unwearied in pursuing his fortune, and making the full use of
any successe, according to that marke that *Lucan* gives of *Iulius
Cæsar: Nil credens actum cum quid superesset agendum.* Hee was so
severe in punishing their offences, that hee began (so great a resem-
55   blance sometimes has vice with vertue) to be taxed of cruelty, till the
wiser sort had fully [O6] considered the quality of his actions, and
the necessity of such proceedings. How prevalent he was in the
managing of warres (to omit those great & high exploits, which he
afterwards atchieved when hee was King of England) by this one sad
60   observation we may somewhat iudge; after the untimely deaths of his
two brothers, *Henry* and *Geoffrey*, when hee onely of the Sonnes
was left at mans estate; and unnaturally warred against his father; as-
sisted onely by *Philip* King of France, hee more prevailed then his
brother *Henry* with a farre greater confederacy had beene able to doe
65   in the foregoing warres. *Henry* the Sonne had many and great
Princes (as before wee shewed) that sided with [O6v] him. And yet
so victorious an end did old King *Henry* make of that businesse, that

hee saw his greatest and most glorious times after the conclusion of
that warre; but when *Richard* revolted from him, assisted onely by
70   *Philip* of France, the father was inforced to suffer more, and stoope
lower than any imagined that a Prince of so great a spirit and power
could ever have bin brought unto. By which finally his heart was
broken, and a period set to all his worldly glory. *Richard* in that was
more unhappy than his brother *Henry*, that his unnaturall wars were
75   able to give so deepe and uncurable a wound to his fathers heart, and
lent him no time at all to obtaine his pardon, as *Henry* had done,
nor [O7] could the father liue to bee a witnesse of *Richards* sorrow
and true repentance, as hee had beene of the others. Which notwith-
standing was many wayes, after the death of old King *Henry*, testi-
80   fied by *Richard;* and last of all, when himselfe was dying, he com-
manded his servants to bury him at *Fonteverard;* and lay him acrosse
at his fathers feet, to whom his disloyalty and unnaturall revolt (as
hee with griefe acknowledged) had beene so great a crosse.

FINIS.

Textual Notes

SIGLA

MS   British Library Royal Manuscript 18.C.XII (copy-text)
C   Corrector of manuscript
P   Printed edition (London, 1633), Huntington Library copy

TITLE PAGE OF THE MANUSCRIPT

bookes] Bookes. / By his Majesties Command. *P, not in MS*
Tho: May.] *extended from* T. M.; *the added characters have a less set appearance than the script of the title, and their ink looks more faded*
excitat,] *comma added with faded ink*
Auson:] *later addition, presumably by the same hand that extended the author's name*

IMPRINT 1633 PRINTED EDITION

LONDON, / Printed by *A. M.* for *Benjamin Fisher*, / dwelling in Aldersgate-streete at the / signe of the *Talbot*. 1633.

PRELIMINARIES ADDED TO THE PRINTED EDITION

Frontispiece
Line engraving with half-length, full face portrait of Henry II, turned slightly to the left, sceptre in right hand, globe in left. Oval frame, lettered]
HENRICVS II ANGLIÆ REX, DVX NORMA:*[nniæ]* ET AQVITA.

[niæ] CO:*[mes]* PICTA:*[viæ]* ET ANDIGA:*[viæ]* D*[omin]*[us] HIBERN.
[iæ]. Signed] R*[obert]* Vaughan fecit
At the top two insets of shields of arms; at the bottom an engraved subscription]
Henry the 2.[d] surnam'd Short mantle, King of / England, Duke of
Normandy and Aquitaine, Earle / of Poicteres. and Anjou: Lord of Ire-
land. [etc]

Dedication
TO / THE SACRED / MAIESTIE / OF / CHARLES, / BY THE
GRACE OF / GOD, KING OF GREAT / Brittaine, France, /
AND Ireland, DEFEN- / DER OF THE / FAITH, &c / / THIS
HISTORICALL / Poem, BORNE BY HIS / COMMAND, AND
NOT / TO LIVE BVT BY HIS / GRATIOVS ACCEPTA- / TION,
IS HVMBLY / DEDICATED BY / THE AVTHOR, / / His Majesties
most obedient / Subject and Servant / / Tho. May.

Book I
Title] THE REIGNE OF / King Henry the Second. / *The Hirst* [sic]
Booke. P
The first booke / Argument] The Argument of the first Booke. P *[between
single rules]*
34 Henry] *interlined C*
93 King] *P*, braue *MS*
106 strengths] strength *P*; *plural* -s *inserted in MS*
136 prudent] *P*, glorious *MS*
153 much] must *P (foul case? cf. P VII, 121)*
154 brother] brothers *P*
202 hills] s *inserted*; theire] i *inserted*
208 And leaves] *P*, Leauing *MS*
215 to] too *P*
237 spatious] *P*, wealthy *MS*
239 sees,] *comma inserted*
243 lough] *P*, Lough *MS*
244 folds] *P*, *cancelled* feilds *MS over caret*, flockes *C*
269 shapes] s[1] *corrected*
325 yeares] a *corrected (from e?)*
348 hoast] a *interlined over caret*
357 loue.] ~, *P*
361 people] o *interlined over caret*
362 alarmes] *P*, ~; *MS*

367 more] e *inserted in secretary hand* C
395 changes] c *corrected from* t
408 oft] t *added with metallic ink*
433 receiv'd] P, reciu'd MS
441 Saracens] P, dearest Turkes MS
450 those foes ... Palæstine] P, the threats of dreadfull Saladine MS
466 Vice] *majuscule* V *corrected from minuscule* v; such] P, so MS
472 ensnaring] n *interlined over caret*
494 through] u *interlined*
523 lay;] *semicolon inserted*, ~, P
526 liberty] t *corrected (from c)*
527 adore,] *comma inserted*, ~ₐ P
532 And] nd *interlined* C *over caret*
542 crawl] w *written over erased* ll
546 Mycenæ's balefull tragœdies] *It is hard to distinguish between the scribe's digraphs æ and œ; May himself spells 'tragœdy' (for instance on the title page of his autograph fair copy of* The Tragœdy of Cleopatra)
559 hoast] a *corrected (from s?)*
560 haire] ir *corrected*
563 doo] o² *corrected (from e)*
568 marke,] P, ~ₐ MS
575 they,] P, they ₐ MS
583 now, ... King,] *commas inserted*
587 giues.] ~, P
594 be sure in this] P, in this bee sure MS

Book II
Title] THE REIGNE OF /King HENRY the Second. / *The Second Booke.* P
The second booke / Argument] The Argument of the second Booke. P [*between single rules*]
6 shine.] P, ~ₐ MS
16 Scotland,] P, ~ₐ MS
20 Yorkes] P, yorkes MS
38 himselfe] P, hinselfe MS
60 weare,] P, ~ₐ MS
61 That from the burden of a King art free] P, And from the Regall power and office free MS
70 Tantalized] T *corrected from* t *produces in effect an* F
75 magnificence,] *comma inserted*, ~ₐ P

78 Princes,] *comma inserted*
87 the adioyning] th'adjoyning *P*
88 Naiades] Najades *P*
90 beauteous] eau *interlined with caret by C over* oun, beautious *P*
95 And] *loop of* d *widened, probably for calligraphic reasons*
113 Yorkes] *P*, yorkes *MS*
122 imperiall] i² *inserted*
153 *bold*] Bold *P*, loose *MS*
154 *Sweete reconciled*] Sweete reconciled *P*, *Bold Theft, becomming MS*
159 Approaching] a *interlined C over caret*, Approching *P*
165 coming,] *comma inserted*, ~ₐ *P*
190 laugh'd] d *corrected from* t
196 Rosamond] d *has been given a more flourished loop in darker ink*; single]
    n *interlined C*
221 is] *P*, i's *MS*
232 *dittographic* the *cancelled in metallic ink before* thrall
233 to] to, *P*
238 A change … to learne] *P*, A change in him, but are afraide to learne /
    The cause, nor dare they aske it him; and hee / (Perchance too long) con-
    ceales his malady *MS, comma after* him¹ *inserted*
253 And] nd *interlined C over caret*
274 him)] *interlined C over caret*
327 begann,] *comma inserted*
345 heauen] a *corrected (from u?)*
355 wore] o *corrected (from e?)*
378 take] *interlined C over caret*
382 thence may] ence m *written over erasure*
390 great,] *comma inserted*, ~ₐ *P*
394 right,] *P*, ~ₐ *MS*
409 Princes] Prince his *P*
417 bee] b *altered from* h
423 rule,] *comma inserted C*, ~ₐ *P*
446 waken'd] *cancellation* [e?] *in metallic ink before* a

Book III
Title] THE REIGNE OF /King HENRY the Second. / *The Third Booke. P*
The third booke / Argument] The Argument of the third Booke. *P* [*be-*
    tween single rules]
6 peace] e *corrected with metallic ink (from a?)*

8 two] *interlined in paler ink with caret over cancelled* tow *by C*

38–41 Againe ... to give] *P*, Againe did beautious Rosamund appeare / To his sick eyes; but how and whence it came / (Since old historians doo so darkely name / The circumstances of her loue and fate) / Doo thou, my faithfull Erato, relate. / [*Indent.*] Declare most louely Muse, thou, that to give *MS*

43 th'Elizian] *smear between* h *and* E *(erased* e*?) makes apostrophe illegible*

47 weare] *interlined in paler ink C over caret*

49 Poets] o *corrected (from* e*?)*

77–80 Thou saw'st ... love and fate] *P*, In curious sort within that shady bower, / Thou saw'st the second Henry's paramour / Th'almost forgotten English beauty there; / And now return'd from thence, oh doo not feare / My Muse, to tell; 'mongst all whome thou hast found, / Declare the Loue and fate of Rosamund *MS*

133 *dittographic* the *cancelled in metallic ink before* thought

143 They] y *inserted C*

149 boast] a *corrected from* u

216 had] *interlined over caret*

254 Inseparable] a^1 *interlined C over cancelled* e

257 remember] em^2 *interlined C over caret*

263 Be] *The catchword on the preceding page reads* Bee

267 'cause] *P*, cause *MS*

279 at] t *altered (from* s*?)*

294 not;] *P*, ~, *MS*

327–8 And made ... heire] *P*, And happy father by that Earledomes heire, / Of a renowned progeny, whose faire / Branches in severall lands much purchase fame, / And through this Realme and Ireland spread the name. *MS*

335 Contemning] *P*, Or slighting *MS*

342 France,] *comma inserted,* ~$_\wedge$ *P*

379 (if] *parenthesis inserted*

380 stor'd] *Apostrophe smudged; no space between* r *and* d *as in the rhyme-words of the following lines; the scribe may have been irritated by the preceding rhyme-word* record.

382 immunityes] m^2 *inserted C over caret*

397–8 And, ... priviledge, ... vice,] *Commas inserted,* ~$_\wedge$ ... ~, ... ~$_\wedge$ *P*

407 hundred] *interlined over caret (by scribe, not C)*

423 lawes,] *comma inserted*

425 King,] *comma inserted*; badd] *interlined C with metallic ink,* weake *P, MS*

426 weake] *interlined C with metallic ink*, badd *MS*, bad P
447 before] *P*, beefore *MS*
456 Prelates] a *cancelled before* l
458 theire] i *inserted*
465 all,] *comma inserted*
468 sprung,] *P*, ~∧ *MS*
487 fooleryes] *P*, ~. *MS*
492 other] her *smeared due to erasure*
Marg 494 miraculis] Footnote *P*, miraculù *MS*
499–500 Which by . . . Becket rue.] *P*, Which both the King and hee must
    after rue, / As in the storyes sequell shall ensue. *MS*
560 being no] *P*, as a *MS*
580 contestation] n *interlined C over caret*
584 king,] *comma inserted*, ~∧ *P*
595 yeares] s *inserted*

Book IV
Title] THE REIGNE OF / King HENRY the Second. / *The Fourth Booke.*
    P
The fourth booke / argument] The Argument of the fourth Booke. *P* [*be-*
    tween single rules]
10 receiu'd] e² *interlined over caret*
15 Raimond] *P*, Raimun'd *MS*
21 Monarchs] Monar *written over erasure*
41 in] *P*, In *MS*
53 Ocean] O *corrected from* o
54 souldiers] *P*, soulders *MS*
57 selfe] e¹ *corrected* (*from* i?)
59 Fitz-Stephans] ans *corrected*
71 remayn'd] *written partly over erasure*
76 atcheiu'de] u *written over erasure*
77 the] *written over erasure*
81 the] *P*, they *MS*
92 state, . . . dignity,] *commas added*, ~∧ . . . ~∧ *P*
97 God, appeares] *comma inserted*, ar *smeared*
100 daughter] a *corrected from* u
117 Dermot] *smudge after* t
118 hers] s *inserted*
134 pretence,] *comma inserted*

146 gett] *closely attached to the last letter of* could *and* written *in a more cursive script, with secretary* e *and ligature* tt *(added by C?)*

147 Strongbow] S *corrected from* s

151 On] *P,* To *MS*; to bestow] *P,* hee affy'd *MS*

152 were both performed now] *P,* by him were ratify'd *MS*

162 No] N *corrected*

170 force,] *comma inserted*

175 Becket's] e² *corrected (from* i?*)*

181 thought] thought) *MS, P*

189 mongst] *smudge after slightly bolder* t

190 excommunicate] *contraction mark with caret over* m¹

195 Yorkes] *P,* yorkes *MS*

202 at] t *added*

205 knights,] *comma inserted*

211 memoryes,] *comma inserted*

222 is] s *corrected from* t

224 Rome] R *written over erased* r

227 Henry,] *comma inserted*

246 the way] *erasure between* e *and* w (the *probably corrected from* their)

255 knights] *smudge over* n *(corrected from* i?*)*

259 safeguard] *P,* safeguar'd *MS*

261 there] *MS* theire, i *cancelled*

263 (in vayne alasse)] *parentheses added*

264 temple,] *comma inserted,* ~ₐ *P*

285 hee to] *comma inserted after* hee *in stop-press correction of* P *(Folger copy 2; Huntington)*

292 ridiculously] i¹ *corrected from* e *with metallic ink*

316 owne,] *comma added,* ~ₐ *P*

325 dispatch'd] *P,* dspatch'd *MS*

345 port] o *corrected (from* a*) with metallic ink*

351 force,] *comma inserted*

368 theire] *corrected from* there

371 there.] *P,* ~ₐ *MS*

386 Besieg'd] i *corrected from* e

426 doo,] *comma inserted*

431 King,] *comma inserted*

446 his] *written over erasure*

463 plentious] i *corrected (from* e*)*

491 More of . . . at last] *P,* More of theire countrey rites, to vnderstand /

Th'antiquities of his new-conquer'd land, / And nature of the soile; and
thus at last *MS*
494 wisdome] o *corrected from* e *(?)*
500 wrought,] *comma inserted*
514 bowing,] *comma inserted (probably by scribe)*
528 dooing,] *P*, ~ₐ *MS*
537 whensoere] h *corrected over erasure*
571 crimes,] *comma added*
617 Ile,] *comma inserted*
633 hast,] *comma inserted*, ~ₐ *P*
633 water] r *bolder than the rest of the word; quill possibly worn (cf.* old *in line*
      644)
638 Another] *No indentation in P*
644 old] l *bolder than the rest of the word; quill possibly worn (cf.* water *in line*
      633)
645 In] *No indentation in P*
649 Not] *No indentation in P*
694 by night] *interlined (over caret, by scribe, not C)*
723 is] are *P*
752 winde] *interlined C over caret*
758 words,] *comma inserted*, ~ₐ *P*

Book V
Title] THE REIGNE OF /King HENRY the Second. / *The Fift Booke. P*
The fift booke / Argument] The Argument of the fift Booke. *P* [*between*
      single rules]
Arg 1 impious] *P*, warrelike *MS*
Arg 2–3 Raise Warre ... back'd] *P*, Throgh every part of his dominions /
      Raise impious warres; in theire vniust designe / The neighbouring kings
      and forreine Princes ioine, / Besides rebellious Lords. *MS*
Arg 3 th'old] the old *P*
Arg 16 ioyes] *comma inserted*, ~ₐ *P*
7 infest] infect *P*
33–7 King Lewis ... immediate hand] *P*, Lewis king of France first plotted
      that designe, / The King of Scotts, and th' Earle of Flanders ioine, / And
      with the sonnes, armes 'gainst the father take; / This combination seem'd
      so much to shake / Great Henry's state, as nothing but the hand *MS*
44 him,] *comma inserted*, ~ₐ *P*
50 subiects,] *comma inserted*, ~ₐ *P*

61 King Iames ... did behold] *P*, While hee was living, hee beheld *MS*
64 Beheld,] *comma inserted and slightly smeared*
78 Vernoul,] *comma inserted*
87 France,] *comma inserted*
91 From] *no paragraph in P*
104 Lucy,] P, ~∧ *MS*
108 Englands] P, England *MS*
114 which,] *comma inserted,* ~∧ *P*
147 foe] foes *MS*, s *cancelled*
148 From] *P*, from *MS*
194 him,] *comma inserted*
199 Richard, ... Winchester,] *commas added, no punctuation in P*
218 him,] *comma inserted,* ~∧ *P*
228 health,] *comma inserted*
234 deepe,] *comma inserted*
256 pensiue] Pensive *P*, Pensiue *MS*
279 farther] f *written over semicolon;*
279 his] *dittographic second* his *cancelled in metallic ink*
287 of] so *P*
297 pillaging,] *comma inserted,* ~∧ *P*
298 Controll,] *comma inserted*
299 Fiue] *interlined in metallic ink over partly illegible cancellation* (*which the catchword on p. 110 identifies as* Sixe); Yorkeshire] *P*, yorkeshire *MS*
299 marg. Vmfreuille] Vinfriville *P*
302 The] *P*, This *MS*
303 strength] *P*, strenght *MS*
335 receiue] receiv'd *P*
336 Thence] And *P*; on,] thence *P*
356 Yorkeshire] *P*, yorkeshire *MS*
381 greiud? a] *P*, ~? how much hee did abhorre / The iealous rage of cruell Elianor / For that black deede? a *MS*
398–9 armes; / Pale] *P*, armes / In every part; whilest Henry's royall crowne / Did seeme into th'extreamest hazard throwne; / Pale *MS*
407 Shall] S *corrected (from* s*?)*
424 desire,] *comma inserted,* ~∧ *P*
435–7 Medea more ... has done,] *P*, Medea mooue / 'Gainst Iason more, for his disloyall loue / Then I haue done, *MS, commas inserted*
444 impiety,] *comma inserted,* ~. *P*
460 woods,] *comma inserted*

472 or] and *P*
509 all,] *comma inserted*
526 had nere at court] *P*, at court had nere *MS*
540 reft] r *written in bolder ink, possibly over erasure*
571 these,] *comma inserted*
611 read,] *P*, ~; *MS*
629 they view] thy view *P*
678 Sett] Set *P*, sett *MS*
678 ope] o *corrected (from* v?*)*
697 Whoo,] *comma inserted*
701 wrought,] *comma inserted,* ~ₐ *P*
711 remain'd,] *comma inserted*
794 apology,] *comma inserted,* ~ₐ *P*
807 this,] *comma inserted,* ~ₐ *P*

Book VI
Title] THE REIGNE OF /King HENRY the Second. / *The Sixt Booke. P*
The sixt booke / Argument] The Argument of the sixt Booke. *P* [*between*
    single rules]
Arg 6 show'd,] *comma inserted*
12 Enough,] *comma inserted*
77 then] *full stop cancelled after* n
100 laurell] *P*, ~. *MS*
109 Nor dooes] *no paragraph in P*
116 Synod,] *comma inserted,* ~ₐ *P*
173 leagues] *P*, legues *MS*
237 Too] *P*, To *MS*
269 Plantagenet,] *P*, ~ₐ *MS*
280 abide] a *corrected*
283 alterations] n *corrected*
289 from that time] *P*, from time *MS*
300 forth,] *comma inserted*
315 hope;] *semicolon inserted,* ~ₐ *P*
330 God,] *P*, ~ₐ *MS*
352 Richard] Riihard *P*
370–1 seruant, . . . him,] *commas inserted*
379 prepares] *first written with double* rr *(probably in anticipation of rhyme-*
    word warre*), first of these cancelled*
380 Barons,] *comma inserted*

388 a way] *follows cancellation* (away?) *in metallic ink by C*
395 But by] By by *P* (*anticipatory error; these are the first words on fol. L4r;*
    catchword on L3v is, correctly, But)
410 made him iustly] justly made him *P*
434 Saints,] *comma inserted,* ~∧ *P*
442 state,] *comma inserted,* ~∧ *P*
450 a] thy *P* (*possibly eyeskip from 449*)
454 iust,] *comma inserted*
455 lett] t[1] *corrected (from* c?)
458 King,] *comma inserted*
468 wash'd] a *corrected (from* i?)
487 vpp,] *comma inserted*
490 castle,] *comma inserted*
507 time] *interlined with caret over cancelled* him.

Book VII
The Seauenth booke / Argument] The Argument of the seventh Booke. *P*
    [*no title, heading without rules*]
7 greivous] i *inserted, erased letter* (*probably* i) *after* v
10 him,] *comma inserted,* ~∧ *P*
22 leaue,] *comma inserted*
23 pleas'd,] *comma inserted,* ~∧ *P*
52 hee] *lower part of* h *over erasure*
53 Realmes] *P,* Realme *MS*
78 Christian] *P,* christian *MS*
81 brother-Christians] *hyphen* (=) *added*
Marg 86] *P, not in MS*
102 season] a *corrected (from* i?)
108 honour] honours *P*
111 Redeemer,] e *cancelled after* e[1]; mooue] o[2] *inserted*
121 such] sucst *P* (*foul case: ligature* st *for* h)
125 (sure)] *parentheses inserted*
134 zeale,] *comma inserted*
138 all,] *comma inserted,* ~∧ *P*
162 feild,] *comma inserted*
179 Aboade] *illegible letter cancelled in metallic ink before* o (r?)
209 Earle,] *comma inserted*
211 mine] in *corrected over erasure*
217 souldiers] *P,* soulders *MS*

236 Seas,] *comma inserted*
241 Yorke] *P,* yorke *MS*
247 preparations] preparation *P*
319 Sadd] *no indentation in P*
332 honour'd] u *corrected (from* r?)
344 foes,] ~,) *MS P*
358 too] *P,* to *MS*
388 Allegiance] a *corrected (from* e?)
391 heart] e *corrected (from* a?)
426 finde] d *corrected (from* e?)
436 Beyond] y *corrected from* i

DESCRIPTION AND CHARACTERS

THE / DESCRIPTION / OF KING HENRY / THE SECOND, WITH
/ A SHORT SURVEY / of the changes in his / REIGNE. and THE /
SINGLE, AND / COMPARATIVE / CHARACTERS OF / Henry
the Sonne, / and Richard. *P, not in MS*

N4r	l. 63	succeed] *Pen and ink correction in an old hand:* ex *cancelled,* suc= *in the margin of the Huntington copy of P*
O1v	l. 169	that] t² *turned letter in both B.L. copies, corrected in Hunt. copy*
		arose] a./rose *(full stop instead of hyphen)*
	l. 172	*Richard]* R *small capital in both B.L. and Hunt. copies*
O3v	l. 11	*Henry]* H *small capital in both B.L. and Hunt. copies*
O4r	l. 14	*Richard]* R *small capital in both B.L. and Hunt. copies*
O6v	l. 67	*Henry]* H *small capital in both B.L. and Hunt. copies*
	l. 73	*Richard]* R *small capital in both B.L. and Hunt. copies*
O7r	l. 79	*Henry,]* comma added in stop-press correction in P (Folger copy 2; Huntington)*
	l. 80	*Richard]* R *small capital in both B.L. and Hunt. copies*

Explanatory Notes

TITLE PAGE

Invalidas ... Auson:] The epigraph is taken from a poem which Ausonius addressed to Emperor Theodosius, "Domino meo et omnium Augusto Ausonius tuus," lines 13–14 (*Ausonius*, ed. Hugh G. Evelyn White, London, 1951, I, 8). May has exchanged "Rex" for "ipse" in the second line.

PRELIMINARIES ADDED TO THE 1633 PRINTED EDITION

Title Page
By his Majesties Command] This addition to the title of the printed edition (A3r), together with the Dedication (A4r), which is also lacking in the manuscript (see Textual Notes, p. 124), indicates that the poem underwent a process of examination before being sent to the press.

Frontispiece
Artist] The copperplate portrait of Henry II on A2v is signed "R[obert] Vaughan fecit" (for its lettering and subscription see Textual Notes, pp. 123–4). Vaughan (fl. 1622–1663) engraved similar portraits of Edward II (for Sir Francis Hubert, *The Historie of Edward the Second*, 2nd ed. 1629), Edward III (for Thomas May's *The Victorious Reigne of King Edward the Third*, 1635) and Edward VI (for Sir John Hayward, *The Life and Raigne of Edward VI*, 1630). His engravings are discussed by Arthur M. Hind, "The Baziliⱳlogia, 1618, and expanded Baziliⱳlogias," *Engraving in England in the Sixteenth and Seventeenth Centuries. Part II. The Reign of*

Figure 11. Frontispiece from the 1633 edition of *King Henry the Second*
with Robert Vaughan's portrait of the king
(Folger Shakespeare Library, STC 17715 copy 2, the Harmsworth copy).

James I (Cambridge, 1955), 115–39 (a description of the portrait of King Henry is on p. 123) and by Margery Corbett and Michael Norton, *Engraving in England in the Sixteenth and Seventeenth Centuries. A Descriptive Catalogue with Introductions. Part III: The Reign of Charles I* (Cambridge, 1964), II, 48–87; the King Henry portrait is described on page 55 of this volume.

Models] A very similar, only slightly larger portrait (17.5 cm x 10.6 cm, printed from a copperplate) is to be found in William Martyn's *The History and Lives of the Kings of England* (1628), after page 31 (E4), where it precedes a short chapter on "The Historie of King Henrie the Second" (F1r–G1v). Dress and attributes in this portrait are closely similar to those in Vaughan's engraving; only the collar has an additional pendant with three crosses formed by pearls and a jewel in the center, and the crown is given a Saxon aspect by having three fleurs-de-lis and three tapering uprights, each surmounted by a ball, on its rim. The lettering is identical, except that the possessions abbreviated in Vaughan's engraving are extended (partly in small caps) to ANGLIÆ REX: DUX NORMANIÆ ET AQVITANIÆ: CO: PICTAVIÆ ET ANDIGAVIÆ D[us] HIBERNIÆ, the device in the top right corner is a badge, not a shield, and lacks the crown, and the subscription adds after the king's style (which is exactly phrased like the one in *The Reigne of King Henry the Second*): "He raigned 34 years 9 months, died the 6th of July 1189 at the age of 61 yeares, and lieth buried at Fonteverard in Normandy. [In smaller type] Are to be sold by Compton Holland ouer against the Exchange." The age is wrong, but the reference to Holland points to the common origin of both these engravings, a collection of royal portraits: *BAZILIΩLOGIA. A Booke of Kings Beeing The true and liuely EFFIGIES of all our English Kings from the Conquest vntill this present: With their seuerall Coats of Armes, Impreses and Devises. And a briefe Chronologie of their liues and deaths. Elegantly grauen in Copper. Printed for H[enry] Holland, and are to be sold by Comp[ton] Holland ouer against th'exchange.* 1618. The portrait of King Henry in this collection has exactly the same measures as that in *The History and Lives of the Kings of England* and has clearly served as a model for both Martyn and Vaughan. In his description of the collection, Howard Levis counts the portrait of King Henry amongst a group he labels Type A (oval portrait, half-length, badges in the upper corners and a subscription) and ascribes it to Renold Elstrack who engraved most of the originally twenty-seven portraits in the *Baziliωlogia* (or thirty-two—the number of plates varies in the extant copies of the first edition; see Howard C. Levis, *Notes on the Early British Engraved Royal Portraits Issued in Various Series from 1521 to the End of the Eighteenth Century* [London, 1917], 59, 61). A copy of Elstrack's original engraving is in the Rosenwald Collection at the National Gallery of Art in Washington, D.C. (see the frontispiece to this edition).

Inscriptions] The royal style in both legend and subscription is historically accurate except for the title Dominus Hiberniae, which Henry did not wear himself but conferred on his son John before sending him on his Irish expedition in 1185. The title Dominus was given to princes royal before they were formally crowned kings, and John had hoped to exchange it for that of King of Ireland. His mission failed miserably (as Thomas May records at the beginning of Book VII of *The Reigne of King Henry the Second*), but he kept the title of Dominus Hiberniae as part of his style after his coronation as king of England in 1199 (see W.L. Warren, *King John*, 2nd ed. [London, 1978], 35). Thomas May will have known this from John Speed's *Historie of Great Britain*, which is one of his major sources. Speed says of King John: "His Stile in his seale of *Ireland* (though *Houeden* sayth, his father made him *Regem*, a King) was onely, *Sigillum Iohannis filij regis Angliæ Domini Hiberniæ*, Lord of Ireland" (*Historie*, IX, 6 [92], 507; cf. note to II, 425; a reproduction of this seal heads the chapter on King John in Speed's *Historie*, IX, 8, 531). The inscriptions on the seals used by Henry II are without the title Dominus Hiberniae; Speed reproduces several of them in his chapter on the king (Speed, *Historie*, IX, 6 [1], 484 [see Fig. 14, p. 142] and [80], 504). May shows an awareness of such heraldic distinctions when he says that Henry sent his son to the Irish "To rule among them as theire Governour; / But not invested in the Regall power." (VII, 27–8). Apparently Vaughan was not as well versed in historical heraldry as his literary colleagues.

Arms and Devices] The shields set in the upper corners of the engraving are crested with coronets that closely resemble the crown worn by King Henry in the portrait beneath. The one in the upper left corner of the portrait shows three lions passant guardant (for England), crowned. In early Stuart heraldic diction these lions would be called lioncels, for, says a contemporary, the Rouge Croix Pursuivant at Arms, John Guillim, "inasmuch as the *Lion* hath a *Prerogatiue Royall* over all *Beasts*, and cannot endure that any other should participate of the *Field* with him *Quia Principes nolunt pares, Princes will admit no fellowes*, to the impeachment of their *Soueraigntie*; therfore the bearing of diuers *Lions* in one *Field* must be vnderstood of *Lions whelps*, which as yet haue not so great feeling of

Figure 12. Plantagenet shield from the Vaughan frontispiece.

Figure 13. Plantagenet badge from MS Harley 6085, fol. 15v.

their owne *strength*, or *inbred noble courage*, nor apprehension of their ingenerated *Royall Soueraigntie* ouer all *beasts* as *Lions* haue." The exception to this rule is the ensigns of sovereigns. If these show several lions, says Guillim, quoting Leigh (i.e., Gerard Legh) as his authority, "euery one of them is reckoned to be of as great dignitie, as if he were borne diuidedly in so many seuerall *Escocheons*, and that in respect of the *Soueraignetie* of the *Ordinarie* so interposed; for which cause they have the title of *most worthy* partitions." (*A Display of Heraldrie* [London, 1632], BB4r, 193; according to Anthony à Wood, the material for this book came from John Barkham or Barcham, a chaplain to archbishop Bancroft, who also supplied John Speed with material for his Life of King Henry II).

The charge in the shield in the upper right corner, which at first sight looks like a griffon, is a leopard passing between two rushes. This becomes evident in a comparison with the larger portrait in Martyn or the *Bazili ɷlogia*. It is unlikely, however, that Henry should be presented with this charge (unless it is meant to refer to the illegitimate birth of the first Norman king, William the Conqueror) because the leopard is associated with low birth in contemporary heraldry: "The shape of the *Leopard* bewraieth his unkindly birth, forasmuch as hee in all proportion of body more like the *Pardus*, as well in respect of the slendernesse of his body, as of his spots, and wanteth the courage notified by the plentifull mane wherewith *Nature* hath invested the *Lyon*, being the expresse token of his generous and noble spirit" (*Display of Heraldrie*, Lll1r, 259). It seems more likely that the leopard is a lion passant and points to Henry's Norman possessions ("gueules au léopard d'or" being part of the arms of Normandy), and that the rushes are to represent the *plantà genista* his father is said to have added to his badge. The heraldic *planta genista* usually shows an open broom pod; a device similar to·the one used by Vaughan occurs, however, in a heraldic manuscript in the British Library, Harl. MS 6085, which is written on vellum, illuminated and signed by William Segar, Garter Principal King of Arms, and dedicated to King James. It has the title "The VARIATION of the Arms, and Badges of the Kings of England, from the tyme of Brute, vntill y^{is} present yeare of our Lord, 1604." Folios 15v–16r deal with King Henry II; on fol. 15v the exact same lions and brooms are displayed in addition to the escarbuncle of Anjou, as on the Vaughan portrait (although the broom sprigs are left without a shield or crown). Segar's accompanying text on fol. 16r gives the following explanation of the latter devices:

"*Henry.2.* vsed for his device *vne Escarboucle d'or* being an ancient mark of the house of *Anjou*; And for his name of *Plantagenett*, a Beast named a Genett, paßing between two Brome plants. In Frenche, *vng Genette, passant entre deux plantz de Genesté.*"

Portrait] The likeness of Henry II in Renold Elstrack's portrait is not historically accurate, and it seems doubtful that it was ever meant or thought to be. It is an idealized picture of the king that has been heightened with contemporary attributes of royalty. The ermine robe and the jewelry look particularly anachronistic. The stylisation comes out in comparison with the unvarnished illustrations that accompany the life of King Henry in John Speed's *Historie.* Speed made use of the most authentic material available at the time, mainly seals and coins supplied by his learned friends and patrons, in particular John Barkham and Sir Robert Cotton (see Introduction, pp. lxxxvi–xciii, and cf. D. R. Woolf's chapter on "John Speed and the Labyrinth of Ambiguity" in *The Idea of History in Early Stuart England* [Toronto, 1990], 64–72). He prints a number of engravings with heraldic devices at the beginning of his chapter on King Henry II that show some details similar to those used by Elstrack and Vaughan in their portraits (*Historie*, IX, 6 [1], 484; see Fig. 14). The device at the top is a crowned shield with three lions passant guardant which corresponds roughly to the badge in the upper left corner of the portrait. The two sides of a seal reproduced underneath the shield show, on the obverse, the king enthroned, holding a sword in his right hand and an orb in his left; the reverse presents the king mounted, in full chainmail armour, with a sword in his right hand and a shield in his left. Under the seal there are the two sides of a coin showing the king with a short beard and moustache, crowned and sceptered (inscription "HENRICVS R E"), and on the reverse a cross with fleurs-de-lis between its arms and the legend "ORIM ON:S" indicating the name of the moneyer and the mint from which he worked (for similar reproductions, and full explanations, of both the seal and coins see W. L. Warren's Frontispiece and Ill. 15 in his *Henry II*).

The throned figure on the obverse of the seal is that of a youthful king with long hair, but it lacks the beard he wears in the Vaughan portrait. The rim of his crown carries three fleurs-de-lis (the so-called ancient crown) instead of the trefoils and crosses in the portrait. The orb is historically more likely in that it shows a plain sphere with cross-patée and

Figure 14. Great Seal of King Henry II (woodcut by Christopher Switzer in John Speed's *Historie of Great Britain*, IX, 6 [1], 484).

a bird (probably the dove used by Henry I; see below). Generally speaking, the differences, in particular in details of ornament, prove Speed to be less anachronistic than his artistic colleagues.

There is another figure later in Speed's *History* (IX, 6 [80], 504) which presents only the recto side of a Great Seal of Henry II. It shows the king seated on a throne with dog-headed sides, holding an orb with cross-patée on a long stem in his right hand and a scepter with a fleur-de-lis at the top in his left. Here the king is depicted as middle-aged, with a moustache and short beard, and crowned with the same coronet as in the earlier seal. The legend runs: "HENRICVS REX ANGLORV[*M*] DVX NOR[*M*]ANNO[*RVM*] ET COMES ANDEGAVO[*RUM*]." The hairstyle and facial expression of the king come closer to the engraving in *The Reigne of King Henry the Second*, but it still seems unlikely that Vaughan used this illustration as a model for his portrait.

From a modern point of view, not even Speed's representations of King Henry's armorial bearings and regalia are beyond doubt. Though Henry II may have been the first English king to employ heraldic arms, there is little evidence to prove this; the seals that have been preserved show the outside of the shield turned away (see J.H. and R.V. Pinches, *The Royal Heraldry of England* [London, 1974], 20–21). As far as can be established, Henry's son Richard was the first to use the three lions on his second Great Seal (1198), "though from the time of Matthew Paris in the thirteenth century these arms were 'backdated', and sometimes attributed to all the English Kings from William the Conqueror onwards." (Thomas Woodcock and John M. Robinson, *The Oxford Guide to Heraldry* [Oxford, 1990], 187). Lions were associated with members of Henry's family: his grandfather, King Henry I; his wife, Eleanor of Aquitaine; and his illegitimate son, William Longespée, the Earl of Salisbury. The antiquaries of the seventeenth century believed that the lions on the badges of Plantagenet kings represented England, Normandy, and Aquitaine (*Oxford Guide*, 187). The leopard passing through rushes of *planta genista* may have been meant to add to the possessions mentioned in the lettering around his portrait and to point out his Anjou origin.

Regalia] As to the regalia, Cyril Davenport knows of no seal showing Henry with an orb but speculates that he can be assumed to have used the same orb on his seal as Henry I: "On Henry I.'s fourth Great Seal a dove is shown above the cross-patée (fig. 13), and Stephen and Henry II. used the same design." (*The English Regalia* [London, 1897], 17–18). The orb on this seal is a plain mound infixed with the cross and dove. There is no dove on the orb in Elstrack's engraving, and the mound is of a type that came into use only much later. The same applies to the scepter. In Davenport's chapter on English scepters Henry II is not mentioned. The first royal seal to show a scepter is that of Henry III; there were, however, scepters on coins (see the illustrations on p. 19 of *The English Regalia*). The crown worn by King Henry in the Vaughan engraving could be described as a "crown with three crosses-patée alternate with ornamented trefoils, arched" according to Davenport's description of various crown forms in *The English Regalia* (p. 23). Again, Davenport does not mention a crown worn by Henry II, and he shows no early analogue to the one in Vaughan's portrait. Apparently Vaughan has tried to heighten the figure of the medieval king in his engraving; this may not be correct historically, but it is in keeping with the poem it adorns.

Book I

Arg. 3 Enyo] The goddess of war (Lat. Bellona). May invokes her in the verse passages he contributed to the translation of John Barclay's *Argenis* (1629), "with frightfull hayre; and kindling with her brand / The clouds" (V3v; see also Cc8v).

Arg. 8 Stephens reigne] King Stephen, Henry's predecessor on the English throne, reigned from 1135 to 1154.

1 first Plantagenet] Henry II, the son of Geoffrey, Count of Anjou, and Maud, daughter of King Henry I, was the first Plantagenet king (see Genealogical Table I); the surname Plantagenet became attached to his father who wore a sprig of broom as his badge (Lat. *planta genista*, Fr. *plante à genêt*; see also note to Frontispiece, above).

21–2 Your favoures influence] Lucan addresses the emperor Nero in similar terms at the beginning of his epic poem on the civil war between Julius Caesar and Pompey the Great, *De bello civili*, I, 66: "Tu satis ad vires Romana in carmina dandas."

41 by right of birth his due] Stephen was a nephew, Henry a grandson, of King Henry I. After the death of his only son, Henry I had publicly designated his daughter Maud as his successor. Maud's plans to secure the throne for herself, or to act as a protector for her son Henry who was two years old when his grandfather died in 1135, failed to win the support of the barons and led to the civil war of 1136–1153. Stuart genealogists apparently regarded Stephen's claim to the throne as unfounded (see Genealogical Table I).

53–5 His braue atcheiuements … admir'd] Henry was made duke of Normandy at the age of 17 and had to defend the title against his souzerain, King Louis VII. His greatest achievement was marrying Eleanor, divorced wife of King Louis: this brought him half the kingdom of France (see Austin Lane Poole, *From Domesday Book to Magna Carta, 1087–1216*, Oxford History of England, vol. III, 2nd ed. [Oxford, 1955], 162–3).

75 digests] OED, s.v. *digest*, vb. 6b: "To get over the effects of" (arch.).

76 corroborates] OED, s.v. *corroborate*, vb. 2: "strengthen (constitutionally or organically, *especially* of medical agents or applications)" (obs.).

77–81 those troopes of forreiners ... did remaine] See William of New-burgh: "Denique edicto præcepit, ut illi, qui ex gentibus exteris in An-gliam sub rege Stephano prædarum gratia tanquam ad militandum conflu-xerant ... propriis regionibus redderentur, fatalem eis diem constituens, quem in Anglia sustinere certi foret discriminis." (*Historia rerum Angli-carum*, II,i, in *Chronicles of the Reigns of Stephen, Henry II, and Richard I*, vol. I [London, 1884], 101). Holinshed translates "eis diem constituens" as "he appointed them a daie" (*Holinshed's Chronicles of England, Scotland and Ireland* [London, 1807; rpt. New York, 1965], vol. II, 111).

89–92 Or else King Stephen ... theire loyalty] One of the followers thus re-warded was William le Gros, Count of Aumale, whom Stephen had cre-ated Earl of York in 1138. Henry marched against York in the year of his coronation (1154) and forced William to yield the royal properties he had held under Stephen (see W. L. Warren, *Henry II* [Berkeley, 1973], 60).

101 all the Midd-land forts] In order to curb the power of the barons, Henry seized (and partly razed) not only the castles of the adherents of Stephen, but also of supporters of the Angevin cause like Hugh Bigod, Earl of Norfolk and Suffolk. In demolishing these castles Henry laid the seed for the rebellion of the Midland earls of Leicester, Chester, Norfolk and Derby in the great war of 1173–1174 (see Warren, *Henry II*, 364–6).

103–8 Nor, though as yett ... Castles that hee held] Hugh Mortimer for-mally submitted to Henry in July 1154; Holinshed gives the names of the castles as Cleobury, Wigmore and Bridgnorth (*Holinshed's Chronicles of England, Scotland and Ireland* [London, 1807; rpt. New York, 1965], vol. II, 112). Speed names Gloucester, Wigmore, Bridgenorth, and refers to Matthew Paris as his source.

114–27 his royall pedegree ... of Saxon kings] St. Margaret of Scotland was a granddaughter of King Edmund II Ironsides, the next to last Anglo-Saxon king and daughter of his son Edward (called the Outlaw in Gene-alogical Table I). Margaret's daughter Matilda (or Maud) married Henry's grandfather, Henry I. Henry II was knighted by her brother, his great-

uncle, King David of Scotland, in 1149. There is a list of Henry's ances-
tors in the chronicles of Matthew Paris that goes back to Noah ("De
genealogia Henrici regis," *Chronica majora*, ed. Henry Richards Luard
[London, 1854], II, 209–10). So does George Owen Harry's *The Genealo-
gy of the High and Mighty Monarch, James, by the Grace of God, King of
Great Brittayne, &c. with his lineall descent from Noah, by diuers direct lynes
to Brutus, first Inhabiter of this Ile of Brittayne* [etc.] (1604).

127 twenty faire descents of Saxon Kings] The number 20 includes all the
Saxon and Danish kings before William the Conqueror (as counted in
Genealogical Table I), not only the predecessors of Edmund Ironsides.

131 Your ancient right to Englands crowne] Charles I was related to both
the ancient Scottish and the Anglo-Norman kings (via the Stewart and
the Tudor lines; see Genealogical Tables). Sir Robert Cotton, the anti-
quary, had written a treatise on the descent of King James from the
Anglo-Saxon kings (see F. Smith Fussner, *The Historical Revolution: Eng-
lish Historical Writing and Thought 1580–1640* [London, 1962], 128).

135–50 Then to the North ... Malcolmes ancestor] This report of Henry's
North England campaign of 1157 corresponds with Holinshed's *Chronicles*
(II, 113) where it is placed, correctly, after the submission of Henry's
brother Geoffrey of Anjou (1156). Holinshed's account is based mainly
on Newburgh, II, iv, but Holinshed is more precise about names than
Newburgh, who speaks of Malcolm IV only as the king of Scots ("Regi
Scottorum," *Historia*, II, 105) and names the counties ("Northumbriam,
Cumbriam, Westmeriam," ibid.) rather than the cities surrendered by
Malcolm. Speed names "*Carleil, Newcastle* vpon *Tyne*, &c." and refers to
Matthew Paris (*Historie*, IX, 6 [7], 486).

143–6 But least iniustice ... hee giues him Huntingdon] The earldom of
Huntingdon had come to Malcolm's grandfather David with his wife
Maud. The marriage had been arranged by King Henry I (David's
brother-in-law) who later confirmed this and other possessions by a royal
charter (see Warren, *Henry II*, 177). Holinshed says of Henry II that he
"tooke into his possession all that countrie which his mother the empresse
had sometimes granted vnto king Dauid, [...] howbeit [...] he suffred
king Malcolme to enioy the earledome of Huntington, which king Ste-
phan had giuen vnto his father earle Henrie, sonne to king Dauid"
(*Chronicles*, II, 113).

151–80 Yett did one deede ... Pope Adrian] See Holinshed (*Chronicles*, II,
112–3) whose account is based on Newburgh, II, vii. Neither Holinshed
nor Newburgh link Geoffrey's "rebellion" with that of Henry's sons. Hol-

inshed inserts a passage in which he cautions against the breaking of vows and "the impudencie of the pope" (p. 113). The whole of the story of the oaths is questioned by Warren, *Henry II*, 46.

163 Of three the strongest castles in the land] Holinshed names them as "Chinon, Lodun, and Mirabell [i.e., Mirebeau]" (*Chronicles*, II, 112).

171–3 Prince Henry ... before them tooke] Cf. Newburgh, "diu hæsitavit; tandem conclamantibus omnibus, ne ad sempiternum et inexpiabile dedecus corpus patris sinet insepultum tabe corrumpi, victus succubuit ; et sacramentum, quod exigebatur, non sine fletu præstitit (*Historia*, II, vii, 113); Holinshed, "For though Henrie was loth to take his oth, yet bicause his fathers bodie should not remaine unburied, he was contented to sweare" (*Historia*, 112).

178 a yearly pension] Cf. Newburgh: "Fratri humiliato et supplici veniam dedit, castellisque nudato, ut occasionem superbiæ tolleret, terram planam concessit, ex qua fructuum utilitas proveniret" (*Historia*, II, vii, 114); Holinshed: "Howbeit, he gave unto his said brother a pension of a thousand pounds English, & two thousand pounds of the monie of Anjou, with the towne of Lodun, and certeine other lands to live upon" (*Chronicles*, II, 113).

179–90 But though ... a brother done] Holinshed (following Nicholas Trivet) mentions the dispensation and rebukes Henry for his breach of faith: "[Henry] found meanes to procure of pope Adrian the fourth (who was an Englishman borne) a dispensation for that oth: wherevpon (hauing got licence to depart from the office both of right, law and equitie) neglecting his fathers ordinance, he passed ouer into Normandie, and making war against his brother the said Geffrey, easilie expelled him out of those places, which were assigned him by bequest in his fathers testament, and so tooke the earldome of Aniou into his owne possession" (*Chronicles*, II, 113). May replaces this with his preview of the rebellion of Henry's sons in 1173–4.

192 stubborne Wales] Cf. Newburgh, "gentem inquietam et barbaram" (*Historia*, II, v, 106).

198–9 Rough woods ... high and craggy mountaines] Cf. Newburgh, "illi silvosis montibus vallibusque suis plus justo confisi" ... "delitescebant in silvis" (*Historia*, II, v, 106); not in Holinshed; Speed mentions only that Henry cut his army a way through the Welsh forests.

208–10 And leaves ... conquests there] Holinshed says (with a reference to Matthew Paris) that Henry built the castles of Rutland [i.e., Rhuddlan] and Basingwerk after the subjection of the Welsh (*Chronicles*, II, 114; cf.

Matthew Paris, *Chronica majora*, II, 214). They did not prove as lasting as May implies but were taken by Owain of Gwynned after Henry's abortive second Welsh campaign in 1167 (see Warren, *Henry II*, 164).

222 Europe then possest a happy peace] Newburgh says that after the North England campaign England enjoyed a period of peace: "His ita compositis, Anglia in cunctis finibus suo otio et securitate pro tempore fruebatur" (*Historia*, II, iv, 106).

223–9 This peace . . . prospects] Ben Jonson gave similar sentiments to the chief witch in his *Masque of Queenes* "I hate to see these fruicts of a soft peace, / And curse the piety gives it such increase" (lines 144–5), *Ben Jonson*. Ed. C. H. Herford & Percy and Evelyn Simpson. Vol. VII [Oxford, 1941], 288.

235–8 Great Henry's large dominions . . . Pyrenes death] Newburgh: "Regis autem supra omnes qui hactenus in Anglia regnasse noscebantur latius dominantis, hoc est ab ultimis Scotiæ finibus ad montes usque Pyrenæos, in cunctis regionibus nomen celebre habebatur" (*Historia*, II, iv, 106).

238 Pyrenes death] Pyrene, a Spanish princess, was raped by Hercules and gave birth to a dragon (or serpent). The sight of this offspring drove her into the mountains named after her.

251–8 A Spatious cave . . . speech againe] Ulysses, to whose kingdom the island of Dulichium belonged, is called "dux Dulichius" in Ovid's *Metamorphoses* (XIV, 226); in Homer's *Odyssey* Circe advises him to descend into Hades and call the shades of the dead by an offering of sheep's (not bullock's) blood (Books X, 487–540; XI, 13–50; Aeneas sacrifices bullocks on the shore of lake Avernus before descending into Hades, *Aeneid*, VI, 243–54). Homer places the entrance to Hades on the Cimmerian coast, i.e., in Southern Italy (*Odyssey*, XI, 13–9). May's contemporaries located it somewhere near the Scythian Bosporus, but May is not the first to find something similar nearer home; commenting on the Cimmerian darkness in the Cave of Sleep George Sandys calls attention to the fact that "there be vallies in *Wales*, wherein the sun shines not for six months together" ("Upon the Eleventh Book," *Metamorphoses*, 395).

261–7 The groue of Proserpine . . . so sadd a shore] Birds are kept off the cave that leads into Hades in Virgil's *Aeneid*, VI, 237–40: "Spelunca alta fuit vastoque inmanis hiatu, / scrupea, tuta lacu nigro nemorumque tenebris, / quam super haud ullae poterant inpune volantes / tendere iter pennis." The atmosphere in May's grove resembles that in Ovid's Cave of Somnus: "Est prope Cimmerios longo spelunca recessu, / Mons cavus, ignavi domus et penetralia Somni, / Quo numquam radiis oriens mediusve cadensve / Phoebus adire potest; nebulae caligine mixtae / Exhalantur humo dubiaeque crepuscula lucis" (*Metamorphoses*, XI, 592-6).

265-6 No Tritons play'd ... Halcyon breede] Proteus and the Tritons are deities of the sea and the shore; they are often named together (for instance in Ovid's *Metamorphoses*, XIII, 918-9; cf. II, 89-90 and note). Halcyon birds (i.e., kingfishers) were supposed to breed on the sea; they are called dear to the Nereids by Theocritus in his *Idyll* No 7, lines 57ff. May refers to them again in VI, 110.

279 In adamantine cavernes] In Drayton's *Polyolbion* Saturn is said to be tied with "Adamantine chaines" (Song I, lines 26–30; *Works*, ed. Hebel, IV, 2). Milton's Satan also lies in "adamantine chains," *Paradise Lost*, I, 48.

293-8 And as sterne Aeolus ... with the land] The simile is based on Virgil's description of the Cave of Winds, *Aeneid*, I, 50–63.

298 Confounding Neptune's kingdome with the land] Virgil says of Aeolus that he has to restrain the winds lest they create chaos: "Ni faciat, maria ac terras caelumque profundum / Quippe ferant rapidi secum verrantque per auras" (*Aeneid*, I, 58–9).

333-4 faire Margaret ... affy'de] In 1160, "the mariage was solemnized betwixt Henrie the kings sonne being seven yeares of age, and the ladie Margaret daughter to the French king, being not past three yeares old" (Holinshed, *Chronicles*, II, 116). Henry managed to obtain a special dispensation to arrange this marriage from the papal legates present in France to promote the cause of Pope Alexander (see Johann Baptist Sägmüller, "Eine Dispens päpstlicher Legaten zur Verehelichung eines Siebenjährigen mit einer Dreijährigen im Jahre 1160," *Theologische Quartalsschrift* 86 [1904], 556–75).

334 Brittaines heire] The heir of Brittany was Constance, daughter of count Conan IV. It took three campaigns (1166, 1167, 1168) to reconcile the Breton barons to her union with young Geoffrey. The actual marriage was not consummated before 1181.

339-40 Nor that hee did ... fertile Aquitaine] Eleanor was the former wife of King Louis VII of France. Henry married her in 1152; she brought him Aquitaine, Poitou and Auvergne.

348-9 The Empresse Mawde ... her royall right] The Empress landed at Arundel in September 1139. Speed mentions in a marginal note that Gervase of Canterbury names Portsmouth as the landing place (*History*, IX, 5 [19], 472).

351 different passions] May uses the same expression in his *King Edward*: "And both the hoasts with passions different / Together joyne" (N5r).

360 they imagin'd prodigyes] Cf. Lucan's remark on the panic that strikes
through Rome on the eve of the Civil War: "His se stimulis dolor ipse
lacessit" (De bello civili, II, 42).

364–74 At Lincolne wholly ... turn'd the state] The battle of Lincoln took
place "vpon Candlemas day [i.e., February 2], and yeare of Christ Jesus
one thousand one hundred fortie one" (Speed, Historie, IX, 5 [23], 473).

369 Augustaes right] Augusta was a byname of the Empress.

370 renowned Gloster] Robert, Earl of Gloucester, an illegitimate son of
Henry I, had entered the ranks of Matilda in 1139.

372 rare valour] Stephen's valour in personal combat is highly acclaimed by
Matthew Paris; Speed gives a translation of the relevant passage in his
Historie (IX, 5 [28], 476).

380–2 his weeping Queene ... all in vayne] Stephen's queen, who was also
named Matilda, sent a chaplain to a church council summoned by Henry
of Blois, Stephen's brother and bishop of Winchester, in which she de-
manded the release of her husband (Warren, Henry II, 26); see Speed,
"the now-dejected vnfortunate Stephen, whose sorrowful wife Queene
Maud, incessantly sollicited the Empress in her Husband's behalfe, desir-
ing his libertie, but not his Crowne, which he was now contented to let
her enjoy" (History, IX, 5 [32], 477).

382–92 the warres ... sett each other free] The empress Matilda was driven
out of London in 1141 ("sine subdolorum instinctu, sine Dei nutu," as
Hoveden puts it, Annales, ed. Savile, 487, 52–3) and made her escape to
Gloucester; the Earl of Gloucester, however, was taken prisoner in Win-
chester and exchanged for Stephen later that year.

399–403 The countreys pillag'de ... burn'd with fire] "King Stephen after
the robbing of many churches, burning and robbing of townes and vil-
lages by the hands of the Fleming souldiers, he and his brother Henry
bishop of Winchester builded a castle of the nunry of Wilton, to represse
the incursions of them of Salisbury. Earle Robert the first of July fell
sodainely vpon them at Wilton, and set the town on fire. The king with
the Bischop fledde with shame, the Earles men tooke the kings people, &
sackt his plate and other things:" (Stow, Annales, 1631, N1v, 146).

402 As Wiltons pittyed sacke] Speed mentions the sack of Wilton in half a
sentence only: "Then was Oxford vpon conditions yeelded to the King;
and Wilton fired by the bastard Earle Robert:" (History, IX, 5 [39], 479).

404 faire Worster] Stow refers to the unsuccessful siege laid to the castle of
Worcester by King Stephen (Annales, N2r, 147). In fact, Worcester was
sacked by Miles of Gloucester, an ally of Maud, in 1139; Stephen took

the town (but not the castle) in 1150 (see R. H. C. Davis, *King Stephen.*
1135–1154 [1967; 3rd ed. London, 1992], 40, 110–11).

409–11 What neede I tell ... Wilton Abbey] "Anno gratiæ 1142. qui erat
annus septimus regni regis *Stephani*, idem rex *Stephanus* construxit cas-
trum apud Wintoniam. Tunc superueniens multitudo nimia hostium ex
insperato, cum regii milites congressionibus bellicis incepissent, & non
potuissent resistere: regem in fugam compulerunt" (Roger of Hoveden,
Annales, ed. Savile, 488, lines 10–14; for the treasure see above, note to
lines 399–403).

411–14 how the Empresse ... So to escape] See Speed, "and thence to the
Castle *Diuize*: where vnderstanding that shee was still in hazard to be
surprised, shee deuized, (as what will not necessitie endure, and a womans
wit deuize?) to be laid in a coffin as dead, bound fast with Cordes; and
so, as if it had beene her corse, carried in a Horse litter to the citie of
Glocester; in which bonds of her owne distresse, shee had good occasion
to remember the chaines of King *Stephens* captiuitie" (*History*, IX, 5 [36],
478).

414–33 what neede I ... to Wallingford] This famous incident occurred in
1143: "Eodem anno rex obsedit Imperatricem apud Oxenfordam. post
festum Sancti *Michaelis*, vsque ad aduentum Domini, & parum ante natale
fugit imperatrix per Tamensem glaciatam, circumamicta vestibus albis; re-
uerberatione niuis, & similitudine fallentibus oculos obsidentium, fugit ad
castellum *Wallingford*" (Roger of Hoveden, *Annales*, ed. Savile, 488, 15–
19). May probably used Speed's more colourful rendering of the incident,
as indicated by a few verbal parallels ("congealed" and "joy"): "The Em-
presse in his [i.e., Robert, Earl of Gloucester's] absence, had well fortified
her selfe in *Oxford*. ... till at length great penurie enforced to think of a
surrender; but shee, a woman (whose sexe hath often deceiued wise-men)
resolued once again to ouer-reach her foe by witte, whom shee could not
by force: whereto the time did fit her wishes; for being a Winter sharpe
aboue measure, the Riuer *Thamisis* that runnes by the Citie walls, was
then congealed with a strong crusted Ice, and besides a great Snow did
then cõtinue, & had couered the ground. *Maude* vpon these aduantages,
put in practice a most dangerous attempt: for cloathing her selfe, and
some choise of her company, in white linnen-garments, to deceiue the
eyes of the Sentinels, issued secretly by night out of a posterne-gate, and
passing the frozen Riuer, ranne on foote, through ice, and snow, ditches,
and vallies, for fiue miles, euen to *Abington*, the falling snow still beating
in their faces; and there taking horse, the same night got to the Castle of

Wallingford, to the great joy, and also admiration of all that were therein."
Speed, (*History*, IX, 5 [38], 479).

434–6 Nor then did England ... in right of her] Geoffrey of Anjou (Maud's
second husband) gradually conquered Normandy in the early 1140s; King
Louis VII of France recognized him as duke of Normandy after the fall
of Rouen in 1144. Geoffrey transferred the title to his son Henry early in
1150 (see Poole, *OHE*, III, 161; Warren, *Henry II*, 38).

441–50 Thy Saracens ... that threaten Palæstine] The narrator raises Luci-
fer's spirit again in Book VII, when the crusade planned by Henry and
Philip is frustrated: "But what malignant spiritt then did reigne, / To
make so pious an entention vayne?" (VII, 245–6). In Holinshed's *Chroni-
cles* the failure of the crusade is ascribed to "the working of some wicked
spirit" (II, 193).

449 Salems feeble king] This points forward to 1185 when the throne of
Jerusalem was held by Baldwin IV, a leper, and his son Baldwin V, a boy
of delicate health. A delegation was sent to England to ask for Henry's
support against Soldan Saladine. The mission is dealt with in detail in
Book VI, 211–78.

458–9 ere many yeares / Into themselves revolue agayne] A Latinism; see,
for instance, Virgil's *Georgica*: "in se sua per vestigia volvitur annus" (II,
402; May, who translated the *Georgics*, was fond of the phrase; cf. II, 369).

465–566 There in her denn ... Henry's sonns] The description of the un-
derworld, which is mainly based on a similar scene in Virgil's *Aeneid*, VI,
takes on an almost medieval aspect: some of the characters would fit in a
miracle play. The Digby *Mary Magdalene*, for example, has a scene in
which the World, the Flesh, and the Devil discuss which Vice to set on
the Magdalen; they send Luxury in the end. Classical and medieval ele-
ments had been mixed in both epic and elegiac narrative poetry before,
for instance in Sackville's "Induction" to *The Mirror for Magistrates* and
Spenser's *Faerie Queene*.

475–6 Fetter'd was ... the Persian beare] this refers to the prophet Daniel's
vision of the four beasts; the first three of these are a lion, a leopard, and
a bear (Dan 7.2–6); Daniel explains them as representing four Kings in
7.17, but he does not give the names of their kingdoms.

485–7 There Ninus image ... free till then] The warrior-king Ninus found-
ed the Assyrian empire.

489 Sesostres] Sesostris, king of Egypt, set out to conquer the world; in a
list of ambitious emperors, Lucan mentions that he had his chariot drawn
by captive kings (*De bello civili*, X, 276–7).

489–96 there the sonn . . . theire natiues bloods] Lucan calls Alexander the
Great the mad son of Philip ("proles vaesana Philippi," *De bello civili*, X,
20); he compares him to a plague that fills rivers with blood and strikes
with lightning force: "ignotos miscuit amnes / Persarum Euphraten, Indo-
rum sanguine Gangen: / Terrarum fatale malum fulmenque, quod omnes
/ Percuteret pariter populos" (X, 32–35).

492 Swift as the lightning] The lightning is also Julius Caesar's emblem in
Lucan's *De bello civili*, I, 151-7. Swiftness of motion had been attributed
to martial men since Mars: Homer's Ares is the swiftest of the gods
(*Odyssey*, VIII, 330 f.). Dio Cassius had called it Caesar's prime asset as
a general (*Roman History*, Book 42); May points to this passage in an
explanatory note to his *Continuation of Lucan* (D5r, note h). He himself
is fond of ascribing the quality to his hero (see II, 454; IV, 753–5; V, 91,
211, 214); in Henry's case it seems to be based on fact: Peter of Blois says
that "he frequently rode four or five times as far in a day as a normal day's
journey" (quoted from Poole, *OHE* III, 334), and King Louis of France
is said to have marvelled that he seemed "rather to fly than to travel by
horse or ship," a remark that May picks up in Book V (see note to V,
213–15).

497–8 Next him that Roman . . . Captiu'de his countrey] The Roman is
Julius Caesar; he is said to have "sought vnkindly to captiue his countrie"
in Ben Jonson's *Seianus his Fall*, I, 96 (*Ben Jonson*, ed. Herford and Simp-
son, IV [Oxford, 1932], 358); the parallel was pointed out by William D.
Briggs in "The Influence of Jonson's Tragedy in the Seventeenth Cen-
tury," *Anglia* 35 (1912): 297.

510–2 Which Iacobs cruell sonnes . . . were sacrific'de] See Gen. 34. Simeon
and Levi, sons of Jacob, killed the Shechemites in revenge of their sister
Dinah's rape by Shechem in spite of the fact that the rapist repented of
his deed and offered to affiliate his people with Jacob's as an act of atone-
ment. Jacob's sons accepted the offer on the condition that all the She-
chemites be circumcised first. The Shechemites complied, but were killed
nevertheless a few days later "when they were sore."

513–14 There the slayne youth . . . vengefull butchery] The Roman emperor
Antoninus Basianus Caracalla was noted for his cruelties. When the
people of Alexandria objected to his marriage with his mother and com-
pared him to Oedipus, he had them slaughtered by the thousands.

515–22 The captiu'de fate . . . the lustfull Roderike] The fate of Roderick,
last king of the Visigoths, is the subject of William Rowley's tragedy
All's Lost by Lust (acted 1619; printed 1633). Roderick rapes Jacinta, the

daughter of his general Julianus who in revenge betrays him and his country to the Muslims.

529–32 aboue his denn ... bold tribunes] The Ephors were senior magistrates in ancient Sparta who were elected annually by the citizens of the five Spartan towns and had far-reaching powers, including the supervision of the king's activities. The tribunes were elected by the plebeians of ancient Rome to take care of their interests, mainly by vetoing laws and regulations of the Senate and its magistrates. Cicero may have given the clue for linking Ephors and Tribunes; see his *De legibus*; "quare nec ephori Lacedaemone sine causa a Theopompo oppositi regibus nec apud nos consulibus tribuni" (III, 16; *Cicero: De re publica. De legibus*, ed. Clinton W. Keyes [London, 1928], 476).

534–5 Such as the Gracchis ... In ancient Rome] The brothers Tiberius and Gaius Sempronius Gracchus initiated agrarian reforms that widened the split between *populares* and *optimates* in Rome; they both found violent deaths in rebellious actions.

546 There were ... tragœdies] Mycenae was the seat of the dynasty of the Atrides; many of its rulers, from Atreus to Agamemnon, found violent deaths.

547 And all the woes ... had wrought] The Theban kings were famous for their misfortunes, most notably Oedipus and his sons Eteocles and Polynices; see also II, 30 and note.

548–54 There false Medea ... from Iasons face] Medea, daughter of Æetes and endowed with magical faculties, helped Jason win the Golden Fleece from her native Colchis and ran off with him. When Æetes pursued them, she cut her brother Absyrtus to pieces and scattered his limbs in her father's way. Later, when Jason left her for Glauce, she killed two of her sons in the presence of their father and fled in a chariot drawn by winged dragons.

555–60 There strong Alcathoë ... purple haire] Alcathoë is another name for Megara. In Ovid's *Metamorphoses* it is the place where Scylla betrays her father Nisus, "in urbe / Alcathoë, quam Nisus habet" (VIII, 7–8). The town was besieged by Minos of Crete, with whom Scylla fell in love. There was an oracle that the fate of Megara depended on a purple hair (or lock) on Nisus' otherwise silver head. Scylla cut it off to win the favour of Minos, and Megara was conquered.

582–4 Soone as his feasts ... solemnityes] In 1170, "the king held his Easter at Winsor, whither William the Scotish king came with his brother Dauid" (Holinshed, *Chronicles*, II, 130).

589 By Becket . . . has beene fledd] Becket left England after the Council of
Northampton in 1164; see below, Book III, 569–74, and notes.

Book II

8 young Henry's coronation day] The coronation took place at Westminster
Abbey; Holinshed dates it on "the foureteenth daie of June 1170" (Hol-
inshed, *Chronicles*, II, 130), but this is doubtful (see Anne Heslin, "The
Coronation of the Young King in 1170," *Studies in Church History*, Vol.
II, ed. G. J. Cuming [London, 1968], 165–78).

15–18 but king William . . . Dauid bring] The Scottish princes had done
homage to young Henry before; in 1163 "the king of Scots did homage
vnto Henrie the yonger, and deliuered his yonger brother Dauid to the
king his father"; (*Chronicles*, II, 118); now old King Henry again "caused
. . . the king of Scots and his brother Dauid, to doo homage vnto his said
sonne" (131).

19–20 in banish'd Becket's stead . . . vpon his head] The coronation cere-
mony was a prerogative of the archbishop of Canterbury, at that time
Thomas Becket; "but bicause he was banished the realme, the king ap-
pointed the archbishop of Yorke to doo it, which he ought not to have
doone" (*Chronicles*, II, 130).

24 a fatall prodigy] "which deed turned him to much trouble, as after shall
appeare" (*Chronicles*, II, 130). The dire consequences of this ceremony are
repeatedly anticipated in the course of the scene: "The cause (alas) of
woes that must ensue, / And thy great father too too soone shall rue"
(71–2); "his ill-presaging minde" (102); "that shall breede a sadd confu-
sion" (240). The coronation exasperated not only Becket, but also the
Pope and the French king (see below, 254–76).

25–31 How ill . . . did stayne] The passage is modelled on Lucan's *De bello
civili*, I, 92–5: "Nulla fides regni sociis, omnisque potestas / Inpatiens
consortis erit. Nec gentibus ullis / Credite, nec longe fatorum exempla pe-
tantur: / Fraterno primi maduerunt sanguine muri." For Lucan, imperial
impatience is one of the seeds of civil war. Holinshed applies the idea
(and Lucan's phrase) to the rivalry between the Irish chiefs (*Chronicles*, II,
138).

30 Vpon the Theban brothers tragœdyes] Eteocles and Polynices agreed to
share the reign of Thebes by alternation, but Eteocles broke the agree-
ment. This led to the siege of Thebes and eventually their deaths by each
other's hands.

31 Or brothers blood, that Romes first walls did stayne] Remus was slain by his brother Romulus (or at his command) when he jumped in scorn over the wall that Romulus had built on the Palatine hill.

33 Brook'd not old Saturne and his Iupiter] Jupiter won his reign by defeating the Titans, who were led by his father Saturn. May is probably following Lucan's hint at "Titana labores" in *De bello civili*, I, 90.

51 A prudent King ... vpp from ground] Source not identified. Matthew Paris reports that Henry, after one of his own coronations (the third), deposed his crown on the altar of Worcester Cathedral, never to wear it again (*Chronica majora*, 215). Speed connects this incident with similar scruples in Canute and Geoffrey of Bouillon (*Historie*, IX, 6, [9], 486).

81–90 Such cates as those ... theire beauteous Queene] The description is based on that of the bridal feast of Thetis and Peleus in Catullus's *Carmen 64*.

85–8 Where aged Chiron ... Were search'd] Cf. Catullus: "Quorum post abitum princeps e vertice Pelei / Advenit Chiron portans silvestria dona: / Nam quoscumque ferunt campi, quos Thessala magnis / Montibus ora creat, quos propter fluminis undas / Aura parit flores tepidi fecunda Favoni, / Hos indistinctis plexos tulit ipse corollis, / Quo permulsa domus iocundo risit odore. / Confestim Penios adest, viridantia Tempe, / Tempe, quae silvae cingunt super impendentes, / Meliasin linquens claris celebranda choreis, / non vacuos" (*Carmen* 64, 278–88).

89–90 Palæmon, Glaucus, and the greene / Sea-nymphs] The lesser sea-gods accompany Neptune in Virgil's *Aeneid*, V, 823 (together with nymphs and Tritons); Glaucus compares himself to young Palaemon in Ovid's tale of Scylla and Glaucus, *Metamorphoses*, XIII, 918–9; in Claudian's *Epithalamium de nuptiis Honorii Augusti* Palaemon, Glaucus and the Nereids throng around Venus and bring gifts for the newly-wedded pair (165–71). Similar companies are often met with in Elizabethan poetry; Thetis, Glaucus and Palaemon, for instance, are feasted in Neptune's bower near the end of Thomas Lodge's epyllion *Scillaes Metamorphosis* (1589), 751–62.

98 those sumptuous cates] cf. *Continuation*, F1v "with rare / And sumptuous cates".

99–127 King Henry wanton ... from such a pride] In France, it was customary to settle the succession by an early coronation; see Warren, page 19. The sewer anecdote goes back to Matthew Paris, who leaves no doubt about his opinion of the ceremony. "De coronatione regis Henrici III. Junioris nimis detestanda" (*Historia Anglorum, sive, ut vulgo dicitur, Historia minor*, ed. Sir Frederick Madden, vol. I [London, 1866], 352–3).

This was paraphrased in Holinshed's *Chronicles* (II, 130–1) and in Speed's *Historie* (IX, 6 [36–7], 493). May refers to Polydore Vergil as his source (see marginal note to line 118); he took his material, however, from Speed, including the source reference: his sidenote is identical with that in Speed's *Historie* ("*Polydor. Virg. in H.2.*"; Holinshed refers only to "*Polydor*"); like Speed he calls Henry's mock office that of a "servitor," whereas Holinshed uses the more technical term "sewer," and he gives, like Speed, the episode a lighter touch ("the Prelate gently smyl'd"; Speed: "the Archbishop of York saying in pleasance to the young King"). Holinshed leaves Polydore Vergil's "ioci causa" untranslated but keeps his stern comment: "Thus the yoong man of an euill and peruerse nature, was puffed vp in pride by his fathers vnseemelie dooings" (Speed, *History*, IX, 6 [37], 493; for full source texts see App. 1, pp. 229–32).

136–7 There like a fire … could make] In pre-Copernican terms, aether was the Fifth Element, lighter and more refined than earthly fire, and found only in the region of the stars.

143 Amidd'st those sparkling beautyes] May uses the same expression for the ladies that resort to the court of Edward III (*King Edward the Third*, 1635, L7r).

147–57 on the state … And all the rest] There is a flight of Amoretti fluttering about the head and shoulders of a statue of Venus in Spenser's *Faerie Queene*, IV, x, 42. May's model, however, is Claudian's *Epithalamium*, 77–83 where a thousand Cupids ("gens mollis Amorum," 73) play around the palace of Venus. The *Epithalamium* suggested the whole scene; Claudian personifies Licentia, Ira, Excubiae, Lacrimae, Pallor Audacia, Metus, Voluptas and "lasciva Periuria"; May's addition of "ruffes or tires" gives it a boudoir atmosphere not unlike that in Pope's *Rape of the Lock*.

157–64 They say … wings display] The description of Venus and her train resembles a decorative passage at the center of Spenser's *Prothalamion*, lines 37–126; but Venus is a frequent guest at weddings; see for instance Ovid's *Metamorphoses*, IX, 796; X, 295.

160 on a sounding Triton's backe] In Claudian's *Epithalamium* Triton is summoned (or bribed) to carry Venus to the court of Honorius (129–30); a swarm of Cupids follows them (lines 151–4).

163–4 The siluer Swanns … wings display] Venus is traditionally associated with swans. The swans in Spenser's *Prothalamion*, for example, are also alternately snow white and silvery (lines 40–1, 56).

168–73 Some high exploit … the Shepheard] This list of Cupid's pranks is modelled on Claudian's *Epithalamium*, where Venus asks her son what mischief he is up to now: " 'Quid tantum gavisus?' ait; 'quae proelia sudas / Improbe? quis iacuit telis? iterumne Tonantem / Inter Sidonias cogis mugire iuvencas? / An Titana domas? an pastoralia Lunam / Rursus in antra vocas? durum magnumque videris / Debellasse deum.' " (111–16).

169–70 As that ... Europaes loue] Jupiter took on the shape of a bull to carry off the beautiful Europa. This is only one of his disguises; see the catalogue of his amorous adventures below, III, 111–20.

171 rough Neptune] In Ovid's *Metamorphoses*, V, 365–70, Venus mentions that Cupid has vanquished both Jupiter and Neptune with his weapons. Drayton links Jupiter's seduction of Io with Neptune's of Amymone in his *Heroicall Epistles* ("Rosamond to King Henry," 154–66; "Henry to Rosamond," 171–6). May picks up Claudian's "durum ... deum," (see note on 168–73) but leaves open which of Neptune's amorous adventures he has in mind.

172–3 Or warm'd ... the Shepheard] Cynthia, the goddess of the moon and of chastity, fell in love with the shepherd Endymion, whom she watched sleeping naked on Mount Latmos, and descended from the sky to join him.

193 How much ... the rest] The idea that Cynthia outshines the stars is commonplace; see Leander's prayer to Cynthia in Ovid's *Heroides*, "quantum, cum fulges radiis argentea puris, / Concedunt flammis sidera cuncta tuis" (XVIII, 71–2), and cf. Spenser's "Cynthia doth shend / The lesser starres" (*Prothalamion*, 121–2). May had used it before in his tragedy *Julia Agrippina*, IV, 424–7.

193–5 So golden Venus ... Achilles heart] Aphrodite is habitually called "golden" in the Homeric Hymns. When Deidamia first appears to Achilles, Statius compares her to Venus; "sed quantum virides pelagi Venus addita Nymphas / obruit, aut umeris quantum Diana reliquit / Naiadas, effulget tantum regina decori / Deidamia chori pulchrisque sororibus obstat" (*Thebais*, I, 293–6).

207–8 Even blacke it selfe ... of the light] Cf. Sidney's *Astrophel and Stella*, Sonnet 7: "When Nature made her chiefe worke, Stella's eyes, / In colour blacke why wrapt she beames so bright?" or his description of Philoclea, "with the sweet caste of her black eye" in *The Old Arcadia* (ed. Jean Robertson [Oxford, 1973], 37).

245 That soveraigne beauty] Samuel Daniel makes the idea that "Loue and Maiestie dwell ill togither" one of the main points in his *Complaint of Rosamond*; "*Henry* the second, that so highly weigh'd me, / Found well

(by proofe) the priuiledge of beauty, / That it had powre to counter-
maund all duty" (868, 166–8; ed. Grosart, *Works*, I, 112, 87).

254 Swift-winged fame] Virgil calls Fama "swift-winged" ("pedibus celerem
et pernicibus alis," *Aeneid*, IV, 180).

261–3 That reason ... theire prey] The courtiers are, apparently, May's
invention. In Speed's *Historie*, furies fire the king's indignation: "Adde
hereunto, that this vnlucky Coronations triumphs, were celebrated with
bon-fires kindled by the furies in *Normandie*; which *Lewis* the *French*
King inuaded with fire and sword, because his daughter *Margaret* was not
crowned as well as the young king her husband" (Speed, *Historie*, IX, 6
[38], 493).

311 Her birth and countrey] Rosamond was the daughter of Walter de
Clifford, an Anglo-Norman with estates in Herefordshire and Wiltshire.

317–26 So when ... Calisto's there] In Ovid's *Metamorphoses* (II, 409–40),
Jupiter's conquest of Callisto is very much a matter of *veni, vidi, vici*: he
meets her while inspecting the damage done to Arcady by the rash Phae-
ton, approaches her disguised as Diana, and carries her by surprise and by
force ("sed quem superare puella, / Quisve Iovem poterat," 436–37). Jupi-
ter's predilection for Arcady is older than his passion for the nymph (cf.
Metamorphoses, II, 405–6). There was a tradition that he was raised in
Arcady, not on Crete. Jupiter's longing for Callisto appears to be May's
invention. He may have taken it from Ovid's Venus who prefers Adonis
to her heavenly abode, "caelo praefertur Adonis" (*Metamorphoses*, X, 532).

335–7 No roses ... vpon the flower] This may be an attempt to erase, by
wordplay, the infamous pun on Rosamond's name in an epitaph that, ac-
cording to Ranulf Higden, once disfigured Rosamond's tomb: "Hic jacet
in tumba Rosa mundi non rosa munda, / Non redolet sed olet quod redo-
lere solet" (*Polychronicon*, VII, xxii, 54); a similar pun is made in Gerald
of Wales's *De principis instructione*, II, iv, 165 (see note to V, 403–4, for
an extract).

347–51 Honours bright Goddesse ... The warrlike lance] Pallas Athene,
traditionally the rival of Venus, is habitually represented as wearing a
plumed helmet and a spear.

355–6 her eyes ... humane sight] This is another reference to the Ptolemaic
notion of an uncorrupted sphere beyond the sublunary world, but also a
hint at the traditionally winking eyes of coquettes, for instance the "amo-
rous blenking / Of fair Cresseid" in Henryson's *Testament of Cresseid*
(503–4).

357–9 Nor did shee ... to make] Goddesses do not walk; a floating movement is one of their "divini signa decoris" and betrays them even in disguise, as it does Venus and Iris in Virgil's *Aeneid* (I, 405; V, 649).

361 Forgettfull Henry] Aeneas is roused in similar terms by Mercury in Virgil's *Aeneid* when he is about to forget his divine duty in the arms of Dido, "heu regni rerumque oblite tuarum" (IV, 267). Mercury also reminds Aeneas of his reputation and the future of his offspring (IV, 272-6).

369 Ten yeares ... agayne] A Latinism; see, for example, "volventibus annis," Virgil, *Aeneid*, I, 22, and cf. note to I, 458-9.

370-80 Since that late Pope ... affection chuse] This refers to the Bull "Laudabiliter" in which Pope Adrian IV († 1159) sanctioned in advance Henry's conquest of Ireland. John of Salisbury carried it from Rome to England. The original of the Bull is now lost, but Gerald of Wales has a transcript in his *Expugnatio Hibernica* (*Opera*, ed. Dimock, V, 317-8). Gerald also says that John brought a golden ring: "Per quem etiam idem papa Anglorum regi annulum aureum in investituræ signum præsentavit" (*Expugnatio*, 316); John of Salisbury had mentioned an emerald ornament on this ring ("smaragdo Annulum optimo decoratum," 316, n. 2).

403-4 To graspe great France ... vncontroll'd possession] May anticipates the successful campaigns of Edward III and Henry V during the Hundred Years War. Edward III captured the French king at Poitiers in 1356; this is treated at length in May's epic poem on Edward's life, *King Edward III* (1635). It is worth remembering that English monarchs in May's time claimed to be kings of France and retained the style shown in the lettering of Vaughan's frontispiece to the printed edition of *King Henry* (see Fig. 11, p. 136).

405-11 When Cæsar's deeds ... Alexia taken] The references are to the last phase of Julius Caesar's conquest of Gaul, 52-51 B.C.

408-9 his strongest enemy / Stout Vercingentorix] Vercingetorix was the chief of the Arverni. He led the revolt of Gaul against Rome in 52 B.C.

410 Arvaricum's fam'd sacke] Avaricum, now Bourges sur Yèvre, was besieged and taken by Caesar in 52 B.C. (see C. Julius Caesar, *De bello gallico*, VII, 14-33).

411 Alexia taken] Vercingetorix was enclosed and eventually captured in Alesia or Alexia, now Alise-Sainte Reine (see Caesar, *De bello gallico*, VII, 68-90).

412 Of Cressy, Poictiers, Agincourt] These famous English victories, all gained during the Hundred Years War (1346, 1356, and 1425), had been the subjects of two historical poems written shortly before May's *Reigne*

of King Henry the Second, Michael Drayton's *The Battaile of Agincourt* (1627, reissued 1631) and Charles Aleyn, *The Battailes of Cresy and Poictiers* (1631, expanded 1633).

418–24 Oft horrid warres ... wholly vindicate] The Tudor conquest of Gaelic Ireland was accomplished by two Elizabethan generals, Mountjoy and Carew, who defeated the combined Irish forces of Tyrone and O'Donnell and parts of a Spanish expeditionary corps under Alonzo del Campo at Kinsale in 1601.

425 There wise King Iames ... English law] This credit is given to King John, among others, in a passage of Speed's *Historie* which provides several points of comparison with May's eulogy on the Stuarts: "The first, who planted *English Lawes* and *Officers* in *Ireland*, & both annexed that *Kingdome*, and fastned *Wales* to the Crowne of *English Monarchs*, he was the *first* who enlarged the *Royall* style, with *Lord of Ireland*: a matter of greater import for *Englands Peace*, then all the *French* Titles euer yet haue prooued" (IX, 8 [63], 572). For Ben Jonson, both King John and the Tudors had won nothing but titles in Ireland; he praises King James for achieving the ultimate conquest and appeasement in one of *The Speeches for Prince Henrie's Barriers* (1610): "*Ireland* that more in title, then in fact / Before was conquer'd, is his *Lawrels* act." (lines 347–8, *Ben Jonson*, ed. Herford & Simpson, VII [Oxford, 1941], 333).

431 The long wish'd ... lands] The dynastic union of England and Scotland brought about by James VI of Scotland and I of England.

436–42 Renowned Charles ... as in royalty] The rigid manners and morals which Charles I introduced at his court differed sharply from the lax practices of his father's (see Kevin Sharpe, "The Image of Virtue: The Court and Household of Charles I, 1625–1642," in David Starkey et al., *The English Court: From the Wars of the Roses to the Civil War*, London, 1987, 226–60). Even the Puritan Lady Lucy Hutchinson had to admit that "the temperate and chast and serious" Charles cleansed the court of its excesses (quoted from David Norbrook, *Poetry and Politics in the English Renaissance* [London, 1984], 249).

Book III

7–22 at Vendosme ... dignity] Roger of Hoveden dates the interview at Vendôme 22 July 1170; "pacem fecit cum *Lodowico* rege, in colloquio apud Wendoniam in festo *S. Maria Magdalenæ*, promittens quod in proximo iterum faceret filium suum coronari, & uxorem suam cum eo" (*Annales*, ed. Savile, 518, 24–6). May's phrasing suggests that he followed

Holinshed's translation; "both the kings came to an enteruiew at Uendosme, where at length they were accorded, vpon promise made by king Henrie, that he would cause his sonne to be crowned againe, and with him his wife the said Margaret the French kings daughter as queene" (*Chronicles*, II, 131). Young Henry was crowned again, with his wife Margaret, at Winchester in August 1172 (see Warren, *Henry II*, 111).

26–34 And in his noble breast ... On fitter tearmes] Dermot MacMurrough, the king of Leinster, had been expelled from Dublin by the king of Connaught and looked to Henry for support. He eventually met him in Aquitaine in 1167 and obtained permission to recruit mercenaries and adventurers for an invasion of Ireland. Holinshed links the idea of an Irish campaign with the difficult situation after the murder of Becket, early in 1171: "About which time it came into the kings mind, to make a conquest of Ireland upon this occasion" (*Chronicles*, II, 138). Speed is even more explicit: "*Henry* therefore, among so many perplexities rising out of the Archbishops murther, saw no way so ready for the calming his owne perturbations, or for the auerting mens thoughts from the consideration of that scandalous Tragedie, as to vndertake some great and noble enterprise, which now offered it selfe very seasonably" (*Historie*, IX, 6 [46], 495). May leaves no doubt about the nobility of the enterprise by placing the resolution for a conquest of Ireland before his account of the Becket scandal.

41 Erato] The Muse of lyric, and in particular amorous, poetry.

45 That farre renowned shade of Mirtles] Elysium is a part of the Weeping Fields in Hades where love's victims mourn their fates hidden in a forest of myrtle trees (see *Aeneid*, VI, 440–4).

51–2 Such as the pale-fac'de Daffadill ... did come] Narcissus, who spurned the love of Echo, was drowned following his own reflection and changed into a daffodil.

53–4 And purple Hyacinth ... Spartan youth] Apollo accidentally killed the boy Hyacinthus with a disk; the flower grew from the boy's blood. Hyacinth was worshipped at Amyclae, south of Sparta.

55–7 Adonis ... there appeare] Adonis was killed by a boar; Venus, who had fallen in love with him, shed tears over his corpse; May refers to Ovid's version of the myth: Venus sprinkles nectar on the blood of the hunter and thus raises the short-lived anemone (*Metamorphoses*, X, 717–39).

58 The pining Clyties ... violett] Clytia unhappily loved Phoebus Apollo, and even when changed into a sunflower (or a tagetes) followed his daily

course. The colours are taken from Ovid's description, "partemque coloris / Luridus exsangues pallor convertit in herbas; / Est in parte rubor violaeque simillimus ora / Flos tegit" (*Metamorphoses*, IV, 266–9).

62–4 Thou saw'st ... ambitious love] Semele was a daughter of Cadmus, the founder of Thebes. Jupiter fell in love with her, and jealous Juno brought about her death by making her ask her lover to appear in his divine shape. Jupiter did so reluctantly, and she was burnt to death.

65–6 There with ... mistaking hand] Procris was killed by a spear flung by her husband Cephalus who mistook her for a beast of prey.

67–8 Faire Dido too ... was left] Dido, the queen of Carthage, killed herself with the sword that the Trojan hero Aeneas left behind when he sailed for Italy.

69–71 And there ... Cleopatra walk'd] Cleopatra killed herself by applying an asp to her breast rather than falling into the hands of Octavian, the rival of her lover Marc Antony.

72 Lesbian Sappho] The poetess Sappho threw herself from the cliff of Leucas when Phaon spurned her love.

72 sadd Eryphile] Eriphyle was the wife of Amphiaraus who went into hiding to escape being drafted into the Argives' campaign against Thebes because he knew that would be his death. When Eriphyle allowed herself to be bribed into disclosing his hiding place Amphiaraus ordered his son Alcmaeon to kill her as soon as he received news of his death. Alcmaeon obeyed.

73 The wailing Phædra] Phaedra fell in love with her stepson Hippolytus; when he spurned her advances, she sent him to his death and killed herself in despair.

73 sham'd Pasiphaë] Pasiphae was the Cretan queen in whom Neptune kindled a passion for a bull.

74 Chast Thisbe] Thisbe stabbed herself in despair when she found the torn garment of her lover Pyramus and believed him killed by a lion.

74 incestuous Canace] Canace had a child by her brother Macareus; her father forced her to kill herself when the trespass was discovered.

75 the much lamented Sestian Maide] Hero, a priestess of Venus, threw herself from the tower of Sestos when her lover Leander was drowned in the Hellespont.

84 to waite on Elianor the Queene] There is little evidence to support the suggestion that Rosamond was employed in the royal household; Wilfred Warren has found "a possible reference to a mistress of Henry employed in Queen Eleanor's household" in the Pipe Roll 30 Henry II, 134–5,

where a large sum is allowed by the king himself "for the clothes of the queen and of Bellebelle" (*Henry II*, 601–2, note 3).

91–6 When hee . . . at second sight] Long absence is one of the remedies of love recommended by Ovid: "lentus abesto" (*Remedia amoris*, 243).

101–3 For him . . . proudly plead] In Daniel's *Complaint of Rosamond*, Henry employs similar means of persuasion: "Thither he daily messages doth send, / With costly Iewels (Orators of Loue,) / Which (ah, too well men know) doe women moue" (376–8). May himself had ascribed similar powers to Antony, "his fame and glory, / His power, and gifts the strongest Oratory / Had woo'd, and wonne the Queene to his delight" (*Continuation of Lucan*, C6v).

104 As second causes serve the will of Ioue] The difference between the first cause (or Creator) and secondary causes (which govern the natural world) was a matter of debate in Renaissance philosophy (Giordano Bruno, Francis Bacon). May uses it with almost Popean joviality.

111 When hee . . . would for Europa bee] Jupiter took on the shape of a bull to abduct Europa, cf. above, II, 169–70.

112 A showre of gold for beautious Danaë] Jupiter visited Danae, whom her father had shut away in a brazen bower, in the shape of a shower of gold; see also below, 204.

113 A Swann for Leda] Jupiter took on the likeness of a swan and, pretending to be pursued by an eagle, sought shelter in the arms of Leda.

136 Cupid's golden shaft] In his tale of Apollo and Daphne, Ovid gives Cupid two darts, a golden one to excite love, and a leaden one to expel it (*Metamorphoses*, I, 468–71).

169–75 No Beldame . . . the Troian's bedd] This refers to a scene in Homer's *Iliad* which shows Helen watching the battlefield from the walls of Troy. Aphrodite approaches her in the guise of an old Spartan woman and lures her away into the bed of Paris whom she has just rescued from the attacks of wrathful Menelay. May's wording is close to Chapman's translation of the incident: "To give her errand good success, she [i.e., Aphrodite] tooke on her the shape / Of beldame Graea who was brought by Helen in her rape / From Lacedaemon and had trust in all her secrets still, / Being old, and had (of all her maids) the maine bent of her will, / And spun for her the finest wooll" (*Iliad*, III, 403–7).

181–4 No farther . . . a forrest] In Daniel's *Complaint of Rosamond* the consummation of Henry's love takes place in a "sollitarie Grange" (373).

191–6 Such was that bower . . . care away] Venus' visit to Mount Ida, and her union with Anchises, is recounted in one of the Homeric hymns to

BOOK III

165

Aphrodite (V, 53–90). Phineas Fletcher wrote an epyllion on *Venus and Anchises* (publ. anonymously in 1628) that contains a lavish description of the grove and bower in which the goddess is discovered by the shepherd. In the Homeric hymn (as in May's epic) the union is consummated in a stately house rather than a grove; Aphrodite's head touches the roof when she rises from the couch (172–5). In his selection from May's poem Henry Headley reminds his readers (with a reference to Spenser's Sonnet 70) that "bower" meant "retreat" in May's time (*Select Beauties*, I, 156).

193–5 About this house ... ever blow] Claudian describes the surroundings of the palace of Venus on Cyprus in similar terms: "Intus rura micant, manibus quae subdita nullis / Perpetuum florent, Zephyro contenta colono" (*Epithalamium*, 60–1; Zephyrus is the West Wind).

195–6 faire youth ... care away] Cf. Claudian's "alta cervice Iuventas / Excludit Senium luco" (*Epithalamium*, 84–5).

204 Danaë in the brazen tower] See above, note to 112. In Daniel's *Complaint of Rosamond* it is the beldame who compares Henry to Jove (239–42).

209–51 Into a spatious gallery ... Turn'd her to stone] In Drayton's *Heroicall Epistles* the palace in Woodstock has a gallery with a picture of chaste Lucrece that Rosamond notices with obvious moral effect: when a maid asks her about its subject, Rosamond can hardly answer her for shame ("The Epistle of Rosamond to King Henry the Second," 93–104). May's main source for the motif is, however, Daniel's *Complaint of Rosamond*, where Henry sends Rosamond a casket decorated with mythological scenes, in particular the rapes of Amymone and Io. In her Complaint, which she speaks from Hades, Rosamond reads these pictures as foreshadowing her own fate.

218–20 the seuerity ... hee spy'de] In Drayton's *Heroicall Epistles* Rosamond mentions a statue of Diana that adorns a fountain in Woodstock Park. It makes her feel pursued by her guilt as Actaeon was by his hounds ("Epistle of Rosamond," 140–7).

221–6 Yett this ... lovers payne] Virgil mentions that Pan used a white fleece to lure Diana into the forest of Arcady and seduce her there (*Georgica*, III, 391–3); May had translated the passage as follows: "So with a snowy fleeced Ram (if we / Trust fame) did *Pan* the god of Arcady / Deceiue thee *Luna*, nor didst thou disdaine / Within the Woods to ease a Louers Paine" (*Virgill's Georgicks Englished* [London, 1628], F6v).

227–231 See Atalanta ... to Hippomenes] Swift-footed Atalanta challenged

her suitors to a running contest and killed the losers. Hippomenes outran
her by dropping three golden apples in her course. In Daniel's *Complaint*
Rosamond compares her falling for the "glittering pompe" of Henry's
court to Atalanta's stooping (360-8).

244–51 behold that cruell fate ... to stone] The story of Iphis and Anaxa-
rete is told in Ovid's *Metamorphoses*; scorned by Anaxarete, Iphis hangs
himself from the posts of her door (XIV, 764).

271 kings haue greater soules] Magnanimity is one of the royal virtues; this
goes back to classical philosophy, and in particular to Aristotle, who de-
fines *megalopsychia* in his *Nicomachian Ethics*, 1123 b.2. Drayton attributes
the virtue to heroes in his foreword "To the Reader" of the 1619 edition
of his *Heroicall Epistles* (ed. Hebel, *Works*, II, 130).

291–7 a divorce may doo it ... Rome bee wonne] Eleanor had been married
to Louis VII for 14 years before they were divorced on the ground of
consanguinity or, "for consanguinitie and adulterie (saith Paris)" (Speed,
Historie, IX, 5 [42], 480). The papal decree came in March 1152; a
month later, Henry was married to Eleanor. Gervase of Canterbury re-
ports that in October 1175 Henry bribed the papal legate Uguccione to
support a divorce (*The Chronicle of the Reigns of Stephen, Henry II, and
Richard I, Historical Works*, I, 257). Gerald of Wales mentions that Henry
contemplated divorcing Eleanor when he was enamoured of Alice, the be-
trothed of his son Richard (*De principis instructione*, III, ii, ed. Warner,
Opera, VIII, 232).

305 Nor had shee leisure to dispute the case] In Daniel's *Complaint of Rosa-
mond* the concubine remembers that she had ample time to "ballance" her
state, but proved too weak to follow her conscience (358).

321 so fresh a Rose] This may be another hint at the epitaph on Rosa-
mond's tomb; see above, note to II, 335–7.

324–28 A brave and noble offspring ... Earledomes heire] Henry had two
known illegitimate sons, but both were born before his marriage; one of
them was William Longsword (see Warren, *Henry II*, 119). There is no
clear evidence, but it was widely believed that William was Rosamond's
son. May probably took his information from Speed's *History*: "*William*,
the naturall sonne of *King Henry*, borne of *Rosamund*, was surnamed in
French, *Longespee*, in *English*, Long-sword. Hee was Earle of *Salisbury*, in
right of *Ela* his Wife, Daughter and heire of *William*, heir of that county,
sonne of Earl *Patrick*; by whom hee had issue *William* Earle of *Salisbury*,
Stephen Earle of *Vlster*, *Ela* Countesse of *Warwicke*, *Idâ* Lady *Beacham* of
Bedford, and *Isabell* Lady *Vescie*: his sonne Earle *William* the second, had

Earle *William* the third, Father of *Margaret*, wife of *Henry Lacie* Earle of *Lincolne:* he dyed in the Castle of old *Salisbury*, and was buried in the Cathedrall Church of the new City, in the ninth yeere of the raigne of King *Henry* the third." (IX, 6 [112], 512).

339–45 the Pope is discontent . . . desire] "In this mean while Thomas the archbishop of Canturburie remained in exile almost six yeares, and could not be restored, till partlie by swelling threats of the pope, and partlie at the earnest suit of Lewes the French king, Theobald earle of Blois, and others king Henrie began somewhat to shew himselfe conformable towards an agreement" (Holinshed, *Chronicles*, II, 131–2).

355–64 A sumptuous bower . . . this beautious Paragon] The bower and maze at Woodstock are first mentioned in Ranulf Higden's *Polychronicon* (c. 1350): "Huic nempe puellæ spectatissimæ fecerat rex apud Wodestok mirabilis architecturæ cameram opere Dædalino sinuatam" (ed. Joseph Lumby, VIII, 52). In a note to his "Epistle of Rosamond" Drayton says that the ruins of the labyrinth are still extant (*Heroicall Epistles*, ed. Hebel, *Works*, II, 139). Camden, however, had reported them lost as early as 1586 in his *Britannia* (see Heltzel, *Fair Rosamond*, 7–8).

367 neere Ambois] Holinshed is not very precise about the place of the final meeting ("at length another meeting was assigned at a certeine place neere the confines of Normandie," *Chronicles*, II, 133), nor is Speed; Roger of Hoveden, however, gives an exact date and place: "Facta est autem pax ista inter Archiepiscopum & regem Angliæ, quarto Idus Octobris feria secunda, in monte laudato, qui est inter Turonim & Ambasium" (*Annales*, ed. Savile, 520, 9–10).

380 Of Monkes then living] Contemporary chronicles, of which there are many, dealing with the events that led up to the martyrdom of Thomas Becket, were, of course, mostly written by monks, but had been put to use nevertheless by generations of post-Reformation historians. Holinshed's main sources are William of Newburgh's *Historia rerum Anglicarum* and the chronicles of Matthew Paris. Speed, too, rests his treatment of the "main controuersie betwixt *Regnum & Sacerdotium*, the *Crowne* and the *Mitre*," as he calls it (*Historie*, IX, 6 [14], 488) on "the reports of two learned Monkes who then liued (for such Authors onely wee will herein follow, as shall be vnpartiall)." A marginal note names "Will of Newburgh & Matthew Paris" again (*Historie*, IX, 6 [11], 487). May's marginal note refers to William only ("The Monke of Nuborough lib: 2. has all this," III, 380, marg.); the form of the reference and its precision point to Speed as his immediate source. Holinshed usually calls William "Parvus"

and rarely gives a book or other specification; Speed calls William "the
Monke of *Nuborough*" in his text and refers to "*Gul. Nubrig. lib 2.c.16*" in
a sidenote (*Historie*, IX, 6 [11], 487).

386–90 Whoo dooes not know . . . Arabia yett] There are similar references
to the "dark ages" in IV, 279–96 and V, 277. In his appreciation of the
Middle Ages Thomas May sides with Francis Bacon, who had treated
them as a period of scientific decline, rather than with Samuel Daniel,
who had stood by them in his *Defence of Rhyme*. May's lines resemble a
passage in Bacon's *Novum Organon* which extols three eras of scientific
advancement, the Greek, the Roman and the Renaissance, but depreciates
medieval scholars: "Media mundi tempora, quoad scientiarum segetem
uberem aut laetam, infoelicia fuerunt. Neque enim causa est, ut vel Arabum
vel Scholasticorum mentio fiat: qui per intermedia tempora scientias potius
contriverunt numerosis tractatibus, quam pondus earum auxerunt." (*The
Works of Francis Bacon*, ed. James Spedding, Robert Leslie Ellis, and Doug-
las D. Heath [London, 1858], I, 186); for Daniel's attitude see May McKi-
sack, *Medieval History in the Tudor Age* (Oxford, 1971), 120–1, 234–5.

391 wisest writers of those tymes] Chief of these would be Roger Hoveden,
William of Newburgh, and Matthew Paris, all favourably mentioned by
Speed. Early Stuart historiographers like Speed were less suspicious of
chronicles from the age of "fatall darkenesse" than their Tudor forerun-
ners such as Foxe and Holinshed; Foxe, for instance, approaches New-
burgh with more caution: "And, although scarcely any testimony is to be
taken of that age, being all blinded and corrupted with superstition, yet
let us hear what Neuburgensis, an ancient historiographer, saith . . ." (*Acts
and Monuments*, ed. Townsend, II, 247); cf. Stubbs, ed. Hoveden, "Pref-
ace," lxx, and Poole, *OHE*, 203.

393–404 The powerfull Prelates . . . of people sought] William of Newburgh
dates this development from the time of the prelates' return from the
Council of Tours (May, 1163): "Regressis a concilio ad proprias sedes
episcopis, regnum et sacerdotium in Anglia disceptare cœperunt, et facta
est turbatio non modica super prærogativa ordinis clericalis. Regi quippe
circa curam regni satagenti, et malefactores sine delectu exterminari ju-
benti, a judicibus intimatum est, quod multa contra disciplinam publicam,
scilicet furta, rapinæ, homicidia, a clericis sæpius committerentur, ad quos
scilicet laicæ non posset jurisdictionis vigor extendi" (*Historia rerum
Anglicarum*, II, xvi, 140).

407–415 An hundred murders . . . punish them] "Denique ipso audiente de-
claratum dicitur, plusquam centum homicidia intra fines Angliæ a clericis

sub regno ejus commissa. Quamobrem acri motu turbatus, in spiritu vehe-
menti contra malefactores clericos posuit leges, in quibus utique zelum
justitiæ publicæ habuit, sed fervor immoderatior modum excessit" (New-
burgh, *Historia Rerum Anglicarum*, II, xvi, 140); the passage is translated
with slight modifications in Holinshed's *Chronicles*, II, 119. Like Holins-
hed, May tones down Henry's "immoderate" zeal.

416–23 King Henry weighing ... royall power] Holinshed relates how
Henry, at the Council of Westminster, asked the bishops "whether they
would obserue his roiall lawes and customes, which the archbishops and
bishops in the time of his grandfather did hold and obeie or not?"
(*Chronicles*, II, 119; his source is Gervase of Canterbury). This demand
was fixed in the preamble to the Clarendon Constitutions.

423–24 those lawes ... had slept] Stephen reigned, with intervals, from
1135 to 1153; his title was doubtful. After his accession, he sought and
obtained a confirmation of his title by Pope Innocent II.

428 the tyme for Papall claymes] In later editions of Speed's *Historie* these
claims are linked with the pamphlet war after the Gunpowder Plot, when
Catholics were asked to take an oath of allegiance to the crowne, which
was condemned by the Pope. Speed suggests that the political situation at
the beginning of King John's reign was so explosive that the smoke has
not yet been dispelled, "all which, like so many Tragicke fire-breathing
Furies, set this State in so horrible combustion, as that the smoake is not
as yet, so many ages after, quite allayed." A marginal note makes the allu-
sion specific by naming some of the prominent Catholic pamphleteers:
"In *Baronius, Bellarmine, Becauus, Gretser, Shioppius*, and other Papall pre-
tenders to the English Crowne." (Speed, *History*, IX, 8 [1], 532; for the
pamphlet war see the chapter "The Gunpowder Plot and the Oath of
Allegiance" in Robert Lockyer's *The Early Stuarts: A Political History of
England 1603–1642* [London, 1989], 284–7).

433–34 Hee thought ... stept in] Stephen's main antagonist and rival for
the English title was the empress Maud, Henry's mother, who had been
designated as heiress to England and Normandy by her father, Henry I.
The successors of Pope Innocent, Celestine II and Eugenius III, sup-
ported her cause (see Poole, *OHE*, III, 192–5). When Stephen tried to
secure the English succession for his son Eustace, the archbishop of
Canterbury refused to consecrate the prince, "by commandement from the
Pope," as Speed says, adding in an aside "(whose holy See can deale on
both sides, as makes most for their aduantage)" (*Historie*, IX, 5 [42],
480).

435–50 So in the age ... the satisfaction] Innocent III laid an interdict on England in 1208 and in 1209 excommunicated King John, who had to resign his kingdoms and do homage to the Pope in order to be released (see Poole, *OHE*, 456–7).

449–50 To Arthur ... the satisfaction] After the death of King Richard, there was a brief struggle for the succession between John and his nephew Arthur who was backed by the chiefs of Anjou, Maine, and Tours. John was suspected of having murdered his nephew in the course of this struggle.

451–66 Those wholesome lawes ... the Kings request] The Council of Westminster was held on 1 October 1163. The terminology may be significant here. Gervase of Canterbury calls it a convocation, "convocatis episcopis apud Westmonasterim simul cum archiepiscopo de criminosis clericis" (*The Chronicle of the Reigns of Stephen, Henry II, and Richard I*, ed. William Stubbs, *Historical Works*, Vol. I [London, 1879], 174). Holinshed speaks of "a parlement at Westminster" (*Chronicles*, II, 119) and mentions bishops and clergy as participants. May, who adopts Holinshed's term and uses it again in III, 563, introduces peers and commoners, thus isolating the clergy and evoking the atmosphere of a parliamentary debate. There was, of course, no parliament in any strict sense of the term in the middle of the twelfth century, at best it was a Great Council attended by barons and bishops as at Clarendon and Northampton in 1164 (see Warren, *Henry II*, 303). The question of the antiquity of parliaments was a matter of debate in the early seventeenth century. Sir Robert Cotton, for instance, had written a treatise on "The Antiquity and Dignity of Parliaments," and May himself was to publish a *Discourse Concerning the Success of Former Parliaments* (1642) which attempts to prove, in the words of the antiquarian William Oldys, "the esteem that English Parliaments were anciently held in" (quoted from Allan Chester, *Thomas May: Man of Letters*, 175). The Elizabethan opinion, held by chroniclers like Holinshed and apparently shared by May, was that Henry I summoned the first parliament at Salisbury in 1116. The date was questioned in Stuart times but not the belief that from the beginning English parliaments had included representatives of the Commons; for details of the debate see E. Evans, "Of the Antiquity of Parliaments in England: Some Elizabethan and Early Stuart opinions," *History* 23 (1939): 206–21.

456–9 Some Prelates only ... the Kings desire] "Nempe episcopi [...] arbitrantur obsequium se præstare Deo et ecclesiæ," Newburgh, *Historia*, II, xvi, 141. Newburgh does not refer to the council of Westminster

specifically; the chroniclers who do (such as Hoveden and Holinshed),
attest that the bishops were united in their refusal of the king's desire
(Hoveden, *Annales*, 492,51–4; Holinshed, *Chronicles*, II, 119). It was only
later in the year that Henry was able to win some of them over to his side.
468 Calliope] The Muse of rhetoric and heroic poetry.
469–72 A London citizen ... for dignity] For this short portrait, May went
to William of Newburgh's *Historia rerum Anglicarum*: "Sane idem Thomas
Lundoniis oriundus, vir acris ingenii et competentis eloquii, vultu et mori-
bus elegans, in efficacia quoque rerum agendarum nulli secundus" (II, xvi,
139); cf. Holinshed, who introduces Becket without mentioning his mental
endowments (*Chronicles*, II, 117). Becket was born in London in 1118, the
son of a Norman merchant. He rose through the service of Theobald, his
predecessor as archbishop, who appointed him archdeacon of Canterbury.
475–6 from thence the warre ... an able souldier] Becket took part in
several campaigns in France, in particular the unsuccessful one against
Toulouse in 1159. Becket's role as a warrior was played down in later
chronicles, but William FitzStephen has two chapters on his military ser-
vice, "Qualiter Cancellarius regis servierit in sua gerra de Tolosa" and
"Item qualiter se habuerit in guerra Francorum" (*Materials for the History
of Thomas Becket*, ed. James Craigie Robertson, vol. III [London, 1877],
33–5).
479–80 Whoo when hee first ... Lord Chancellour] "Cum autem Henricus
secundus, defuncto Stephano, ... regnum hereditarium suscepisset, virum
coram regibus stare idoneum sibi deesse non passus, sublimitatis regiæ
fecit cancellarium" (Newburgh, *Historia*, II, xvi, 139). Henry was crowned
in October 1154; he made Becket his chancellor in the same year.
485–8 Thou had'st not ... Deify'de] May anticipates some of the results of
Becket's martyrdom; see below, IV, 220–6, 273–96.
489–90 But Canturburyes Prelate ... in his stead] See Newburgh, "voluntate
regia Cantuariensis ecclesiæ pontificatum sortitur" *Historia rerum Angli-
carum*, II, xvi, 139–40). Archbishop Theobald died in April 1161; Becket
was nominated his successor in May 1162 and consecrated 3 June.
491–3 Though the wise Empresse ... Mislik'de the choyse] There is dis-
agreement about the amount of resistance against Becket's election.
William of Canterbury has a chapter "De contradictione electionis" in his
Vita, but names only Gilbert Foliot, the bishop of London, as an oppo-
nent (*Materials*, I, 9; cf. Poole, *OHE*, 200, and Warren, *Henry II*, 454–5);
May's version is based on a letter in which the suffragan bishops of Can-
terbury reminded Becket of the benefices he received from Henry, "et

dissuadente matre sua, regno reclamante, ecclesia Dei, quoad licuit, suspi-
rante et ingemiscente, vos in eam qua praeestis dignitatem modis omnibus
studuit sublimare" ("Thomae Cantuariensi Archiepiscopo Clerus Angliae,"
Epistle CCV in *Materials for the History of Thomas Becket*, ed. James Crai-
gie Robertson, Vol. V [London, 1881], 410). Roger Hoveden gives a copy
of the letter in his *Annales* (ed. Savile, 509–11, 510); Speed ascribes it to
Gilbert Foliot and says that "the King, till he found the contrary, thought
himselfe assured of his *Thomas*, whom (if *Gilbert* Bishop of *London* said
true) he aduanced to that dignity against the liking as well of *Matildis* the
Empresse his mother, as of the Clergy and people" (*Historie*, IX, 6 [18],
489; a marginal note refers to "*Epist. ad Th. apud Rog. Houeden*").

494 *marginal note*] There is no *Chronicon de passione et miraculis* by Roger of
Hoveden; the note refers to two different sources. May adopted it from
Speed who gives several references on the margin adjoining his report of
Becket's election: "Houeden. / *Chron. de Passione / & mirac. beati / Th.
MS. / Fox. p. 287*." (Speed, *History*, IX, 6 [11], 487). This was probably
meant to point to three different sources: Hoveden's *Annales*, an anony-
mous chronicle *De passione et miraculis*, and Foxe's *Acts and Monuments*.
Foxe, in fact, refers to an anonymous manuscript in terms which may
have prompted Speed's marginal note: "And first to begin with the tes-
timony of one of his own religion, and also not far, as it appeareth, from
his own time, who, writing of his martyrdom and miracles, thus testifieth
of the judgement and sentence of divers concerning his promotion and
behaviour. The chronicle being written in Latin, and having the name of
the author cut out, thus beginneth: '*Quoniam vero multi, &c.*'" This
manuscript is reprinted as "Auctore anonymo II" in Robertson's *Materials*,
IV, 80–144. Foxe then gives a lengthy quotation from this manuscript (in
Latin and English) which Speed paraphrases in his *Historie*: "Which to be
true, a *Legender* of his Miracles can best relate. *Nonnullis tamen, etc. Many*
(saith he) *judged his promotion not Canonicall, because it was procured more
by the importunitie of the King, then by the voyces of Clergie, or People; and
it was noted as presumption and indiscretion in him, to take vpon him to
guide the Sterne, who was scarce fit to handle an Oare, and that being skil'd
onely in worldly affaires, he did not tremble to ascend vnto that sacred toppe
of so great dignitie*." (*Historie*, IX, 6 [11], 487).

495 a Courtier and a souldier] See Speed, "the Monkes objected against
Becket, that *neither a courtier nor a Souldier* (as he had been both) *were fit
to succeede in so high and sacred a function*." On the margin, Speed refers to
"Foxe, p. 264" as his source (*Historie*, IX, 6 [11], 487).

503–4 the other Bishops . . . party fall] This is Newburgh's version, "ita om-
nes usque ad unum vel pellexit blanditiis vel infregit terroribus" (*Historia
rerum Anglicarum*, II, xvi, 141); Hoveden names three submissive bishops
and adds "& alios . . . prælatos" (*Annales*, ed. Savile, 493,1–3).

505 Hee stiffely stands alone] "But the archbishop stood stiflie in his opin-
ion" (Holinshed, *Chronicles*, II, 119).

507–12 Pope Alexander . . . Henryes loue] See Speed, "Pope *Alexander* very
desirous to keepe the Kings loue (though secretly wishing well to *Beckets*
attempts)" (*Historie*, IX, 6 [19], 489). Emperor Frederick Barbarossa had
promoted the election of an antipope (Victor IV) in 1159; Pope Alexan-
der was exiled to France where he found the support of King Louis and,
eventually, Henry II.

513–14 Hee therefore wrote . . . the Kings entent] Roger of Hoveden and
Holinshed report that the pope sent his letter by the abbott of L'Aumône
(*Annales*, ed. Savile, 493, 5; *Chronicles*, II, 119); Speed names him as "one
Philip, his Almoner" (*Historie*, IX, 6 [19], 489).

515–18 Becket repaires . . . the lawes] See Holinshed, "he came first to
Woodstocke, and there promised the king to obserue his lawes, Bona
fide, Faithfullie, and without all collusion or deceit" (*Chronicles*, II, 119),
who follows Hoveden (*Annales*, ed. Savile, 493, 11–12).

522 A Councell straight hee calls at Clarendon] This "great council" was
held in January 1164.

525–8 Becket revolts . . . sinne no more] "*Becket*, relapsing againe from his
promise giuen to the King, said, that he had greeuously sinned in making
that absolute promise, and that he would not sinne therein any more"
(*Historie*, IX, 6 [20], 489). May prefers this short account of Becket's
manoeuvres at Clarendon, which goes back to Roger of Hoveden, to Hol-
inshed's circumstantial report (*Chronicles*, II, 120) which is based on Ger-
vase of Canterbury and Matthew Paris.

538–50 King Henry's fill'd . . . wrath-enflamed mynde] The passage enlarges
on a sentence in William of Newburgh's *Historia rerum Anglicarum*, II,
xvi: "Tunc vero tanto vehementius in eum furor efferbuit, quanto ipse re-
gali magnificentiæ ratione dati et accepti magis obnoxius videbatur" (142).

551–74 At last resolu'de . . . Papall throne] "Tunc mandavit ei rex per mili-
tes suos, vt sine dilatione veniret, & redderet ei plenariam computationem
de omnibus receptis, quae receperat de redditibus regni, quamdiu Cancel-
larius eius fuit" (Roger of Hoveden, *Annales*, ed. Savile, 495, 14–16). In
his account of the council of Northampton, May relies mainly on Holins-
hed's paraphrase of the passage, some of whose phrases, such as "dis-

obedience" or "his goods confiscat" he adopts (*Chronicles*, II, 120, 121).

560–2 But (being no layman) ... of Rome] "I am not bound to answer, neither will I. [...] I refuse to stand to the iudgement either of the king, or of any other, and appeale to the pope, by whome (vnder God) I ought to be iudged" (Holinshed, *Chronicles*, 122). Roger of Hoveden makes Becket use stronger words: "Quibus Archiepiscopus respondit: prohibeo vobis ex parte omnipotentis Dei, & sub anathemate, ne faciatis hodie de me iudicium, quia appelaui ad præsentiam domini Papæ" (*Annales*, ed. Savile, 495, 28–30).

563–4 the Parliament / (Then at Northampton)] May's note refers to Matthew Paris, *Historia minor*: "Item, apud Norhamtonam tractus in causam, super actis quæ in cancellaria egerat, presentiam suam exhibuit iii.° idus Octobris" (ed. Madden, I, 328–9). The expression "Parliament," however, is taken from Speed, who also refers to "Matth. Paris" in a marginal note (*Historie*, IX, 6 [23], 490).

565–9 the Bishopps ... obedience to him] Hilary, Bishop of Chichester, is quoted by Gervase of Canterbury as accusing Becket of perjury, "iccirco te reum perjurii dicimus, et perjuro archiepiscopo de cætero obedire non habemus" (*Chronicle of the Reigns of Stephen, Henry II, and Richard I*, ed. Stubbs, I, 188). Speed translates this as "the Prelates themselues by joynt consent adjudged him of Perjury, & by the mouth of the Bishop of *Chichester*, disclaimed thence-forward all obedience vnto him, as their Arch-Bishop." Speed, (*Historie*, IX, 6 [23], 490). He gives "Geruasius" as his source in a sidenote.

573 in disguise] See Holinshed, "he fled awaie disguised in a white vesture and a moonks coule" (*Chronicles*, II, 123).

577 How Becket to the Pope resign'd his Pall] A similar (but doubtful) incident is reported by William of Newburgh as having occurred during the Council of Tours in 1163 (i.e., before Becket's confrontation with Henry [see *Historia*, II, xvi, 140]). Holinshed renders it in a phrase closely resembling that of May, "the archbishop resigned his pall vnto the pope" (*Chronicles*, II, 125). Speed, who also relies on Newburgh, uses more disparaging words: "Becket *secretly surrendred his Arch-bishopricke* ... into the Popes hands" (*Historie*, IX, 6 [11], 487).

578–9 How in his wrath ... allyes and kinn] "The king on the other part banished out of England, and all parts of his other dominions, all those persons that were knowen to be of kin vnto the archbishop, both young and old" (Holinshed, *Chronicles*, II, 127). This appears to be a less pathetic version of Roger of Hoveden's: "Idem Rex *Henricus* expulit ab Anglia, & ab omnibus terris suæ dominationis, omnes homines & fœminas, quoscunque inuenire potuit de cognatione beati *Thomæ* Cantuariensis: Pueros etiam in cunis vagientes, & adhuc ad vbera matrum pendentes, misit in exilium" (*Annales*, ed. Savile, 500, 11–14). Speed retains the pathetic appeal: "Neither was this [i.e., the confiscation of Becket's goods] all, for he banished out of the Realme, all the kindred of the Arch-bishop, man, woman, Childe, and sucking babes" (*Historie*, IX, 6 [26], 491).

585–7 how oft ... fear'd in England] Roger of Hoveden reports one such critical moment for 1169: "Eodem anno *Henricus* rex Angliæ timens, quod beatus *Thomas* Cantuariensis Archiepiscopus in personam ipsius excommunicationis sententiam, & in regnum eius proferret interdictum, appellauit pro se, & regno suo ad præsentiam summi pontificis; & missis ad eum legatis, petiit mitti in Angliam à latere suo vnum, vel duos legatos" (*Annales*, ed. Savile, 515, 23–6).

592 fruitlesse Legacies] Immediately after Becket's flight Henry sent a delegation headed by the archbishop of York "to the number of 15. to pass in ambassage vnto the pope, that they might excuse his dooings" (Holinshed, *Chronicles*, II, 123); this was only the first of a series of missions which culminated in the two meetings of the opponents in 1169 (see below, note to 594).

593 How many dayes of bootlesse parleys sett] King Louis arranged no less than twelve meetings with Henry during Becket's exile; ten were actually held (Poole, *OHE*, 209). Speed gives a detailed account of the negotiations in his *Historie*, IX, 6 [24–39], 490–4.

594 How oft with him the King in person mett] There were two meetings of the antagonists before their sudden reconciliation in 1170, one in January 1169 at Montmirail, the other in November of that year at Montmartre (Poole, *OHE*, 213).

595–6 Seaven yeares ... banish'd man] Cf. Speed, "in the seauenth yeare of *Beckets* banishment," (*Historie*, IX, 6 [39], 493).

597 At Pointinew, and St Columba] Both these abbeys are mentioned in Holinshed's *Chronicles* (II, 125, 127). Becket stayed at Pontigny from 1164 to 1166, when after excommunicating some of Henry's ministers he was obliged to seek refuge at St. Columba near Sens, which lay on the territory of the King of France.

599 Flanders Lord] This could be either Count Thierry (1128–1168) or Count Philip (1168–1191) of Flanders; Hoveden does not mention him as a negotiator at this point.

601 But now accord ... is made] This was at Fréteval on 22 July 1170.

602–5 For though … agreement make] See Holinshed, "at the earnest suit
of Lewes the French king, Theobald earle of Blois, and others king Hen-
rie began somewhat to shew himselfe conformable towards an agreement"
(*Chronicles*, II, 132).

605–6 and Becket … to his See] "Then the archbishop departing out of
France, came into England, and landed at Sandwich about the first of
December" (i.e., 1170; Holinshed, *Chronicles*, II, 133).

608–9 Seldome is … by death] According to Holinshed, King Louis had
his doubts about the reconciliation and warned Becket: "For he perceived
by King Henries words & countenance such a deepe rooted displeasure in
his hart, that he agreed to receiue him into fauour rather by compulsion
and against his will than otherwise" (*Chronicles*, II, 133).

Book IV

1 Faire Floraes pride] Flora is the goddess of flowers and loses her splen-
dour, of course, with the approach of winter.

13–18 Fame had … the Ilands feare] King Dermot of Leinster had re-
cruited the half–brothers Robert FitzStephen and Maurice FitzGerald to
help him regain his kingdom (see III, 26–34), and these Norman-Welsh
adventurers had captured Wexford in 1169. In 1170 another recruit,
Richard, Earl of Strigoil, called Strongbow, sent his kinsman Reimond
over with a small contingency which laid siege to Waterford; Earl Rich-
ard himself followed later that year with a strong force and overran
Waterford and Dublin. These invasions are treated at length below. The
main source is Gerald of Wales's *Expugnatio Hibernica*, Book I. This
treatise, in parts a first-hand report, is incorporated in a printed collection
of manuscripts usually ascribed to William Camden, *Anglica, Hibernica,
Normannica, Cambrica, a veteribus scripta* (Frankfurt, 1602). Camden
probably only supplied (bad) exemplars for this compilation (see James F.
Dimock, ed., *Giraldi Cambrensis opera*, V, "Introduction," lxxix–lxxx); the
full title claims no more than that the chronicles come "ex bibliotheca
Guilielmi Camdeni"; nevertheless, the collection was reprinted in 1603.
Holinshed attached a translation of the *Expugnatio* ("The Conquest of
Ireland") by John Hooker alias Vowell to the 1587 edition of his *Chroni-
cles* (Vol. VI in the reprint of 1807). From this reprint the English quota-
tions in these notes are taken because it still is the most readily available
edition. May's transcription of the Irish names suggests that he used not
only the Latin text and Hooker's translation but also Speed's account of

the conquest of Ireland in his *Historie*, IX, 6 [46–62]; see notes to lines 17, 58, and 435–40.

17 Earle Strongbow] The byname Strongbow is not used in the known manuscripts of the *Expugnatio*. Hooker calls him Strangbow in a note to Chap. I, ii of his translation (*Chronicles*, VI, 127). There is an addition, "dictus Strongbow, fortis arcus" ["Strangbow" in the 1603 edition], attached to Earl Richard's name "comes Strigulensis Ricardus, Gilleberti comitis filius" in Book I, chap. ii, of the *Expugnatio* in Camden's *Anglica* (which Dimock took to be its first occurrence; ed. *Giraldus*, V, 228, and note 4). May probably followed Speed, who always calls Earl Richard Strongbow.

27–28 Pompey's laurell'd charriot] Plinius gives an impression of the pomp of Pompey's third triumph, which was held in 61 B.C., in his *Natural History*, XXXVII, vi, 12–14. Francis Bacon deals with the Roman triumph, "the type of all true Honour and Renowne," in his essay "Of the Greatness of Kingdoms" (*Essays*, ed. Michael J. Hawkins [London, 1972], 96–7). For the laurelled chariot see note to VI, 87–92.

29–30 Cæsar's triumphs] In his *Cleopatra* Thomas May mentions "those fower rich triumphs which hee [i.e., Julius Caesar] held at Rome" (I, ii, 103; ed. Denzell. S. Smith, 13). May probably knew Andrea Mantegna's magnificent series of canvases on *The Triumphs of Caesar* which Charles I had bought in 1629; they served as models for James Shirley's Inns of Court Masque, *The Triumph of Peace*, which was presented in February 1634 (see J. S. A. Adamson, "Chivalry and Political Culture in Caroline England," in *Culture and Politics in Early Stuart England*, ed. Kevin Sharpe and Peter Lake [London, 1994], 170).

31–40 Shee did record ... clearly knowne] The references to Rome's early heroes are taken mainly from Virgil's description of the shield of Aeneas which Vulcan is said to have decorated with prophetic scenes from the history of the empire (*Aeneid*, VIII, 626–51; similar lists of imperial heroes are in Livy, *Ab urbe condita*, I, 3, and Ovid, *Fasti*, 4,39). May adds the less martial pair of Numa and Egeria. On the application of Roman examples to political programmes in the visual arts see John Peacock, "The Politics of Portraiture," in *Culture and Politics*, ed. Sharpe & Lake, 213–15.

32 Quirinus ... 'gainst Tatius] Quirinus is Romulus deified; he accorded a peace with Tatius, king of the Sabines, who had almost conquered Rome.

33 Tullus ... 'gainst Alba] Tullius (Hostilius), king of Rome, destroyed Alba (Longa).

34 Numa and Aegeria] Numa Pompilius, the second king and first lawgiver of Rome courted and (peacefully) captured the nymph Egeria. Ovid tells a version of their story in *Metamorphoses*, XV, 479–551.

35–6 Porsenna ... Clœlia swumme] When Tarquinius Superbus was expelled from Rome, he appealed to Porsenna for help. Porsenna besieged and almost captured Rome but lifted the siege, impressed by valiant Romans such as Cocles and Cloelia.

45–7 The yeare before, ... the spring] Gerald gives the date as "circa kalendas Maii," that is on or shortly before 1 May 1169 (*Expugnatio Hibernica*, I, iii, 230).

48–9 In aide ... engag'de before] According to Gerald, Dermot had secured FitzStephen's help by promising him possession of the town of Wexford (*Expugnatio Hibernica*, I, ii); see also below, line 150.

50–6 The braue Fitz-Stephens ... arrivall fam'de] "In the meane time Robert Fitzstephans, not vnmindfull nor carelesse of his word and promise, prepareth and prouideth all things in a readinesse, and being accompanied with thirtie gentlmen of seruice of his owne kinsfolks & certeine armed men, and about three hundred of archers and footmen, which were all of the best chosen and piked men in Wales, they all ship and imbarke themselues in three sundrie barkes, and sailing towards Ireland, they land about the calends of Maie at the Banne" (*Expugnatio Hibernica*, trl. Hooker, *Chronicles*, VI, iii, 127). May's addition, "A little Creeke neere Wexford, then scarce nam'de, / But ever since by his arrivall fam'de" (55–6), is an indication that he consulted Hooker's translation, for Hooker explains in a footnote to *Banne*: "The Banne is a little creeke lieng in the countie of Wexford, [...] the same being the place of the first receipt of Englishmen, there were certeine monuments made in memorie thereof, and were named the Banna & the Boenne, which were the names (as the common fame is) of the two largest ships in which the Englishmen there arrived" (*Chronicles*, VI, 129). Speed takes the name of the river to be Irish and gives it a prophetic quality: "a place called by the *Irish*, *Bann*, [...] which in our language signifies *Sacred*: a word which (so much as names may be presages of things) did as it were hallow the attempt of the *English* with a lucky and gratious omination" (*History*, IX, 6 [54], 498).

52–3 his stout brother ... (Fitz-Girald)] "Maurice Fitzgerald, [...] his halfe brother[s] by the mothers side" (*Chronicles*, VI, 126). Their mother was, as Gerald informs us in *Expugnatio*, I, ii, the Welsh Lady Nesta, a former mistress of King Henry I (see Warren, *Henry II*, 192–3).

58 Maurice de Pendergast] Both Giraldus and Hooker spell the surname
"Prendelgast" (*Expugnatio*, I, iii), but Speed has the same spelling as May.
In his most antiquarian manner Speed refers on the margin to a manu-
script in the keeping of Patrick White ("*Manusc. Clonmel in Custod.
Patric White*"), and mentions another source in a further note: "The name of
Pendergast yet remaines in *Ireland*: taken first (as seemeth) from a town
of that name in Pembrokeshire. Pendergasts coat of Armour, was Gules,
a Saltoyr Varie, as my learned friend, Master *Bolton* (whose notes haue
giuen me much light in this king's life, and diuers others) himselfe ob-
serued in the Friers Church at Clonmell" (*Historie*, IX, 6 [55] 498).
Edmund Bolton propagated the establishment of a Royal Academy of
Antiquaries in the early seventeenth century. Patrick could be the Chris-
tian name of the person whom Bolton entered with his surname White
only on his list of eighty-four proposed members in 1626; see Ethel M.
Portal, "The Academ Roial of King James I," *Proceedings of the British
Academy*, 1915–1916, 189–208, 208. See also Introduction, p. xcii.

66–8 The country neere … bestow'd] May relies on Speed's patriotically
heightened rendering of Gerald here: "*Dermot*, to whose vse the *English
Generall* had taken it, bestowed the Citie it selfe, and the Countrey about
vpon Robert Fitz-Stephen, at his pleasure to be disposed of: and there the
first Colony of our Nation was planted, which hath euer since immoouea-
bly maintained their abode among innumerable changes in the World,
retaining at this day the ancient attire of the *English*, and the language
also it selfe, though brackish with the mixture of vulgar *Irish*, which
therefore by a distinct name is called *Weisford* speech" ("Conquest," I, iii;
Historie, IX, 6 [55], 498).

78 Hee sends his frend the valiant Reimond ore] "he sendeth ouer before
him into Ireland, a gentleman of his owne houshold and familie named
Reimond le grosse" ("Conquest," I, xiii, *Chronicles*, VI, 141).

80–2 The noble Earle … hee wonne] Strongbow arrived "in the kalends of
September on the vigill of saint Bartholomew" and captured Waterford
"vpon saint Bartholomew's daie" (i.e., 24 August 1170; "Conquest," I, xvi,
Chronicles, VI, 145–6).

83–93 Thither King Dermot … celebrated now] "Mac Morogh, who was
also come thither […] gaue his daughter Eua, whom he had then
brought thither with him, to be maried to the earle according to the first
pact and couenant" ("Conquest," I, xvi, *Chronicles*, VI, 146). The marriage
pact is mentioned in *Expugnatio*, I, 2.

94–106 Mars smooth's … spatious lands] According to Catullus, it was not unusuall in heroic times for the gods to visit the houses of mortals (*Carmen* 64, 384–6). Zeus himself descends with his wife and children to attend the wedding of Peleus and Thetis in that poem (298–9). In Claudian's marriage song, Venus leaves her home on Paphos, orders the god of war to be kept out of the way, directs Hymen to choose the festal torches, and acts as *pronuba* herself (*Epithalamium*, 184–5; 190–2; 202; 254; 285).

96–7 The Paphian Queene ... the Thracian God] the Thracian god is Mars; he is the lover of Venus, the Paphian queen.

109–52 A Ladyes loue ... performed now] May recapitulates here what Gerald had sketched in at its proper point in the course of events near the beginning of his *Expugnatio* (I, i). Gerald may have prompted May to add an epic touch to his account: he had applied the most notorious line from Virgil's book of Dido, "varium et mutabile semper / femina" (*Aeneid*, IV, 569–70) to the conduct of the wife of Tiernan O'Rourke, the king of Meath. Gerald had also called Egypt and Troy to witness: "Such is the variable & fickle nature of a woman, by whome all mischiefes in the world (for the most part) doo happen and come, as maie appeare by Marcus Antonius, and by the destruction of Troie" ("Conquest," I, i, *Chronicles*, VI, 121. Dimock identifies O'Rourke's wife as Devorgilla in a note to his edition of the *Expugnatio*, *Opera*, V, 226).

128 And drew ... to Ilion] A variation on Christopher Marlowe's famous strong lines, "Helen, whose beauty summoned Greece to arms, / And drew a thousand ships to Tenedos" (*Tamburlaine the Great, Second Part*, II, iv, 87-8); May had used them before in his comedy *The Heire* (1620): "I tell thee, sweet, a face not halfe so faire / As thine hath arm'd whole nations in the field, / And brought a thousand ships to Tenedos" (E1v, 1633 ed.).

129 his fatall Hellen] Speed compares Devorgilla to the Spartan Queen in identical terms: "*Dermot Mac Murgh*, being in possession of this fatall *Hellen* (the adulterous wife of *Rotherick*) was persued so eagerly with the reuenging sword of his enemie ..." (*History*, IX, 6 [50], 496).

131–2 ambitious Rotherike ... Irelands monarch] Cf. below, 163–4, and note to 443.

150 Wexfords seignory] The fulfilment of this promise has already been mentioned above, 48–9.

154 The revells ended all] An echo of Prospero's "Our revels now are ended" (*The Tempest*, IV, i, 148)?

163–9 Proud Roderike ... to Dublin came] "Rotherick himselfe was well

contented (notwithstanding his lately vsurped, and swelling title of Mon-
arch of *Ireland*) to hold himselfe within the bogs & fastnesses of his
peculiar Realme, the wilde, and mountainous Connaught; meane while,
Strong-bow keepes on his way ouer the bosome of *Ireland* to the principall
Citie thereof, *Dublin*" (Speed, *Historie*, IX, 6 [58], 499).

167 Connagh] The usual spelling in both versions of the poem is Con-
naught; in this line, however, both manuscipt and print have this peculiar
spelling.

169 Till hee at last to Dublin came] Dublin fell into the hands of the in-
vaders about a month after Strongbow's landing near Waterford (Poole,
OHE, III, 306).

188–96 And to his See . . . Canturburyes See] There are divergencies among
the authorities concerning Becket's actions immediately after his return to
England, which are duly recorded in Holinshed's *Chronicles*. May follows,
like Holinshed, Gervase of Canterbury's account: "It shuld seeme yet by
Ger. Dorober. that the archbishop of Yorke, and the bishop of Durham
were suspended, and the bishops of London, Salisburie, and diverse other
excommunicated" (*Chronicles*, II, 134).

195 that office] See note to II, 19–20.

197–8 Nor would hee . . . Henry were] Matthew Paris says that young King
Henry refused to see Becket and asked him to return to his church when
Becket was on his way to visit him at Woodstock (*Chronica majora*, 278;
Historia minor, 359).

199–201 While this . . . greivances] The bishops met Henry at Bures where
he was lodging for the Christmas season of 1170/71 (see Warren, *Henry
II*, 508).

203–4 Such words . . . impression tooke] May leaves Henry's exact words to
the imagination of his reader; Holinshed dramatises Gervase of Canter-
bury's indirect speech: "The king [...] was so displeased in his mind
against archbishop Thomas, that in open audience of his lords, knights,
and gentlemen, he said these or the like words: 'In what miserable state
am I, that can not be in rest within mine owne realme, by reason of one
onelie preest? Neither is there any of my folkes that will helpe to deliuer
me out of such troubles'" (*Chronicles*, II, 134); cf. Gervase, *Chronicle of the
Reigns of Stephen, Henry II, and Richard I*, "rex plusquam suam deceret
majestatem iratus, et fere jam extra se positus, cœpit se miserum con-
clamare, asserens se ignobiles et ignavos homines nutrivisse, quorum nec
unus tot sibi illatas injurias voluerit vindicare" (*Historical Works*, ed.
Stubbs, I, 224). Speed only mentions "some words slipping from him

[i.e., King Henry], and arguing his great discontent" (*History*, IX, 6 [41], 494).

205–6 Foure knights . . . Fitz-Vrse] "There were some also of the kings seruants, that thought after an other maner of sort to reuenge the displeasure doone to the kings maiestie, as sir Hugh Moreuille, sir William Tracie, sir Richard Britaine, and sir Reignold Fitz Urse, knights" (*Chronicles*, II, 134). Speed names the assassins as "Hugh Moruill, William Traci, Hugh Brito, and Richard Fitz-Vrse, Knights and Courtiers" (*History*, IX, 6 [41], 494).

238–47 In lookes . . . retire from him] Holinshed creates an elaborate question-and-answer scene out of Becket's first encounter with the knights; May takes a shortcut via William of Newburgh's *Historia rerum Anglicarum*: "Quibus ille non territus, furentibus granditerque frementibus mira libertate atque fiducia loquebatur. Unde magis accensi concite egressi sunt" (II, xxv, 162). Speed is even more succinct but sets off the "butcherly" crime of the knights against the "blind" cult that was to spring up around the martyr (*Historie*, IX, 6 [41], 494, see excerpt below, note to 287–92).

255–65 While thus . . . his person] "Suasum est venerando pontifici a suis, ut in sacram se basilicam recipiens, inhumane sævientium rabiem declinaret. Cumque non facile acquiesceret, paratus ad subeundum discrimen, tandem irrumpentibus atque urgentibus adversariis, amica suorum violentia ad sacri loci munimina trahebatur" (Newburgh, *Historia rerum Anglicarum*, II, xxv, 162–3).

265–70 but not all . . . deadly sinne] "Insecuti enim satellites diaboli neque sacri ordinis, neque sacri vel loci vel temporis reverentiam, ut Christiani, habuerunt" (*Historia rerum Anglicarum*, II, xxv, 163).

273–96 How much . . . pray to thee] Protestant historians, and in particular church historians such as John Foxe, tended to question the validity of medieval hagiography. See note on III, 391, and Foxe's savage onslaught on the sanctity of Becket's life and the miracles said to attest it; one of his crown witnesses against the saint is Caesarius of Heisterbach, a Cistercian monk and near-contemporary of Becket's, who had mentioned a theological debate in the University of Paris in which Becket's sanctity had been called in question (*Dialogus magnus visionum atque miraculorum*; discussed in *Acts and Monuments*, ed. Townsend, II, 246–52). Prompted by Foxe, John Speed paraphrases this report : "Some other learned men there were, who liued nere to that time, whose censure was far sharper than that *Monks* [i.e., Newburgh's, whose skeptical remarks had also been quoted by Foxe]: such were some of those Diuines of *Paris*, mentioned by *Cæsarius* the Monke, who saith, The question was debated to and fro amongst the Doctors, in the Vniuersitie of *Paris*, whether *Thomas* were damned or saued: amongst whom *Rogerius* the *Norman* auowed, that hee deserued death and damnation, for his contumacie against his King, the Minister of God: but *Petrus Cantor* alleadged, that his miracles were signes of his saluation, etc. And indeede if all be true which one man hath written in fiue Bookes, containing his 270. Miracles, we cannot but acknowledge him, both the greatest Saint, and the merriest too, that euer got into heauen; so ridiculous are many things recorded of him" (*History*, IX, 6 [43], 494–5). A marginal note identifies the "one man" as "*Monach. Cant. de miraculis B. Thomae.*" It seems likely that this Monk was Benedict of Peterborough, whose *Miracula* Foxe must have read, possibly in a manuscript now kept at Lambeth (MS 135).

285–6 Even hee . . . worshipp thee] See below, V, 267–71.

287–92 Whose gorgeous . . . ridiculously-holy shoo] This was prompted by a passage in Speed's account of the murder where he criticises the exalted worship of the martyr saying "that not onely the basest part of his *Shrine* was pure gold, and his old *Shoe* was deuoutly kissed by all passengers, but also shamelesse and numberlesse Miracles blindely ascribed vnto him" (*Historie*, IX, 6 [41], 494).

294–6 Nay in her danger . . . pray to thee] "Yea, euen a *Bird, hauing beene taught to speake, flying out of her cage, and ready to be seized on by a SparHauke, said onely, S. Thomas helpe mee, and her enemie fell presently dead, and she escaped*, and (belike) reported it" (Speed, *Historie*, IX, 6 [43], 495), with a marginal reference to "*The Printed golden Legend in vit. Thom.*" which May appears to have latinized.

299–302 And fill'd . . . was wrought] "King Henrie doubtlesse was right pensiue for his death, bicause he wist well inough that it would be iudged, that he himselfe was priuie to the thing" (Holinshed, *Chronicles*, II, 137).

309–12 into the North . . . vntimely came] There is disagreement about the fate of Becket's murderers; "in aquilonales Angliæ partes secesserunt," says Newburgh (*Historia rerum Anglicarum*, II, xxv, 163); "in Occidentales partes Angliæ secesserunt," Roger of Hoveden (*Annales*, ed. Savile, 522, 46–7); Holinshed leaves open which direction their flight took, "despairing vtterlie of pardon, fled one into one place, and another into another, so that within foure yeares they all died an euill death (as it hath beene reported)." Holinshed also records the tradition that they died on a crusade imposed upon them by the Pope (*Chronicles*, II, 136).

313–23 King Lewis ... a sonne] Holinshed mentions only the love the French princes bore the archbishop, "king Lewes, and Theobald the earle of Blois, as they that loued him most deerelie were most sorowfull for it, and [...] wrote their letters unto pope Alexander, giving him to vnderstand both of the slaughter, and how king Henrie had caused it to be put in execution, requiring most instantlie, that such an iniurie doone to the Christian religion, might speedilie be punished" (*Chronicles*, II, 137). William of Newburgh doubts, like May, their motives, "et Francorum maxime principes, qui felicitatis ejus æmuli semper exstiterant, adversus eum, tanquam in verum certumque tantæ enormitatis auctorem, sedem Apostolicam instigarent" (*Historia rerum Anglicarum*, II, xxv, 164).

325–31 But Henry ... sadd a cause] "At length, he sent his ambassadors to Rome, partlie to purge himselfe of the archbishops death, partlie to excuse his fault, [...] & partlie to require the pope to send his legats into England, to make inquirie both for the death of the archbishop, and also of the state of the clergie" (Holinshed, *Chronicles*, II, 137).

341–48 And, fearing ... crosse the Seas] Holinshed says that "the king stood in great feare least his land should be interdicted, in so much that he commanded the wardens of the ports both on this side the sea and beyond, to take good heed, least any coming with letters of interdiction should passe into England" (*Chronicles*, II, 138).

355–8 At Milford hauen ... follow Henry ore] According to Roger of Hoveden, Henry assembled 400 ships in Milford Haven to transport his army to Ireland (*Annales*, ed. Savile, 527,26; Holinshed, *Chronicles*, II, 139).

359–61 Whose lustre ... possession there] In Holinshed, Strongbow is said to have attacked Dublin for a very similar reason, "he thought to worke some feat, whereby he might make his name famous, & cause the Irishmen to haue him in feare" (*Chronicles*, II, 139). May uses the same motive again with respect to Henry's Christmas celebrations in Dublin; see below, 457–60.

373–6 For which ... Irish shore] Henry "by proclamation restreined all his subiects from passing into Ireland with any kind of merchandize, prouision of vittels, or other commodities whatsoeuer" (Holinshed, *Chronicles*, II, 139).

377–8 And that ... returne agayne] This clause is not in Holinshed, but Speed, "and commands all English to returne before Easter" (*Historie*, IX, 6 [59], 499; both rely on Gerald, *Expugnatio*, II, xix).

385–92 How Strongbow ... with victory away] Giraldus relates at length how Strongbow and most of his fellow adventurers were besieged in

Dublin by an Irish army under Rory O'Connor, king of Connaught, and a fleet from the Isle of Man led by King Gottred. The town was saved by a sally of three small troops under Reimond, Miles Cogan, and Maurice FitzGerald (*Expugnatio*, I, xxii–xxiv).

393 Or how Miles Cogan chas'd the King of Meth] The king was "Ororike, the one eied king of Meth" ("Conquest," I, xxx [xxix in Gerald], *Chronicles*, VI, 158).

396–403 Or how ... Fitz-Stephans body] Gerald reports in detail how the Irish besieged FitzStephen in Wexford and, being unable to capture the town, brought two bishops and several other clerics to the moat and made them swear by a number of saints' relics that Dublin had surrendered to Roderick and that his troops were on their way to Wexford. They then promised FitzStephen and his men free leave for Wales before Roderick's arrival (*Expugnatio*, I, xxv).

409–20 Nouembers cold ... a King] Henry sailed on 16 October 1171, landed the following day, and entered Waterford on St. Luke's day (18 October). May's date is prompted by the Latin calendar ("circa kalendas Novembris, die videlicet sancti Lucæ," *Expugnatio*, I, xxx, 275; Hooker translates "in the kalends of Nouember, being saint Luks daie," *Chronicles*, VI, 159).

422–6 So soone ... Limericke] "Then Dermon Mac Arth prince of Corke came to the king of his owne free will, submitted himselfe, became tributarie, and tooke his oth to be true and faithfull to the king of England" ("Conquest," I, xxxii [xxxiii in Gerald], *Chronicles*, VI, 160. Donald of Limerick did the same two days later at Cashel [ibid.]).

431–2 The King ... the towne] "These things thus doon at Waterford, the king left Robert Fitzbarnard there" ("Conquest," I, xxxiii; *Chronicles*, VI, 161).

435–40 The greatest Lords ... Gillemeholoch] The spelling suggests that May took the names of the Irish chiefs from Hooker's translation, "the great men & princes, as namelie Machelan Ophelan prince of Ossorie, Mache Talewie, Othwelie Gillemeholoch, Ochadese, O Carell of Uriell & Ororike of Meth: all which yeelded & submitted them selues to the king in their owne persons, & became his vassals, & swore fealtie" ("Conquest," I, xxxiii; *Chronicles*, VI, 161–2); the splitting up of *Othwely*, *Gillemeholoch*, however, may be due to Gerald, who uses slightly Latinized versions of the names, "Otuetheli, Gillemoholmoch" (*Expugnatio*, I, xxxiii, 278); the Camden volume has also partly Latinized spellings: "Machelanus Ophelan, Machtalewy, Othweteli, Gillemoholmoch, Oeadhesi, Ocaruelwriensis, & Ororitius Medensis" (*Hibernia expugnata*, Cap. xxxii, 776, 1602 edition). Speed gives no names but mentions only "petty-Kings, and principall persons" (*History*, IX, 6 [46], 499).

443–52 But Rotherike ... to Henry's name] This passage appears to be conflated from Holinshed and Speed. Rory O'Connor's titles come from Speed: "Rotherick the Great ... hauing already inuaded the Title and Stile of KING AND MONARCH OF IRELAND" (*History*, IX, 6 [46], 495; cf. "the style of Irelands Monarch," IV, 132); the refusal to do personal homage to Henry from Holinshed, "but Rothorike the monarch came no neerer than to the riuer side of the Shenin, which diuideth Connagh from Meth, & there Hugh de Lacie and William Fitzaldeline by the kings commandement met him, who desiring peace submitted himselfe, swore allegiance, became tributarie, and did put in (as all others did) hostages and pledges for the keeping of the same" (*Chronicles*, VI, 162). Both versions rely on Gerald (*Expugnatio*, I, xxxiii).

457–60 That those rude Irish ... vnusuall lustre] Cf. above, 359–61.

463–4 While plentious ... the lands affoords] One of the delicacies offered was crane's meat, and it took some special pleading to make the Irish taste it, "carne gruina, quam hactenus obhorruerunt, regia voluntate passim per aulam vesci coeperunt" (*Expugnatio*, I, xxxiii, 280).

465–80 Downe with ... sweetly sing] This passage on the royal banquet at Dublin borrows heavily from Statius' "Eucharisticon" on a banquet given by Emperor Domitian (*Silvae*, IV, ii).

466–9 So show'd ... gorgeous court] See Statius: "Hic cum Romuleos proceres trabeataque Caesar / Agmina mille simul iussit discumbere mensis" (*Silvae*, IV, ii, 32–3).

467 barbarous kings] Cf. Statius, "talem quoque barbarus hostis / Posset et ignotae conspectum agnoscere gentes" (*Silvae*, IV, ii, 44–5).

475–7 While they behold ... Giue cupps] Ganymede, the Olympian cupbearer, was a son of Tros, founder of Troy; Spenser calls him "that ympe of Troy" (*Faerie Queene*, III, xii, 7); in Statius' "Eucharisticon" his service is referred to as "Iliaca porrectum sumere dextra immortale merum" (*Silvae*, IV, ii, 11–12).

477–80 and ravish'd ... sweetly sing] Phoebus Apollo here appears in his office as Musagetes, conductor of the Muses. Homer describes an Olympian feast at the end of Book I of the Iliad with musical accompaniment by Apollo (on the lyre) and the Muses as choristers (594–5). The rural deities may be a reminiscence of the marriage of Peleus and Thetis in Catullus's *Carmen*, 64 (see note to 94–106).

479 his nine daughters] "his" refers to Jove; the Muses are his daughters.

480 Pallenæan triumphs] In the "Eucharisticon" of Statius, Jupiter bids Phoebus sing the triumph of Pallene, "Pallenaeos triumphos" (IV, ii, 56). It was at Pallene or Phlegra that Jupiter finally overcame the giants.

488 When wyne and Cates had weakned appetite] This phrase and the following scene are modelled on an Egyptian episode in Lucan's *De bello civili*, where Caesar, after a sumptuous meal, asks the aged priest Acoreus to tell him of the origins of the Egyptian nation: "Postquam epulis Bacchoque modum lassata voluptas" (X, 172); May's translation is: "When wine, and cates had tir'd their glutted pleasure" (*Lucans Pharsalia*, S3r).

507 scorched Affricke] A veiled reference to the African (Lybian and Egyptian) parts of Lucan's *De bello civili*, Books IV and IX, on which May drew this episode.

508 breeding wonders] In May's play *Cleopatra*, Caesar is said to have listened to Cleopatra's father talk "of all / The mysteryes of religion, and the wonders / That Aegypt breedes" (6v).

532 The freedome of that great Creator] In his commendatory verses to Hodgson's *The Divine Cosmographer* (Cambridge, 1640), May admonishes "vain Cosmographers," who seek to measure and describe the creation, not to forget "to view through this varietie / Of creatures the Creatours majestie" (x3r).

553–704 Ireland is faire ... could runne] This description of the wonders of Ireland is taken from Gerald of Wales's *Topographia Hibernica* (quotations in the following notes are from Dimock's edition, *Giraldi Cambrensis opera*, vol. V, London, 1867), with admixtures from Lucan's *De bello civili*. May went to his medieval source directly. The English translation by John Hooker, which was added to the 1587 edition of Holinshed's *Chronicles*, covers only a small part of the *mirabilia* listed by Gerald. Most of them are simply ignored by the translator while others are questioned. See for instance Hooker's comment on the life-preserving qualities of the *Insula viventium*: "For my part, I haue beene verię inquisitiue of this Iland, but I could neuer find this estrange propertie soothed by anie man of credit in the whole countrie. Neither trulie would I wish anie to be so light, as to lend his credit to anie such feined gloses, as are neither verefied by experience, nor warranted by anie colourable reason" (Holinshed, *Chronicles*, VI, 38; cf. below, 596–616). May's dramatic device of having the Irish *mirabilia* related by a venerable inhabitant enables him to let them stand, thus preserving a sense of wonder.

562–70 Although shee want ... diamonds gather'd] In Lucan's *De bello civili* the rough Libyans ("Incultes Garamantes") are said to lack Eastern gems and Roman gold (IX, 511–21).

565–70 Although the silkewormes ... her flocks] Gerald says of the East: "Habet quidem, vermiculorum beneficio, lanuginem sericam vario colore fucatam. Habet pretiosa metallorum genera: habet gemmas perlucidas" (*Topographia*, I, xxxiv, 68).

573–4 Shee brings ... often hold] "Nec tantum cibaria et pocula [...] veneno suspecta sunt" (*Topographia*, I, xxxvi, 69).

575 no balefull hearbs] May mixes in an element from Vergil's utopian vision of the New Age in his *Bucolica*: "Occidet et serpens, et fallax herba veneni / Occidet" (Ecloga IV, 24–5).

576 Nor Aconite ... gather here] Gerald lists venom among the evils of the East, which he contrasts with innocuous Ireland: "Item et novercæ privigno, et matronæ offensæ marito, et coci corrupti domino, venenosa manus est formidanda" (*Topographia*, I, xxxvi, 69). The reference to aconite (wolfsbane), however, is taken from Book I of Ovid's *Metamorphoses*, where he describes the evils of the Iron Age: "Inminet exitio vir coniugis, illa mariti; lurida terribiles miscent aconita novercae" (*Met.*, I, 146–7).

577 Arachnes poison] Arachne is the mythological name of the spider.

578–80 Nor those sadd plagues ... the Gorgons head] Lucan retells the myth of Medusa, one of the Gorgons, to account for the plagues, and in particular the snakes, of Libya. Perseus slew Medusa, whose hair had been turned into snakes, in the Libyan sands, and snakes grew from her blood (*De bello civili*, IX, 619–99). Gerald gives a quotation from *De bello civili* when enumerating the asps, vipers, dragons, etc. of the East (*Topographia*, I, xxxvi, 69).

581–4 Most æquall temper ... without a shade] Gerald comments in several chapters on the salubrity of the Irish climate (*Topographia*, I, iii; xxxiii, xxxvii ['De aeris nostri clementia incomparabili']); in Chap. xxxiii he uses astronomical terms similar to May's: "Terra terrarum hæc omnium temperatissima. Non cancri calor exæstuans compellit ad umbras; non ad focos capricorni rigor urgenter invitat" (66).

585–88 In winters cold ... winter know] "Sicut æstivo, sic et hiemali tempore herbosa virescunt pascua. Unde nec ad pabula fena secari, nec armentis unquam stabula parari solent" (*Topographia*, I, xxxiii, 66–7).

596–616 In Mounsters Northern part ... there straight they dye] See Gerald, *Topographia*, II, iv "De duabus insulis; in quarum altera nemo moritur; in alteram feminei sexus animal non intrat" (80–1). Of the latter, Hooker observes dryly: "This Iland were a place for one that were vexed with a shrewd wife" (Holinshed, *Chronicles*, VI, 38).

617–34 Another Ile . . . instantly they dy] See Gerald, *Topographia*, II, vi, "De insula, ubi hominum corpora sub divo posita non putrescunt" (83–4).

635–7 A Well . . . a hoary dye] "Est fons in Momonia, cujus aquis si quis abluitur, statim canus efficitur" (*Topographia*, II, vii, 84).

638–44 Another fountaine . . . bathed there] "Est e contra fons in Ultonia ulteriore, quo si quis abluitur non canescet amplius. Hunc autem fontem feminæ frequentant, et viri canitiem vitare volentes" (*Topographia*, II, vii, 84).

645–8 In Connaught . . . doo ebb away] "Est in Connactia fons dulcis aquæ, in vertice montis excelsi, et procul a mari; qui die naturali bis undis deficiens, et toties exuberans, marinas imitatur instabilitates" (*Topographia*, II, vii, 84).

649–56 Not farre . . . evermore] See Gerald, *Topographia*, II, xxxii, "De ratis, per sanctum Yvorum a Ferneginan expulsis" (120).

657–70 A spatious quantity . . . all withstand] See Gerald, *Topographia*, II, xxxi, "De pulicibus, a sancto Nannano deportatis" (119; see Appendix 2, p. 233); May gives the pest an Old Testament turn by making it a plague and leaving out the intercession of St. Nannan.

671–78 Some other meadow . . . truly yeild] See Gerald, *Topographia* (II, xxxvi, 121–2): "Sunt et hic campestria pulcherrima, quæ Brigidæ pascua vocantur: in quæ nullus aratrum ausus est mittere. De quibus pro miraculo ducitur, quod licet provinciæ totius animalia solo tenus herbam corroserint, mane facto non minor herbositas apparebit; tanquam de pascuis illis dictum fuerit, 'Et quantum longis carpunt armenta diebus, / Exigua tantum gelidus ros nocte reponit.'" May excludes the reference to St. Brigid, but keeps the one to Virgil's *Georgics*, II, 201–2.

680–1 wolues haue . . . whelped beene] "De lupis in Decembri catulos habentibus" (Gerald, *Topographia*, II, xxvi, 112).

682 And young-hatch'd Crowes . . . seene] See Gerald: "Circa Natale [. . .] pluribus in Hibernia locis, et præcipue circa partes Mediæ, corvi et ululæ pullos habuere" (*Topographia*, II, xxvii); May leaves out the prodigious character of these phenomena, "alicujus forte novi et præmaturi facinoris prognosticantes eventum. Sicut eodem anno, terræ illius dominatoris, Hugonis scilicet de Laci, perniciosa suorum malitia est protestata" (111–13).

683–90 What neede . . . powerfull prayer] "Sanctus igitur Keivinus cum apud Glindelachan vita et sanctitate claruisset, puer quidam nobilis, quem alumnum habuerat, ægrotans forte poma desiderabat. Cui sancto compatiente, et orationem ad Dominum fundente, salix quædam non procul ab ecclesia poma protulit, tam puero quam aliis ægrotantibus salutifera. Et usque in hodiernum diem tam salix illa, quam aliæ ex ea circa cœmiterium transplantatæ more pomerii, salicis tamen alias per omnia tam foliis quam frondibus natura manente, singulis annis poma producunt" (Gerald, *Topographia*, II, xxviii, 113).

691–8 Or to your sacred eare... exceeding those] See Gerald, "De insula, cujus pars una bonis, altera malis spiritibus est frequentata" (*Topographia*, II, v, 82–3).

710–18 And that ... Christian purity] May returns to political events, and Gerald's *Expugnatio*; the Synod was held at Cashel in November 1171, that is, before the Christmas festivities at Dublin described earlier (*Expugnatio*, I, xxxiv; *Chronicles*, VI, 16).

733 as mischeifes ever ioyne] Hooker, the translator of the *Expugnatio*, is more colloquial, "for commonlie good lucke commeth alone, but ill haps come by heapes and by huddels" ("Conquest," I, xxxvii; *Chronicles*, VI, 165).

734–42 Albert and Theodine ... forthwith appeare] "For there were come into Normandie from pope Alexander the third two cardinals in an ambassage, the one of them being named Albertus, and the other Theodinus, to make inquirie of the death of Thomas archbishop of Canturburie [...] who were fullie determined to haue interdicted, not onelie England, but also all the whole dominions subiect vnto the king, if he himselfe had not the sooner come and met with them" ("Conquest," I, xxxvii; *Chronicles*, VI, 165).

744–6 King Henry greiu'd ... well settled] "Yea, and it greeued him verie much, that he being minded and determined the next summer then following to settle Ireland in some good staie, and to fortifie the same with holds and castels, he should now be compelled and driuen to leaue the same vndoone" ("Conquest," I, xxxvii; *Chronicles*, VI, 165).

749–51 Makes Hugh de Lacy ... hee leaues] The distribution of Ireland among the Anglo-Norman captains is given in detail in *Expugnatio*, I, xxxviii, and *Chronicles*, VI, 166. The term *iustitiar*, however, is only used by Holinshed in his "Henrie the Second," "He gaue also vnto the same Hugh, the keeping of the citie of Dublin, and made him cheefe iusticer of Ireland," (*Chronicles*, II, 141); Holinshed quotes from Roger of Hoveden, "& constituit eum iusticiarium Hyberniæ" (*Historia rerum Anglicarum*, II, 528,59–529,1); on the political motives behind the division and the doubtful term justiciar, see Warren, *Henry II*, 200–1.

753–5 but making ... To Normandy] This is taken from Holinshed, "and landed neere to S. Dauids in south Wales, from thence (without delaie) he hasted foorth to Douer" (*Chronicles*, II, 141). Gerald interpolates a pil-

grimage to St. David's church and a prophetic incident at the Speaking
Stone there (*Expugnatio*, I, xxxviii). As to Henry's speed, see note to I,
492, with further references.

756 And dooes ... sweare] The oath was taken in a public ceremony on 21
May 1172 in the cathedral of Avranches (see Warren, *Henry II*, 531).

758–60 But for those words ... black tragœdy] "Sane non negavit homicidas
illos ex aliquibus forte verbis ejus incautius prolatis occasionem ausumque
tanti furoris sumpsisse" (William of Newburgh, *Historia rerum Anglica-
rum*, II, 165).

761–2 Hee is contented ... to submitt] "neuertheles he was contented to
doo the penance inioined him" (Holinshed, *Chronicles*, II, 167).

Book V

1–3 Now did ... England bleede] The physiological metaphors could have
been suggested by Speed, who makes more drastic use of them: "Now
beganne the wombe of rebellion, and vnnaturall conspiracies to disclose
the mischiefes which were ordained to exercise this right redoubled King
and Warriour, hatched heere at home by the malice (some say) of *Eleanor*
his Queene, at such a time as he was absent in *Ireland*, so that as one
writes *God stirred vp the Kings owne bowels against himselfe*" (Speed, *His-
tory*, IX, 6 [64], 500, with marginal note referring to "Math. Paris").

2 more then ciuill warres] The wars are "more then ciuill" because the com-
batants are not only countrymen but kinsmen like Caesar and Pompey (cf.
Lucan's "Bella per Emathios plus quam civilia," *De bello civili*, I, 1). May
repeats the allusion to Lucan in 45–6. He was not the first to see the af-
finity; the comparison is also drawn in William of Newburgh's *Historia
rerum Anglicarum*, "Bellum igitur plusquam civile inter patrem et filium,
cum tanto multorum discrimine gestum, hunc finem accepit" (II, xxxviii,
198), and Gerald of Wales's *Expugnatio*, "Rex ergo [...] bella plusquam
civilia per biennium sustinens" (I, xlv, 298–9). For reflections of this
famous line in Tudor and early Stuart poetry and drama see Werner von
Koppenfels, " 'Our swords into our proper entrails': Lucan und das Bild
des Bürgerkriegs in der Shakespearezeit," *Bild und Metamorphose. Paradig-
men einer europäischen Komparatistik* (Darmstadt, 1991), 87–118.

8 Megæra] In a passage dealing with precedents to the civil war in Rome,
Lucan mentions the furies that excited the Theban Brothers and fright-
ened even Hercules; one of them is Megaera (Lucan, *De bello civili*, 572–
7). She is associated with impiety (and a family feud) in Seneca's *Thyestes*

when Atreus calls on her to help him in his revenge on his brother (lines 247–54).

13 Pelops sonns] Atreus and Thyestes, two of the ill-fated descendants of Tantalus. Atreus was killed by Thyestes' son Aegisthus.

14 the Theban brothers] See note on II, 30.

15 Atrides] Patronym for the descendants of Atreus; it usually refers to Agamemnon, who was slain by his adulterous wife Clytemnestra. He was revenged by his son Orestes, who killed both his mother and her lover Aegisthus.

21–4 in that blacke designe ... Elianor the Queene] "Mox idem Henricus junior [...] partes Aquitaniae clam adiit, et duos fratres impuberes ibidem cum matre consistentes, Ricardum scilicet et Gaufridum sollicitatos, connivente, ut dicitur, matre, in Franciam secum traduxit" (William of Newburgh, *Historia rerum Anglicarum*, II, xxvii, 170–1). Holinshed and Speed leave no doubt about the queen's intentions, "she [...] cared not what micheefe she procured against him" (*Chronicles*, II, 149); "violently vindicatiue for wrong done vnto her Bed" (*Historie*, IX, 6 [64], 500).

25–7 With them ... rebells ioine] "Tunc multi potentes et nobiles [...] a patre ad filium paulatim cœperunt deficere, et ad motus se bellicos modis omnibus præparare, comes scilicet Leicestrensis, comes Cestrensis, Hugo Bigotus, Radulfus de Fougeriis, aliique complures amplitudine opum et firmitate munitionum terribiles" (Newburgh, *Historia*, II, xxvii, 171).

35 Philip Earle of Flanders] Newburgh does not give the Christian name at this point; he mentions Philip by title only, "Comitem quoque Flandrensem" (*Historia*, II, xxvii, 171). So does May in the manuscript version ("th' Earle of Flanders")—the Christian name was, apparently, added in a revision, possibly with the aid of Holinshed, who dwells at length on the formation of the league against Henry and gives the full name, "Philip, earle of Flanders" (II, 150), or of Speed who gives an extensive list of conspirators which includes the full name of the earl of Flanders and all the others mentioned by May (IX, 6 [65], 500). Count Philip, an intimate friend of Young Henry in the seventies, had become attached to Philip, the young king of France, in 1179. Towards the end of Henry's reign the earl sought an alliance with England (Warren, *Henry II*, 147–8, 224). May reports that he tried in vain to mediate between the French and English kings at Gisors in 1188 (see VII, 95–8).

37–8 nothing almost ... make him stand] Cf. Gerald, "divina potius quam humana potentia victor ubique videretur" (*Expugnatio*, I, xlv, 299).

39–54 Why doo you Princes ... subiects of his owne] William of Newburgh is in no doubt about the princes' motives: they pretend to support young Henry's cause, "sub obtentu quidem quasi pro filio æmularentur contra patrem, qua nimirum æmulatione nil stultius, re autem vera proprii vel odii, ut rex Francorum, vel emolumenti, ut comes Flandrensis, negotium porrecta occasione agentes" (*Historia rerum Anglicarum*, II, xxviii, 172-3).

45–6 Your arming ... no more] See note to line 2.

64 his funerall] James I died on 27 March 1625 and was buried on 7 May.

71–82 The foes ... marches speedily] Speed has a similarly condensed account of the opening moves in the Civil War: "The particular accidents of the warres would fill a volume. At one time *Normandie, Guyen,* and *Britaine* were inuaded by the confederates in *France,* and at the same time *Cumberland* by the *Scots.* But the King of *England* had friends in all those parts, and himselfe hearing that *Vernuil* was besieged by the *French* King in person, he beganne at last to kindle" (*History*, IX, 6 [67], 501). Like Speed, May gives a sketch of the overall strategic situation before following the different campaigns. The chroniclers are more precipitate; in Hoveden, for example, we first meet Chester and Fougères when they have occupied most of Brittany (*Annales*, ed. Savile, 535,30–2).

79 Thus like a Lyon rowz'd on every side] Cf. Speed, who says that Henry kindled only after "hauing, like a sleeping Lyon, sitten still all that while" (*History*, IX, 6 [67], 501). The simile, though commonplace, may have been prompted by their common source: Newburgh applies it to the French, who had roared like lions when they entered the field but left it running like hares on Henry's approach: "Sicque illi qui paulo ante ferocibus animis, et grandium rugitu verborum leones videbantur, tanquam lepores cedendo fugiendoque repente inventi sunt" (*Historia*, II, xxviii, 175).

81–4 and first ... fledd away] King Louis laid siege to Verneuil in June 1173 ("mense Junio, quando solent reges ad bella procedere," as Newburgh puts it; *Historia*, II, xxviii, 172). In July he managed to occupy parts of Verneuil during a truce but lost heart when Henry came to the rescue (Holinshed has a detailed report, *Chronicles*, II, 151). Louis's flight from Verneuil (9 August 1173) ended the Norman rising.

91 with winged speede] Another instance of Henry's rapidity of movement; see also below, 211, 214 and above, I, 492, and note.

93–8 But Chesters Earle ... of note] "Ibi quippe comes Cestrensis, et Radulfus de Fougeriis, aliique nobiles fere centum, in manus regis, quem atrocissimis fuerant odiis insectati, Dei judicio inciderunt" (Newburgh, *Historia*, II, xxix, 176). The capture of the rebels in Dôle (26 August

1173) ended the revolt in Brittany. The number of prisoners is taken
from Holinshed ("eighty knights," *Chronicles*, II, 153). Speed gives no
number but speaks of "very many other prisoners of especiall note and
Nobility" (*History*, IX, 6 [68], 501).

99–184 While thus in France ... that victorious day] May follows the out-
lines of Speed in his account of the battle of Fornham: "But God, who
meant to chastise the King, and not to deliuer him vp into his enemies
hands, destroyed those hopes that mooued the sonnes to their vnnaturall
attempts; for it was not long after, when newes came into *Normandie*, that
his faithful friends and seruants, *Richard de Lucie*, and *Humphrey de Bo-
hun* high Constable of *England*, together with the powers of *Reignald* Earle
of *Cornwall* the Kings Vncle, *Robert* Earle of *Gloucester* and *William*
Earle of *Arundell*, not farre from *Burie*, couragiously encountred with the
Earle of *Leicester*, and his *Flemings*, of whome aboue fiue thousand were
slaine, or taken, and among the prisoners was the Earle himselfe, and his
Amazonian Countesse, whose persons at his commandement were not
long after brought ouer into *Normandie*" (*History*, IX, 6 [70], 501–2).
Speed, however, does not name Fornham as the site of the encounter, he
has no battle speeches, and he halves the number of Flemings slain (or
captured). May turned to other sources, for instance Hoveden's *Annales*,
Holinshed's *Chronicles*, and Lucan's *De bello civili*, to flesh out his report.

102–6 The Northren parts ... warrelike king] For an account of the
Northern campaign, which is barely mentioned by Speed, May turns to
Hoveden and/or Holinshed: "In tempore autem illo *Richardus* de Luci
iustitiarius Angliæ, & *Humfredus* de Boun regis constabularius, profecti
fuerant cũ exercitu magno in Lonais terrã regis Scotiæ ad deuastandã
eam" (Roger of Hoveden, *Annales*, ed. Savile, 536, 41-3; Holinshed
speaks of King William's invasion of Northumbria but names the leaders
of the English counterattack only in retrospect, *Chronicles*, II, 153, 154).

108–11 in Englands Easterne parts ... Norfolke ioyne] "Comes enim Leice-
strensis cum classe hostili ex Flandria apud Orientales Anglos applicuit,
susceptusque a complice proprio, Hugone scilicet Bigoto" (Newburgh,
Historia, II, xxx, 178).

112–7 There theire ... Easterne parts] "Qui cũ audissent aduentum Comitis
Leicestriæ in Angliam, timuerunt valde. Et omnibus aliis negotiis postpo-
sitis dederunt, & coeperũt inducias à rege Scotiæ, datisq; hinc & inde
obsidibus de pace seruãda, vsque ad festum sancti *Hillarii*, festinato cursu
peruenerunt ad sanctum *Eadmundum*" (Roger of Hoveden, *Annales*, ed.
Savile, 536, 43-5).

119–20 The loyall Earles ... are mett] "Veneruntque illuc ad eos *Reginaldus* Comes Cornubiæ auunculus regis, & *Robertus* Comes Gloucestriæ, & *Willielmus* Comes de *Arundel*" (Roger of Hoveden, *Annales*, ed. Savile, 536, 46–7).

123 The Lords all mett, to Farneham march away] The battle of Fornham St. Genevieve near Bury St. Edmunds, which ended the Leicester War, was fought on 17 October 1173.

126–7 with different hopes, / Though æquall fury] Lucan says of the armies that met at Pharsalia, where the outcome of the Roman civil war between Caesar and Pompey was decided: "Ergo utrimque pari procurrunt agmina motu / Irarum; metus hos regni, spes excitat illos" (VII, 385–6).

128 The Flemmings prey, the English freedome sought] "his pro gloria, illis pro salute certantibus" (Newburgh, *Historia*, II, xxx, 179). Leicester led an army of Flemish mercenaries, mainly weavers who could expect no mercy from the English soldiers or the English peasants who feared for their wool (see Poole, *OHE*, 336).

131–58 When thus ... theire spiritts gaue] In Lucan's epic, Caesar cheers his army with similarly patriotic arguments before the battle at Pharsalia (*De bello civili*, VII, 269–87). The juster cause in the eyes of the author, however, is that of Pompey, though he commands an army of foreigners (cf. Pompey's rousing answer, in particular VII, 349–51).

177 Ten thousand of them] "Et ceciderunt in prælio illo plusquam decem millia Flandrensium" (Roger of Hoveden, *Annales*, ed. Savile, 536, 57–8). There were conflicting reports about the number of Flemings slain at Fornham; Holinshed discusses the differences in his *Chronicles*, II, 155 while Speed settles for 5000 (*History*, IX, 6 [70], 501; see above, note to 99–184).

179 his Amazonian Countesse] Her name was Petronilla; Newburgh only mentions her manly courage, "virilis animi femina" (*Historia*, II, xxx, 179), the title "Amazonian" comes from Speed; see above, note to 99–184.

181–3 Whoo by ... old Henry brought] Only those capable of raising ransom money were thus taken care of, "& cæteri ditiores qui cum eis capti fuerant missi sunt in Normanniam ad regem patrem" (Roger of Hoveden, *Annales*, ed. Savile, 536,59–537,1).

191 The King forbeares revenge] Gerald praises (with an Ovidian quotation) the king's clemency, "vincens animos iramque suam qui caetera vincit, hostibus undique victis et triumphatis vitam reddidit et honorem" (*De principis instructione*, II, iv, ed. Warner, *Opera*, VIII, 165; cf. Ovid, *Heroides*, III, 85).

198–9 For second newes ... elect of Winchester] "Thither came vnto him out of *England, Richard* (the Elect of *Winchester*) sent with all hast by the Kings Iusticiaries" (Speed, *Historie*, IX, 6 [73], 502). Holinshed mentions that Richard of Worcester, archdeacon of Poitiers, was given the bishopric of Winchester in 1173 (*Chronicles*, II, 155), but not that he acted as messenger. Richard, more often called of Ilchester, was one of the *familiares* at the court of Henry II, who employed him in various offices; see Warren, *Henry II*, 311–14.

204 Norwich was with fire destroy'd] "Item Comes *Hugo Bigot* infregit ciuitatem de Noretwiz & combussit" (Hoveden, *Annales*, ed. Savile, 537, 55–6). In Holinshed and Speed Norwich is "assaulted" and "spoyled" but not burnt down.

206–8 That th' Earle ... they had made] "Interea rex Angliæ filius & *Philippus* Comes Flandriæ venerūt cum magno exercitu usque *Gravelinges*, parati ad transfretandū in Angliam" (Roger of Hoveden, *Annales*, ed. Savile, 538, 48–9). While adverse winds kept back young King Henry and his fleet at Gravelines, his father embarked at Barfleur on 7 July and arrived safely at Southampton; see below, note to 220–54.

211 accustom'd speede] May applies the same expression to Caesar in his *Continuation of Lucan*, H5v; see also I, 492; II, 454; V, 91, 214.

213–15 (For all his acts ... not goe but fly] "*Lewis* said, that, *hee seemed not to goe but to flie*, hee went with such celeritie from one place and Kingdom to another" (Speed, *Historie*, IX, 6 [72], 502). Ralph of Diceto mentions that King Louis once remarked: "Rex Angliæ modo in Hybernia, modo in Anglia, modo in Normannia, volare potius judicandus est quam vel equum vel navem conscendere" ("Ymagines Historiarum," MCLXXII, *Opera Historica*, ed. William Stubbs [London, 1876], I, 351).

217–9 And takes aboord ... many moe] "adduxit secum [...] *Robertum*, Comitem Leicestriæ, & *Hugonem*, Comitem Cestriæ, quos statim custodiæ mancipauit" (Hoveden, *Annales*, ed. Savile, 539,3–5). Ralph of Diceto names the Countess, not the Count of Leicester: "Comitem quoque Cestrensem, Legecestrensem Comitissam, et alios plures quos habuit in vinculis," *Opera Historica*, I, 382.

220–54. But when hee hois'd ... sett on shore] The prayer and the accompanying gestures are apparently taken from Ralph of Diceto directly: "Sed cum rex ventum ex directo venire, navem cursum in Angliam via recta dirigere, flatus creberrimos vehementer ingravescere didicisset, erectis in coelum luminibus palam omnibus ait, 'si quæ ad pacem sunt cleri et populi habeam in proposito, si pacem in adventu meo reformandam Rex coelorum disposuit, tunc pro Sua misericordia portum michi indulget salutis. Si autem fuerit aversus et regnum in virga visitare decreverit, numquam michi datum sit vel fines regionis attingere.' Orationem ejus auditam sui satis præsumere potuerunt, quoniam ipsa die qua navem ascenderat, hora diei vesperascente, cum indempnitate rerum apud Hamonis Portum appulsus est" ("Ymagines historiarum,"MCLXXIV, *Opera Historica*, I, 382–3). Speed translates the prayer but leaves out the gestures: "but the winde changing, and he compelled to stay in harbour at *Barbfleet* in *Normandie*, where he had taken shipping, he is said (God touching his heart) to haue vttered these words with much remorse, in the presence of all; 'If my purpose in this voyage be for the peace of the Clergie and people, and if the King of Heauen shall vouchsafe to quiet and calme these troubles at my arriuall, then for his mercies sake wee beseech him to send vs a prosperous winde: But if it be against it, and hath resolued to visit the Kingdome of *England* with the rod of his fury, let him grant me neuer to touch the shore of that Country more.' His prayer thus vttered from the depth of soule, was seconded with a fresh pery of winde: wherupon setting sayle, hee arriued safe the same day with all his Nauie at the Port of *Hampton* in *England*" (*History*, IX, 6 [74], 502). For a contrast (which May must have had in memory) see Caesar's defiant speech before his frustrated attempt at crossing the Adriatic Sea (Lucan, *De bello civili*, V, 577–93).

255–84 Departing thence ... but the age] Henry's penitential walk to Canterbury is taken almost literally from Hoveden's account in *Annales*, ed. Savile, 539, 6–19; Speed also translates from Hoveden, "what it was, let *Houeden* report," but adds details from Matthew Paris, "*Matthew Paris* can tell you more plainely what that *Discipline* was" *(Historie*, IX, 6 [75], 502–3). See Appendix 3, pp. 233–4.

283–4 A strange example ... but the age] Speed censures the penitential practices of the monks in harsh terms: "To such height was the Papall tyranny and pride growne towards those, of whom God had said expressly, *Touch not mine Annointed*" (*History*, IX, 6 [75], 503).

286–8 (as if ... him fortunate)] William of Newburgh attributes the change in Henry's fortunes to God's providence, "quia Deus sic voluit, ut voluntati magis divinæ, quam potentiæ prudentiæve humanæ, ascriberetur eventus" (Newburgh, *Historia*, II, xxxiii, 184); Speed says that "some Monkes" attributed the reversal in Henry's fortunes to his penitence (Speed, *Historie*, IX, 6 [76], 503). May's epic mode helps him avoid a polemical note; cf. below, "And twas the hand of heauen, not Henry, fought" (372).

290–332 That Scotlands King ... is captive borne away] This incident, which occurred on 13 July 1174, is told after Holinshed (*Chronicles*, II, 157–8) who took it from William of Newburgh's *Historia* (II, xxxiii, 183–5; see Appendix 4, pp. 235–6). Speed mentions it only in passing.

294–8 And so much wracke ... round about] Both Hoveden and Newburgh give more vivid accounts of the devastation wreaked by the Scottish army; Hoveden is moved to one of his few exclamations: "rex Scotiæ inde recedēs obsedit *Alnewic* castellū *Willielmi* de Vesci & diuidens exercitum suum in tres partes, vnam secum retinuit [...] Et præcepit vt ipsi circumiacentes deuastarent prouincias, homines interficerēt, & prædas abducerent. Proh dolor! Tunc audires clamorem mulierū, vlulatus senū, gemitus morientium, desperationem iuuenum" (*Annales*, ed. Savile, 538,43–8). Newburgh is even more detailed and more passionate (*Historia*, II, xxxii, 182–3).

299–300 Five gallant ... Castell came*] The list given in the marginal note derives from Holinshed, who conflated it from similar lists in Hoveden, Newburgh, and Polydore Vergil: Hoveden names six knights as defendors of Prudhoe castle, "*Robertus* de *Stuteuile* vicecomes Eboraci, & *Willielmus* de Vesci, & *Ranulphus* de *Glamuile*, & *Radulfus* de Tilli constabularius familiæ *Rogeri* Eboracensis Archiepiscopi, & *Bernardus* de Bailol, & *Odonellus* de *Vmframuile* (*Annales*, ed. Savile, 538,40–42); William of Newburgh gives only four names, "Robertus de Stutevilla, Ranulfus de Glanvilla, Bernardus de Baliolo, Willelmus de Vesci" (*Historia* II, xxxiii, 184). Holinshed follows Newburgh, but adds "Odonet de Umfreiuille" in brackets from Hoveden's list (*Chronicles*, II, 157); he will have taken the spelling "Ursie" from Polydore Vergil, who has a Reginald Urcy in an otherwise different list: "Hugo Moriuilla, Gulielmus Tracius, Ricardus Britto, & Reginaldus Vrcius" (*Anglicae historiae libri*, 218, t2v); Holinshed mentions Polydore Vergil in a sidenote to his account of the wasting of Kendal, which immediately precedes his own list of English captains. As in the case of the Earl of Flanders and the Archbishop of Tyre, May probably added his note in a revision, perhaps with Holinshed's *Chronicles* at hand (Speed only mentions the fact and the date of the king's capture).

317–21 the King ... leaue] Holinshed, who is May's authority for this episode, does not single out William's bravery: "The king with a few other (who at the first had begun the battell) was taken" (*Chronicles*, II, 158).

329 Guarded ... souldiers] The marginal note correctly points to Newburgh's *Historia* as source for the number of soldiers, "in hostili vero exercitu plusquam octoginta armatorum millia æstimari" (II, xxxiii, 183), but

the note may simply have been taken over from Holinshed who habitually refers to William as "Parvus."

334 From thence] That is from Canterbury, where Henry received the news that "Scotlands King was taken prisoner" (290).

341 Huntingdon Castle's yeilded] "profectus est Huntendoniam, & castellum obsedit: quod traditum est ei die Dominica proximo sequenti" (i.e., 19 July 1174; Roger of Hoveden, *Annales*, ed. Savile, 539,44).

342–7 Nor durst Earle Bigot . . . there obtain'd] "In crastino venit ad eum Comes *Hugo Bigot*, & facta cum eo pace reddidit ei castellum de *Fremingham* & castellum de *Bungaie*, & cum magna difficultate impetrauit à rege, vt Flandrenses qui cum eo erant sine impedimento possent repatriare" (*Annales*, ed. Savile, 539,49–52). The castle of Framlingham was levelled (see Warren, *Henry II*, 235).

348–50 The like did Ferrers . . . long had held] "Et comes de Ferreres reddidit ei castellū de *Tutesberie*, & de *Duffeld*" (*Annales*, ed. Savile, 540,1).

351–2 As much stout Mowbray . . . his castle too] "Venit etiam ibidem ad regem *Rogerus* de *Mubrai*, & reddidit ei castellū de *Tresk*" (*Annales*, ed. Savile, 539,59–540,1).

353 So did the forts then kept in Leisters name] Hoveden names the castles as Leicester, Mountsorel, and Groby (*Annales*, ed. Savile, 540,2).

354–5 And to Northampton . . . the King] "Venitque illuc ad eum *Hugo* Dunelmensis Episcopus, & tradidit ei castellum de *Dunelmia*, & castellum de *Norham*, & castellum de *Aluertun* nouum" (*Annales*, ed. Savile, 539,56–7).

356–8 Thither did then . . . Henry's prisoner] May does not mention, as his authority Hoveden does, that they brought William with his legs tied under his horse, "adductus est ei *Willielmus* rex Scottorum sub ventre equi compeditus" (*Annales*, ed. Savile, 539,55–6).

390 Melpomene] The Muse of tragedy.

397–644 Whilest England . . . neuer gain'd] Eleanor's jealousy and vengeance is a late medieval addition to the Rosamond legend. The earlier chroniclers record at most the fact, first mentioned by Gerald of Wales, that after the rebellion of his sons Henry lived in open adultery with Rosamond (see note to 403–4). A first (chronologically misplaced) version of Eleanor's vengeance appears in *The French Chronicle of London*, where her namesake Eleanor of Provence, the wife of King Henry III, is said to have bled to death her husband's concubine Rosamond; the clue of thread and the cup of poison are still later accretions (see Virgil B. Heltzel, *Fair Rosamond: A Study of the Development of a Literary Theme* [rpt. New York], 1970, 1–11, for details).

399 Pale Nemesis] In later antiquity, Nemesis is the goddess of vengeance.

403–4 'Mongst which ... loue of Rosamund] Gerald says that Henry incar-
cerated Eleanor and acknowledged Rosamond as his concubine, "olim
incarcerata sponsa sua Alienora regina in pœnam forte maritalis excidii
primi consensusque secundi, qui adulter antea fuerat occultus, effectus
postea manifestus, non mundi quidem rosa juxta falsam et frivolam nomi-
nis impositionem, sed immundi verius rosa vocata palam et impudenter
abutendo" (*De principis instructione*, II, iv, 165–6).

416 Rhamnusia] Another name for Nemesis.

435–39 What could ... fathers eyes] Medea is invoked here as a paragon of
female cruelty; besides dismembering her brother and slaughtering her
children (see above, I, 548–54), she caused the death of her rival Creusa:
when Creusa was about to marry Jason, Medea sent her a poisoned gar-
ment that burnt her to death.

461–90 About those places ... persuasiue straines] This rustic interlude
shows some affinities with the pastoral drama of the period. See below,
note to 485–90.

463 the huntresse Queene] Diana.

467–81 Theire iolly May-games ... the merryest lasses] Country sports and
games were preached against by Puritan divines; at court, however, they
were considered harmless. A proclamation to support the games, first
published by King James in 1618, was reissued in 1633 as *The Kings
Maiesties Declaration to his Subjects, Concerning Lawfull Sports to Bee Vsed*.

483 But sitts at home with folded armes] Headley sees a parallel here with
Shakespeare's ship-wrecked Fernando: "His arms in this sad knot" (*Se-
lected Beauties*, 151; *The Tempest*, I, ii, 224).

485–90 Cupid, they say ... straines] Cupid's escapade into Arcady forms the
framework for Torquato Tasso's pastoral comedy *Aminta*. In the prologue,
Cupid addresses the audience in the habit of a shepherd and discloses
that he is hiding from his mother Venus, who wants to keep him on
Olympus in order to have his arrows entirely at her own disposal. There
had been translations of the *Aminta* by Abraham Fraunce in 1591 and by
Henry Reynolds in 1628 (the latter was published by Augustine Math-
ewes, who also printed May's *King Henry the Second*).

525–27 Oh then shee wish'd ... Henry's eye] Headley compares this to a
reflection in Daniel's *Complaint of Rosamond*, 680–6 (*Select Beauties*, 153).

531–3 The cry was ... Her Ladyes life] A silk thread that leads the queen
into Rosamond's bower is first mentioned by Robert Fabyan: "But the
common fame telleth, that lastly the queene wan to her by a clewe of

threde, or silke, & delt with her in such maner, that she liued not long after" (*The Chronicle of Fabyan*, 1559, G1r–v, 350–1). Holinshed took the clue and spun it out in the "Character" which concludes his Life of King Henry. There, the thread is no longer cleverly spun but accidentally drawn out: "But the common report of the people is, that the queene in the end found hir out by a silken thread, which the king had drawne after him out of hir chamber with his foot, and dealt with hir in such sharpe and cruell wise, that she liued not long after" (*Chronicles*, II, 200). Speed follows Holinshed, but lets Rosamond accidentally draw out the thread herself and thus guide the queen to her hiding place in a "Character" of Rosamond attached to his *Historie* (IX, 6 [102], 509).

536–49 Oh whoo can tell ... her bedd forsooke] From Ovid's *Metamorphoses* onwards, a timely transformation is the way out of distress for damsells in the epyllion tradition. Usually, however, they are turned into living things like a laurel (Daphne) or a reed (Syrinx); to be changed into a statue usually is a form of punishment (as with Aglauros, Niobe, and Anaxarete).

548 Least Henry should haue turn'd Pigmalion] This is an ingenious reversal of the myth of the sculptor Pygmalion, whose passionate prayers turned his favourite statue into a living woman.

557–9 Heere take ... presently] John Stow was the first to report (parenthetically) the rumour that Rosamond was brought to death by poison in the 1592 edition of his *Annales*, "(poisoned by Queene *Elianor*, as some thought)" (*Annales*, 1631, N5v, 154). From him (if not by oral tradition) it passed into the verse history of William Warner, *Albions England*, 1592, and Samuel Daniel's *Complaint of Rosamond*, 1592 (see Tillotson, ed. Drayton, *Works*, V, 102).

581 poisonous leprosyes] This is the punishment the gods decree for Cressida in Robert Henryson's *Testament of Cresseid*, 304–43. In a lover's complaint entitled "The Fruits of Jealousy or, A Love (but not Loving) Letter," Robert Tofte groups Rosamond with Cressida, "a Lazer foul in sight," and "SHORES wretched wife," the concubine of Edward IV (*The Blazon of Jealousy*, 1615, 81).

610–16 for when the story ... you sought] Rosamond's story was read in many versions. By May's time, it had passed into balladry; see "On the Death of Fair Rosamond," preserved in the 1607 edition of Thomas Deloney's *Strange Histories*, but probably much older. For the literary afterlife of Rosamond see Heltzel, *Fair Rosamond*, chapters II and III.

629–32 There well ... had mistooke] There is an emblem of Cupid and

Death in Alciati's and many later emblem books. Du Bellay wrote a well-known elegiac poem on the subject; the first two distichs are: "Mutarunt arma inter se Mors, atque Cupido: / Hic falcem gestat, gestat at illa facem / Afficit haec animum, corpus se conficit ille: / Sic moritur iuvenis, sic moribundus amat." Geoffrey Whitney reproduced Alciati's emblem in his *Choice of Emblemes and other Deuises* (1586, No 132) and quoted these lines by Du Bellay on the margin of the *descriptio* (Geoffrey Whitney, *A Choice of Emblems*, ed. Henry Green [1866; rpt. Hildesheim], 1971, lxiii).

635–7 Her hearse ... remaine] Higden first mentions the burial at Godstow Nunnery, "illa cito post obiit, et apud Godestowe juxta Oxoniam in capitulo monialium sepulta est" (*Polychronicon*, VII, xxii, 52–4). In 1191 Bishop Hugh of Lincoln ordered her to be disinterred because her tomb had become a place of worship for the nuns (see [Benedict of Peterborough], Gesta Regis *Henrici Secundi*, II, 231–2). Her remains were then buried outside the church. She may have been reentombed at some later date in the chapter house; Leland reports that "Rosamundas tumbe at Godestow nunnery was taken up a late" (*Itinerary*, ed. Lucy T. Smith [London, 1907], I, 328; quoted from Heltzel, *Fair Rosamond*, 9, n. 30). May does not mention the epitaph on this tomb, which most of the chronicles give in both Latin and English: "Hic iacet in tumba, Rosa mundi, sed non rosa munda / Non redolet sed olet, que redolere solet." (Fabyan, *Chronicle*, 1559, Vol. I, G1v, 351; cf. Stow, *Annales*, 1631, N5v–6r, 154–5, and Speed, *Historie*, IX, 6 [102], 509–10). There may be allusions to the epitaph in II, 335–7, III, 321 (see notes to these lines and to V, 403–4).

641–4 This act was cause ... neuer gain'd] Eleanor was kept in custody from about 1173 (well before Rosamond's supposed death) to 1185 (see Heltzel, 3, and Warren, *Henry II*, 118–21).

656–61 But first with care ... close custody] "For the king after this happie atchieuement of his warlike affaires, being ruled by reason and aduise (as it is likelie) would not that so smoking a fierbrand (as queene Elianor had prooued hirselfe to be) should still annoie his eies, and therefore (whether in angrie or quiet mood, that is doubtfull) he committed hir to close prison, bicause she had procured his sons Richard and Geffrey to ioine with their elder brother against him their father" (Holinshed, *Chronicles*, II, 159). Rosamond is not mentioned at this point in the *Chronicles*.

662–4 Then musters ... crosses ore] May follows Newburgh, "rex cum ingentibus copiis celeriter transfretavit, ducens secum paulo ante sibi exhibitum regem Scottorum, comitemque Leicestrensem, aliosque captivos insignes" (*Historia*, II, xxxvii, 195). The comparison to Caesar turns this journey into the triumph mentioned in 665; Newburgh suggests something similar in his description of Henry's entry into Rouen: "Rothomagum in conspectu hostium pompatice ingressus est. Hostes [. . .] sunt repentino et triumphali ex Anglia reditu stupefacti" (ibid.)

674–6 and first convey'd . . . followed then] "Et in crastino præmisit rex Franciæ debiliores exercitus sui in terram suam mane: & permissione regis Angliæ, eodem die secutus est eos" (Roger of Hoveden, *Annales*, ed. Savile, 540,25–6). Louis abandoned the siege of Rouen on 14 August 1174. May does not mention the breach of promise involved in the king's retreat (he failed to honour an engagement for peace talks with Henry) which Hoveden reports a little later (540, 30–1) and Speed takes up in his *Historie* (IX, 6 [78], 503).

677–9 For vncontroll'd . . . stopp'd the way] See Hoveden, "ecce rex Angliæ pater veniens de Anglia portas ciuitatis, quas burgenses obstruxerant, reserauit, & exiens cum militibus & seruientibus, fossata, quæ facta fuerant inter exercitum regis Franciæ & ciuitatem, fecit impleri lignis, lapidibus, & terra, & in planum redigi" (*Annales*, ed. Savile, 540,20–3).

691 A reverend bishopp] Hoveden and Holinshed name him as William, Archbishop of Sens (*Annales*, ed. Savile, 540,28–9; *Chronicles*, II, 161).

699–706 Then to Gisors . . . Lewis conclude] The meeting was held on 8 September 1174 ("in natiuitate S. *Mariæ*," *Annales*, ed. Savile, 540,33–4).

702–3 For young prince Richard . . . in Poictou] "Quo cum venissent, non potuit inter eos conuenire propter *Richardum* Comitē Pictauiæ, qui tempore illo erat in Pictauia expugnās castella & homines patris sui" (*Annales*, ed. Savile, 540,34–5). Holinshed and Speed do not specify Richard's activities in Poitou at this point.

713–26 This is that Heroë . . . the Pagan name] Richard I became famous for his exploits during the Third Crusade, which led him within sight of Jerusalem and made him popular as the absentee king of the Robin Hood legends.

721 From him the dreadfull Saladine shall fly] In the course of the Third Crusade, a Christian army under Richard's command beat Saladine's saracens in the Battle of Assur (7 September 1191).

727–86 After the truce . . . pœnitence alone] See Hoveden, "rex Angliæ pater promouit exercitū suū in Pictauiam. Cuius aduentum *Richardus* Comes Pictauiæ filius eius non ausus expectare fugit de loco in locum. Et cum constaret illi, quod rex Franciæ & rex frater suus exclusissent eum à treugis indignatus est inde. Et cū lachrymis veniens cecidit pronus in terram ante pedes regis patris sui, & postulans veniam in sinu patris recipitur" (*Annales*, ed. Savile, 540,39–43). Polydore Vergil extended this passage and added a dry hint suggesting that Richard's apparent repentance might have been calculated: "Quæ res ita Ricardum terruit, vt viribus suis diffidens evagari cœperit, nec vspiã hostes sequentes expectare auderet: quinimò cùm videret ad extremũ, res esse in discrimen adductas, cum primis sociorum ingratos animos incusans, quòd immemores datæ fidei se deseruissent, ac nõnihil sibi de patria pietate pollicitus, statuit mutare sententiam, séque totum ad parentis voluntatem nutúmque cõvertere, id quod ei saluti fuit: quippe sic posteriores cogitiones, vt aiunt, sapientiores esse solent" (*Anglica historia*, V3v, 232). The insinuation is reflected in Holinshed's *Chronicles*: "At length when he had considered his owne state, and weied how vnthankfullie the French king and his brother had dealt with him, in hauing no consideration of him at such time as they tooke truce, he determined to alter his purpose, and hauing some good hope in his fathers clemencie, thought best to trie it, which he found to be the best waie that he could haue taken" (II, 161).

787–815 So much king ... his sonne away] In his version of the reconciliation scene May stresses Richard's offer to go on a peace mission. There is nothing like it in Newburgh or in Hoveden; in Holinshed's *Chronicles* the initiative is old King Henry's who sends "this Richard vnto king Lewes, and to his other sonne Henrie, to commen with them of peace" (II, 161). Speed comes closest to May: "*Richard* ... put himselfe most humbly into his Fathers mercy, and throwing himselfe with tears at his feete, obtained the pardon he begd, and a full restitution to his most inward grace & fauour. A most Christian, fatherly, wise, and happy Act; for *Richard* ouercome with this vnexpected and incredible goodnesse, neuer desisted till he had brought the young King to a finall attonement" (*History*, IX, 6 [79], 504).

807 I, that have sinned happily] The idea of a happy sin (*felix culpa*) is often applied to Adam's fall, the first sin, which eventually provoked the coming of Christ.

Book VI

2–5 With such ... Ambois and Tours] See note to V, 787–815.

14–27 The causes ... when the warre begann] The clauses of the peace agreement are listed in Hoveden, *Annales*, ed. Savile, 540,49–541,41 and Holinshed, *Chronicles*, II, 162.

24–5 every prisoner ... sett free] Four of Henry's chief opponents were, in fact, kept in custody and released only after paying heavy fines: William, King of Scots, in December 1174, the earl of Leicester, the earl of Chester, and Ralph de Fougères probably in 1177 (see Warren, *Henry II*, 138–9).

30–2 Adela ... in Henry's custody] "Herewith also the peace was renewed betwixt king Henrie and king Lewes, and for the further confirmation, a new aliance was accorded betwixt them, which was, that the ladie Adela the daughter of king Lewes should be given in mariage vnto earle Richard the sonne of king Henrie, who bicause she was not yet of age able to marie, she was conueied into England to be vnder the guiding of king Henrie, till she came to lawfull yeares", Holinshed, *Chronicles*, II, 162. In fact, Adela (or Alice, as she is also called) was betrothed to Richard as early as 1161 when she was three and Richard seven years old (Speed has the correct ages, *Historie*, IX, 6 [85], 505). At three, Alice was not only below the legal age for marriage, but also for betrothal; therefore, a special dispensation had to be sought from the Pope; see Johann Baptist Sägmüller, "Eine Dispens päpstlicher Legaten zur Verehelichung eines Siebenjährigen mit einer Dreijährigen im Jahre 1160," *Theologische Quartalsschrift* 86 (1904), 556–75.

34–8 Richard and Geoffrey ... in regall dignity] "Thus the peace being concluded, king Henrie [...] brought home his sons, [...] where Richard and Geffrey did homage to him, receiuing their othes of allegiance according to the maner in that case required. But king Henrie the sonne did no homage, for his father (in respect that he was a king) would not suffer him" (Holinshed, *Chronicles*, II, 162–3).

39–43 White-winged Concord ... to light] Lucan has an apostrophe to Concordia to mark a lull in the the the Roman civil war (*De bello civili*, IV, 189–92). Holinshed ruminates at length on the theme "Discordia fit charior concordia" (*Chronicles*, II, 163). In May's translation of one of the verse passages in John Barclay's *Argenis* (1629) Peace and Piety descend "with snowy wings" from heaven (N6r).

44–6 With her ... earth againe] Lucan links Concordia with love rather than with piety. The goddess *Pietas* is a late addition to the classical pantheon; the first temple of Piety was erected in 181 B.C. (according to Livy, *Ab urbe condita*, 40, 34, 4–6). Cicero defines her function as "Iustitia adversus Deos" (*De natura deorum*, I, 186), but, as the example of "pius Aeneas" shows, this was soon extended to the duties owed to one's family and nation.

48–50 As once ... his mourning light] The horrid feast of Atreus, who killed the children of his brother Thyestes and served them up as a dish, has been handed down in several versions from Aeschylus to Ovid; a detailed treatment is found in Seneca's *Thyestes*, 682–788.

57–60 his two younger sonns ... his Aquitaine] "Rex vero pater misit *Richardum* filium suum in Pictauiam, & *Gaufridum* filium suum in Brittaniam" (Roger of Hoveden, *Annales*, ed. Savile, 542,34–5).

63–7 The two king Henrys ... whole againe] If we can follow Holinshed, who lists many of the stations, this progress, which went on from about Christmas 1174 to Easter 1175, took the kings through the heartland of their continental possessions (*Chronicles*, II, 163–4).

72–81 Or show ... Theire happinesse] See Holinshed, "landing at Portsmouth [...] they tooke their iournie streight to London, all the waies being full of people that came to see them, and to shew themselues glad and ioifull of their concord and happie arriuall. At their comming to the citie they were receiued with great reioising of the people, beseeching God long to preserve them both in health and honour" (Holinshed, *Chronicles*, II, 164).

76–8 And Sol from Taurus ... with the men] The Bull (Taurus) is the second sign of the Zodiac and reigned from 12 April to 11 May in the old style calendar; according to Holinshed, the two Henrys landed on 9 May 1175.

84 Two Sunns at once] Three suns appear in the air before the battle of Towton in Shakespeare's *Third Part of King Henry VI*, II, i, 25, five suns in his *King John*, IV, ii, 182.

87–92 Nor could ... envy'd gloryes] There are several references to the Roman triumphs of Pompey and of Caesar in Lucan's *De bello civili*; after the Spanish campaign, Caesar quells a mutiny of his war-weary soldiers by asking if they would not like to join in his future triumph procession: "Lauriferos nullo comitetur volnere currus" (V, 332); before the battle at Pharsalus, Lucan surveys Pompey's multiracial army and asks him to rob Caesar of the subjects for future triumphs by slaying all of mankind: "Eripe victori gentes et sanguine mundi / Fuso, Magne, semel totos consume triumphos" (*De bello civili*, VII, 233–4). In his *Continuation of Lucan's Historical Poem* (1635) May later described in detail Caesar's four triumphs, which made kings from several nations "waile in chaines their common overthrow" (G3v). In his *Cleopatra*, May describes in Marlovian diction what Caesar did to the Armenian king Artanasdes, "Whome through the streetes of Alexandria / Hee ledd in triumph bound with golden chaines" (9r).

103 blew Neptunes watery armes] May calls all the sea-gods "bluish" in one

of the verses he contributed to the translation of John Barclay's *Argenis* (T1v); Neptune, in particular, is apostrophized as "he that does in his blue armes enfold / Earth's Globe" (C1r; see also "blue Neptune," S8r). It is a classical topos: "Caeruleos habet unda deos," Ovid, *Metamorphoses*, II, 8.

107 th' Oebalian frendly starres] The stars are Castor and Pollux; their mother Leda was a Spartan queen, and Sparta was founded by King Oebalus. May found the expression, which is very rare, in a valedictory poem by Statius, in which the author asks Neptune to send good weather for the sea voyage of a patron's son: "Proferte benigna / Sidera et antemnae gemino considite cornu, / Oebalii fratres" (*Silvae*, III, ii, 8–10).

110 The Halcyon dayes] Days of calm, originally the days when kingfishers (*alcyones*, named after Alcyone and her husband) were said to breed on the sea; cf. above, I, 265–6 and note. In a prophetic passage of his *Edward the Third* May uses the same expression to point forward to the Stuart reign: "And after him [i.e., King James], more to confirme those blest / And Halcion dayes, shall *Charles* from heaven be sent" (K2r). The 1630s were often called Halcyon years; it may be of topical interest that Charles I, like Henry II, tried to settle an ecclesiastical dispute in those years.

114–17 the sinne of Simony ... did restraine] Simony was declared a heresy in one of the articles decreed at the synod of London: "Hæc Symoniacæ hæresis esse detestata est sancta synodus, & anathematizauit" (Roger of Hoveden, *Annales*, ed. Savile, 543,30–1).

121–4 And many Castles ... Huntington] The list of castles is taken from Speed, who says of Henry that "hee threw to the Earth sundry Castles which had beene formerly kept against him, as *Leicester, Huntington, Walton, Groby, Stutesbury*, &c" (Speed, *Historie*, IX, 6 [83], 505, with marginal reference to "Matth Paris / Roger Wend. / Manusc."). Huntingdon and Walton are listed by Fabyan (*Chronicle*, 154), but not by Holinshed, Hoveden, or Benedict.

125–38 To deedes of Iustice ... Henry's name] This reform was brought forward at the Assize of Northampton (1176).

129–31 England hee diuides ... Iustices itinerant] See Speed, "hee caused *England* to be diuided into sixe circuits, and to each Circuit three Iusticiars Itinerants deputed" (Speed, *Historie*, IX, 6 [83], 505).

151 Calliope] The Muse of epic poetry. With this apostrophe May embellishes an invitation to pause and reflect on Henry's achievements which Speeds inserts in his *Historie* after the relief of Rouen in 1174: "Let the greatnesse and felicitie of this King be now but sleightly looked vpon, and it will appeare, that no Prince of those times was hitherto so much bound

to God for manifold fauours as hee" (X, 6 [78], 503).

163–8 That King of Connaught, Roderike] Rory O'Connor, the Irish high-king, had refused to do personal homage to Henry in Dublin in 1171; see above, IV, 443–50. The new negotiations led to the treatise of Windsor (1175), which made him the king of England's man (see Warren, *Henry II*, 201).

172–82 Embassadours ... in Henry's stately Court] The year of these embassies is 1176; the list of ambassadors goes back to Matthew Paris, *Chronica majora*, who names in addition the archbishop of Trier: "In eisdem sane diebus, nuncii Manuelis Constantinopolitani imperatoris, nuncii Romani imperatoris Fretherici, nuncii Willelmi Treverensis archiepiscopi, nuncii Henrici ducis Saxonici, nuncii Flandrensis comitis Philippi" (II, 299). Matthew does not include the king of Sicily. In Speed's *Historie*, however, the list is followed by a reference to the Sicilian match of one of Henry's daughters, which was celebrated in the same year (IX, 6 [78], 503; see excerpt in the note to "The Description of King Henry the Second," lines 141–57, below). Perhaps May extrapolated an embassy from this coincidence. He mentions the Sicilian match later on (see lines 207–10 and note).

184 as to Salomon] The comparison is prompted by Speed ("like another Salomon," *Historie*, IX, 6 [78], 503); Matthew Paris only marvels at the wisdom and glory of the king ("quantae rex Henricus sapientiae fuerit quantaeque magnificentiae," *Chronica majora*, II, 300).

186–94 As two great Kings ... both obey] Holinshed calls them "Alfonse king of Castile and Garsias king of Nauarre" (confusing the latter with his son, *Chronicles*, II, 174); Speed does not give the Christian names of the two (Speed, *History*, IX, 6 [78], 503). May could have found his version of the incident either in the *Chronica majora* of Matthew Paris (II, 299) or, more likely, in Roger of Hoveden's *Annales*: "Eodem anno *Aldefonsus* rex Castellæ, & *Sanctius* rex Nauarræ auunculus eius, post multas & magnas debellationes inter eos habitas, compromiserunt se in regem Angliæ patrem, de controuersiis & calumniis, quæ inter illos erant" (561,31–4). Both Matthew and Roger offer substantial accounts of the case.

195–202 And young Alphonso ... celebrate] Both Roger of Hoveden (*Annales*, ed. Savile, 555,42–3) and Holinshed (*Chronicles*, II, 170) say that Eleanor was given away in the year of Henry's Solomonic judgment (1176), but they do not suggest a connection between these events; Warren accepts 1176 as the year of their marriage (*Henry II*, 222); Poole places it in 1170 (Poole, *OHE*, 329).

203–6 His eldest daughter . . . shall come] This marriage had been arranged in 1165 and was celebrated in 1168 (Poole, *OHE*, 328); it produced Emperor Otto IV.

207–10 And in this . . . solemnity] "The same yeare [i.e., 1176] the ladie Johan the kings daughter was giuen in marriage vnto William king of Sicill" (Holinshed, *Chronicles*, II, 170, and see above, note to 172–82; the marriage of Joan and William II took place in 1177).

218–31 Great Saladine . . . conquest on] "Interim *Saladinus* rex Babyloniæ, associatis sibi regibus, & principibus Paganorum, [. . .] intrauit terram Christianorum, & non longe à sancta ciuitate Ierusalem sua fixerunt tentoria" (Roger of Hoveden, *Annales*, ed. Savile, 566,19–22).

225 Entitled King of Kings and Lord of Lords] Perhaps suggested by William of Newburgh, "nactus est nomen grande supra nomen aliorum magnorum qui sunt in terra" (*Historia rerum Anglicarum*, III, x, 241), or by Giraldus, "Saldini cujusdam, viri magni in gente sua et magnifici, nimis amplam potentiam, qui, Damasco Babiloniam, Alexandriam, necnon et Ægyptum totam adjiciens bellicosisque Parthorum populis potenter imperans" (*De principis instructione*, II, xxii, 200).

231–4 great feare . . . of late] May is mistaken about the sequence of events: King Baldwin IV died in 1185; he initiated the consultations about the state of Jerusalem himself and sent Heraclius to muster support in 1184. The mistake may have been prompted by Newburgh's *Historia*, which in Chap. III, xii seems to imply that the consultations took place after the death of Baldwin the Leper. Hoveden is right about the initiative, but assigns it to 1185: "Eodem anno, *Baldewinus* leprosus rex Ierusalem, & Templares & Hospitalares miserunt ad regem Angliæ, filium *Matildis* Imperatricis, *Heraclium* sanctæ ciuitatis Ierusalem Patriarcham" (*Annales*, ed. Savile, 628,14–6).

235–6 a childe . . . five yeares old] Newburgh makes Baldwin V a nine-year-old (*Historia rerum Anglicarum*, III, xii, 244); Hoveden simply calls him a boy (*Annales*, ed. Savile, 631,32–3). May's information probably comes from Matthew Paris: "Mortuo interea Baldewino rege Jerosolimorum leproso, regnavit pro eo Baldewinus, puer quinque annorum, nepos ejus ex sorore Sibilla, et Willelmo marchione Montis Ferrati genitus" (*Chronica majora*, II, 322).

239–58 the Princes all . . . Ierusalem] "Cum ergo res Ierosolymitanæ indies languescerent [. . .] prudentes terræ illius crebra cogitatione versarent; generali providentia statutum est ut vir magnus, cujus cum quantitate negotii moveret auctoritas, Sanctæ scilicet Resurrectionis patriarcha, petendi contra immanissimum hostem Saladinum auxilii gratia, ad Christianos principes in Europam mitteretur, et maxime ad illustrem Anglorum regem, cujus efficacior et promptior opera sperabatur" (Newburgh, *Historia*, III, xii, 244–5).

247–58 And for Embassadour . . . Ierusalem] Heraclius presented the insignia at Reading on 29 January 1185. Speed conflates this first meeting with the council which Henry called to Clerkenwell for March 10, 1186, when he reports that he "had brought with him (for memorable signes, that the suite was by common consent of the Countrey) the *Keyes* of the places of Christes *Natiuitie, Paßion,* and *Resurrection;* of *Dauids Tower,* and of the holy *Sepulchre;* and the humble offer of the *Kingdome* of *Hierusalem,* with the *Ensigne* or *Standard* of the *Kingdome*" (*History*, IX, 6 [90], 506).

265–70 Although . . . Palæstine] Speed says that Heraclius offered the ensigns of Jerusalem to Henry "as duely belonging to him, who was the right heire therunto; to wit, the sonne of *Geffrey* Earle of *Anjou,* whose brother *Fulke* was King of *Hierusalem*" (*History*, IX, 6 [90], 506).

272 Persuasiue letters] William of Newburgh, Roger of Hoveden, and Gerald of Wales reproduce copies of the Pope's letter (*Historia*, III, xii, 245–7; *Annales*, ed. Savile, 628–29; *De principis instructione*, II, xxv, 204–6).

277–8 sadd newes . . . Ierusalem] Jerusalem surrendered on 3 October 1187. May uses the same phrase again in VII, 73–4.

285 That happy Genius] Concordia or Piety, both mentioned at the beginning of Book VI (39–46).

295 Fortunes restlesse wheele] Gerald of Wales attributes the change in Henry's fortunes to his refusal to come to the aid of Jerusalem; when Henry declined the offer of the keys to the holy city, he says, Heraclius prophesied: "From hensefoorth shall your glorie be turned into sorrow" (*Expugnatio*, II, xxvii; trl. Hooker, Holinshed, *Chronicles*, VI, 214). In his *De principis instructione* Gerald devotes a whole chapter to the prophecies of Heraclius and their fulfilment: "De patriarchæ monitis et comminationibus in regem Henricum quasi prophetico spiritu ter prolatis," II, xxviii, 210–2).

298–304 The stormy Ocean . . . as Acheron] The tempestuous simile may owe something to the storms in Virgil's *Aeneid* (III, 564–5) or Ovid's *Metamorphoses* (XI, 497–500).

299 Aeol's adamantine caues] Cf. above, note to I, 279.

330–32 God . . . their impietyes] Speed expresses a similar sentiment shortly before the collapse of the rebellion: "But God, who meant to chastise the

King, and not to deliuer him vp into his enemies hands, destroyed those hopes that mooued the sonnes to their vnnaturall attempts" (Speed, *Historie*, IX, 6 [70], 501).

335–8 Richard ... commanded so] "Post natale Domini præcepit rex regi filio suo accipere homagium à *Richardo* Comite Pictauiæ fratre suo, & à *Gaufrido* Comite Brittanniæ fratre suo. Ipse vero obediens patri recepit homagium *Gaufridi* fratris sui, & cum à *Richardo* fratre suo recipere vellet, noluit ei *Richardus* homagium facere, & postmodum cum *Richardus* offerret ei homagium facere, noluit rex filius recipere" (Roger of Hoveden, *Annales*, ed. Savile, 618,35–40). This was at Le Mans in 1183; May has taken a step back in time.

352–5 Richard in wrath ... is pursu'd] The phrasing suggests that May turned to Holinshed's close translation of Hoveden: "Richard departed from the court in great displeasure, & comming into Poictow, began to fortifie his castels & townes, that he might be in readinesse to stand vpon his safegard, if his father or brethren should come to pursue him" (*Chronicles*, II, 183).

358–9 To craue ... repaires] "Cum ergo *Richardus* vidisset se non posse resistere fratribus suis, misit ad regem suum pro auxilio, qui magno congregato exercitu festinanter aduenit" (Roger of Hoveden, *Annales*, ed. Savile, 618,45–6). Holinshed's translation has no equivalent for Hoveden's "festinanter," such as May's "straight."

370–2 Once a true seruant ... traitour found] Hoveden places the incident in the vicinity of Limoges; "sui eum pessime receperunt; quia in eum miserunt sagittas, ita vt etiam super tunicale suum crudeliter perforarent, & quendam militem suum coram oculis eius vulnerarent" (Roger of Hoveden, *Annales*, ed. Savile, 619,27–29).

372–7 and when againe ... to save his master, dy'd] The adjoining castle was Limoges; "præsentibus filiis suis præfati castelli satellites sagittas direxerunt lethiferas: adeo vt equum, quo rex pater ferebatur, in capite vulnerarēt, & nisi equus ad aduentum sagittæ altius caput eleuasset, sagitta in regio pectore profundius descendisset" (Roger of Hoveden, *Annales*, ed. Savile, 619,32–5).

381–92 But that ... a sonne] The pious reflection is inspired by Speed, "behold the hand of God by taking away the young king at *Martell* [...] gaue an end to this odious, foule, and intricate contention" (*Historie*, IX, 6 [86], 505–6).

393–9 Now young king Henry ... his vitall part] "Paucis post elapsis diebus rex filius [...] in grauem incidit infirmitatē in villa, quæ dicitur Martel

[. . .]. Primo [e]n[im] arripuit eum febris, deinde fluxus ventris" (Roger of Hoveden, *Annales*, ed. Savile, 620,41–4).

400–82 Oppressed nature . . . slaughter'd sonne] For the deathbed scene May turns mainly to Speed; "certainely his death was not inglorious, but worthy to be set out in Tables at large, as a patterne to disobedient Children: for his Father refusing to visite him, (fearing his owne life,) but sending his Ring in signe of forgiueness; the dying Prince most humbly with flouds of teares kissing the same, made a most sorrowfull confession of his sinnes, and feeling death approache, would needs be drawne (as an vnworthy sinner) out of his owne bed, and laid vpon another, strewed with ashes, where his Soule departed in a most penitent manner from his body; which being related to the Father, hee fell vpon the earth, weeping bitterly, and (like another *Dauid* for his *Absolon*) mourned very much, *O quam nefandum est!* saith one most grauely: *O how hainous a thing it is for sonnes to persecute the father! for neither the sword of the fighter, nor, the hand of any enemie, did auenge the fathers wrong, but a feuer and a flux with excoriation of the bowels* (*History*, IX, 6 [87], 506). The various ways in which this early death is moralised by various authorities is worth comparing; see Newburgh, *Historia*, III, vii, 234; Hoveden, *Annales*, 620,43–621,3; Holinshed, *Chronicles*, II, 184–45).

405 Now late alas (though not too late)] Cf. Holinshed's more colloquial "(better late than neuer)," *Chronicles*, II, 184.

422–3 the kingly roabes . . . sackcloath on] "Deinde depositis mollioribus indumentis, cilicium induit, & ligato fune in collo suo, dixit" (Roger of Hoveden, *Annales*, ed. Savile, 620,49–50). May omits the halter; in his last words Henry prays to be forgiven like the penitent robber on the cross (but does not mention his filial or imperial duties).

455–6 How ere . . . excluded bee] May turns into a last will what is stated as post mortem fact in Holinshed: "He is not put in the number of kings, bicause he remained for the more part vnder the gouernance of this father" (*Chronicles*, II, 185).

462 And night . . . his eyes] Young Henry died at Martel on 11 June 1183.

472 As holy Dauid did to Absalon] Young King Henry is twice compared to Absalon in Newburgh's *Historia*; both times stress is laid on his crimes rather than his father's grief: first for his role in the rebellion of 1173–1174, "quominus jus violaret naturæ, exemplo non est territus scelestissimi Absalonis" (II, xxvii, 170); then after his death: "Foedaverat enim adolescentiam suam nævo inexpiabili, id est, similitudine scelestissimi Absalonis" (III, vii, 233).

483–90 The greife ... all the land] For his rendering of the siege of Li-
moges, May makes use of Holinshed's close translation of Hoveden:
"King Henrie (after his sonne the king was thus dead) inforced his power
more earnestlie than before to winne the citie and castell of Limoges
which he had besieged, and at length had them both surrendered into his
hands, with all other castels and places of strength kept by his enimies in
those parts" (*Chronicles*, II, 186).

492–4 Prince Geoffrey ... punishment] "*Gaufridus* vero Comes Britanniæ
regis filius rediit ad patrem suum, & pacem fecit cum illo" (Roger of Ho-
veden, *Annales*, ed. Savile, 621,35–6).

499–510 at a turneament ... hee shortly after dy'd] "Eodem anno *Gaufridus*
Comes Brittanniæ filius *Henrici* regis Angliæ in conflictu militari pedibus
equinis contritus Parisiis obiit" (Roger of Hoveden, *Annales*, ed. Savile,
631,56–7); the year was 1186.

Book VII

19–20 The Realme ... youngest sonne] "Deinde venit rex *Oxeneford* & in
generali concilio ibidem celebrato constituit *Iohannem* filium suum regem
in Hybernia, concessione & confirmatione *Alexandri* summi pontificis"
(Roger of Hoveden, *Annales*, ed. Savile, 566,49–51). Hoveden dates the
council correctly as 1177, Speed gives 1185. It is altogether doubtfull
whether the decision to make John king of Ireland was taken at this
council (when John was nine years old). In any case it took effect only
eight years later when John was knighted by his father (see Warren,
Henry II, 204–6).

20–3 and to that end ... in Irelands gouernement] "Eodem anno *Henricus*
rex Angliæ misit nuntios suos ad Vrbanum Papam, & multa ab eo impe-
trauit, quibus Papa *Lucius* fortiter resistebat; quorum vnum hoc fuit, quod
ab eo impetrauit, Quod vnus, quem vellet de filiis suis coronaretur de
regno Hyberniæ; & hoc confirmauit ei dominus Papa bulla sua" (Roger of
Hoveden, *Annales*, ed. Savile, 631,8–11). The pope had to approve of the
creation of a new kingdom, and since Pope Lucius III refused to do so,
Henry had to wait until Urban III was elected. Urban complied, but his
bull reached England only after John's return (see Warren, *Henry II*, 599).
It was the third privilege concerning Henry's right to rule over Ireland
after Pope Adrian's bull Laudabiliter (probably granted in 1155) and its
confirmation by Pope Alexander III (in 1174 or 1175); the first two are
paraphrased in Gerald of Wales's *Expugnatio*, II, v, ed. Dimock, V, 315–
19.

25 (But twelue yeares old)] John was, in fact, in his eighteenth year when he was sent into Ireland in March 1185. May's information is probably based on Hooker's translation of Gerald's *Expugnatio*, "Iohn at this his first arriuall into Ireland was of the age of 12 yeres" (Holinshed, *Chronicles*, VI, 220), or Sir John Davies, *Discovery of the True Causes why Ireland Was Never Entirely Subdued*, "This young Prince the Kings sonne, being but twelue years of age" (1612, 19). In the manuscripts of the *Expugnatio* John's age is given as "anno ætatis suæ duo de vicesimo." As Dimock suggests, Hooker may have translated from a copy that misread "duo de vicesimo" as "duodecimo" (*Expugnatio*, II, xxxii, 381, note 5).

28 But not ... Regall power] May follows Speed and rejects, like Speed, Roger of Hoveden's statement that Henry made his son King of Ireland; see note on the frontispiece above, page 138. Speed also suggests that Henry delayed the coronation pretending to wait for the necessary number of cardinals to attend it, "whereupon the King gaue the same [i.e., the crowne of feathers sent by Pope Urban III] to his sonne *Iohn*, whose Coronation (stung with the like before) his father onely did delay, at such time as two Cardinalls offered to celebrate that solemnity" (*History*, IX, 6 [91], 507).

39–41 The youthfull gallants ... did deride] "But our new men & Normans, who had not before beene in those parties, making small account of them, did [...] mocke them, and laugh them to scorne" (*Expugnatio*, trl. Hooker; Holinshed, *Chronicles*, VI, 224).

53–66 Now daily quarrels ... they raise] "The French king [...] threatned to destroie the countrie of Normandie, and other lands on that side the sea, except king Henrie would deliuer into his hands the towne of Gisors, with the appurtenances, or cause his sonne Richard earle of Poictou to take to wife his sister Alice, according to his promise" (Holinshed, *Chronicles*, II, 192). Demands concerning Alice's marriage were raised with increasing frequency and urgency; see also notes to VI, 30–2; VII, 59–60, and 295–302. Gisors was part of the dowry of young king Henry's wife Margaret; it should have reverted to King Philip II, Margaret's brother, on young King Henry's death in 1183. In a conference held at Gisors in March 1186 King Philip agreed to transfer the dowry to his sister Alice, and Henry promised to have Richard and Alice speedily married (see Warren, *Henry II*, 598).

60 Of perfect age] Alice had been betrothed to Richard since 1161 (see VI, 30–2); Henry had taken her in custody at his court, as was usual, until she reached legal age, which was twelve years for girls. Her father Louis had

tried in vain to enforce the fulfilment of the contract (see Poole, *OHE*, III, 339). By the mid-1180s her marriage was long overdue; Gerald of Wales reports rumours that Henry seduced her after the death of Rosamond: "Dicebatur etenim, et murmur populi fuerat, quia de veritate non alleviabitur hic quippiam, quod post mortem Rosomaundæ puellæ, quam rex adulterinis amplexibus nimis adamaverat, et virginem istam, domini sui filiam et fidei suæ ab eodem fiducialiter commissam, nimis impudice nimisque infideliter dehonestaverit" (*De principis instructione*, III, ii, 232). Holinshed and Speed accept this rumour on the authority of Polydore Vergil (*Chronicles*, II, 196; *Historie*, IX, 6 [85], 505; see also note to III, 291–7).

78–9 These wofull tydings ... In Europe flew] "the heauy newes of *Jerusalem* lost, flew into Christendom" Speed, (*History*, IX, 6 [94], 508).

86 one of greatest name] In the printed edition, a footnote identifies the prelate as William, Archbishop of Tyre. Neither Hoveden nor Holinshed give his full name (Hoveden, "Archiepiscopus Tyri," *Annales*, ed. Savile, 641,19; Holinshed, "the archbishop of Tire," *Chronicles*, II, 192); Matthew Paris, however, says that the Pope made William of Tyre his legate to propagate the crusade in the West (*Chronica majora*, II, 330; *Historia minor*, I, 446), and the extra information found its way into Speed's *Historie*, May's probable source: "Vpon these newes *Henry* and *Philip* meete, and for the honor of God, laying downe displeasure, in presence of *William* Archbishop of *Tyre*, at which time some say a Crosse appeared in the ayre, take vpon them, as Souldiers of Christ, the badge of the Crosse" (IX, 6 [95], 508). Speed does not name the place where William preached; this could be found in Hoveden, however ("inter Gisortium, & Trie"), to whom Speed refers in a marginal note that gives the exact folio number of the 1596 edition of the *Annales* in Savile's compilation *Rerum Anglicarum scriptores*, fol. 365. May's misspelling of the name of the archbishop could be due to a confusion with the place of the meeting "betwixt Gisors and Try."

139–43 Behold ... seruice shew'd] This could be taken from a letter of the Patriarch of Antioch to King Henry: "Mementote laudis, & nominis vestri, vt Deus, qui vos subleuauit in regnum, per vos exaltetur, & si huic tam digno operi volueritis manum apponere, vt veniatis, vel optatum nobis mittatis succursum, totius terræ sanctæ liberatio vobis post Deum imputabitur, & nos ipsi in quantum possumus lugentes, & rea pectora nostra percutientes ad Deum clamamus, vt ipse donet vobis, & velle, & posse id ipsum sic perficiendi ad laudem, & gloriam sui nominis; quatenus in hoc mortis articulo terræ sanctæ, & nobis clementer succuratis" (Hoveden, *Annales*, ed. Savile, 643, 53–9).

159–82 If Homers Poëm ... Xanthus was] Troy and its sites, the scenes of Homer's *Iliad*, are compared to the holy places in and around Jerusalem; epic poems on biblical subjects had been advocated by Du Bartas, particularly in his *La muse chrestienne*, which King James had translated as *The Uranie, or, Heavenly Muse* in his apprentice years. Du Bartas asks his fellow poets to look for subjects in the Scriptures (in King James's words): "Then consecrat that eloquence most rair / To sing the lofty miracles and fair / Of holy Scripture" (237–9), and gives examples such as this: "I had farr rather *Babell* tower forthsett, / Then the thre *Grecian* hilles on others plett / To pull doun gods afraide, and in my moode, / Sing *Noës* rather then *Deucalions* floode (269–72; *The Poems of King James I*, ed. J. Craigie, STS [Edinburgh, 1958], II, 31, 33).

162 And lend each feild, each stone a pleasing name] When Lucan's Caesar wanders around in the ruins of Troy, he finds that no stone is without a legend, "nullum est sine nomine saxum" (*De bello civili*, IX, 973).

167–9 Instead of Idaes hill ... to grace] May has mentioned the hill and grove on Mount Ida himself as antecedents of Rosamond's bower (see above, III, 191–2); Venus descended there to lie with Anchises, and Aurora to carry off Tithonus (cf. Ovid, *Heroides*, XVI, 201–4).

173–6 Instead of Priam's pallace ... Hesion' stood] During his visit to Troy Caesar comes across Hesione's rock, the marriage chamber of Anchises and the cave in front of which Paris sat in judgment over the goddesses: "Aspicit Hesiones scopulos silvaque latentes / Anchisae thalamos; quo iudex sederit antro" (Lucan, *De bello civili*, IX, 970–1).

178–9 Which once ... Aboade on earth] St. John baptized "in Aenon near to Salim," on the bank of the river Jordan (John 3:23).

179–80 or where Elias ... lifted vpp] Elias stood on the bank of the river Jordan when he was taken up into heaven in a chariot of fire (2 Kings 2:7–11).

194–6 let it become ... honour first] This is taken from a letter reproduced in Hoveden's *Annales* in which King Henry promises the patriarchs of Antioch to come to their aid: "Inter cæteros autem principes ego, & filius meus, reiecta huius mundi gloria, & spretis voluptatibus vniversis, omnibusque quæ mundi sunt postpositis, in propriis personis totis viribus vos cito, auctore Domino, visitabimus" (*Annales*, ed. Savile, 644,35–7). Speed translates it more literally in his *Historie*, IX, 6 [96], 508.

216–20 And that a difference ... the Flemmings greene] Both Holinshed and Speed record this agreement; the more succinct version is in Speed's *Historie*, "and there the better to distinguish thēselues, it was agreed that the *French* should weare redde Crosses, the *English* white, and the *Flemish* greene" (IX, 6 [95], 508).

225–33 For when they tooke ... for preparation] "Dispositum est autem à regibus, & Archiepiscopis, [...] quod omnes illi tam clerici, quam laici, qui hoc iter non arrripient, decimas reddituum [...] dabunt. [...] Dispositū est etiam, quod omnes clerici, milites, & seruientes, qui hoc iter arripient, decimas terrarum suarum & hominum suorum habebunt, & nihil pro se dabunt" (Roger of Hoveden, *Annales*, ed. Savile, 641,51–8). This contribution, one of the few direct taxes levied during Henry's reign, came to be known as the Saladin Tithe (see Warren, *Henry II*, 377).

236–42 And thence ... all townes to doo] "Et tunc Dominus rex misit seruientes suos clericos, & laicos per singulos Comitatus Angliæ ad decimas colligendas secundum prædictam præordinationem in terris suis transmarinis constitutam, sed de singulis vrbibus totius Angliæ fecit eligi omnes ditiores, videlicet de Londonia .200. & de Eboraco .100. & de aliis vrbibus secundum quantitatem & numerum eorum" (Roger of Hoveden, *Annales*, ed. Savile, 642,35–39).

245–6 But what ... entention vayne] "But by the working of some wicked spirit (as we may well thinke) which enuied the aduancement of the christian common-wealth, that good meaning of the two kings was broken and disappointed" (Holinshed, *Chronicles*, II, 193).

249–66 Alas, what starres ... vnlook'd for change] There is a similar, but much longer, exclamatory passage in Gerald's *Expugnatio*, which begins: "O quam feliciter successisse probaverim [...]" (II, xxxi, 378–80). Both passages reflect on the opportunity missed for a happy ending of Henry's career ("vitæ temporalis comœdiam felici fine compleverit," says Gerald, p. 378). A shorter version of Gerald's *exclamatio* is in Speed's *History*: "Who would not haue thought, that this stirring Prince, should haue had opportunitie to end his dayes in peace and glory? but it was otherwise ordained by God, and ancient Writers hold, he was principally scourged, for being drawne, by seeming reasons of State, to put off an holy enterprise, the occasion whereof, was laid as it were at his foote" (IX, 6 [88], 506).

267–70 Reimond Tholouses Earle ... an alteration] Holinshed mentions that English and French chroniclers disagree about who broke the treaty that should have guarded the peace and enabled the French and English kings to participate in the crusade; he then opts for Roger of Hoveden, who simply states that Raymond made war against Richard; May apparently knows the petty preliminaries to this war as reported in Benedict (*Gesta regis Henrici secundi*, II, 34–6), but cuts them short; see note to 268.

268 Although but slight] The wrongs were slight only from a detached point of view; hostilities started with Raymond maltreating a number of merchants from Poitou, "de quibus plures privavit oculis et testiculis; quosdam vero illorum interfecit, et quosdam illorum incarceravit" (Benedict, *Gesta regis*, II, 34). Hoveden speaks of "mala multa" (*Annales*, ed. Savile, 642,56), Holinshed of "manie displeasures" (*Chronicles*, II, 194).

271–4 For fierce young Richard ... surprising castles there] "Comes autem *Richardus* cum magno exercitu intrauit terram Comitis de sancto *Egidio*, & deuastauit eam igne & gladio, & castella illius prope Tolosam obsedit, & cepit" (Roger of Hoveden, *Annales*, ed. Savile, 643,11–13); there is no equivalent to "igne & gladio" (as in May's "With fire and sword," 274) in Holinshed's *Chronicles*, which otherwise paraphrases Hoveden's account.

277–9 wrathful Philip ... suddainely] "Howsoeuer this matter went, certeine it is, that king Philip taking weapon in hand, vpon a sudden entred into Berrie, and tooke from king Henrie Chasteau Raoull, Brezancois, Argenton, Mountrichard, Mountresor, Vandosme, Leprose, Blanc en Berrie, Culan and Molignon" (Holinshed, *Chronicles*, II, 194); Roger of Hoveden gives no names.

280–1 whoo straight ... army goes] Henry landed at Harfleur on 11 July 1188. May omits Henry's last-minute attempt to find a diplomatic solution of the conflict: "with all speed possible he sent Baldwin archbishop of Canturburie, and Hugh bishop of Durham over into France, to appease the French kings displeasure with courteous words and reasonable persuasions" (Holinshed, *Chronicles*, II, 194).

295–302 Philip ... all the Lords] "Eodem anno rex Angliæ, & rex Franciæ habuerunt colloquiū inter Bonimoltus, & Suleinni 14. Kal. Septembris, feria sexta, in quo colloquio rex Franciæ obtulit regi Angliæ, quicquid ceperat de eo per Guerrā, tali cōditione: quod tradidisset *Alais* sororem suam Comiti *Richardo* filio suo in vxorem, & permisisset ipsi *Richardo* hæredi suo fieri homagia, & fidelitates ab hominibus terrarū suarum" (Roger of Hoveden, *Annales*, ed. Savile, 649,40–4). The conference at Bonmoulins was in November 1188.

302–4 that Iohn ... in Palæstine] This demand was raised at a meeting in La Ferté-Bernard at Whitsuntide in 1189: "In quo colloquio rex Franciæ petiit à rege Angliæ *Alesiam* sororem suam donari in vxorem *Richardo*

Comiti Pictauiæ, & vt fidelitates terrarum suarum eidem *Richardo* fierent, & vt *Iohannes* frater suus accepta cruce Ierosolymã iret" (Roger of Hoveden, *Annales*, ed. Savile, 652,35–7).

307–9 In indignation ... his side] "Vnde Comes *Richardus* plurimum indignatus, sine consilio, & voluntate patris sui deuenit homo regis Franciæ" (Roger of Hoveden, *Annales*, ed. Savile, 649,46–7).

313–8 When now ... a parley more] "Deinde habito inter illos colloquio apud Gisortium, cum inter illos de pace facienda non potuissent conuenire: rex Franciæ in iram & indignationem commotus succidit vlmum quandam pulcherrimam inter Gisortium & Trie, vbi colloquia haberi solebant inter reges Franciæ, & duces Normanniæ: iurans, quod de cætero nunquam ibi colloquia haberentur" (Roger of Hoveden, *Annales*, ed. Savile, 645,26–30). Gisors was a fortress on the border between Normandy and Champagne; the elm had served as a meeting point in cases of dispute between the kings of France and the dukes of Normandy (now also kings of England).

329–33 Those old religious trees ... this stately Elme] Cf. Lucan, *De bello civili*, "Exuvias veteres populi sacrataque gestans / Dona ducum" (I, 137–8); May translates: "Great Conquerers spoyles, and sacred Trophæs bore" (*Lucans Pharsalia*, A3v). Lucan's tree, an ancient oak which totters under its own weight, becomes an emblem of Pompey's (and Republican Rome's) impending fall.

334–6 The Druides ... superstition] Lucan addresses the Druids who revive their rites on Caesar's return to Rome: "Et vos barbaricos ritus moremque sinistrum / Sacrorum, Dryadae, positis repetistis ab armis" (*De bello civili*, I, 450–1); May translates: "You Druides now freed from warre maintaine / Your barbarous rites, and sacrifice againe" (*Pharsalia*, A8r).

350, 359 his beloued City Mauns ... that beloued towne] The assault on Le Mans, "ibi natus fuerat, & ciuitatem illam plus cæteris diligebat" (Roger of Hoveden, *Annales*, ed. Savile, 653,3–4), came on 12 June 1189.

355 For but ... guard theire King] "cum septingentis militibus aufugit" (Roger of Hoveden, *Annales*, ed. Savile, 653,1–2). Holinshed does not mention the number of knights.

364 Curses ... his sonne] Holinshed gives a fuller version of "the words of King Henrie in displeasure": "Sith thou hast taken from me this daie the thing that I most loued in this world, I will requite thee, for after this daie, I shall deprive thee of that thing which in me should most please thee, euen mine owne hart" (*Chronicles*, II, 197).

366 surprising Tours] "Hostes autem [...] urbem quoque Turonicam cum
arce ejus, procurrente impetu expugnaverunt" (Newburgh, *Historia*, III,
xxv, 278). Tours was taken on 3 July 1189.

365–424 Philip ... farthest Aquitaine] The account of Henry's capitulation
and death is based on Roger of Hoveden's *Annales*, ed. Savile, 653–4,
mediated, in parts, through Holinshed's *Chronicles*, II, 19–8, and Speed's
Historie, IX, 6 [98–9]; see Appendix 5, pp. 236–41.

369–77 where, although ... held him vpp] "It is written that at the meeting
of these two Kings the sky being cleare, a thunderbolt strok betweene
them, and after a little pause comming together againe, it thundered more
terribly, so that *Henry* had falne off his horse, but that his people sus-
tained him; whereupon he came presently to an end, though it were to his
vnspeakable griefe; his Kingly heart being vsed to giue, not to take condi-
tions" (Speed, *Historie*, IX, 6 [98], 508); see Appendix 5 for the wider
context.

369 Not farre from Turwyn] May is mistaken about the name of the town;
Turwyn (Thérouanne) is a small town in Artois, famous for King Henry
VIII's victory over the French in 1513 (when it was razed), but far from
the field of the earlier Henry's last stand; May probably misread Turonim
(acc. of Turonis, Lat. for Tours) in his source, Roger of Hoveden's *An-
nales*; Roger speaks of a "colloquium inter Turonim & Arasie" (ed. Savile,
653,49). In Holinshed's *Chronicles* the meeting takes place "not farre from
Towrs", Vol. II, 197; see Appendix 5). Speed gives no location at all.
This would mean that May went to the Latin source for his account of
the meeting.

390 Two thousand marks to Philip] Roger of Hoveden (and Holinshed)
speak of 20,000 marks: "viginti millia marcarū argēti" (*Annales*, ed. Savile,
653,52), "20. thousand markes" (*Chronicles*, II, 197); Speed does not men-
tion this condition.

410–16 Hee curst ... to peace] On this point, the divines in Roger's *Annales*
are less effective: "maledictionem Dei, & suam dedit filiis suis, quam
numquam relaxare voluit, licet Episcopi, & cæteri viri religiosi eum ad
relaxationem maledictionis suæ sæpius commouissent" (*Annales*, ed. Savile,
654,9–11), and this is preserved in Speed's *Historie*, "hee bitterly cursed
the howre of his birth, laying Gods curse and his vpon his sonnes, which
he would neuer recall, for any perswasion of the Bishops and others" (IX,
6 [99], 509). Roger mentions, however, that Henry gained absolution of
his sins in the end; this is dropped by Holinshed (but not by Speed; see
App. 5).

421–2. And of so great ... a tombe containes] Fabyan quotes the following
epitaph from Henry's tomb at Chinon: "Sufficit hic tumulus, cui non suf-
fecerit orbis. / Res breuis est ampla, cui fuit ampla breuis. / Rex Henricus
eram: mihi plurima regna subegi / Multiplicique modo, duxque comesque
fui, / Cui satis ad uotum non essent omnia terræ / Climata, terræ modo
sufficit octo pedum. / Qui legis hec, pensa discrimina mortis: & in me /
Humane speculum condicionis habe. / Quod potes instanter operare bo-
num, quia mundus / Transit, & incautos mors inopina rapit" (Fabyan,
Chronicle, 1559, Vol. I, G4r, 356). The sentiment expressed in these dis-
tichs is old; Statius, for instance, meditates in similar terms on the re-
mains of Alexander the Great: "Sic natum Nasamonii Tonantis / post
ortus obitusque fulminatos / angusto Babylon premit sepulcro" ("Geneth-
liacon Lucani ad Pollam," "Ode to Polla in Honour of Lucan's Birthday,"
93–5; *Silvae*, II, vii, ed. J.H. Mozley, London, 1961, I, 134). Shakespeare
applies it to Hotspur (*Henry IV*, Part 1, V, iv, 88–91) and Prince Arthur
(*King John*, IV, ii, 99–100).

The Description of King Henry the Second
May's "Description of King Henry the Second," which he added to the
printed edition of *The Reigne of King Henry the Second*, is based mainly on
a portrait, "Descriptio Anglorum regis Henrici secundi," which forms
Cap. xlvi, the final chapter, of Gerald of Wales's *Expugnatio Hibernica*,
Liber I (ed. Dimock, *Opera*, V, 301–306). A shortened version of this de-
scription found its way into Gerald's *De principis Instructione*, II, xxix.
Hooker's translation of the former is in Holinshed's *Chronicles*, VI, 175–9
(see App. 6, pp. 241–3, for extracts); a summary of Henry's virtues and
vices is in Holinshed's *Chronicles*, II, 199–201. May passes over Gerald's
eulogy on the achievements of the king in the *Topographia Hibernica*, "De
victoriis Anglorum regis Henrici secundi" (Cap. xlvii) and "De titulis et
triumphis ejusdem variis recapitulatio brevis" (Cap. xlviii), and he makes
no use of a similar list in Chapter III, xxvi of Newburghs *Historia*, "De
moribus regis Henrici." There are indications that May went to the Latin
text of the *Expugnatio* for his material: one such indication is his trans-
lation of "oculis glaucis, ad iram torvis," Gerald's description of the ex-
pression of Henry's eyes (see note to lines 14–6); glaucus can mean either
"grey" or "red." Hooker has an explanatory note on the term in which he
argues in favour of "red" (or rather "fierie, red"). He justifies this with
Gerald's statement about Henry's irefulness, which immediately follows
the description ("ad iram torvis"). He is probably right, for Gerald had

called Henry "grey-eyed" already ("caesius") and it seems odd that he should repeat that information in the same sentence. May translates "his eyes gray, whose aspect was terrible in his anger"; unless he had the earlier "caesius" in mind, this would argue for a somewhat hasty translation from the Latin without the help of Hooker's learned note.

9 of a just stature] This is May's translation of: "Statura vir erat inter mediocres" (*Expugnatio*, I, xlvi, 303).

9–14 a strong and healthfull constitution ... all his exercises] Though Gerald, who knew Henry personally, draws no more than the outlines of a portrait, he gives a graphic description of Henry's physique: "corpore carnoso, et naturæ magis quam gulæ vitio, citra tumorem enormem et torporem omnem, moderata quadam immoderantia ventre præamplo. Erat enim cibo potuque modestus ac sobrius, et parcimoniæ, quoad principi licuit, per omnia datus. Et ut hanc naturæ injuriam industria reprimeret ac mitigaret, carnisque vitium animi virtute levaret, bello plusquam intestino tanquam in se conjurans, immoderata corpus vexatione torquebat" (Gerald, *Expugnatio*, I, xlvi, 302).

14–16 Hee was of a ruddy complexion ... hoarse and hollow] "Erat igitur Anglorum rex Henricus secundus vir subrufus, cæsius, amplo capite et rotundo, oculis glaucis, ad iram torvis, et rubore suffusis, facie ignea, voce quassa" (*Expugnatio*, I, xlvi, 302).

16–18 Hee was a Prince ... his whole conversation] "Citra animi turbationes et iracundiæ motus, princeps eloquentissimus: et quod his temporibus conspicuum est, literis eruditus. Vir affabilis, vir flexibilis et facetus: nulli prorsus hominum, quicquid intus palliaverit, urbanitate secundus" (*Expugnatio*, I, xlvi, 303). Hooker gives an almost literal translation of the passage but omits the facetiousness that May retains (cf. *Chronicles*, VI, 176).

19–22 The best histories ... perfectly] "Quicquid aliquando memoria dignum audierat, nunquam a mente decidere poterat. Unde et historiarum omnium fere promptam notitiam, et cunctarum propemodum experientiam rerum, ad manum habebat" (*Expugnatio*, I, xlvi, 306).

23–25 couragious in warre ... a battell] "In armata militia strenuus, in togata perprovidus. Semper tamen rebus in martiis ambigua bellorum fata reformidans: et ex summa prudentia, juxta comicum illud, omnia prius quam arma pertentans" (*Expugnatio*, I, xlvi, 303). The comedy alluded to is Terence's *Eunuchus*, the line is spoken by Captain Thraso, the *miles gloriosus* of the play (correctly it runs "omnia prius experiri quam armis sapientem decet," 789).

27–30 honouring the memories ... they were dead] "Amissos in acie plus principe plangens; et humanior extincto militi, quam superstiti; longeque majori dolore mortuos lugens, quam vivos amore demulcens" (*Expugnatio*, I, xlvi, 303).

32–3 Though in private ... magnificence] "Largus in publico: parcus in privato" (*Expugnatio*, I, xlvi, 303).

33–6 his bountie ... wisely provident] "Incomparabilis elemosinarum largitor, et præcipuus terræ Palestinæ sustentator" (*Expugnatio*, I, xlvi, 304).

37–8 his too too often breaking of his promises] "Naturali quadam inconstantia, verbi spontaneus plerumque transgressor" (*Expugnatio*, I, xlvi, 304).

39–45 Hee was exceeding ... a Monarch] "Legitimæ prolis pueritiam naturali affectu plusquam pater amplectens, provectiores ejusdem annos plusquam vitricus oblique respiciens. Et quanquam filios tam inclitos habens et illustres, magno tamen absolutæ felicitatis impedimento, forsan ex meritis, semper odio persequens successores" (*Expugnatio*, I, xlvi, 305).

42–3 Yet there ... greatest crosses] Gerald spins the paradox out in a series of puns, "unde gaudium habere debuerat, inde gladium, unde securitatem inde securim, unde pacem inde pestem," and so on (*Expugnatio*, I, xlvi, 305).

53–5 But perchance ... addicted] "Unde aliquo vel maritalis copulæ vitio, vel parentum criminis cujuslibet vindicta videtur accidere, quod nec patris in filios, nec filiorum in parentem, nec fratrum inter se vera concordia" (*Expugnatio*, I, xlvi, 306). Speed had criticised King Henry, saying that he was "immoderately addicted to varietie of loues" (*Historie*, IX, 6 [64], 500).

57–61 but especially ... wanton affections] "Post gravem, matris, ut fertur, instinctu, filiorum in patrem offensam, publicus legitimi foederis violator" (*Expugnatio*, I, xlvi, 304).

67 consider it ... five Acts] This division cuts across the seven-book structure of the epic. Gerald divides Henry's thirty-five-year reign in seven "lustra" (*Expugnatio*, II, xxvii, 364). The comparison of man's life to a play was fluent not only in theatrical circles; the Oxford philosopher John Case, for instance, applies it to his own life in an address to the readers of his *Lapis philosophicus* (1600), "quinto iam actu vitae meae peracto" (9r; quoted from J.W. Binns, *Intellectual Culture in Elizabethan and Jacobean England: The Latin Writings of the Age* [Leeds, 1991], 545, n. 63).

67–8 *Tanquam fabula est vita hominis*] This is a commonplace notion of long standing; it is to be found, for example, in the *Zodiacus vitae* of

Palingenius ("Si recte aspicias, vita haec est fabula quaedam") and the *Short Dictionary of Latin and English* of John Withals ("Vita haec est fabula quaedam"). Baldwin has followed its traces in his *Small Latine and Lesse Greeke* (I, 652–5). The comparison with a comedy (*fabula*) does not strictly apply to Henry's life, of course (both Gerald and May acknowledge in their comments the tragic turn of Henry's career).

141–57 Let the fourth Act ... *Sicily* and *Arragon*] This summary owes much to a eulogy on "The great felicitie of King *Henry*," as it is called in a marginal note, which Speed gives after recording Henry's victory in the civil war: "Let the greatnesse and felicitie of this King be now but sleightly looked vpon, and it will appeare, that no Prince of those times was hitherto so much bound to God for manifold fauours as hee. The King and power of *France*, after so many attempts with the young King of *England*, and all their forces, flying at his presence without any stroke strucken, the valiant King of *Scotland* prisoner, and the chiefest of his Rebels vnder foote, *England* assured, *Scotland* dismayed, *Ireland* retained, *Wales* ministering souldiers, *Normandy* in possession, and all the coasting Regions, *Britaine*, *Anjou*, *Poictou*, *Main*, *Tourain*, *Limosin*, *Gascoign*, *Guian*, &c. from thence as farre as the Mountaines which separate *Spaine* from *France*, vnder his Dominion; and the Blessing of Peace, shortly after ensuing, vpon such termes as himselfe could reasonably wish, made him like another *Salomon* to be sought vnto: his Wisdome & Magnificence being in such high credite through the Christian World, that the Kings of *Castile* and *Nauarre* chose him sole Arbiter in their debate, which to both their contentment he most wisely determined; and then at one time in his Palace at *Westminster* were seene together, the Ambassadours of *Manuel* Emperour of *Constantinople*, of *Fredericke* Emperour of *Romans*, of *William* Archbishop for *Triers* in *Germany* (a mightie Prince) of the Duke of *Saxonie*, and of *Philip* Earle of *Flanders*. Moreouer he had the Gouernment of *France* for a time, the Kingdome of *Jerusalem* offered him, but refused, and two of his daughters married to the two Kings of *Castile* and *Sicilie*" (*History*, IX, 6 [78], 503, with marginal references to "Math. Paris. / Ypodig. Neustr. [i.e., Thomas Walsingham's *Ypodigma Neustriae*]/ Rog. Houed.").

The Single, and Comparative Characters of Henry the Sonne, and Richard These "Characters" of King Henry's sons, like the preceding "Description" of their father, go back to Gerald of Wales; the final chapters of the *Topographia Hibernica* deal with King Henry's children. There is one chapter on Young Henry, "De titulis filiorum: et primo de Anglorum rege Henrico tertio" (III, xlix), one on Richard, "De titulis Pictaviensis" (III, l), and one that compares the two, "De diversitate duorum" (III, li; see Dimock's edition, *Opera*, V, 193–9). Again, parts of these chapters were worked into the *De principis instructione*. The "Character of Richard," for instance, is inserted almost verbatim in the later work ("De titulis Ricardi comitis Pictaviæ occasionaliter hic intersertis," *De principis instructione*, III, viii; ed. Dimock, *Opera*, V, 246–50).

7–17 They were both tall ... a terror to all offenders] "Ambo igitur staturæ grandis, pauloque plusquam mediocris; et formæ dignæ imperio. Strenuitas illis et animi magnitudo fere par; sed via virtutis valde dispar. Ille lenitate laudabilis et liberalitate, iste severitate spectabilis et stabilitate: ille suavitate commendabilis, hic gravitate: illi facilitas, huic constantia laudem peperit: ille misericordia conspicuus, iste justitia: ille miserorum et male meritorum refugium, iste supplicium: ille malorum clipeus, iste malleus: Martiis ille ludis addictus, hic seriis" (*Topographia*, III, li, 198).

17–21 Two Princes ... full of varietie] "Tantos ab uno principe duos, et tam diversissimos, nec præsens ætas nec ulla recolit antiquitas. Tanta nimirum et tam varia virtutum incrementa, longeque si fieri posset ampliora, diversi diversa plene et abunde nobili poterant a stirpe contrahere. Quicquid enim in utroque fere virtutis invenias, noveris in ramos a radice transfusum" (*Topographia*, III, li, 198).

34–8 So many rich gifts ... so good a father] "Unde et quoniam nihil humanum omni ex parte perfectum esse potest, tantam naturalium bonorum gratiam in unum congeri livida natura detrectans, tandem tamen niveo candori nævum adjecit, splendidissimum virum solius ingratitudinis vitio, et optimi patris vexatione, notabilem reddens" (*Topographia*, III, xlix, 194–5).

42–50 The severity ... had ever done] "Sequens [i.e., Richard] vero, cujus digna laudum præconia vox præconis non silebit, provida patris dispositione paternæ nomen, maternæ stirpis honorem statim adeptus, terram hactenus indomitam in tenera ætate tanta virtute rexit et domuit, ut non tantum ipsam per omnes ejus anfractus longe plenius et tranquillius solito pacificaret, verum etiam mutilata dudum et dispersa redintegrans, strenua virtute pristinos in status singula revocaret" (*Topographia*, III, l, 195).

50–53 so was hee constant ... *agendum*] "Fortunam siquidem urgens, et se in anteriora protendens, tempora sibi contemperans, et semper successibus instans, Cæsarque secundus 'Nil credens actum cum quid superesset agendum'" (*Topographia*, III, l, 196). Gerald employs it again in his *De prin-*

cipis instructione, III, viii ("De titulis Ricardi comitis Pictaviæ occasio-
naliter hic intersertis"), page 246. The reference is to Lucan's *De bello
civili*, II, 657 (correctly "Nil actum credens" etc.).

53–7 Hee was so severe . . . proceedings] "in male meritos juris rigore desæ-
viens, unde non indigne laudem a dignis promereri debuerat, lividorum
latratibus coepit in commune crudelitate notari" (*Topographia*, III, l, 196).

80–3 and last of all . . . a crosse] This probably comes from Matthew Paris,
"Corpus vero suum apud Fontem Ebraudi, secus pedes patris sui, cujus
proditorem se confitebatur, sepeliri jubens" (*Chronica majora*, II, 451).
Speed gives an extended version in his *Historie*, "commaunding further,
that when he was dead, his bowels should be buried at *Charron* among
the rebellious *Poictouins*, as those who had onely deserued his worst parts;
but his Heart to be enterred at *Roan*, as the citie, which for her constant
loyalty had merited the same; and his Corps in the Church of the Nun-
nerie at *Font-Euerard* in *Gascoigne*, at the feete of his Father King *Henry*,
to whom hee had beene sometime disobedient" (IX, 7 [69], 529).

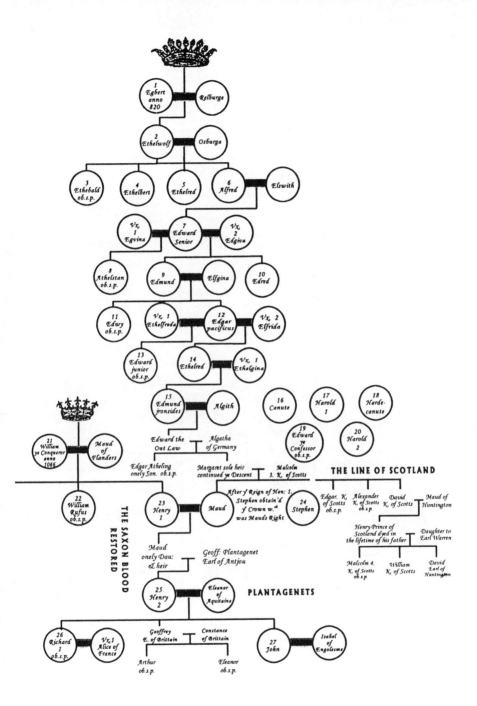

Table I: Saxons and Normans.
Redrawn from Lansdowne MS 884 (1682).
Reproduced by permission of the British Library

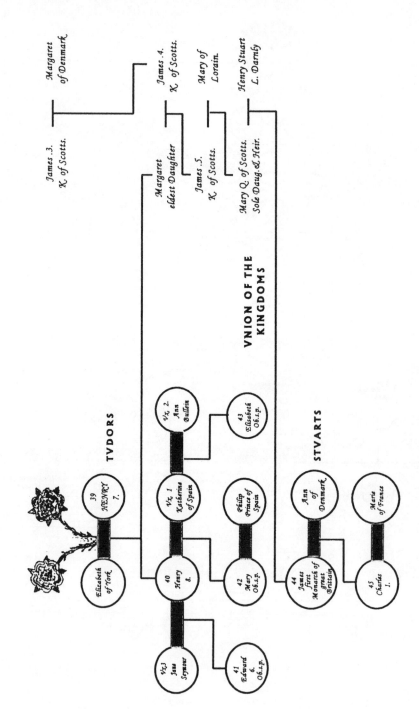

Table II: Tudors and Stuarts.

Redrawn from Lansdowne MS 884 (1682). Reproduced by permission of the British Library

Appendices: Excerpts from Source Texts

Short extracts from medieval and Renaissance chronicles, parts of which have been taken over almost verbatim in some of the key passages of the poem, meant to illustrate May's treatment of his sources.

1. THE CORONATION OF YOUNG HENRY
(CF. II, 99–127)

Matthew Paris[1]

Anno quoque sub eodem, idus Julii, convenerunt ad mandatum regis Henrici apud Westmonasterium, Rogerus, Eboracensis archiepiscopus, et omnes suffraganei Cantuariensis ecclesiæ episcopi, ad coronationem Henrici, filii regis primogeniti. Qui, patre jubente, coronatus est a Rogero, Eboracensi archiepiscopo, et aliis episcopis regni, xiiii°. kalendas Julii, contra prohibitionem papæ, in enormemque ecclesiæ Cantuariensis læsionem. Quantumque Deo displicuit hæc præsumptio, mors ipsius elegantissimi juvenis festina evidenter edocuit. Præterea, ipsa die coronationis, dum a dextris novi regis in menso pompose prandentis sederet archiepiscopus Eboracensis Rogerus, rex pater formam senescalli ministrantis sibi assumpsit. Et stans coram eis, palam protestatus est coram omnibus, se deinceps non esse regem, sed filium suum

---

[1] "De coronatione regis Henrici III. Junioris nimis detestanda." *Historia Anglorum, sive, ut vulgo dicitur, Historia minor*. Ed. Sir Frederic Madden (London, 1866), Vol. I, 352–3.

Henricum. Et cum primum ferculum ipsemet dapifer egregius, tubis præviis, bajularet et poneret ante novum regem filium suum, scilicet caput aprinum magnum, dixit archiepiscopus Rogerus ipsi juveni regi jocose, "Exulta satis et merito gratulare. Non enim est aliquis in mundo, qui tantum habeat in mensa ministrum, sicut tu hodie." At juvenis non æquo ovulo archiepiscopum intuens, respondit, "Non est dispersonatus, degradatus, minoratus vel degeneratus, si mihi minstret. Ego enim sum filius regis et reginæ, ipse vero non." Quod cum aures regis non sine offendiculo attigisset, ilico doluit se fecisse quod fecit, et instillans auribus archiepiscopi demissa voce dixit, "Poenitet me fecisse hominem." Et statim postea alii, sibi proximo, "Filium enutrivi et exaltavi, ipse autem jam sprevit me." Et quasi præsaga mente suspicabatur et augurabatur, et jamjam palam confitebatur se infeliciter errasse. Unde, ultore Deo Domino ultionum, postea in vita patris non cessavit ficta filii dilectio vel persecutio manifesta patrem inquietare.

Polydore Vergil[2]

Dedit eo ipso die rex quo filius regia insignia accepit, epulum, in quo honoris gratia, primū ferculum, ipse iuueniliter exultans filio discumbenti apposuit. Ex quo facto, adolescens aliquantò superbior effectus, cùm insolentius solito circunstantes intueretur, Eboracensis antistes qui assidebat, ioci causa, ad eum conversus, Gaude, inquit, optime fili. non est enim alter in toto orbe princeps, qui talem habeat in mensa administrum. Ad ea ille stomachatus respōdit: Quid miraris? non putat pater id facere, suae minus esse dignitatis, quādo quidem ille materno duntaxat genere clarus mihi administrat, qui & patre rege & matre regina natus sum. Ita Henricus filius malo prauòque ingenio præditus, in patrem ex tempore cauillatus est. At pater Henricus hæc audiens, ingenti affectus dolore, antistiti dismissa voce ait: Pœnitet, inqā, pœnitet extulisse hominem. Iam inde prospexit futurū, vt filius sibi adversaretur. Verumtamē etsi se malè fecisse cruciabatur, cùm factum infectum reddi non posse videret, curauit, vt omnes principes regni vnà cum rege Scotorū in verba eius more maiorum, iurarint, sed noluit illos iureiurando liberatos, quo se iampridem ei obligarant.

---

[2] *Polydori Vergilii Urbinatis Anglicae Historiae libri vigintiseptem* (Basle, 1570), Lib. XIII, 215–16.

Raphael Holinshed[3]

Upon the daie of coronation king Henrie the father serued his sonne at the table as sewer, bringing vp the bores head with trumpets before it, according to the manner. Whervpon (according to the old adage,

Immutant mores homines cùm dantur honores)

the yoong man conceiuing a pride in his heart, beheld the standers-by with a more statly countenance than he had béen woont. The archbishop of Yorke, who sat by him, marking his behauior, turned vnto him, & said; "Be glad my good sonne, there is not an other prince in the world that hath such a sewer at his table." To this the new king answered, as it were disdainefullie, thus: "Why doost thou maruell at that? My father in doing it, thinketh it not more than becommeth him, he being borne of princelie bloud onlie on the mothers side, serueth me that am a king borne hauing both a king to my father, and a queene to my mother." Thus the yoong, man of an euill and peruerse nature, was puffed vp in pride by his fathers vnseemelie dooings.

But the king his father hearing his talke, was verie sorrowfull in his mind, and said to the archbishop softlie in his eare: "It repenteth me, it repenteth me my lord, that I haue thus aduanced the boy." For he gessed hereby what a one he would prooue afterward, that shewed himselfe so disobedient and froward alreadie. But although he was displeased with himselfe in that he had doone vndiscréetlie, yet now when that which was doone could not be vndoone, he caused all the Nobles and lords of the realme togither with the king of Scots and his brother Dauid, to doo homage vnto his said sonne thus made fellow with him in the kingdome: but he would not release them of their oth of allegiance, wherein they stood bound to obeie him the father, so long as he liued.

John Speed[4]

After all this, it came into King *Henries* mind, to sweeten these his many cares with some solace, and to crowne his eldest sonne, young *Henry* King of *England*, now in his owne life time. *A counsell not more temerarious, then*

---

[3] *Chronicles of England, Scotland and Ireland* (1807; rpt. New York, 1965), Vol. II, 130–1.

[4] *The Historie of Great Britaine.* Book IX, chap. 6, §§ 36–8 (London: J. Dawson for G. Humble, 1632), 493.

infortunate: but of which yet he did hope to reape this consolation; that it was done in contempt of *Becket* (whose office it was to haue crowned the King,) with some aduantage also toward the perpetuation of the *Auitall Customes*, and that also without scruple of conscience, his sonne *receiuing the Crowne without caution, to preserue the Churches libertie, either by him put in, or by others exacted.* Yea rather, an Oath minstred, and by the young King taken, to maintaine those *Auitall Customes* to the vttermost.

This solemnity was perfomed at *Henrie* the Fathers commandement, by *Roger* Arch-bishop of *Yorke*, (the anciently riuall See of *Canterbury*) contrary to the Popes expresse Inhibition, the father himselfe King *Henrie* being present thereat, though without any fortunate presage in comming, or cause of consolation in the action. For he, in his inauspicious passage out of *Normandy*, arriuing not without very great perill, at *Portsmouth*, the best and newest ship he had was suncke in the stormes, and therin, besides *Henry de Agnellis* and his two Sonnes, *Gilbert de Sullemni*, Master *Ralfe de Bealmunt*, the Kings Physition and fauourite, with about foure hundred men and women more, were deuoured of the working waues. And at the feast, the joyfull father himselfe, carrying the first dish, and the Archbishop of *Yorke* saying in pleasance to the young King: *Reioyce my faire sonne, for there is no Prince in the world, hath such a seruitor attending at his Table as you. The vnnaturall young man answered; why? wonder you at that? my Father knowes he doth nothing that misbecomes him, for so much as he is royall borne but of one side, but our selfe are royall borne both by Father and Mother.*

Adde hereunto, that this vnlucky Coronations triumphs, were celebrated with bon-fires kindled by the furies in *Normandie*; which *Lewis* the *French* King inuaded with fire and sword, because his daughter Margaret was not crowned as well as the young King her husband: but the father speeding into those parts, quencht this flame with a promise to re-crowne his Sonne, and then his daughter *Margaret* should be honoured with like Ceremonies. Thus the fathers patience was exercised on euery hand, & worse things were feared.

2. THE FLEAS BANISHED BY ST. NANNAN
(CF. IV, 657–70)

Gerald of Wales[5]

De pulicibus, a sancto Nannano deportatis.

Est in Connactia vicus quidam, quem sancti Nannani illustrat ecclesia. Ubi ab antiquo tanta pulicum excreverat multitudo, ut ea pestilentia locus ille fere desertus et habitatoribus vacuus extitisset, donec intercessione sancti Nannani in pratum quoddam proximum sunt deportati. In tantum igitur meritis sancti istius locum illum vis divina mundavit, ut nec unus postmodum hic reperiri potuisset. In prato vero tanta superabundat copia, ut non tantum hominibus, verum etiam bestiis semper maneat inaccessibile.

3. KING HENRY'S PENITENTIAL WALK TO CANTERBURY
(CF. V, 255–84)

Roger of Hoveden[6]

In crastino autem ad beatum *Thomam* Cantuariensem martyrem peregre profectus est. Et cum appropinquasset, ex quo Ecclesiam videre potuit, in qua corpus beati martyris sepultum est, equum in quo sedebat, deseruit, & extractis calceamentis, nudus, pedes, & in pānis laneis per tria milliaria profectus vsq; ad sepulchrum martyris, in tanta humilitate, & cordis compunctione, vt credatur illius opus sine dubio extitisse, qui respicit terram, & facit eam tremere. Vestigia autem eius in via qua ambulabat intuentibus apparuerunt sanginolenta, & erant. sanguis enim multus à teneris pedibus eius lapidibus duris incisis, profluebat in terram. Cum autem ad tumbam veniret, pium erat intueri afflictiones quas faciebat cum fletu singultuoso, & disciplinas, qua de manu Episcoporum, sacerdotumq; plurimorum & monachorum recepit. Ibidem etiam ante sepulchrum beati martyris in oratione, in ieiunio, & plāctu pernoctauit adiutus plurimorum sanctorum virorum suffragiis.

---

[5] "Topographia Hibernica." *Giraldi Cambrensis opera.* Ed. James F. Dimock (London, 1867), Vol. V, Distinctio II, cap. xxxi, 119.

[6] "Rogeri Hovedeni annalium pars prior & posterior." *Rervm Anglicarvm scriptores post Bedam præcipvi, ex vetvstissimis codicibus manvscriptis nvnc primvm in lvcem editi.* Ed. Sir Henry Savile (Francofvrti, 1601), 539, lines 6–19.

Dona autem & redditus, quos Ecclesiæ illi in remißionēm peccatorum suorum contulit, à memoria Ecclesiæ nulla poterunt ratione diuelli. In crastino autem summo mane Missa audita inde receßit, tertio Idus Iulij, sabbato, Lundonias iturus. Et quoniam memor fuit Domini in toto corde suo, dedit illi Dominus victoriam de inimicis suis, & tradidit eos captiuos in manu sua.

John Speed[7]

The next day he took his journey towards *Canterbury*, where (as it appeareth) the residue of his penance enioyned him at his Absolution, was to be performed. For, besides the fore-mentioned conditions, the *Legates enioyned him* (saith the Author of *Beckets* life) *some other othings [sic] secretly, which came not to our knowledge*; yea, the Legates themselues wrote in their owne letters, *that he then promised to doe voluntarily*, (if yee list to beleeue it) *some things which was not fit for them to lay open in writing*. And well might they be ashamed thereof; but if it were so vnfit to be written, how vnfit was it to be imposed on such a Soueraigne Prince? what it was, let *Houeden* report. The King comming towardes the Church, where the late Archbishop was buried, clad all in woollen, *went three miles bare-footed, in so much that the verie ground where he went, was bloudy, as was euidently seene, much bloud running from his tender feete which were cut with the hard stones*. Neither yet was this the worst; for after all this, *he receiued Discipline at the hands of the Bishops, of a great many Priests, and of the Monkes. Geruasius* names *Abbots* also, whereby appeares, that euery seuerall sort were to haue a hand in that seruice. *Matthew Paris* can tell you more plainly what that *Discipline* was: *viz.* he *receiued the Discipline of rods on his bare flesh, receiuing of euery religious man, (a great multitude of them being there gathered) three or fiue jerkes a peece*: whence wee may easily beleeue, *Baronius* and his Author spake within compasse, who acknowledge hee receiued eightie lashes. To such height was the Papall tyranny and pride growne towardes those, of whom God had said expresly, *Touch not mine Annointed.*

---

[7] John Speed. *The Historie of Great Britaine.* Book 9, chap. 6, § 75 (London: J. Dawson for G. Humble, 1632), 502–3.

4. THE CAPTURE OF KING WILLIAM OF SCOTLAND
(CF. V, 285–332)

Raphael Holinshed[8]

This enterprise which he made into Northumberland, he tooke in hand chéeflie at the suit and request of Roger Mowbray, from whome Geffrey (who after was bishop of Lincolne) K. Henries eldest base son had taken two of his castels, so that he kept the third with much adoo. He had giuen his eldest sonne in hostage vnto the said king of Scots for assurance of such couenants to be kept on his behalfe as were passed betwixt them. In the meane time one Duncane or Rothland, with an other part of the Scotish armie entred into Kendall, and wasted that countrie in most cruell wise, neither sparing age nor sex, insomuch that he brake into the churches, slue those that were fled into the same for safegard of their liues as well preests as other. The English power do horsseman which passed not the mumber of 400. was assembled at Newcastell, vnder the leading of Robert de Stoute-uille, Rafe Glanuille, William Ursie, Bernard Balliolle [and Odonet de Um-freiuille.]

These capteines hauing knowledge that Duncane was in one side of the countrie, and king William in another, determinned to issue foorth and trie the chance of warre, (which is doubtfull and vncerteine, according to the old saieng,

Fortuna belli semper ancipiti in loco est)

against the enimies, sith it should be a great rebuke to them to suffer the countrie to be wasted after that sort without reuengement. Herevpon riding foorth one morning, there arose such a thicke fog and mist that they could not discerne any waie about them, so that doubting to fall within the laps of their enimies at vnawares, they staied a while to take aduise what should be best for them to doo. Now when they were almost fullie resolued to have turned backe againe, by the comfortable words and bold exhortation of Ber-nard Balliolle, they changed their purpose, and rode forward, till at length the northerne wind began to waken, and droue awaie the mist, so that the countrie was discouered vnto them, and perceiuing where Alnewike stood, not knowing as yet whether the Scots had woone it or not, they staied their pace, and riding softlie, at length learning by the inhabitants of the countrie,

---

[8] *Chronicles of England, Scotland and Ireland* (London, 1807; rpt. New York, 1965), Vol. II, 157–8.

that the Scotish king desparing to win Alnwike, had raised his siege from thence the same day, they turned streight thither, and lodging there all night, in the morning got to their horsses verie earelie, riding foorth towards the enimies that were spred abroad in the countrie to forey the same. They had anon espied where the king was, and incontinentlie compassed him about on euerie side, who perceiuing the English horssemen readie thus to assaile him, with all diligence called backe his men from the spoile; but the more part of them being staied far off through the swéetness they found in getting of preies, could not heare the sound of the trumpets, yet notwithstanding with those his horssemen which he could get togither, he encountred the English men which came vpon him verie hastilie.

The battell was begun verie fiercelie at the first, and well fought for a time, but the Scotish horssemen being toiled before in foreieng the countrie, could not long continue against the fierce assault of the English, but were either beaten downe, or else constreined to saue themselues by flight. The king with a few other (who at the first had begun the battell) was taken. Also manie of the Scots that being far off, and yet hearing of the skirmish, came running toward the place, & were taken yer they could vnderstand how the matter had passed. This taking of the king of Scots was on a saturdaie, being the euenth [sic] of Julie.

The English capteines hauing thus taken the Scotish king in the midst of his armie, conteining the number of 80000 men, returned to Newcastell, greatlie reioising of their good successe, aduertising king Henrie the father hereof with all speed, who as then was come ouer from Normandie, and was (the same day that the Scotish king was taken) at Canturburie, making his praiers there before the sepulture of the archbishop Becket (as after shall appéere.)

5. KING HENRY'S DEATH (CF. VII, 343–424)

Roger of Hoveden [9]

Conuenerunt igitur prædicti rex Franciæ & rex Angliæ, & *Richardus* Comes Pictauiæ cum Archiepiscopis & Episcopis Comitibus & Baronibus suis circa

---

[9] "Rogeri Hovedeni Annalium pars prior & posterior." *Rervm Anglicarvm scriptores post Bedam præcipvi, ex vetvstissimis codicibus manvscriptis nvnc primvm in lvcem editi.* Ed. Sir Henry Savile (Francofvrti, 1601), 653–4.

festum Apostolorum Petri & Pauli ad colloquium inter Turonim & Arasie, vbi rex Angliæ ex toto posuit se in concilio, & voluntate regis Franciæ. Tunc vero rex Angliæ iterum fecit homagium regi Franciæ, quia ipse in principio istius guerræ quietum clamauerat regi Franciæ dominum suum; & rex Franciæ quietum clamauerat ei homagium suum. Tunc prouisum est à rege Franciæ, quod *Alesia* soror eius, quam rex Angliæ in custodia habuit, reddita esset, & tradita in custodiam vnius de quinque, quos Comes *Richardus* elegerit. Deinde prouidit rex Franciæ, quod per sacramentum hominum terræ assecuratum esset, quod prædicta soror sua tradita sit Comiti *Richardo* in reuersione sua de Ierusalem; & quod Comes *Richardus* haberet fidelitates hominum de terris patris sui circa mare & ultra, & nullus baronum vel miles, qui in hac guerra à rege Angliæ recesserit, & ad Comitem *Richardū* venerit, de cætero redibit ad regem Angliæ, nisi in vltimo mense ante motionem suam versus Ierusalem. Et terminus motionis erat in media Quadragesima: ita quod prædicti reges, & *Richardus* Comes Pictauiæ erunt ad illum terminum apud Wireliacum, & omnes burgenses de dominicis villis regis Angliæ erunt quieti in tota terra regis Franciæ per rectas consuetudines suas, & nō implacitabūtur de vlla re, nisi foris fecerint in felonia. Et rex Angliæ dabit regi Franciæ viginti millia marcarū argēti, & omnes barones regis Angliæ iurabunt, quod si rex Angliæ nouerit has conuētiones tenere, quod ipsi tenebunt cū rege Franciæ & Comite *Richardo*, & eos adiuuabunt pro posse suo contra regē Angliæ. Et rex Franciæ & Comes *Richardus* tenebunt in manu sua ciuitatē Cenomannis, & ciuitatem Turonis, & castellū Ligidi, & castellum de Trou: vel si rex Angliæ maluerit, rex Franciæ & Comes *Richardus* tenebunt castellū de Gisortio, & castellum de Pasci, & castellum de Nouacurt tamdiu, donec omnia fiant, quæ diuisa sunt superius per regem Franciæ, & dum prædicti reges ore ad os loquerentur, intonuit super eos Dominus, & ictus fulmineus cecidit inter illos duo, sed nullam intulit illis læsionem; at plurimum perterriti ab inuicem separati sunt, & omnes, qui aderant, multum mirati sunt, quod tam subito auditus est tonitrua, cum nulla nubium præceßisset obscuritas. Iterum paulo facto ineruallo, conuenerunt reges simul locuturi, & iterum auditus est tonitrus maior, & terribilior priore, die permanente in pristina serenitate, vnde rex Angliæ plurimum conturbatus in terram corruisset ab equo, in quo sedebat, nisi manib. circumstantium sustentatus fuisset. Et ex tunc ex toto posuit se in voluntate regis Franciæ, & pacem superscriptā conceßit postulans, vt nomina eorū omnium, qui illo relicto, adhæserunt rego Franciæ, & Comiti *Richardo*, scripto cōmendarentur, & sibi traderentur. Quod cū factum fuisset, inuenit *Iohannem* filium suum scriptum in principio scripti illius. & admirans supra modum venit ad Chinonem, &

tactus dolore intrinsecus maledixit diei, in qua natus fuit, & maledictionem
Dei, & suam dedit filiis suis, quam nunquam relaxare voluit, licet Episcopi,
& cæteri viri religiosi eum ad relaxationem maledictionis suæ sæpius com-
mouissent. Qui cum ægrotasset vsq; ad mortem, fecit se deferri in Ecclesiam
ante altare, & ibi communionem corporis & sanguinis Domini deuote susce-
pit, cõfitens peccata sua, & ab Episcopis, & clero absolutus obiit, anno 35.
regni sui, in Octauis Apostolorum Petri et Pauli, feria 5. Regnauerat enim
34. annos, & menses 7. & dies 4. Quo defuncto, omnes reliquerunt eum,
diripientes opes illius; vere mel muscę; lupi caduera, frumētum formicæ; non
hominem, sed prædam sequebatur hæc turba. Tandem redierunt ministri eius,
& sepelierunt eum more regio. In crastino autem obitus illius, cum porta-
retur ad sepeliendum in Ecclesia Sanctimonialium Fontis *Ebrandi*, Comes
Richardus filis suus & hæres venit ei obuiam, & misertus illius fleuit amare.
Sanguis autem continuo fluebat de naribus regis superueniniente filio. Filius
vero processit cum corpore patris sui, vsq; ad abbatiam Fontis *Ebrandi*, & ibi
eum sepeliuit in choro Sanctimonialium, & sic ipse inter velatas velabatur.

Raphael Holinshed[10]

Being thus driven to leaue the defaced citie of Mauns, he repaired vnto
Chinon, the citizens whereof being left destitute of aid, yéelded themselues
to the French king, who taking a great pride in his dooings for that victorie,
passed ouer Loire, and wan the citie of Towrs, wherein he placed a garison,
and so hauing sped his businesse with good successe, brought home his
armie laden with preies & booties. King Henrie being thus put to the
worsse, and not perceiuing anie readie meane how to recouer his losses, be-
gan to despaire in himself, and therfore of necessitite thought it best to
séeke for peace, but his suit was in vaine: for the enimie hauing now the ad-
uantage, would not grant to agrée vpon any reasonable conditions.

At the last Philip the earle of Flanders and William archbishop of
Reimes, with Hugh duke of Burgoine, came to king Henrie to moue waies
of agréement, and to conclude the same betwixt him on the one partie, and
the French king and earle Richard on the other partie. Earle Richard had
the Britaines and them of Poictou confederate with him vnder such condi-
tions, as he might not agrée with his father, vnlesse they might be com-
prised in the agréement. At length they agreed vpon conditions, not al-

---

[10] *Holinshed's Chronicles of England, Scotland and Ireland* (London, 1807; rpt. New
York, 1965), Vol. II, 197–8.

togither aduantageable to the king of England, yet in the end, Chateau Raoul was restored to king Henrie with all that had béene taken from him since the time that the French king & he tooke vpon them the crosse: on the other part king Henrie did homage to the French king, which in the beginning of this warre he had surrendred and renounced. He was bound also to paie to the French king 20. thousand markes for the aid which earle Richard had receiued of him: moreouer to resigne and acquite vnto the French king, all that which either he or his predecessours held or possessed within Aluergne. Other articles there were which king Henrie agréed vnto sore against his will , as the deliuerie of the ladie Alice or Adela, and such other, which (as not much materiall) we passe ouer.

This peace was concluded not farre from Towrs, in a place appointed conuenient for both the kings to méet in, about the feast of the apostles Peter and Paule. And (as writers record) there chanced great thunder and lightening at the verie time when the two kings came to enteruiew and talke togither, so that the thunderbolt did light betwixt them two: & yet (notwithstanding such thunder & lightening) the aire was cleare and nothing troubled. The two kings parted a sunder through feare therof for that day, and on the next day the like chance happened, greatlie to the terrour of them both. Which mooued king Henrie the sooner to condescend to the agreement.

Moreouer this is not to be forgotten, that when all matters were quieted and accorded amongst them, King Henrie required to haue all their names deliuered vnto him in writing, which had promised to take part (and were joined as confederates) with the French king and earle Richard. This was granted, and when the roll was presented vnto him he found his sonne John the first person that was named in that register, wherewith he was so troubled and disquieted in his mind, that comming to Chinon he felt such gréefe hereof, that he cursed euen the verie daie in which he was borne, and as was said, gaue to his sonnes Gods cursse and his, the which he would neuer release, although he was admonished to doo it both of sundrie bishops and other religious and godlie men. Thus saith Houeden.

Howbeit, it is not like that earle Richard at this time had procured his brother John to be confederate with him in his rebellious dealings, but rather bicause earle Richard had some suspicion, least his father would make John his heire and successour in the kingdome, it might be a policie wrought by the French king and earle Richard, to alienate his fathers mind from the said John.

These euils were estéemed to fall vnto king Henrie by the iust iudgment

of God, for that being admonished diuerse waies, as well by diuine reuela-
tion, as by the wholesome aduise of graue men, as Hugh bishop of Lincolne
and others, he would not reforme his licentious appetite of heaping vp sinne
vpon sinne, but still wallowed therein to his owne destruction. Wherevpon
being brought to such an extremitie as ye haue heard, he was taken with a
greeuous sicknesse, which bringing him to vtter desperation of recouering of
health, he finallie departed this life, though more through verie anguish and
gréefe of his late losse and troubles susteined, than by the force of his
bodilie disease (as writers haue affirmed.) But howsoeuer it was, he ended
his life the sixt of Julie in the 61. yeare of his age, and after he had reigned
34. yeares, nine moneths, and two daies, which was in the yeare after the
birth of our sauiour 1189. and of the creation of the world 5155. His bodie
was buried at Founteuerard, which is an abbeie situate not farre from the
towne of the eagle within the dutchie of Alanson.

John Speed[11]

The effect whereof was, that former good fortunes forsaking King *Henry*,
hee sustained many losses by the Armies of King *Philip* and *Richard*, and
was driuen out of *Mentz* in *Main*; (the city where hee was borne, and which
hee loued aboue all other places) by firing of the Suburbs before the enemie
came, being casually consumed, he was glad to yeeld to such conditions as
it pleased *Philip* to prescribe. It is written that at the meeting of these two
Kings the sky being cleare, a thunderbolt strok betweene them, and after a
little pause comming together againe, it thundered more terribly, so that
Henry had falne off his horse, but that his people sustained him; whereupon
he came presently to an end, though it were to his vnspeakable griefe; his
Kingly heart being vsed to giue, and not to take conditions.

Fearefull was the speech which King *Henry*, when hee abandoned *Mentz*
by reason of the fire, vttered against *Richard*, which was, "That sith hee had
taken from him that day the thing that he most loued in this world, he
would requite him, for after that day hee would depriue him of that thing
which in him should best please a Child, to wit, his *Heart*." But after the
peace concluded (vpon meditation [1623 edition: vpon mediation]) betweene
the sides, another thing strucke neerer; for finding the name of his sonne
Iohn first in the Catalogue of the Conspiratours against him in that action,

---

[11] John Speed. *The Historie of Great Britaine*. Book 9, chap. 6, §§ 98–99 (London:
J. Dawson for G. Humble, 1632), 508–9.

hee bitterly cursed the howre of his birth, laying Gods curse and his vpon his sonnes, which hee would neuer recall, for any perswasion of the Bishops and others: but comming to *Chinon*, fell there grieuously sicke, and feeling death approach, hee caused himselfe to bee borne into the Church before the Altar, where after humble confession, and sorrow for his sinnes, he departed this life.

6. THE CHARACTER OF KING HENRY

Gerald of Wales [12]

Erat igitur Anglorum rex Henricus secundus vir subrufus, cæsius, amplo capite et rotundo, oculis glaucis, ad iram torvis, et rubore suffusis, facie ignea, voce quassa, collo ab humeris aliquantulum demisso, pectore quadrato, brachiis validis, corpore carnoso, et naturæ magis quam gulæ vitio, citra tumorem enormem et torporem omnem, moderata quadam immoderantia ventre præamplo. Erat enim cibo potuque modestus ac sobrius, et parcimoniæ, quoad principi licuit, per omnia datus. Et ut hanc naturæ injuriam industria reprimeret ac mitigaret, carnisque vitium animi virtute levaret, bello plusquam intestino tanquam in se conjurans, immoderata corpus vexatione torquebat. Nam praeter bellorum tempora, quæ frequenter imminebant, quibus, quod rebus agendis supererat, vix id tantillum quieti dabat, pacis quoque tempore, sibi nec pacem ullam nec requiem indulgebat. Venationi namque trans modestiam deditus, summo diluculo equo cursore transvectus, nunc saltus lustrans, nunc silvas penetrans, nunc montium juga transcendens, dies ducebat inquietos: vespere vero domi receptum, vel ante cœnam vel post, rarissime sedentem conspexeris. Post tantas namque fatigationes, totam statione continua curiam lassare consueverat. Sed quoniam hoc "adprime in vita utile, ut ne quid nimis," nullumque remedium simpliciter bonum, cum tibiarum pedumque tumore frequenti, recalcitrantium ad hæc jumentorum ictibus aucta læsione, ceteras id ipsum corporis incommoditates accelerabat; et si non aliam, matrem malorum omnium ac ministram certe vel senectutem.

Staturæ vir erat inter mediocres: quod nulli filiorum contingere potuit;

---

[12] "Descriptio Anglorum regis Henrici secundi." *Expugnatio Hibernica. Giraldi Cambrensis opera.* Ed. James F. Dimock (London, 1867), Liber I, Cap. xlvi, 302–3.

primævis ambobus paulo mediocritatem excedentibus, junioribus vero duobus infra subsistentibus.

Citra animi turbationes, et iracundiæ motus, princeps eloquentissimus: et quod his temporibus conspicuum est, literis eruditus.

Vir affabilis, vir flexibilis et facetus: nulli prorsus hominum, quicquid intus palliaverit, urbanitate secundus.

Princeps adeo pietate spectabilis, ut quoties armis vicerat, ipse quoque magis pietate vinceretur.

In armata militia strenuus, in togata perprovidus.

Semper tamen rebus in martiis ambigua bellorum fata reformidans. Et ex summa prudentia, juxta comicum illud, omnia prius quam arma pertentans.

Amissos in acie plus principe plangens; et humanior extincto militi, quam superstiti; longeque majori dolore mortuos lugens, quam vivos amore demulcens.

Urgentibus incommodis, nemo benignior: resumpta securitate nemo rigidior.

Acer in indomitos: clemens in subactos.

Durus in domesticos: diffusus in extraneos.

Largus in publico: parcus in privato.

Quem semel exosum habuerat, vix in amorem; quem semel amaverat, vix in odium revocabat.

Avium, quarum victus ex præda, volatu plurimum; canumque, feras narium sagacitate persequentium, tam voce sonora et consona, quam cursu veloci, ultra modum delectatus. Et utinam tam devotioni deditus, quam venationi.

Raphael Holinshed[13]

Henrie the second, king of England, was of a verie good colour, but somewhat red: his head great and round, his eies were fierie, red, and grim, and his face verie high coloured; his voice or speech was shaking, quiuering, or trembling, his necke short, his brest brode and big, strong armed, his bodie was grosse, and his bellie somewhat big, which came vnto him rather by nature than by anie grosse feeding or surfetting. For his diet was very temperat, and to saie the truth, thought to be more spare than comelie, or for the state of a prince: and yet to abate his grossenesse and to remedie this fault of nature, he did as it were punish his bodie with continuall exercise,

---

[13] "The description of king Henrie the second." *Chronicles of England, Scotland and Ireland* (Ireland, 1808; rpt. New York, 1965), Vol. VI, 176.

and did as it were kéepe a continuall warre with himselfe. For in the times of his warres, which were for the most part continuall to him, he had little or no rest at all; and in time of peace he would not grant vnto himselfe anie peace at all, nor take anie rest; for then did he giue himselfe wholie vnto hunting, and to follow the same he would verie erlie euerie morning be on horssebacke, and then into the woods, sometimes into the forrests, and som-times into the hilles and fields, and so would he spend the whole daie vntill night. In the euening when he came home, he would neuer or verie seldome sit either before or after supper. For though he were neuer so wearie, yet still would he be walking and going. And forsomuch as it is verie profitable for euerie man in his life time, that he doo not take too much of anie one thing; for the medicine it selfe which is appointed for a mans helpe & remedie, is not absolutelie perfect and good to be alwaies vsed; euen so it befell and happened to this prince; for partlie by his excessiue trauels, and partlie by diuerse bruses in his bodie, his legs and féet were swollen and sore. And though he had no disease at all, yet age it selfe was a breaking sufficient vnto him. He was of a resonable stature, which happened to none of his sons; for his two eldest sons were somwhat higher, & his two yoonger sons were somewhat lower and lesse than was he. If he were in a good mood, and not angrie, then would he be verie pleasant and eloquent: he was also (which was a thing verie rare in those daies) verie well learned: he was also verie affable, gentle, and courteous; and besides so pitifull, that when he had ouercome his enimie, yet would he be ouercome with pitie towards him.

In warres he was most valiant, and in peace he was as prouident and cir-cumspect. And in the wars mistrusting and doubting of the end and euent therof, he would (as Terence writeth) trie all the waies and meanes he could deuise rather than wage the battell. If he lost anie of his men in the fight, he would maruellouslie lament his death, and séeme to pitie him more being dead than he did regard or account of him being aliue, more bewailing the dead than fauouring the liuing. In times of distresse no man more courteous, and when all things were safe no man more hard or cruell. Against the stub-borne & vnrulie no man more sharpe, nor yet to the humble no man more gentle; hard toward his owne men and houshold, but liberall to strangers, bountifull abrode, but sparing at home; whom he once hated, he would neuer or verie hardlie loue; and whom he once loued, he would not lightlie be out with him, or forsake him; he had great pleasure and delight in hawk-ing and hunting. Would God he had béene as well bent and disposed vnto good deuotion!

Bibliography

MANUSCRIPTS

Bodleian Library

Add. MS C. 165. Richard Hooker, *The Lawes of Ecclesiastical Politie.*
Laud MS 582. Part II of Roger of Hoveden's *Chronica.*
Smith MS 34. Papers originally belonging to Patrick Young, the Royal Librarian from c. 1605–1649, with a list of "Books and Manuscripts of King Charles."

British Library

Add. MS 12049. Sir John Harington. Epigrams.
Add. MS 12049. Sir John Harington. Translation of *Orlando furioso.*
Add. MS 36789. Catalogue of the Cotton Library.
C.120.h.6 (1–7). Catalogues of the Old Royal Libraries.
Cotton MS Julius. C. III. Letters addressed to Sir Robert Cotton.
Harley MS 6018. List of borrowers from Sir Robert Cotton's library.
Harley MS 6085. William Segar. "The Variation of the Arms, and Badges of the Kings of England."
MS Lansdowne 884. "A Genealogicall Table of the Successions of the Kings of England."
Royal MS 14.C.II. Part I of Roger of Hoveden's *Chronica.*
Royal MS 16.E.XXXVIII. Henry Peacham. A book of emblems based on the *Basilikon Doron.*

Royal MS 17.C.XXXV. Butler, Thomas, and John Nodes. "A Description of Fire Works."

Royal MS 18.A.XXXI. John Marston. "The Argument of the Spectacle presented to the Sacred Maiestys of great Britain, and Denmark, as they Passed through London."

Royal MS 18.A.XLV. Ben Jonson. "The Masque of Queenes."

Royal MS 18.A.LXXI. Edmund Bolton. The Proposal for a Royal Academy.

Royal MS 18.A.LXXII. Samuel Daniel. "A Panegyricke Congratulatorie to the King."

Royal MS 18.C.VII. Thomas May. "The Tragœdy of Cleopatra."

Royal MS 18.C.XII. Thomas May. "The Reigne of King Henry the Second."

Edinburgh University Library

MS De.3.69. Samuel Daniel. "Hymen's Triumph."

Huntington Libary

MS HM 180. Catalogue of the Library at St. James's Palace, London.

EDITIONS, SOURCES, AND ANALOGUES

Aleyn, Charles. *The Battailes of Crescey and Poictiers*. London: T. Purfoot for T. Knight, 1631; 2nd ed. 1633.

———. *The Historie of that Wise Prince, Henrie the Seventh*. London: T. Cotes for W. Cooke, 1638.

Ausonius. Decimus Maximus A. *Ausonius*. Trl. Hugh G. Evelyn White. Loeb Classical Library. London, 1951.

Bacon, Sir Francis. *The Historie of the Raigne of King Henry the Seventh*. London: W. Stansby for M. Lownes and W. Barret, 1622.

———. *The Works of Francis Bacon*. Ed. James Spedding, Robert Leslie Ellis, and Douglas D. Heath. London, 1858, Vol. I.

———. *Essays*. Ed. Michael J. Hawkins. London, 1972.

Benedict of Peterborough. "Miracula Sancti Thomae Cantuariensis auctore Benedicto Petriburgensi abbate." *Materials for the History of Thomas Becket, Archbishop of Canterbury*. Ed. James Craigie Robertson, 21–281. Vol. II. London, 1876.

———. "Passio Sancti Thomae Cantuariensis auctore Benedicto Petriburgensi abbate." *Materials for the History of Thomas Becket, Archbishop of Canterbury.* Ed. James Craigie Robertson, 1–19. Vol. II. London, 1876.

Blundeville, Thomas. *The True Order and Method of Writing and Reading Histories* (1574). Ed. Hugh G. Dick, *Huntington Library Quarterly* 3 (1940): 149–70.

Bolton, Edmund. *Hypercritica, or: A Rule of Judgment for Writing or Reading our Histories.* Ed. Anthony Hall. Oxford, 1712. Ed. J. E. Spingarn. *Critical Essays of the Seventeenth Century.* Vol. I: 1605–1650, 82–115. Oxford, 1908.

Brydges, Sir Egerton. *Censura Literaria: Containing Titles, Abstracts, and Opinions of Old English Books.* Vol. X. London, 1809.

Caesar. Caius Julius. *Gallic War.* Trl. H. J. Edwards. Loeb Classical Library. London, 1917.

Calendar of State Papers, Domestic Series, of the Reign of Charles I. Ed. J. Bruce. London, 1858–97.

Camden, William, ed. *Anglica, Normannica, Hibernica, Cambrica, a veteribus scripta.* Francofurti: Impensis Claudij Marnij et haeredibus Iohanni Aubrij, 1602.

———. *Britannia* (1695). Ed. Edmund Gibson. Intr. by Stuart Piggott. Newton Abbot, 1971.

Catullus. *Catullus, Tibullus and Pervigilium Veneris.* Trl. F. W. Cornish. Loeb Classical Library. London, 1912.

Chamberlain, John. *The Letters of John Chamberlain.* Ed. N. M. McClure. 2 vols. Philadelphia, PA, 1939.

———. *The Chamberlain Letters: A Selection of the Letters of John Chamberlain Concerning Life in England from 1597 to 1626.* Ed. Elizabeth McClure Thomson. Preface by A. L. Rowse. London, 1966.

Cicero, Marcus Tullius. *Cicero: De re publica. De legibus,* Trl. Clinton W. Keyes. Loeb Classical Library. London, 1928.

———. *De natura deorum.* Trl. H. Rackham. Loeb Classical Library. London, 1933.

Claudianus, Claudius. "Epithalamium de nuptiis Honorii Augusti." *Claudian.* Trl. Maurice Platnauer, 240–67. Loeb Classical Library. London, 1956.

Cotton, Sir Robert Bruce. *A Short View of the Long Life and Raigne of Henry the Third.* London, 1627.

Daniel, Samuel. *The Complete Works in Verse and Prose.* Ed. Alexander B. Grosart. 5 vols. 1885–96; rpt. New York, 1963.

Davenant, Sir William. *Sir William Davenant's Gondibert.* Ed. David Gladish. Oxford, 1971.

Davies, Sir John. *A Discoverie of the True Causes why Ireland Was Never Entirely Subdued untill his Majesties Raigne.* London: W. Jaggard for J. Jaggard, 1612.

D'Ewes, Sir Simonds. *The Autobiography and Correspondence of Sir Simonds D'Ewes.* Ed. J. O. Halliwell. 2 vols. London, 1845.

Digby, Sir Kenelm. "Concerning Spenser that I Wrote att Mr. May his Desire." *Spenser. The Critical Heritage.* Ed. by R. M. Cummings, 148–9. London, 1971.

Drayton, Michael. *The Works.* Ed. William Hebel, Kathleen Tillotson and B. H. Newdigate. 5 vols. Oxford, 1931–41.

Fabyan, Robert. *The Chronicle of Fabyan Continued to thende of Queene Mary.* London: J. Kingston, 1559.

[Foliot, Gilbert]. "Thomae Cantuariensi Archiepiscopo Clerus Angliae," *Materials for the History of Thomas Becket.* Ed. James Craigie Robertson. Vol. V: 410. Epistle CCV. London, 1881.

Foxe, John. *The Acts and Monuments.* Ed. George Townsend. Vol. II, s.d.; rpt. New York, 1965.

Gerald of Wales. "De principis instructione liber." *Giraldi Cambrensis opera.* Rolls Series, 21. Vol. VIII, ed. George F. Warner. London, 1891.

———. "Expugnatio Hibernica." *Giraldi Cambrensis opera.* Rolls Series, 21. Vol. V, ed. James F. Dimock. London, 1867.

———. "Topographia Hibernica." *Giraldi Cambrensis opera.* Rolls Series, 21. Vol. V, ed. James F. Dimock. London, 1867.

Gervase of Canterbury. "The Chronicle of the Reigns of Stephen, Henry II, and Richard I." *The Historical Works of Gervase of Canterbury.* Ed. William Stubbs. Rolls Series, 73. Vol. I. London, 1879.

Guillim, John. *A Display of Heraldrie. The Second Edition; Corrected and Much Enlarged by the Author Himselfe in his Life Time.* London: Richard Badger for Ralph Mab, 1632.

Harington, Sir John. *The Sixth Book of Virgil's Aeneid. Translated and Commented on by Sir John Harington* (1604). Ed. Simon Cauchi. Oxford, 1991.

Harry, George Owen. *The Genealogy of the High and Mighty Monarch, James, by the Grace of God, King of Great Brittayne, &c. With his Lineall Descent from Noah, by Diuers Direct Lynes to Brutus, First Inhabiter of this Ile of Brittayne* [etc.]. London: S. Stafford for T. Salisbury, 1604.

Hayward, Sir John. *The First Part of the Life and Raigne of King Henrie IIII.* London: [E. Allde and T. Judson] for J. Woolfe, 1599.

———. "The Lives of the Three Normans, Kings of England: William the First, William the Second, and Henry the First" (1613). *The Harleian*

Miscellany, or A Collection of Scarce, Curious, and Entertaining Pamphlets and Tracts. Vol. III: 115-68. London, 1809.

———. *The Life and Raigne of King Edward the Sixt.* London: J. Lichfield? for J. Partridge, 1630.

Hazlitt, W. C., ed. *Select Collection of Old English Plays.* 4th ed., vol. XII. London, 1875.

Henry of Huntingdon. *The Chronicle of Henry of Huntingdon: Comprising the History of England from the Invasion of Julius Caesar to the Accession of Henry the Second.* Ed. and trl. Thomas Forester. 1853; rpt. Lampeter, 1991.

Henryson, Robert. *Poems.* Ed. Charles Elliott. 2nd ed. Oxford, 1974.

Herbert of Cherbury, Lord Edward. *The Life and Reigne of King Henry the Eighth.* London, 1649.

Higden, Ranulf. *Polychronicon Ranulphi Higden Monachi Cestrensis.* Ed. Joseph R. Lumby. Rolls Series, 41. Vol. VIII. London, 1882.

Hodgson, William. *The Divine Cosmographer. A Tractate on the VIII. Psalm.* Cambridge: R. Daniel, 1640.

Holinshed, Raphael. *Holinshed's Chronicles of England, Scotland and Ireland.* 6 vols. 1807–1808; rpt. New York, 1965.

Holland, Henry, the Bookseller. *Baziliωlogia. A Booke of Kings Beeing the true and liuely Effigies of all our English Kings from the Conquest vntill this present: With their seuerall Coats of Armes, Impreses and Devises. And a briefe Chronologie of their liues and deaths. Elegantly grauen in Copper.* London: Printed for H. Holland, 1618.

Homer. *The Odyssey.* Trl. A. T. Murray. 2 vols. Loeb Classical Library. London 1919.

Hooker, Richard. *Of the Laws of Ecclesiastical Polity.* Book V. Ed. W. Speed Hill. The Folger Library Edition of the Works of Richard Hooker, 2. Cambridge, MA, 1977.

[Hubert, Sir Francis]. *The Deplorable Life and Death of Edward the Second.* London: for R. Michell, 1628.

James VI and I. *The Kings Maiesties Declaration to His Subjects, Concerning Lawfull Sports to Be Vsed.* London: Bonham Norton and John Bill, 1618.

———. "The Essayes of a Prentise and Poeticall Exercises at Vacant Houres." *The Poems of James VI of Scotland.* Ed. James Craigie. Vol. I. Scottish Text Society. Edinburgh, 1955.

———. *New Poems by James I of England from a Hitherto Unpublished Manuscript (Add. 24195) in the British Museum.* Ed. Allan F. Westcott. New York, 1911.

Jonson, Ben. *Seianus his Fall. Ben Jonson*, ed. C. H. Herford and Percy Simpson, Vol. IV. Oxford, 1932.

———. "The Masque of Queenes." *Ben Jonson*. Ed. C. H. Herford & Percy and Evelyn Simpson. Vol. VII: 265–319. Oxford, 1941.

———. "The Speeches at Prince Henry's Barriers." *Ben Jonson*. Ed. C. H. Herford & Percy and Evelyn Simpson. Vol. VII: 321–36. Oxford, 1941.

Kett, Henry, ed. *Henry Headley's Select Beauties of Ancient English Poetry: A New Edition, To which Are Added his Original Poems.* Vol. I. London, 1810.

Legenda Aurea. *The Legende Named in Latyn Legenda aurea that is to Say in Englysshe the Golden Legende.* London: Wynkyn de Worde, 1527.

Livius, Titus. *Livy.* Trl. B. O. Foster. Loeb Classical Library. Vol. XII, London, 1938.

Lodge, Thomas. "Scillaes Metamorphosis." *Elizabethan Narrative Verse.* Ed. Nigel Alexander, 33–55. London, 1967.

Lucanus, M. Annaeus. *The Civil War (Pharsalia). Lucan.* Trl. J. D. Duff. Loeb Classical Library. London, 1928.

Marlowe, Christopher. *Tamburlaine.* Ed. J. W. Harper. London, 1971.

Marston, John. *The Poems of John Marston.* Ed. Arnold Davenport. Liverpool, 1961.

Martyn, William. *The Historie and Lives, of the Kings of England: From William the Conqueror, vnto the end of the Raigne of King Henry the Eighth.* London: [H. Lownes] for John Boler [and for G. Tompson], 1628.

Materials for the History of Thomas Becket, ed. James Craigie Robertson. Vol. I–V. Rolls Series, 67. London, 1875–81.

May, Thomas. *The Old Couple* (1619?). Ed. W. C. Hazlitt, *A Select Collection of Old English Plays,* 4th ed. Vol. XII. London, 1875.

———. *The Heire an Excellent Comedie.* London: 1620; 2nd ed. A. Mathewes for T. Jones, 1633.

———, trl. *Lucan's Pharsalia: or The civill warres of Rome, betweene Pompey the great, and Julius Cæsar. The three first bookes.* London: J. N[orton] and A. M[athewes], 1626; with additions, *Lucan's Pharsalia: The whole ten Bookes.* A. M[athewes] for T. Jones and J. Marriott, 1627; 2nd edition, A. M[athewes] for T. Jones, 1631.

———. *Virgil's Georgicks Englished.* London: [H. Lownes] for T. Walkley; [A. Mathewes] for T. Walkley, 1628.

———, trl. *John Barclay his Argenis. Translated ovt of Latin into English. The Prose vpon his Maiesties Command by Sir Robert Le Grys, Knight: And the Verses by Thomas May, Esquire.* London: Felix Kyngston for Richard Meighen and Henry Seile, 1629.

————, trl. *Selected Epigrams of Martial*. London: [H. Lownes] for T[homas] Walkley, 1629.

————. *A Continvation of Lucan's historicall poem till the death of Iulius Cæsar*. London: [J. Haviland] for J. Boler, 1630; 2nd ed. [T. Cotes] for J. Boler, 1633.

————, trl. *The Mirrour of Mindes. Or, Barclay's Icon Animorum*. London: I[ohn] N[orton] for Thomas Walkley, 1631; 2nd ed. I[ohn] B[eale] for Thomas Walkley, 1633.

————. *The Tragedy of Antigone, The Theban Princesse*. London: Thomas Harper for Benjamin Fisher, 1631. Ed. Edward J. Lautner, Ph.D. diss., Case Western Reserve University, 1970.

————. *The Reigne of King Henry the Second, Written in Seaven Bookes*. London: A[ugustine] M[athewes and J. Beale] for Benjamin Fisher, London, 1633.

————. *The Tragedie of Cleopatra*. London: T. Harper for T. Walkly, 1639. Ed. Denzell S. Smith. Ph.D. diss., University of Minnesota, 1965; printed New York, 1979.

————. *The Tragedy of Julia Agrippina*. London: R. Hodgkinsonne for T. Walkly, 1639. Ed. F. Ernst Schmid, Diss. University of Straßburg, 1910; printed Louvain, 1914.

————. *Supplementum Lucani Libri VII*. Lugduni Batavorum: Typis Wilhelmi Christiani, 1640.

Milton, John. *Poetical Works*. Ed. Douglas Bush. London, 1966.

Ovid. Publius O. Naso. *Metamorphoses*. Trl. Frank Justus Miller. Loeb Classical Library. 2 vols. 2nd ed. 1921; rpt. London, 1958.

————. *Heroides and Amores*. Trl. Grant Showerman. Loeb Classical Library. London, 1914.

————. *The Art of Love and Other Poems*. Trl. J. H. Mozley. Loeb Classical Library. London, 1929.

————. *Ovid's Metamorphosis Englished, Mythologiz'd, and Represented in Figures* [by George Sandys]. Oxford: J. Lichfield, 1632.

Paris, Matthew. *Matthaei Parisiensis, Monachi Sancti Albani, Historia Anglorum, sive, ut vulgo dicitur, Historia Minor*. Rolls Series, 44. Vol. I, AD 1067–1189. Ed. Sir Frederic Madden. London, 1866.

————. *Matthaei Parisiensis Chronica Majora*. Rolls Series, 57. Vol. II, AD 1067 to AD 1216. Ed. Henry Richards Luard. London, 1874.

Polydore Vergil. *Polydori Vergilii Urbinatis anglicae historiae libri vigintiseptem. Ab ipso autore postremùm iam regogniti, àdque amussim, salua tamen historiæ veritate, expoliti*. Basileae: Apud Thomam Guarinum, 1570.

Prynne, William. *Histrio-mastix. The Players Scourge.* London, E. A[llde], A. Mathewes, T. Cotes and W. J[ones] for M. Sparke, 1633.

Ralph of Diceto. *Radulfi de Diceto Opera Historica.* Ed. William Stubbs. Rolls Series, 68. London, 1876.

Roger of Hoveden. *Chronica Magistri Rogeri de Houedene.* Ed. William Stubbs. 8 vols. Rolls Series, 51. London, 1868–71.

Roger of Hoveden (?). *Gesta Regis Henrici Secundi Benedicti Abbatis.* Ed. William Stubbs. 2 vols. Rolls Series, 74. London, 1867.

Rowley, William. *A Tragedy Called All's Lost by Lust.* London: T. Harper, 1633.

Savile, Sir Henry, ed. *Rervm Anglicarvm scriptores post Bedam præcipvi, ex vetvstissimis codicibus manvscriptis nvnc primvm in lvcem editi. Willielmi Monachi Malmesburiensis de gestis regum Anglorum lib. V. Eiusdem historia Nouella li. II. Eiusdem de gestis Pontificum Angl. lib. IIII. Henrici Archidiaconi Huntindoniensis Historiarum lib. VIII. Rogeri Hovedeni Annalium pars prior & posterior. Chronicorum Ethelwerdi lib. IIII. Ingulphi Abbatis Croylandensis historiarum lib. I.* Francofvrti, 1601.

Seneca, Lucius Annaeus. *Tragedies.* 2 vols. Trl. Frank Justus Miller. Loeb Classical Library. London, 1917.

Shakespeare, William. *The Arden Shakespeare.* Second Series. London, 1946–82.

Sidney, Sir Philip. *The Old Arcadia.* Ed. Jean Robertson. Oxford, 1973.

———. *The Poems of Sir Philip Sidney.* Ed. William A. Ringler, Jr. Oxford, 1962.

Slatyer, William. *Genethliacon sive Stemma Jacobi.* London: G. Miller, 1630.

———. *The History of Great Britanie to this Present Raigne.* London: W. Stansby for R. Meighen, 1621.

Speed, John. *The Historie of Great Britaine.* London: J. Dawson for G. Humble, 1632.

Spenser, Edmund. "The Faerie Queene." *The Poetical Works of Edmund Spenser.* Ed. J. C. Smith and E. de Selincourt. 1912; rpt. London, 1957.

Stafford, Thomas. *Pacata Hibernia. Ireland Appeased and Reduced.* London: A. Matthewes for R. Milbourne, 1633.

Statius, Publius Papinius. *Statius.* Trl. J. H. Mozley. 2 vols. Loeb Classical Library. 1928; rpt. London, 1961.

Stow, John. *Annales, or: Generall Chronicle of England. Continued unto 1631. By E. Howes.* London: [J. Beale, B. Alsop and T. Fawcet, and], A. Mathewes, imp. R. Meighen, 1631 (1632).

Tasso, Torquato. *Aminta: Favola boschereccia.* Ed. C. E. J. Griffiths. Manchester, 1972.

Terentius, Publius T. Afer. *Terence.* Trl. John Sargeaunt. 2 vols. Loeb Classical Library. 1912; rpt. London, 1953.

Theocritus. *The Greek Bucolic Poets: Theocritus, Bion and Moschus.* Trl. J. M. Edmonds. Loeb Classical Library. London, 1912.

Tofte, Robert. *The Blazon of Jealousie.* London: T. S [nodham] for J. Busbie, 1615.

Virgil. Publius V. Maro. *Virgil.* Trl. H. Rushton Fairclough. 2 vols. 1916; rev. Loeb Classical Library. London, 1935.

Warner, William. *Albions England.* London, 1612.

Whitney, Geoffrey. *A Choice of Emblems.* London: [W. Stansby] for G. P[otter], 1586. Ed. Henry Green. 1866, rpt. Hildesheim, 1971

William of Newburgh. *Historia rerum Anglicarum. Chronicles of Stephen, Henry II, and Richard I.* Ed. Richard Howlett. Rolls Series, 82. 4 vols. London, 1853-1858.

STUDIES AND REFERENCE WORKS

Adamson, J. S. A. "Chivalry and Political Culture in Caroline England." *Culture and Politics in Early Stuart England.* Ed. Kevin Sharpe and Peter Lake. London, 1994, 161–97.

Baldwin, Thomas W. *Shakespere's Small Latine and Lesse Greeke.* 2 vols. Urbana, 1944.

Barlow, Frank. *Thomas Becket.* London, 1986.

Beal, Peter, compiler. *Index of English Literary Manuscripts.* Vol. II, 1625–1700. Part 1 Behn-King. London, 1987.

Bierstadt, Edward Hale. *Catalogue of the Library of the Late Edward Hale Bierstadt.* New York, 1897.

Binns, J. W. *Intellectual Culture in Elizabethan and Jacobean England: The Latin Writings of the Age.* Leeds, 1991.

Birrell, T. A. *English Monarchs and their Books: From Henry VII to Charles II.* The Panizzi Lectures 1986. London, 1987.

Blissett, William. "Samuel Daniel's Sense of the Past." *English Studies,* 38 (1957): 49–63.

Brettle, R. E. "Notes on John Marston." *Review of English Studies,* NS 13 (1962): 390–3.

Briggs, William Dinsmore. "The Influence of Jonson's Tragedy in the Seventeenth Century." *Anglia* 35 (1912): 277–337.

Bruère, R. T. "The Latin and English Versions of Thomas May's *Supplementum Lucani.*" *Classical Philology* 44 (1949): 145–63.

Burroughs, Franklin G., Jr. "Marvell's Cromwell and May's Caesar: 'An Horation Ode' and the Continuation of the Pharsalia." *English Language Notes* 13 (1975): 115-22.

Butt, John. "The Facilities for Antiquarian Study in the Seventeenth Century." *Essays and Studies* 24 (1938): 64–79.

Carlton, Charles. *Charles I: The Personal Monarch.* London, 1983.

Casley, David. *A Catalogue of the Manuscripts of the King's Library. An Appendix to the Catalogue of the Cottonian Library; Together with an Account of Books Burnt or Damaged by a late Fire.* London, 1734.

Chambers, Frank M. "Some Legends Concerning Eleanor of Aquitaine." *Speculum* 16 (1941): 459–68.

Chester, Allan Griffith. *Thomas May: Man of Letters 1595–1650.* Philadelphia, PA, 1932.

———. "Dryden and May." *Times Literary Supplement* (19 July 1934): 511.

Corbett, Margery and Michael Norton. *Engraving in England in the Sixteenth & Seventeenth Centuries: A Descriptive Catalogue with Introductions,* Part III, "The Reign of Charles I." Cambridge, 1964.

Croft, Peter J. *Autograph Poetry in the English Language.* 2 vols. London, 1973.

Darbishire, Helen. *The Manuscript of Paradise Lost. Book I.* Oxford, 1931.

Davenport, Cyril. *English Heraldic Book-Stamps.* London, 1909.

———. *Royal English Bookbindings.* London, 1896.

Davies, Godfrey. *The Early Stuarts, 1603–1660.* Oxford History of England, vol. X. 2nd ed., Oxford, 1945.

Davis, R. H. C. *King Stephen. 1135–1154.* 1967; 3rd ed. London, 1992.

Dean, L. F. "Francis Bacon's Theory of Civil History Writing." *Journal of English Literary History* 8 (1941): 161-83.

———. *Tudor Theories of History Writing.* The University of Michigan Contributions in Modern Philology, Nr. 1. Ann Arbor, 1947.

Dilke, O. A. W., "Lucan and English Literature." *Neronians and Flavians. Silver Latin I,* ed. D. R. Dudley (London, 1972): 83–112.

Donnelly, M. L. "Caroline Royalist Panegyric and the Disintegration of a Symbolic Mode." *"The Muses Common-Weale": Poetry and Politics in the Seventeenth Century.* Ed. Claude J. Summers and Ted-Larry Pebworth. Essays in Seventeenth-Century Literature, 3. Columbia, MO, 1988, 163–76.

Dowling, Margaret. "Sir John Hayward's Troubles over his Life of Henry IV." *The Library,* 4th ser. (1931): 212–24.

Evans, E. "Of the Antiquity of Parliaments in England: Some Elizabethan and Early Stuart Opinions." *History* 23 (1939): 206–21.

Evans, Joan. *A History of the Society of Antiquaries.* Oxford, 1956.

Evans, Robert C. *Ben Jonson and the Poetics of Patronage.* Lewisburg, PA, 1989.

Ferguson, Arthur B. *Clio Unbound: Perception of the Social and Cultural Past in Renaissance England.* Durham, 1979.

———. "The Historical Thought of Samuel Daniel." *Journal of the History of Ideas* 32 (1971): 185–202.

Ferguson, W. Craig. *Valentine Simmes.* Bibliographic Society of the University of Virginia. Charlottesville, 1968.

Fichter, Andrew. *Poets Historical: Dynastic Epic in the Renaissance.* New Haven, CN, 1982.

Foot, Mirjam. *The Henry Davis Gift. A Collection of Bookbindings.* Vol. I : Studies in the History of Bookbinding. London, 1978. Vol. II: A Catalogue of North-European Bindings. London, 1983.

———. "Some Bindings for Charles I." *Studies in Seventeenth-Century English Literature, History and Bibliography.* Festschrift for Professor T. A. Birrell on the Occasion of His Sixtieth Birthday. Ed. G. A. M. Janssens and F. G. A. M. Aarts. Amsterdam, 1984, 95-106.

Fox, Levi, ed. *English Historical Scholarship in the Sixteenth and Seventeenth Centuries: A Record of the Papers Delivered at a Conference Arranged by the Dugdale Society to Commemorate the Tercentenary of the Publication of Dugdale's "Antiquities of Warwickshire."* Oxford, 1956.

Fussner, F. Smith. *The Historical Revolution: English Historical Writing and Thought, 1580–1640.* London, 1962.

Gardiner, Samuel Rawson. *History of England from the Accession of James I to the Outbreak of the Civil War, 1603-1642.* 10 vols. London: 1884; rpt. New York, 1965.

Gaskell, Philip. *A New Introduction to Bibliography.* Oxford, 1972.

———. *From Writer to Reader: Studies in Editorial Method.* Oxford, 1978.

Gilson, Julius P., and George F. Warner. *Catalogue of Western Manuscripts in the Old Royal and King's Collections in the British Museum.* 4 vols. London, 1921.

Godshalk, William L. "Daniel's *History.*" *Journal of English and Germanic Philology* 63 (1964): 45–57.

Goldberg, Jonathan. *James I and the Politics of Literature: Jonson, Shakespeare, Donne and their Contemporaries.* Baltimore, MD, 1983.

Goldberg, S. L. "Hayward's 'Politic' Historian." *Review of English Studies* 6 (1955): 233–44.

Gottfried, Rudolf B. "The Early Development of the Section on Ireland in Camden's *Britannia.*" *Journal of English Literary History* 10 (1943): 117–30.

Gransden, Antonia. *Historical Writing in England c. 550–c. 1307.* London, 1974.

———. *Historical Writing in England c. 1307 to the Early Sixteenth Century.* London, 1982.

Greg, Sir Walter Wilson. *The Editorial Problem in Shakespeare.* Oxford, 1941.

———, et al. *English Literary Autographs, 1550–1650.* Part 1, "Dramatists." London, 1925.

Guibbory, Achsah. *The Map of Time: Seventeenth-Century English Literature and Ideas of Pattern in History.* Urbana, IL, 1986.

Hay, Denys. "The Manuscript of Polydore Vergil's *Anglica historia.*" *English Historical Review* 54 (1939): 240–51.

Heal, Ambrose. *The English Writing-Masters and their Copy-Books 1570–1800: A Biographical Dictionary and a Bibliography.* 1931; rpt. Hildesheim, 1962.

Heawood, Edward. *Watermarks Mainly of the 17th and 18th Centuries.* Hilversum, 1950.

Helgerson, Richard. *Self-Crowned Laureates: Spenser, Jonson, Milton and the Literary System.* Berkeley, CA, 1983.

Heltzel, Virgil B. *Fair Rosamond: A Study of the Development of a Literary Theme.* 1947; rpt. New York, 1970.

Herford, C. H., and Percy Simpson, eds. *Ben Jonson: The Man and his Work.* 2 vols. Oxford, 1925.

Heslin, Anne. "The Coronation of the Young King in 1170." *Studies in Church History,* Vol. II. Ed. G. J. Cuming. London, 1968, 165–78.

Higgins, Alison I. T. *Secular Heroic Epic Poetry of the Caroline Period.* Swiss Studies in English, 31. Berne, 1953.

Hill, Christopher. *Change and Continuity in Seventeenth-Century England.* Cambridge, rev. ed. 1992.

Hind, Arthur M. *Engraving in England in the Sixteenth and Seventeenth Centuries. Part II. The Reign of James I.* Cambridge, 1955.

Holden, Edwin Babcock. *Illustrated Catalogue of Early English and Later Literature from the Library of Edwin Babcock Holden.* New York, 1920.

Hulse, Clark. "Samuel Daniel: The Poet as Literary Historian." *Studies in English Literature 1500–1900* 19 (1979): 55–69.

Jackson, William A. *Records of the Court of the Stationers' Company, 1602 to 1640.* London, 1957.

Jayne, Sears. *Library Catalogues of the English Renaissance*. Berkeley, CA, 1956.

———, and F. R. Johnson. *The Lumley Library: The Catalogue of 1609*. London, 1956.

Kelliher, Hilton, ed. *Andrew Marvell, Poet and Politician 1621–1678: An Exhibition to Commemorate the Tercentenary of his Death*. London, 1978.

Kemke, Johannes. *Patricius Junius (Patrick Young). Bibliothekar der Könige Jacob I. und Carl I. von England. Mitteilungen aus seinem Briefwechsel*. Sammlung bibliothekswissenschaftlicher Arbeiten, 12. Heft. Leipzig, 1898.

Koppenfels, Werner von. " 'Our swords into our proper entrails': Lucan und das Bild des Bürgerkriegs in der Shakespearezeit." *Bild und Metamorphose. Paradigmen einer europäischen Komparatistik*. Darmstadt, 1991, 87–118.

LaBranche, Anthony. "Drayton's *The Barons Warres* and the Rhetoric of Historical Poetry." *Journal of English and Germanic Philology* 62 (1963): 82–95.

———. "Poetry, History and Oratory: the Renaissance Historical Poem." *Studies in English Literature 1500–1900* 9 (1969): 1–19.

Lavin, J. A. "John Danter's Ornament Stock," *Studies in Bibliography* 23 (1970): 21–44.

Leidig, Heinz Dieter. *Das Historiengedicht in der englischen Literaturtheorie: Die Rezeption von Lucans "Pharsalia" von der Renaissance bis zum Ausgang des 18. Jahrhunderts*. Europäische Hochschulschriften, Reihe XIV: Angelsächsische Sprache und Literatur, 26. Berne, 1975.

Levine, Joseph M. *Humanism and History: Origins of Modern English Historiography*. Ithaca, 1987.

Levis, Howard C. *Notes on the Early British Engraved Royal Portraits Issued in Various Series from 1521 to the End of the Eighteenth Century*. London, 1917.

Levy, F. J. "The Making of Camden's *Britannia*." *Bibliothèque d'Humanisme et Renaissance* 26 (1964): 70–97.

Lievsay, John L. "Bacon Versified." *Huntington Library Quarterly* 14 (1951): 223–38.

Lockyer, Roger. *The Early Stuarts: A Political History of England 1603–1642*. London, 1989.

Logan, George M. "Daniel's *Civil Wars* and Lucan's *Pharsalia*." *Studies in English Literature 1500–1900* 11 (1971): 53–68.

Love, Harold. *Scribal Publication in Seventeenth-Century England*. Oxford, 1993.

Maas, P. "Notes on the Text of Jonson's Masques." *Review of English Studies* 18 (1942), 464–5.

Madan, Falconer. *A Summary Catalogue of Western Manuscripts in the Bodleian Library at Oxford.* Vol. 3. Clarendon Press. Oxford, 1895.

Marotti, Arthur F. *Manuscript, Print, and the English Renaissance Lyric.* Ithaca, NY, 1995.

Martindale, Charles. *John Milton and the Transformation of Ancient Epic.* Beckenham, 1986.

Maus, Katherine Eisaman. *Ben Jonson and the Roman Frame of Mind.* Princeton, NJ, 1984.

McEuen, Katerine. *Classical Influence upon the Tribe of Ben.* New York, 1968.

McKerrow, R. B., and K. F. S. Ferguson. *Title Page Borders Used in England and Scotland.* London, 1932.

McKisack, May. "Samuel Daniel as Historian." *Review of English Studies* 23 (1947): 226–43.

———. *Medieval History in the Tudor Age.* Oxford, 1971.

Murdoch, W. G. Blaikie. "King Charles the First as a Book-Lover." *Book-Lover's Magazine* 6 (1907): 114–15.

Nearing, Homer, Jr. "English Historical Poetry 1599–1641." Ph.D. diss., University of Pennsylvania, 1945; rpt. [s.l.]: Norwood Editions, 1978.

Nixon, Howard M. *Royal English Bookbindings in the British Museum.* London, 1957.

Norbrook, David. *Poetry and Politics in the English Renaissance.* London, 1984.

———. "Lucan, Thomas May, and the Creation of a Republican Literary Culture," *Culture and Politics in Early Stuart England.* Eds. Kevin Sharpe and Peter Lake, 45–66. London, 1994.

Norden, Linda Van. "The Elizabethan College of Antiquaries." Ph.D. diss., University of California at Los Angeles, 1946.

———. "Sir Henry Spelman on the Chronology of the Elizabethan College of Antiquaries." *Huntington Library Quarterly,* 13 (1950): 131–60.

Parkes, M. B. *English Cursive Book Hands 1250–1500.* 1969; rpt. London, 1979.

Parry, Graham. *"The Golden Age Restor'd": The Culture of the Stuart Court, 1603–42.* Manchester, 1981.

Patterson, Annabel. *Censorship and Interpretation: The Conditions of Writing and Reading in Early Modern England.* Madison, WI, 1984.

———. "Pastoral versus Georgic: The Politics of Virgilian Quotation." *Ren-*

aissance Genres: Essays on Theory, History, and Interpretation. Ed. Barbara Kiefer Lewalski. Harvard English Studies, 14. Cambridge, MA, 1986, 241–67.

————. *Reading Holinshed's "Chronicles".* Chicago, IL, 1994.

Peacock, John. "The Politics of Portraiture." *Culture and Politics in Early Stuart England.* Ed. Kevin Sharpe and Peter Lake. London, 1994, 199–228.

Petti, Anthony G. *English Literary Hands from Chaucer to Dryden.* London, 1977.

Phelps, Wayne H. "Two Notes on Thomas May." *Notes and Queries,* N.S. 26 (Oct. 1979): 412–15.

Pickel, Margaret Barnard. *Charles I as Patron of Poetry and Drama.* Ph.D. diss., Columbia University. London, 1936.

Pinches, J. H. and R. V. *The Royal Heraldry of England.* London, 1974.

Poole, Austin Lane. *From Domesday Book to Magna Carta, 1087–1216.* Oxford History of England, vol. III. 2nd ed. Oxford, 1955.

Portal, Ethel M. "The Academ Roial of King James I." *Proceedings of the British Academy 1915–16,* 189–208.

Reedy, Gerard, S.J. " 'An Horation Ode' and 'Tom May's Death'." *Studies in English Literature 1500-1900* 20 (1980): 137-51.

Rees, Christine. "Tom May's Death and Ben Jonson's Ghost." *Modern Language Review* 71 (1976): 481–8.

Riggs, David. *Ben Jonson: A Life.* Cambridge, MA, 1989.

Rivers, Isabel. *The Poetry of Conservatism, 1600-1745: A Study of Poets and Public Affairs from Jonson to Pope.* Cambridge, 1973.

Russell, Conrad. *Parliaments and English Politics, 1621-1629.* Oxford, 1979.

————. "The Nature of a Parliament in Early Stuart England." *Before the Civil War. Essays on Early Stuart Politics and Government.* Ed. Howard Tomlinson, 123-50. London, 1983.

————. *The Causes of the English Civil War. The Ford Lectures Delivered in the University of Oxford 1987-1988.* Oxford, 1990.

Sägmüller, Johann Baptist. "Eine Dispens päpstlicher Legaten zur Verehelichung eines Siebenjährigen mit einer Dreijährigen im Jahre 1160." *Theologische Quartalsschrift* 86 (1904): 556–75.

Schmid, F. Ernst. *Thomas Mays "Tragedy of Julia Agrippina, Empresse of Rome," nebst einem Anhang: Die Tragödie "Nero" und Thomas May.* Materialien zur Kunde des älteren englischen Dramas, vol. 43. Louvain, 1914.

Schmitz, Götz. *Die Frauenklage: Studien zur elegischen Verserzählung in der englischen Literatur des Spätmittelalters und der Renaissance.* Tübingen, 1984.

————. *The Fall of Women in Early English Narrative Verse.* European Studies in English Literature. Cambridge, 1990.

Sharpe, Kevin. *Sir Robert Cotton 1586-1631: History and Politics in Early Modern England.* Oxford Historical Monographs. Oxford, 1979.

————. "The Personal Rule of Charles I." *Before the Civil War. Essays on Early Stuart Politics and Government.* Ed. Howard Tomlinson, 53-78. London, 1983.

————. *Criticism and Compliment. The Politics of Literature in the England of Charles I.* Cambridge, 1987.

————. "The Image of Virtue: The Court and Household of Charles I, 1625–1642." Starkey, David, et al., *The English Court: From the Wars of the Roses to the Civil War,* 226–60. London, 1987.

————, and Steven Zwicker, eds. *Politics of Discourse: The Literature and History of Seventeenth-Century England.* Berkeley, CA, 1987.

————. *Politics and Ideas in Early Stuart England: Essays and Studies.* London, 1989.

————. *The Personal Rule of Charles I.* New Haven, CT, 1992.

————, and Peter Lake, eds. *Culture and Politics in Early Stuart England.* London, 1994.

Simpson, Evelyn M. "Jonson's Masques: A Rejoinder." *Review of English Studies* 18 (1942): 291–300.

Simpson, Percy. *Proof-Reading in the Sixteenth, Seventeenth and Eighteenth Centuries.* 1935; rpt. Oxford, 1970.

Smith, Hallett. " 'No Cloudy Stuffe to Puzzell Intellect': A Testimonial Misapplied to Shakespeare." *Shakespeare Quarterly* 1 (1950): 18–21.

Smuts, R. Malcolm. "The Puritan Followers of Henrietta Maria in the 1630s." *English Historical Review* 93, (1978): 28-34.

————. "The Political Failure of Stuart Cultural Patronage." *Patronage in the Renaissance.* Ed. Guy Fitch Lytle and Stephen Orgel. Princeton, NJ, 1981.

————. *Court Culture and the Origins of a Royalist Tradition in Early Stuart England.* Philadelphia, PA, 1987.

Sommerville, J. P. *Politics and Ideology in England, 1603-1640.* London, 1986.

Starkey, David et al. *The English Court: From the Wars of the Roses to the Civil War.* London, 1987.

Strong, Roy. *The English Icon: Elizabethan and Jacobean Portraiture.* New York, 1969.

————, and Oliver Millar. *The Age of Charles I.* London, 1972.

———. "England and Italy: The Marriage of Henry Prince of Wales." *For Veronica Wedgwood These. Studies in Seventeenth-Century History*. Ed. Richard Ollard and Pamela Tudor-Craig, 59-87. London, 1986.

———. *Henry Prince of Wales and England's Lost Renaissance*. London, 1986.

Styles, Philip. "Politics and Historical Research in the Early Seventeenth Century." *English Historical Scholarship*, ed. Levi Fox, 49-72. London, 1956.

Summers, Claude J. and Ted-Larry Pebworth. *Classic and Cavalier: Essays on Jonson and the Sons of Ben*. Pittsburgh, PA, 1982.

———, eds. *"The Muses Common-Weale": Poetry and Politics in the Seventeenth Century*. Essays in Seventeenth-Century Literature, 3. Columbia, MO, 1988.

Thompson, E. Maunde. "Handwriting." *Shakespeare's England. An Account of the Life and Manners of his Age*. Ed. Sidney Lee and C. T. Onions. I, 284-310. Oxford, 1916.

Tite, Colin G. C. "A Catalogue of Sir Robert Cotton's Printed Books?" *British Library Journal* 17 (1991): 1-11.

———. *The Manuscript Library of Sir Robert Cotton*. Panizzi Lectures 1993. London, 1993.

Tyacke, Nicholas. *Anti-Calvinists: The Rise of Arminianism c. 1590-1640*. Oxford, 1990.

Wagner, B. M. "Manuscript Plays of the Seventeenth Century." *Times Literary Supplement* (4 October 1934): 675.

Wardrop, James. "Civis Romanus svm: Giovanbattista Palatino and his Circle." *Signature*, N.S. 14 (1952): 3-39.

Warren, Wilfred Lewis. *King John*. 1973; 2nd ed. London, 1978.

Wedgwood, Cicely Veronica. *Poetry and Politics under the Stuarts*. Ann Arbor, MI, 1964.

Wilkinson, C. H. "A Note on Thomas May." *Review of English Studies* 11 (1935): 195-8.

Williams, Daniel. *England in the Twelfth Century*. Woodbridge, 1990.

Wolf, Heinrich. *Thomas May's "Tragedy of Cleopatra, Queen of Aegypt."* Diss. Straßburg, 1914. Materialien zur Kunde des älteren englischen Dramas. Louvain, 1914.

Wood, Anthony à. *Athenae Oxonienses*. 5 vols. 1813-20; rpt. Hildesheim, 1969.

Woodcock, Thomas and John M. Robinson. *The Oxford Guide to Heraldry*. Oxford, 1990.

Woolf, D. R. *The Idea of History in Early Stuart England: Erudition, Ideology, and "The Light of Truth" from the Accession of James I to the Civil War*. Toronto, 1990.

Worden, Blair. "Ben Jonson among the Historians." *Culture and Politics in Early Stuart England*, ed. Kevin Sharpe and Peter Lake, 67–89. London, 1994.

———. "Classical Republicanism and the Puritan Revolution." *History and Imagination. Essays in Honour of H. R. Trevor Roper*. Ed. Hugh Lloyd-Jones, Valerie Pearl, and Blair Worden, 182–200. London, 1981.

Wormald, Francis and C. E. Wright, eds. *The English Library before 1700: Studies in its History*. London, 1958.

Wright, C. E. "The Elizabethan Society of Antiquaries and the Formation of the Cottonian Library." *The English Library before 1700: Studies in its History*. Ed. Francis Wormald and C. E. Wright, 176–212. London, 1958.

Editorial Committee for *The Reigne of King Henry the Second*
Thomas L. Berger, Chair
A. R. Braunmuller
Carolyn Kent

The Renaissance English Text Society was established to publish literary texts, chiefly nondramatic, of the period 1475–1660. Dues are $30.00 per annum ($15.00, graduate students; life membership is available at $500.00). Members receive the text published for each year of membership. The Society sponsors panels at such annual meetings as those of the Modern Language Association, the Renaissance Society of America, and the Medieval Congress at Kalamazoo.

General inquiries and proposals for editions should be addressed to the president, Arthur Kinney, Massachusetts Center for Renaissance Studies, PO Box 2300, Amherst, Mass., 01004, USA. Inquiries about membership should be addressed to William Gentrup, Director of Memberships, Arizona Center for Medieval and Renaissance Studies, Arizona State University, PO Box 872301, Tempe, Ariz., 85287-2301.

Copies of volumes X–XII may be purchased from Associated University Presses, 440 Forsgate Drive, Cranbury, N.J., 08512. Members may order copies of earlier volumes still in print or of later volumes from XIII, at special member prices, from the Treasurer.

FIRST SERIES
VOL. I. *Merie Tales of the Mad Men of Gotam* by A. B., edited by Stanley J. Kahrl, and *The History of Tom Thumbe*, by R. I., edited by Curt F. Buhler, 1965. (o.p.)
VOL. II. Thomas Watson's Latin *Amyntas*, edited by Walter F. Staton, Jr., and Abraham Fraunce's translation *The Lamentations of Amyntas*, edited by Franklin M. Dickey, 1967.

SECOND SERIES
VOL. III. *The dyaloge called Funus*, A Translation of Erasmus's Colloquy (1534), and *A very pleasaunt & fruitful Diologe called The Epicure*, Gerrard's Translation of Erasmus's Colloquy (1545), edited by Robert R. Allen, 1969.
VOL. IV. *Leicester's Ghost* by Thomas Rogers, edited by Franklin B. Williams, Jr., 1972.

THIRD SERIES
VOLS. V–VI. *A Collection of Emblemes, Ancient and Moderne*, by George

Wither, with an introduction by Rosemary Freeman and bibliographical notes by Charles S. Hensley, 1975. (o.p.)

FOURTH SERIES

VOLS. VII–VIII. *Tom a' Lincolne* by R. I., edited by Richard S. M. Hirsch, 1978.

FIFTH SERIES

VOL. IX. *Metrical Visions* by George Cavendish, edited by A. S. G. Edwards, 1980.

SIXTH SERIES

VOL. X. *Two Early Renaissance Bird Poems,* edited by Malcolm Andrew, 1984.

VOL. XI. *Argalus and Parthenia* by Francis Quarles, edited by David Freeman, 1986.

VOL. XII. Cicero's *De Officiis,* trans. Nicholas Grimald, edited by Gerald O'Gorman, 1987.

VOL. XIII. *The Silkewormes and their Flies* by Thomas Moffet (1599), edited with introduction and commentary by Victor Houliston, 1988.

SEVENTH SERIES

VOL. XIV. John Bale, *The Vocacyon of Johan Bale,* edited by Peter Happé and John N. King, 1989.

VOL. XV. *The Nondramatic Works of John Ford,* edited by L. E. Stock, Gilles D. Monsarrat, Judith M. Kennedy, and Dennis Danielson, with the assistance of Marta Straznicky, 1990.

Special Publication. *New Ways of Looking at Old Texts: Papers of the Renaissance English Text Society, 1985–1991,* edited by W. Speed Hill, 1993. (Sent *gratis* to all 1991 members.)

VOL. XVI. George Herbert, *The Temple: A Diplomatic Edition of the Bodleian Manuscript (Tanner 307),* edited by Mario A. Di Cesare, 1991.

VOL. XVII. Lady Mary Wroth, *The First Part of the Countess of Montgomery's Urania,* edited by Josephine Roberts. 1992.

VOL. XVIII. Richard Beacon, *Solon His Follie,* edited by Clare Carroll and Vincent Carey. 1993.

VOL. XIX. An Collins, *Divine Songs and Meditacions,* edited by Sidney Gottlieb. 1994.

VOL. XX. *The Southwell-Sibthorpe Commonplace Book: Folger MS V.b.198,* edited by Sr. Jean Klene. 1995.

Special Publication. *New Ways of Looking at Old Texts II: Papers of the Renaissance English Text Society, 1992–1996,* edited by W. Speed Hill, 1998. (Sent *gratis* to all 1996 members.)

VOL. XXI. *The Collected Works of Anne Vaughan Lock*, edited by Susan M. Felch. 1996.

VOL. XXII. Thomas May, *The Reigne of King Henry the Second Written in Seauen Books*, edited by Götz Schmitz. 1997.